Cracking the

SSAT® & ISEE®

2013 Edition

Elizabeth Silas and Reed Talada

PrincetonReview.com

Random House, Inc. New York

The Princeton Review, Inc.
111 Speen Street
Framingham, MA 01701
E-mail: editorialsupport@review.com

ISBN 978-0-307-94493-1
ISSN 1090-0144

SSAT is a registered trademark of the Secondary School Admission Test Board.
ISEE is a registered trademark of the Educational Records Bureau.
The Princeton Review is not affiliated with Princeton University.

Editor: Calvin Cato
Production Editor: Michelle Krapf
Production Coordinator: Deborah A. Silvestrini

Printed in the United States of America on partially recycled paper.

10 9 8 7 6 5 4 3 2 1

2013 Edition

Editorial

Robert Franek, Senior VP, Publisher
Laura Braswell, Senior Editor
Selena Coppock, Senior Editor
Calvin Cato, Editor
Meave Shelton, Editor

Production

Michael Pavese, Publishing Director
Kathy Carter, Project Editor
Michelle Krapf, Editor
Michael Mazzei, Editor
Michael Breslosky, Associate Editor
Stephanie Tantum, Associate Editor
Kristen Harding, Associate Editor
Vince Bonavoglia, Artist
Danielle Joyce, Graphic Designer

Random House Publishing Team

Tom Russell, Publisher
Nicole Benhabib, Publishing Director
Ellen L. Reed, Production Manager
Alison Stoltzfus, Managing Editor

Acknowledgments

The Princeton Review would like to thank Reesa Graham for her work on the previous editions of the book. We would also like to thank David Stoll for his contributions to this book.

Special thanks to Adam Robinson, who conceived of and perfected the Joe Bloggs approach to standardized tests and many of the other successful techniques used by The Princeton Review.

Welcome

Dear students and parents,

Thank you for choosing The Princeton Review for your test-prep needs. I am sure you will find the book very useful!

If you need additional support, ask us about our classroom courses and private tutoring program.

David Stoll, National Content Director, SSAT and ISEE

Contents

...So Much More Online!

More Information...

- Clear outline of the SSAT and ISEE

- Informational articles about internships, taking time off, summer programs, and summer school

More Good Stuff...

- Learn about exciting summer programs for high school students

- Helpful information about fantastic internships

- Tons of useful college-planning information

...and eventually, College!

- Detailed profiles for hundreds of colleges

- Dozens of Top 10 ranking lists including Quality of Professors, Worst Campus Food, Most Beautiful Campus, Party Schools, Diverse Student Population, and tons more

- Useful information about the admissions process

- Helpful information about financial aid and scholarships

- Learn about more books on college from The Princeton Review— *The Best 377 Colleges, The Complete Book of Colleges, Paying for College Without Going Broke*

princetonreview.com

A Parent's Introduction

HOW CAN I HELP?

Congratulations! Your child is considering attending a private secondary school, and by virtue of the fact that you hold this book in your hands, you have recognized that either the SSAT or the ISEE is an important part of the admissions process. Providing your child with the information contained in this book is an excellent first step toward a strong performance on the SSAT or the ISEE.

As a parent, however, you know well the fine line between support and intrusion. To guide you in your efforts to help your child, we offer a few suggestions.

Have a Healthy Perspective

Both the SSAT and the ISEE are standardized tests designed to say something about an individual student's chances for success in a private secondary school. Neither is an intelligence test; neither claims to be.

Set realistic expectations for your child. The skills necessary for a strong performance on these tests are very different from those a student uses in school. The additional stress that comes from being expected to do well generally serves only to distract a student from taking a test efficiently.

At the same time, beware of dismissing disappointing results with a simple, "My child doesn't test well." While it is undoubtedly true that some students test better than others, this explanation does little to encourage a student to invest time and effort in overcoming obstacles and improving his or her performance.

Know How to Interpret Performance

Both the SSAT and the ISEE use the same test to measure the performance of an eighth-grade student and an eleventh-grade student. It is impossible to interpret scores without considering the grade level of the student. Percentile rankings have much more value than do either raw or scaled scores, and percentiles are the numbers schools use to compare students.

Remember That This Is Not an English or a Math Test

There are both verbal and math questions on the SSAT and on the ISEE. However, these questions are often based on skills and concepts that are different from those used on a day-to-day basis in school. For instance, very few English teachers—at any level—spend a lot of time teaching students how to do analogies or sentence completion questions.

This may be frustrating for parents, students, and teachers. But in the final judgment, our educational system would take a turn for the worse if it attempted to teach students to do well on the SSAT, the ISEE, or even the SAT. The fact that the valuable skills students learn in school don't directly improve test scores is evidence of a flaw in the testing system, not an indictment of our schools or those who have devoted their professional careers to education.

Realize That All Tests Are Different

Many of the general rules that students are accustomed to applying to tests in school do not apply to either the SSAT or the ISEE. Many students, for instance, actually hurt their scores by trying to work on every question. Although these tests are timed, accuracy is much more important than speed. Once your child learns the format and structure of these tests, he or she will find it easier to apply his or her knowledge to the test and will answer more questions correctly.

Provide All the Resources You Can

This book has been written to provide your child with a very thorough review of all the math, vocabulary, reading, and writing skills that are necessary for success on the SSAT and ISEE. We have also included practice sections throughout the chapters and practice tests that simulate actual SSAT or ISEE examinations.

The very best SSAT practice questions, however, are naturally the ones written by Secondary School Admission Test Board (SSATB), the organization that writes and administers the SSAT. The best ISEE questions come from the Educational Resources Bureau (ERB), the organization that writes real ISEE questions. We encourage you to contact both these organizations (addresses and phone numbers can be found on page 5) to obtain any resources containing test questions that you can use for additional practice.

One word of caution: Be wary of other sources of SSAT or ISEE practice material. There are a number of test preparation books available (from companies other than The Princeton Review, of course) that are woefully outdated. The ISEE changed quite substantially in 2010, and many books have not caught up with these changes. In addition to major structural changes like this, both the SSAT and the ISEE change with time in very subtle ways. Thus, we suggest supplementing the information in this book with ERB's "What to Expect on the ISEE," which you can find at **www.erblearn.org**.

Make sure the materials you choose are, to the greatest extent possible, reflective of the test your child will take and not a test that was given years earlier. Also, try to avoid the inevitable confusion that comes from asking a student to follow two different sets of advice. Presumably, you have decided (or are about to decide) to trust The Princeton Review to prepare your child for this test. In doing so, you have made a wise decision. As we have said, we encourage you to provide any and all sources of additional practice material (as long as it is accurate and reflective of the current test), but providing other test preparation advice tends to muddy the waters and confuse students.

The Rules Have Changed
The ISEE, in particular, has changed dramatically. Make sure the practice materials your child uses are up to date!

Be Patient and Be Involved

Preparing for the SSAT or the ISEE is like learning to ride a bicycle. You will watch your child struggle, at first, to develop a level of familiarity and comfort with the test's format and content.

Developing the math, vocabulary, reading, and writing skills that your child will use on the SSAT or the ISEE is a long-term process. In addition to making certain that he or she is committed to spending the time necessary to work through the chapters of this book, you can also be on the lookout for other opportunities to be supportive. An easy way to do this is to make vocabulary development into a group activity. In the vocabulary chapters, we provide an extensive list of word parts and vocabulary words; learn them as a family, working through flash cards at the breakfast table or during car trips. You may even pick up a new word or two yourself!

Important: If your child is in the fourth, fifth, or even sixth grade, you may want to offer extra guidance as he or she works through this book and prepares for the test. Because this book covers preparation for the full range of grade levels taking the tests (fifth through eleventh grades), some of the content review will be beyond the areas that your child is expected to know. It is an excellent idea to work through the book along with your younger child, so that he or she doesn't become intimidated by these higher level questions that should be skipped. Look at the chapter titled "A Student's Introduction" on page 7 to see the suggested schedule.

A SHORT WORD ON ADMISSIONS

The most important insight into secondary school admissions that we can offer is that a student's score on the SSAT or the ISEE is only one of many components involved in the admissions decision. While many schools will request SSAT or ISEE scores, all will look seriously at your child's academic record. Think about it—which says more about a student: a single test or years of solid (or not so solid) academic performance?

Be an Informed Customer
For the most accurate information about their admissions policies, don't hesitate to call the schools to which your son or daughter may apply.

In terms of testing, which is the focus of this book, some schools will specify which test they want applicants to take—the SSAT or ISEE. Others will allow you to use scores from either test. If you are faced with a decision of whether to focus on the SSAT, the ISEE, or both, we encourage you to be an informed consumer. This book contains a practice test for the ISEE and the SSAT, so your child should take both. Then, based on the requirements of your desired school and the results of the practice tests, decide which test best suits your child. The ISEE can be taken only once every six months, and the SSAT can be taken multiple times.

There are some differences in subject matter. The SSAT, for example, contains a section on analogies, which many students find difficult; the ISEE includes a section of sentence completions. On the other hand, Middle and Upper Level ISEE test takers will be faced with a number of quantitative comparison questions in the Math section, and these can be tricky at first, especially for younger students.

Resources

SSAT — Secondary School Admission Test Board (SSATB)
609-683-4440
www.ssat.org
info@ssat.org

ISEE — Educational Records Bureau (ERB)
800-989-3721
www.erblearn.org
isee@erblearn.org

REGISTERING FOR THE SSAT

Before you begin to think about preparing for the SSAT, you must complete one essential first step: **Sign up for the SSAT**. The test is administered about eight times every year—generally in October, November, December, January, February, March, April, and June. Once you decide which test date you prefer, we encourage you to register as soon as possible. Testing sites can fill up; by registering early, you will avoid the possibility of having to take the test at an inconvenient or unfamiliar second-choice location. You can register online at **www.ssat.org**, or call the SSATB at 609-683-4440 to receive a registration form by mail.

The regular registration deadline for the test (at U.S. testing centers) is usually three weeks before the test date. You may return the registration form by mail along with the $116 registration fee for test centers in the United States and Canada (or $225 for international test centers), or you may submit your registration form by fax. If you register online, you can pay the fee with either Visa or MasterCard. In some cases, you may be able to obtain an SSAT fee waiver.

If you forget to register for the test or decide to take the SSAT at the last minute, there is a late registration deadline, usually two weeks before the test date (for U.S. testing centers). If you still have at least two weeks, you can register online late and pay an additional $30 late registration fee.

Even if you miss the late registration deadline, you can be a "walk-in" for the test. The SSAT people refer to this as "standby." To do this, you must go online at **www.ssat.org**. You will be able to search for testing locations that offer standby testing, although not all sites do. You can then register online and pay an additional $60 fee. The deadline to register for standby testing is 8:00 A.M. on the day of the test.

Remember that there is no guarantee that you will be able to walk in to the test, so register in advance if you can. It will not only be less stressful to have a guarantee that you'll be allowed to take the test, but you will also save all those extra fees!

Plan Ahead
Early registration will not only give you one less thing to worry about as the test approaches, but will also help you get your first-choice test center.

Students who need special testing accommodations must register for the test at least three weeks in advance. Sunday testing is available, but only for those students who are unable to take a Saturday test for religious reasons. There is no online registration or standby testing option for Sunday administrations.

REGISTERING FOR THE ISEE

Before you begin to think about preparing for the ISEE, you must do one essential thing: **Sign up for the ISEE.** Your first step should be to get a copy of the most recent ISEE Student Guide, which comes from the Educational Records Bureau (ERB), the organization that writes and administers the ISEE. This publication is available directly from ERB (call 800-989-3721 or download it from the ERB website at **www.erblearn.org**) or from the schools to which you are applying. The test is administered on a regular basis, but test dates differ from one city to the next. The Student Guide lists all available test dates and test centers. The regular registration deadline for the test (at U.S. testing centers) is usually three weeks before the test date. The registration fee is $95. You can either mail in your registration or complete it online at **www.erblearn.org**. If you register online, you can use Visa, MasterCard, or American Express. You can also register late for the ISEE. If you register one week after the official deadline, then you pay an additional $20 fee. You must fax in your request to register late. See the ERB website for additional information on registering late.

In addition to these regularly scheduled test dates, it is possible to take the ISEE by appointment, privately, through a network of educational consultants. The fee for a private administration is from $125 to $140, and a list of those consultants who administer the ISEE is available from ERB. Even if you choose to take the test privately, be sure you make your testing appointment as far in advance as possible.

A Student's
Introduction

WHAT DO I DO WITH THIS BOOK?

You've got a hefty amount of paper and information in your hands. How can you work through it thoroughly, without spending eight hours on it the Saturday before the test?

Plan ahead.

We've broken down the contents of this book into 12 study sessions and suggested a timeline for you to follow. Some of these sessions will take longer than others, depending on your strengths and weaknesses. If any of them takes more than two hours, take a break and try to finish the session the following day. You may want to do one, two, or three sessions a week, but we suggest you give yourself at least a day or two in between each session to absorb the information you've just learned. The one thing you should be doing every day is quizzing yourself on vocabulary and making new flash cards.

Also, don't think that you can work through this book during summer vacation, put it aside in September, and be ready to take the test in December. If you want to start that early, work primarily on vocabulary until about ten weeks before the test. Then you can start on techniques, and they'll be fresh in your mind on the day of the test. If you've finished your preparation too soon and have nothing to practice on in the weeks before the test, you're going to get rusty.

If you know you are significantly weaker in one of the subjects covered by the test, you should begin with that subject so you can practice it throughout your preparation.

At Each Session

At each practice session, make sure you have sharpened pencils, blank index cards, and a dictionary. Each chapter is interactive; to fully understand the techniques we present, you need to be ready to try them out.

As you read each chapter, practice the techniques and do all the exercises. Check your answers in the Answer Key as you do each set of problems, and try to figure out what types of errors you made to correct them. Review all of the techniques that give you trouble.

As you begin each session, review the chapter you did during the previous session before moving on to a new chapter.

When You Take a Practice Test

You'll see when to take practice tests in the following session outlines. Here are some guidelines for taking these tests.

- Time yourself strictly. Use a timer, watch, or stopwatch that will ring, and do not allow yourself to go over the allotted time for any section. If you try to do so on the real test, your scores will probably be canceled.
- Take a practice test in one sitting, allowing yourself breaks of no more than two minutes between sections. You need to build up your endurance for the real test, and you also need an accurate picture of how you will do.
- Always take a practice test using an answer sheet with bubbles to fill in, just as you will for the real test. For the practice tests in this book, use the attached answer sheets. You need to be comfortable transferring answers to the separate sheet because you will be skipping around a bit.
- Each bubble you choose should be filled in thoroughly, and no other marks should be made in the answer area.
- As you fill in the bubble for a question, check to be sure you are on the correct number on the answer sheet. If you fill in the wrong bubble on the answer sheet, it won't matter if you've worked out the problem correctly in your test booklet. All that matters to the machine scoring your test is the No. 2 pencil mark.

If You're Taking the SSAT

All students should follow this syllabus as closely as possible. However, Lower Level SSAT takers (Grades 5–7) are not expected to know all the material in this book. Lower Level students should follow the guidelines provided and skip inappropriate drills—anything marked "Upper Level Only" (UL). Only Upper Level test takers (Grades 8–11) are expected to cover everything in the book as detailed in the syllabus.

Session One

In the Vocabulary chapter (Chapter 1), read the following passages and complete the practice drills.

- Read through the introduction and complete the exercises (pages 22–30).
- Complete the Word Webs for Groups 1, 2, and 3 (pages 33–35).
- Start creating your flash cards and plan how you're going to work on vocabulary every day.
- Read Chapter 5, "Everything You Always Wanted to Know About the SSAT" (pages 165–167), and Chapter 6, "General Test-Taking Techniques for the SSAT" (pages 169–173).

Session Two

- If you have not done so already, contact SSATB at 609-683-4440, or go online to **www.ssat.org**, to obtain a practice SSAT to use toward the end of your preparation. You should be able to buy two practice tests for each level in a booklet called "Preparing and Applying" (it costs $30). If you are unable to get a practice test from SSAT, then save the one in this book to use when you're done with the SSAT chapters, and try to judge your target score by asking the schools you are applying to what their average scores are for incoming students.
- If you were able to get a practice test from SSATB to use later, then take the practice SSAT in this book now (either Lower or Upper Level) using the bubble answer sheet that follows each test. Score it and look at the pacing chart in Chapter 6 to determine your target score for the next practice test.

Review
At the start of each session, quickly review the work you did on the previous session. You should also quiz yourself on vocabulary regularly.

Session Three

In the Fundamental Math Skills chapter (Chapter 2), read the following passages and complete the practice drills.

- Introduction (page 62)
- Math Vocabulary (page 63)
- The Rules of Zero (page 64)
- The Times Table (page 64)
- Working with Negative Numbers (pages 66–70)
- Order of Operations (pages 71–73)
- Factors and Factor Trees (pages 74–75)
- Multiples (pages 75–76)

In the Vocabulary chapter (Chapter 1), complete the following sections.

- Word Webs: Groups 4 and 5 (pages 36–37)
- Hit Parade: "Attempting to Be Funny" (page 47)
- Hit Parade: "Let's Get Together (UL)" (page 47)—(Upper Level Only)

Session Four

In the Fundamental Math Skills chapter, read the following passages and complete the practice drills.

- Fractions (pages 77–78)
- Improper Fractions and Mixed Numbers (pages 79–82)
- Adding and Subtracting Fractions (pages 83–84)
- Multiplying and Dividing Fractions (page 85)

In the SSAT Verbal chapter (Chapter 8), read the following passages and complete the practice and review drills.

- Introduction (pages 236–240)
- Analogies (pages 240–264)

In the Vocabulary chapter, complete the following sections.

- Word Webs: Groups 6 and 7 (pages 38–39)
- Hit Parade: "Make It Official" (page 47)

Session Five

In the Fundamental Math Skills chapter, read the following passages and complete the practice and review drills.

- Decimals (pages 86–87)
- Converting Fractions to Decimals (pages 88–89)
- Percents (pages 90–91)
- More Percents (pages 92–94)
- Exponents and Square Roots (pages 94–95)
- More Exponents (pages 96–97)—(Upper Level Only)

In the Vocabulary chapter, complete the following sections.

- Word Webs: Group 8 (page 40)
- Hit Parade: "Hard to Handle" and "The Perfect Mate" (page 48)
- Hit Parade: "Hard to Handle (UL)" and "The Perfect Mate (UL)" (page 48)—(Upper Level Only)

Session Six

In the Fundamental Math Skills chapter, read the following passages and complete the practice drills.

- Algebra Introduction (page 99)
- Solving Simple Equations (pages 99–100)
- Manipulating an Equation (pages 101–102)—(Upper Level Only)
- Manipulating Inequalities (page 103)—(Upper Level Only)
- Solving Percent Questions (pages 104–105)—(Upper Level Only)

In the SSAT Verbal chapter, read the following passages and complete the practice drills.

- Synonyms (pages 265–288)

In the Vocabulary chapter, complete the following sections.

- Word Webs: Group 9 (page 41)
- Hit Parade: "You Don't Want to Know This Guy" (page 49)
- Hit Parade: "You Don't Want to Know This Guy (UL)" (page 49)—(Upper Level Only)

Session Seven

In the Fundamental Math Skills chapter, read the following passages and complete the practice drills.

- Geometry Introduction (page 106)
- Perimeter, Angles, and Squares and Rectangles (pages 106–112)
- Triangles (pages 113–119)
- The Pythagorean Theorem (page 119)—(Upper Level Only)
- Circles (pages 120–122)—(Upper Level Only)

In the Vocabulary chapter, complete the following sections.

- Word Webs: Group 10 (page 42)
- Hit Parade: "A Bad Scene" and "Simply Perfect" (pages 50–51)
- Hit Parade: "A Bad Scene (UL)" and "Simply Perfect (UL)" (pages 50–51)—(Upper Level Only)

Session Eight

In the Fundamental Math Skills chapter, read the following passages and complete the practice and review drills.

- Word Problems (pages 123–125)

In the SSAT Math chapter (Chapter 7), read the following passages and complete the practice drills.

- Introduction (pages 176–178)
- Working with Answer Choices (pages 179–201)
- Ratios (pages 202–204)
- Averages (pages 205–206)
- Percent Change (pages 207–208)—(Upper Level Only)

In the Vocabulary chapter, complete the following section.

- Hit Parade: "Time to Make a Speech" and "Just Under the Surface" (page 51)

Session Nine

In the SSAT Math chapter, read the following passages and complete the practice drills.

- Plugging In (pages 208–212)
- Plugging In The Answers (pages 213–215)
- Geometry (pages 216–219)

In the SSAT Reading chapter, read the following passages and complete the practice drills.

- Reading (pages 289–304)

In the Vocabulary chapter, complete the following sections.

- Word Webs: Group 11 (page 43)
- Hit Parade: "Hardworking" and "Nice Attitude" (page 52)

Session Ten

In the SSAT Math chapter, read the following passages and complete the practice drills.

- Functions (pages 219–220)
- Charts and Graphs (pages 221–232)
- Math Review (pages 233–234)

In the SSAT Reading chapter, read the following passages and complete the review and practice drills.

- Review—The Reading Plan (pages 304–318)

In the Vocabulary chapter, complete the following section.

- Word Webs: Groups 12 and 13 (pages 44–45)

Session Eleven

Read and complete the exercises in the Writing the Essay chapter (pages 138–161).

Session Twelve

- Take another practice SSAT, preferably an actual released test that you've obtained from the SSAT Board. If you are working from their booklet, "Preparing and Applying," take Practice Test I timed, and score it. (Use Practice Test II as additional timed practice questions, if you have time.)
- If there are questions that are still giving you trouble, review the appropriate chapters.

A Note for Lower Level Students

If you are taking the Lower Level SSAT, there may be some problems at the end of each practice set that are too difficult for you. Don't be discouraged—they will be difficult for everyone in your grade level. Just do your best and work on as many problems as you can.

If You're Taking the ISEE

Upper Level, Middle Level, and Lower Level test takers should all follow this syllabus. Sections that cover material meant only for Upper Level and/or Middle Level test takers are marked accordingly. Upper Level test takers should do all the work detailed in this syllabus. Lower Level test takers should skip only the sections marked "Middle and Upper Level Only," or "(UL)."

Session One

In the Vocabulary chapter (Chapter 1) read the following passages and complete the practice drills.

- Read through the introduction and complete the exercises (pages 22–30).
- Complete the Word Webs for Groups 1, 2, and 3 (pages 33–35).
- Start creating your flash cards and plan how you're going to work on vocabulary every day.
- Read Chapter 15, "Everything You Always Wanted to Know About the ISEE" (pages 419–421), and Chapter 16, "General Test-Taking Techniques for the ISEE" (423–425).

Session Two

- Take the ISEE practice test contained in this book, according to your grade level.
- If you have not done so already, contact the Educational Records Bureau at 800-446-0320, or **www.erblearn.org**, to obtain any practice materials available to supplement your preparation. You should be able to get a booklet called "What to Expect on the ISEE" (it costs $15, or you can download it for free). This booklet contains sample questions for each test level, and half-length practice tests for Middle and Upper Level tests.

Session Three

In the Fundamental Math Skills chapter (Chapter 2), read the following passages and complete the practice drills.

- Introduction (page 62)
- Math Vocabulary (page 63)
- The Rules of Zero (page 64)
- The Times Table (page 64)
- Working with Negative Numbers (pages 66–70)
- Order of Operations (pages 71–73)
- Factors and Factor Trees (pages 74–75)
- Multiples (pages 75–76)

In the Vocabulary chapter (Chapter 1), complete the following sections.

- Word Webs: Groups 4 and 5 (pages 36–37)
- Hit Parade: "Attempting to Be Funny" (page 47)
- Hit Parade: "Let's Get Together (UL)" (page 47)—(Upper Level Only)

Session Four

In the Fundamental Math Skills chapter, read the following passages and complete the practice drills.

- Fractions (pages 77–78)
- Improper Fractions and Mixed Numbers (pages 79–82)
- Adding and Subtracting Fractions (pages 83–84)
- Multiplying and Dividing Fractions (page 85)

In the ISEE Verbal chapter (Chapter 18), read the following passages and complete the practice and review drills.

- Introduction (pages 492–495)
- Synonyms (pages 496–516)

In the Vocabulary chapter, complete the following sections.

- Word Webs: Groups 6 and 7 (pages 38–39)
- Hit Parade: "Make It Official" (page 47)

Session Five

In the Fundamental Math Skills chapter, read the following passages and complete the practice drills.

- Decimals (pages 86–87)
- Converting Fractions to Decimals (pages 88–89)
- Percents (pages 90–91)
- More Percents (pages 92–94)
- Exponents and Square Roots (pages 94–95)
- More Exponents (pages 96–97)—(Upper Level Only)
- Review Drill 1—The Building Blocks (page 98)

In the Vocabulary chapter, complete the following sections.

- Word Webs: Group 8 (page 40)
- Hit Parade: "Hard to Handle" and "The Perfect Mate" (page 48)
- Hit Parade: "Hard to Handle (UL)" and "The Perfect Mate (UL)" (page 48)—(Upper Level Only)

Session Six

In the Fundamental Math Skills chapter, read the following passages and complete the practice drills.

- Algebra Introduction (page 99)
- Solving Simple Equations (pages 99–100)
- Manipulating an Equation (pages 101–102)—(Middle and Upper Level Only)
- Manipulating Inequalities (page 103)—(Middle and Upper Level Only)
- Solving Percent Questions (pages 104–105)—(Middle and Upper Level Only)

In the ISEE Verbal chapter, read the following passages and complete the practice and review drills.

- Sentence Completions (pages 517–540)

In the Vocabulary chapter, complete the following sections.

- Word Webs: Group 9 (page 41)
- Hit Parade: "You Don't Want to Know This Guy" (page 49)
- Hit Parade: "You Don't Want to Know This Guy (UL)" (page 49)—(Upper Level Only)

Session Seven

In the Fundamental Math Skills chapter, read the following passages and complete the practice drills.

- Geometry Introduction (page 106)
- Perimeter, Angles, and Squares, and Rectangles (pages 106–112)
- Triangles (pages 113–119)
- The Pythagorean Theorem (page 119)—(Middle and Upper Level Only)
- Circles (pages 120–122)—(Middle and Upper Level Only)

In the Vocabulary chapter, complete the following sections.

- Word Webs: Group 10 (page 42)
- Hit Parade: "A Bad Scene" and "Simply Perfect" (pages 50–51)
- Hit Parade: "A Bad Scene (UL)" and "Simply Perfect (UL)" (pages 50–51)—(Upper Level Only)

Session Eight

In the Fundamental Math Skills chapter, read the following passages and complete the practice and review drills.

- Word Problems (pages 123–125)

In the ISEE Math chapter (Chapter 17), read the following passages and complete the practice drills.

- Introduction and General Math Strategies (pages 428–449)
- Ratios (pages 450–451)
- Averages (pages 451–454)
- Percent Change (page 455)—(Upper Level Only)

In the Vocabulary chapter, complete the following section.

- Hit Parade: "Time to Make a Speech" and "Just Under the Surface" (page 51)

Session Nine

In the ISEE Math chapter, read the following passages and complete the practice drills.

- Plugging In (pages 456–464)
- Geometry (pages 465–466)

In the ISEE Reading chapter, read the following passages and complete the practice and review drills.

- Reading (pages 541–572)

In the Vocabulary chapter, complete the following sections.

- Word Webs: Group 11 (page 43)
- Hit Parade: "Hardworking" and "Nice Attitude" (page 52)

Session Ten

In the ISEE Math chapter, read the following passages and complete the practice and review drills.

- Functions (pages 467–468)
- Charts and Graphs (pages 469–474)
- Quantitative Comparison (pages 475–487)—(Middle and Upper Level Only)
- Math Review (pages 488–489)

In the Vocabulary chapter, complete the following section.

- Word Webs: Groups 12 and 13 (pages 44–45)

Session Eleven

Read and complete the exercises in the Writing the Essay chapter (pages 138–161).

Session Twelve

- Take another practice ISEE, preferably an actual test obtained from the ERB.
- If there are questions that are still giving you trouble, review the appropriate chapters.

A Note for Lower and Middle Level Students

If you are taking the Lower Level or Middle Level ISEE, you should NOT complete the sections of this book that deal with quantitative comparison. You should also avoid the vocabulary marked "(UL)." Also note that there may be some problems at the end of each practice set that are too difficult for you. Don't be discouraged—they will be difficult for everyone in your grade level. Just do your best and work on as many problems as you can.

The Day of the Exam

- Wake up refreshed from at least eight hours' sleep the night before.
- Eat a good breakfast.
- Arrive at the test center about half an hour early.
- Have with you all the necessary paperwork that shows you have registered for the test, four No. 2 pencils with erasers, and a working black pen. You may also want to bring juice or water and a small snack like a granola bar. The test center may not allow you to bring food or beverages into the room, but you can leave them in the hall, in case you have a chance to get them during a short break. Do not bring a cell phone or any books, papers, or calculators.
- Remind yourself that you do not have to work out every question on the test to get a good score. Don't let yourself become rushed. Pace yourself.

Part I
The Basics of Both Tests

Chapter 1
What's So Important About Vocabulary?

WHY LEARN NEW WORDS?

Although this book is going to show you many ways to get verbal questions right when you don't know the exact definitions of the words involved, the fastest and most accurate way to answer questions correctly is to know what the words mean! So, while you will learn techniques to help you answer the questions on these tests, you will also need to learn new vocabulary.

Take It Easy
The easiest way to get any question right is to know all the words in it!

Learning new words along with the techniques to answer questions will increase your SSAT or ISEE score much more than just learning the techniques alone. Your vocabulary skills affect not only your verbal score, but also your reading score. And there are many more advantages to learning new vocabulary. Here are just a few to help motivate you.

1. It is arguable whether or not you will need to know the number of degrees in a triangle as an adult, but no matter who you are or what career path you follow, a good vocabulary will always be essential in your everyday life.
2. Impress your friends, teachers, and parents. Nothing says, "Mom, I did my homework; now can I go to the movies?" like using the word *recalcitrant* to describe your former aversion to learning new vocabulary.
3. Insult your enemies without their even knowing it. Let the "troglodytes" know what you really think of them.
4. Want to go to college? Graduate school? Well, guess what you'll need to know? That's right: more vocabulary words.

WHERE TO FIND NEW WORDS

Vocabulary in This Book

We have put together this chapter to get you started on learning new words. You will find two lists here: the **Hit Parade** and **Back-for-More**. The words on the Hit Parade list have shown up often on past tests. Whether you have two weeks or twenty, you will need to learn all the words on this list. The test writers are not terribly original, so they often recycle words from old tests. The Back-for-More list contains more words at the level of vocabulary tested on the SSAT and ISEE. If you are getting started more than ten weeks in advance, you should aim to learn all the words on both these lists.

The section on Word Parts (prefixes, roots, and suffixes) in this chapter is excellent for learning the pieces of words that show up repeatedly in difficult vocabulary. By knowing the roots of the English language, you can often decipher the meaning of an unknown word without looking up its definition. The best way to learn the meaning of a word part is by thinking of the words that you already know that contain the part. Then you can stretch this group of words to include new ones. If you learn words this way, you're more likely to remember them because you've linked them to words you already know.

Finally, the Verbal and Reading chapters have plenty of practice questions and reading passages. Whenever you see a word you don't know, answer the question without looking anything up, and circle the words of which you're not sure. Write the circled words on flash cards, and look them up after you are done.

Everywhere Else

Newspapers, magazines, books, people, and even television are all sources of new words. Once you become aware of how many new words are right around you, you'll be able to identify them quickly and make them your own.

You hear and read words you don't know all the time. How do you keep from running to the dictionary every hour? You figure out what the word means based on the context in which it is used—the other words around it.

> Steve had nervous tics that exposed his anxiety at inconvenient times—during an oral report, one or another of his appendages might start twitching uncontrollably.

What do you think an *appendage* is? _____

How about a *tic*? _____

Now look up these words in a dictionary:

appendage: _____

tic: _____

How close were you? If you surmised that the author meant "parts of the body" when she wrote *appendages*, you were right, and you understood the sentence. But notice that the main dictionary definition of *appendage* is different. The next time you see this word, it may refer to something else—not just a body part. And that brings us to…

The Dangers of Word Definitions

The SSAT and ISEE test dictionary definitions of words, so assuming that you know a word's definition just because you've seen the word before can be very dangerous. Also, some words have more than one definition, and you may not be able to guess all the definitions from the context in which the words are used. So whenever you hear or read a new word, try to figure out what it means from the way it is used, but also write down that word and look up its definition in the dictionary.

Newspapers, Magazines, and Books

Choose a newspaper or magazine that your parents or older siblings read, or just pick one from the following list. Read a few articles from it each week, keeping the dictionary nearby. The Op-Ed pages of major newspapers are a great place to start. If you didn't have to use the dictionary the first week, change your periodical!

Newspapers

Daily Newspapers	Website Addresses
The New York Times	www.nytimes.com
USA Today	www.usatoday.com
Wall Street Journal	http://online.wsj.com

Is your local paper on the Web? Check it out at **www.usnpl.com**.

Magazines

Magazines	Website Addresses
TIME	www.time.com
Newsweek	www.thedailybeast.com/newsweek
National Geographic	www.nationalgeographic.com
Popular Science	www.popsci.com

Books

It's much more fun to learn new words if you are reading a really good book. The books listed are full of great stories and loads of new words. Whenever you see a word you don't know, write it on a flash card. See if you can guess the meaning from its context.

Fiction

Title	Author
Watership Down	Richard Adams
The Outsiders	S. E. Hinton
Great Expectations	Charles Dickens
Pride and Prejudice	Jane Austen
Jane Eyre	Charlotte Brontë
The Call of the Wild	Jack London
The Adventures of Sherlock Holmes	Sir Arthur Conan Doyle
To Kill a Mockingbird	Harper Lee
Animal Farm	George Orwell
The Adventures of Huckleberry Finn	Mark Twain
Things Fall Apart	Chinua Achebe
I Know Why the Caged Bird Sings	Maya Angelou

Science Fiction and Fantasy

Title	Author
The Phantom Tollbooth	Norton Juster
The Hobbit	J. R. R. Tolkien
The Lord of the Rings	J. R. R. Tolkien
I, Robot	Isaac Asimov
Fahrenheit 451	Ray Bradbury
The War of the Worlds	H. G. Wells
Brave New World	Aldous Huxley

Nonfiction

Title	Author
Narrative of the Life of Frederick Douglass	Frederick Douglass
The Diary of a Young Girl	Anne Frank
The Wright Brothers	Russell Freedman
Twenty Years at Hull House	Jane Addams

Vocabulary-Building Books and Websites

If you're starting way ahead of your scheduled test date, or if you want to continue learning new words and making it easier to do so, you may want to check out these resources.

Books
Word Power Made Easy by Norman Lewis
Word Smart and *More Word Smart* by Adam Robinson and the Staff of The Princeton Review (Grades 8–12)
Word Smart Junior and *Word Smart Junior II* by C. L. Brantley and the Staff of The Princeton Review (Grades 6–8)

Websites
www.m-w.com
www.wordcentral.com
www.syndicate.com
www.vocabulary.com
http://freerice.com

Note: These are provided for reference only, and neither they nor any products advertised by them or in their websites are endorsed by The Princeton Review or the authors of this book.

LEARNING THE NEW WORDS

Looking up a new word is only your first step. The next step is even more important: writing it down.

If you write down words and definitions in a list and then read them over periodically, you'll remember a few of them. But why go through all that trouble looking them up and writing them down if you're not able to remember them afterward? You need a better way to make sure your vocabulary time isn't wasted.

Make a flash card for each individual word. You may have used flash cards before, but be sure to read this and the following two pages to learn how to make them really useful.

Step 1: You'll need 3 × 5 index cards. Have them handy while you are working in this book and whenever you read. Stash a few blank ones in your backpack so they're always handy.

Step 2: Whenever you see a word you don't know, write the unknown word on one side of the card. (You can also write down the sentence or phrase in which you heard it.)

Step 3: When you get to your dictionary, look up the word and write down the definition(s) on the other side of the card.

Step 4: To help you remember the definition, you will need to associate the word with what you already know. There are several ways to do this, and you can use whichever method works best for you and the particular word you are learning. Here they are.

- **Make up a sentence connecting the word to someone or something you know.** If you're trying to learn the word *banal* and your friend Jean never seems to have anything original to say, make a sentence for banal that stars Jean.
- **Draw a picture to show the meaning.** If you're trying to remember *mosaic*, sketch tiles laid out in a pattern or picture. The funnier the picture, the easier it is to remember.
- **Make up a sentence or phrase that is a mnemonic.** A mnemonic uses the way a word sounds along with its definition to jog your memory. If you want to be sure you remember that *laud* means to "praise and acclaim," you can imagine a whole congregation proclaiming, "Praise the Laud!" Again, the funnier the mnemonic, the easier it is to remember.
- **Write down the word parts that make up the word you want to remember.** In good dictionaries, the roots and prefixes that are found in a word are right in its entry, after the pronunciation and part of speech. If you're making a card for *benevolent*, write down "bene = good" and write down another "bene" word you know well (like *benefit* or *beneficial*).

Start Now!
Do you know what *banal*, *mosaic,* and *benevolent* mean? If not, time to find a dictionary and make a flash card!

- **Group your cards by their general definitions.** If you've got many cards with words on them that mean bad character traits, put them together.

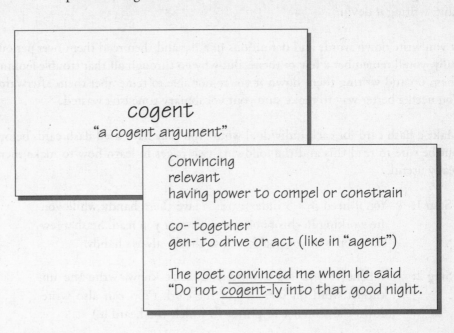

cogent

"a cogent argument"

Convincing
relevant
having power to compel or constrain

co- together
gen- to drive or act (like in "agent")

The poet convinced me when he said
"Do not cogent-ly into that good night.

Step 5:   Now it's time to study. You should review your flash cards at least once EVERY DAY. Don't simply read the word and then its definition. Try to define the word on the card and then check your answer with the definition on the other side. You can either test yourself or have your parents or friends quiz you. The best part about using flash cards is you can study them almost anywhere: in a car or bus on your way to school, while you are waiting for dinner, or right before bed. Carry them in your backpack, and you can work on them wherever you go.

Step 6:   Once you've learned the definition of a word really well, you can move that card into a box or container for safekeeping. You need to go through the cards in the box only once a week to make sure you still remember the definitions of those words.

Step 7:   Try this new lexicon out on your parents, friends, and teachers. You'll be able to get your point across more quickly and accurately with precise verbiage.

Important Tips About Using Flash Cards

- Be sure to have blank cards handy to write down the words in the Hit Parade and Back-for-More lists and anywhere else in this book where you see a word you don't know.
- Don't bite off more than you can chew. You will learn the words and their definitions more quickly if you work on a group of 20 to 25 words at a time. Once you have learned a word, put it in a box of words you know and add a new word to the group you are working on.
- No one says you have to do the whole pile of words at once. Squeeze them in whenever you have time during the day. Work on a few during any spare five minutes you have.
- Try going through the stack two or three times in a row. The first time you go through the stack, put aside every word you correctly defined and return to the stack those that you missed. Repeat this process until you have discarded all your cards.

WORD PARTS

Suffixes

The suffix (the end part of a word) can often tell you what part of speech a word is. Let's quickly review the most basic parts of speech, or you can look them up in a good dictionary:

What is a noun? _____

What is a verb? _____

What is an adjective? _____

What is an adverb? _____

Look at the following suffixes and examples, and add some words of your own that end in each suffix. Then look at all the words that end in that suffix. Which parts of speech are they? Check your answers in the Word Parts Index at the end of this chapter.

-ness: happiness, friendliness _____

-able: perishable, amiable _____

-ous: androgynous, fibrous _____

-ity: animosity, charity _____

-ology: psychology, sociology _____

-ical: tyrannical, hypothetical _____

-archy: monarchy, anarchy, matriarchy _____

-less: fearless, artless _____

Prefixes and Roots

Prefixes come at the beginnings of words, and roots can be anywhere in words. Both types of word parts are very helpful in trying to remember words that are new to you. For example, say you come upon the word *vociferous* (voh-SIF-uh-rus). You make a card for it, and then you try to think of other words that have that same root, *voc*. *Vocal* is a word you know has to do with speaking, and so now, when you see *vociferous* again, you'll remember it has to do with speaking. If you always imagine *vociferous* being shouted, you'll remember the rest of its meaning: "*loud and insistent* in speaking."

Notice that the sound of *voc* is not the same in *vociferous* as it is in *vocal*. Word parts change their sound over time, and most of the words you'll be learning have been around for hundreds of years. Not only do the sounds change, but the meanings also mutate over time, so today's meaning of a word is sometimes far different from the sum of its word parts. Thus, these word parts are to be used to help you remember and group new vocabulary (there's that *voc* again, in a word that has to do with speaking), and not as a substitute for looking up words.

The word parts on each page of this section can be linked together by the meanings of the words that contain them. This is a great way to think about words in general—they're linked by their word parts, and the many links that crisscross build a web.

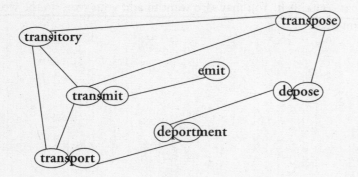

And that's only seven words!

Using the Word Web Pages

On each page in this section, you'll find word parts on the top and words on the bottom. Here's how to use the pages.

1. Start with one of the words from the bottoms of the pages. Write it in the center. Circle the word parts it contains.

2. Now choose another word from the list that contains a matching word part. Write that word out, circling any word parts it contains, and draw a line between the parts that match in each word.

3. Repeat this step until you have linked all the words that were at the bottom of the page, making a web like the one above.

4. As you come across a word you don't know, look it up and make a flash card for it. There will be many words you don't know on these pages. When you look up these words, remember that the word parts and their meanings are at the beginning of the dictionary entries.

5. Now look at the word parts at the tops of the pages. On the first line under each word part, write down what you think it means, from the context of the words you've seen. Check this in the Word Parts Index on pages 59 to 60. The index has abbreviated versions of what each root means. Don't be discouraged if you don't guess correctly at the meaning every time; you may be closer than you think because some word parts have wider meanings than just those we've included.

6. On the second line under each word part, write a word of your own that contains it. You may also want to add your word to the web you drew.

Group 1

ROOT	chron	a	morph	path
meaning				
your word				
ROOT	**anti**	**par**	**dis**	**dign/dain**
meaning				
your word				

synchronize	chronicle	anachronism	amoral
apathy	apartheid	amorphous	metamorphosis
sympathy	empathy	pathos	antipathy
parity	disparate	dissociate	disparity
disperse	dissuade	dissipate	dignify
deign	disdain		

Group 2

ROOT	mis	gyn	phobe
meaning			
your word			
ROOT	phil	techn	anthr/andr
meaning			
your word			

miscreant	misanthrope	mistake	anthropology
philanthropy	androgynous	misogyny	philosophy
technophile	technophobe	technology	technique

Group 3

ROOT	sub	terr	vers/vert
meaning			
your word			
ROOT	extr	super	sed
meaning			
your word			

substantiate	subterranean	subordinate	terrestrial
terrarium	subvert	advertise	extrovert
traverse	extraterrestrial	extrapolate	supervise
superimpose	supersede	sediment	sedate
subside	subservient	introvert	

Group 4

ROOT	vor	carn	in/en/im/em	tract
meaning				
your word				
ROOT	**ante**	**bell**	**am**	**nat/nas/nai**
meaning				
your word				
ROOT	**omni**	**pot**	**sci**	**pre**
meaning				
your word				

voracious	devour	carnivorous	carnage
incarnation	infiltrate	input	inject
ingratiate	incarnate	intractable	protract
tractor	antecedent	antebellum	rebel
belligerent	bellicose	enamored	amorous
amity	amicable	innate	nascent
naive	natal	native	renaissance
omnivorous	omniscient	omnipotent	potential
potent	potentate	prescience	preface
prefix	predestine		

Group 5

ROOT	amb	re	spec	post
meaning				
your word				
ROOT	**circ/circum**	**ven/vent**	**scrib/script**	**man**
meaning				
your word				

ambitious	amble	circumambulate	circumscribe
circumvent	circumspect	redo	repudiate
recirculate	convene	intervene	inspect
auspicious	transcribe	manuscript	postpone
postscript	manual	manufacture	manifest

Group 6

ROOT	uni	anim	equi/equ	ad/at
meaning				
your word				
ROOT	voc	magna	loc/loq/log	neo/nov
meaning				
your word				

unified	unanimous	animosity	magnanimous
equitable	equilibrium	iniquity	equanimity
equivocate	attract	adhere	advocate
vociferous	vocal	convoke	magnificent
magniloquent	eloquent	loquacious	circumlocution
neologism	novice	innovate	neophyte

Group 7

ROOT	epi	hyper	hypo	derm
meaning				
your word				
ROOT	dem	tens/ten	pan	
meaning				
your word				

epiloque	epithet	hypertension	hypodermic
epidermis	dermatologist	tensile	tenuous
epidemic	democracy	demographics	pandemic
panorama			

Group 8

ROOT	eu	phon	dys	bene
meaning				
your word				
ROOT	dic	mal	fac	fic/fig
meaning				
your word				

euphoria	euphemism	eulogy	euphony
utopia	megaphone	cacophony	dystopia
dyslexia	benefit	beneficent	benevolent
benediction	benign	dictionary	dictation
contradict	malediction	malevolent	malicious
malign	maleficent	malodorous	facile
factory	malefactor	manufacture	deficient
proficient	prolific	effigy	soporific

Group 9

ROOT	ex/ej	clu/clo/cla	cis
meaning			
your word			
ROOT	culp	ten	ac/acr
meaning			
your word			

exit	eject	exculpate	excise
exclusive	preclude	cloister	foreclose
recluse	scissors	incisive	concise
culprit	culpable	extenuate	tenable
tentative	tenacious	acrid	acerbic
acumen	exacerbate	acrimonious	

Group 10

ROOT	co/com/con	cur/cour	her/hes	sequ/secru
meaning				
your word				
ROOT	**tact**	**gen**	**homo**	**norm/nym**
meaning				
your word				
ROOT	**hetero**	**fid**	**vi/viv**	**vid/vis**
meanine				
your word				

confide	convivial	cogent	concurrent
convoke	cursory	current	precursor
incur	coherent	cohesive	inherent
consequently	consecutive	tactile	contact
genesis	congenial	progeny	homogenous
homonym	synonym	anonymous	pseudonym
misnomer	ignominy	heterogenous	heterdox
fidelity	infidel	bona fide	diffident
perfidy	fiduciary	vivacious	viable
vivid	vivisection	vista	evident
video	visage	supervise	

Group 11

ROOT	bi	di	ab/abs
meaning			
your word			
ROOT	ad/at	us/ut	ob
meaning			
your word			

bipartisan	bicycle	bisect	dichotomy
digress	diaphanous	divide	dissect
abhor	abdicate	abscond	abstain
attract	adjacent	advocate	abuse
utilitarian	utilize	obsinate	obviate
obscure			

Group 12

ROOT	in/il/im/ir	un/non	cred	mut
meaning				
your word				
ROOT	**pun/pen**	**apt/ept**	**plac**	
meaning				
your word				

illegible	incredible	irresponsible	improper
unusual	nonsense	credible	credence
immutable	permutation	impunity	penalty
punitive	penance	adapt	apt
inept	adept	implacable	placid
placate			

Group 13

ROOT	pro	cli	inter	intra
meaning				
your word				
ROOT	pon/pos	de	port	trans
meaning				
your word				
ROOT	mit/mis	luc/lum/lus	esce	
meaning				
your word				

Flash Cards
Go back to the first part of this chapter for ways to use flash cards creatively and effectively.

propose	produce	recline	proclivity
disinclination	interject	interpose	interlude
intervene	intravenous	transpose	deposit
depose	deport	decipher	defame
deportment	purport	portfolio	transitory
transport	translucent	transmit	emissary
missive	remission	demise	emit
luminescent	illustrious	lucid	lackluster
elucidate	obsolescent	coalesce	quiescent
acquiescent			

HIT PARADE

The words on the Hit Parade list are from released SSATs and ISEE sample questions. These words give you an idea of the level of difficulty of SSAT and ISEE words, and they're likely to appear on future tests as well. The definitions included with them are the ones that have been tested; for additional nuances and secondary meanings, consult a dictionary.

Some words are followed by relevant roots, prefixes, and/or suffixes or by a more familiar variant of the word. These are provided in parentheses for you to use on your flash cards.

How to Use This List

Go through the Hit Parade with one hand covering the definitions, and try to define each word. Write each word that you don't know or can't really define on a flash card. If you already know the word and its definition, you don't need to put it on a flash card.

Lower Level and Middle Level students do not have to know the words marked "UL" (Upper Level), but there is no harm in learning them as well. Upper Level students must know all the words in this list.

ATTEMPTING TO BE FUNNY

Jeer   *to make fun of*

Jest   *to joke (court jester)*

Parody   *a humorous imitation*

Recreation   *something done for fun, a hobby or game*

Skit   *a short comic scene*

LET'S GET TOGETHER (UL)

Adjunct   *an accessory, something added on (ad + junc/join)*

Coalesce   *to come together (esce)*

Congeal   *to thicken, or change from liquid to solid (con)*

Consensus   *an agreement (con)*

Contiguous   *lying side by side (con)*

Fission   *a splitting apart*

Fusion   *a joining together*

Integrate   *to bring together and make whole (integer)*

Juxtapose   *to place side by side*

Pact   *a formal agreement between two countries; a bargain*

Rendezvous   *a meeting, usually secret*

MAKE IT OFFICIAL

Abdicate   *to give up power (ab)*

Accord   *to be in agreement*

Allege   *to declare that something is true without proof*

Assess   *to evaluate or determine the worth of*

Condone   *to forgive or disregard an offense*

Conventional   *traditional, ordinary (con + vent)*

Counsel   *to advise*

Debunk   *to prove false*

Decree   *an order or a command*

Inquiry   *a request for information (in)*

Ratify   *to approve, usually a law*

Sustain   *to support*

HARD TO HANDLE

Ambiguous	*unclear*
Amorphous	*without shape (a + morph + ous)*
Itinerant	*nomadic, constantly moving*
Kinetic	*moving*
Obscure	*hidden or dark, hard to see (ob); to hide*
Remote	*far away, distant (remote control)*
Writhe	*to twist*

HARD TO HANDLE (UL)

Egress	*exit*
Epoch	*a period of time*
Intangible	*not able to be touched or sensed (in + tang + ible)*
Polymorphous	*having many shapes (poly + morph + ous)*
Prolific	*fertile, very productive (pro)*
Scull	*a small rowboat or an oar for a rowboat*
Sporadic	*having no pattern or order*
Surrogate	*a substitute*
Variegated	*having many parts or colors*

THE PERFECT MATE

Akin	*related to or alike*
Amiable	*friendly, good-natured (able)*
Congenial	*agreeable (con + gen)*
Equivalent	*equal (equi)*
Extol	*to praise (ex)*
Placate	*to quiet down, appease (plac)*

THE PERFECT MATE (UL)

Altruistic	*doing good for others*
Aspirant	*someone reaching for something (aspirations)*
Astute	*sharp, shrewd*
Benevolence	*goodness (bene)*

YOU DON'T WANT TO KNOW THIS GUY

Animosity   *hostility (anim + ity)*

Debilitating   *weakening, harmful (de)*

Deficient   *lacking an essential part (de)*

Insolent   *disrespectful, rude (in)*

Irate   *enraged*

Notorious   *known widely and unfavorably*

Profane   *to abuse or put to ill use*

Recalcitrant   *disobedient, stubborn*

Warlock   *a male witch*

YOU DON'T WANT TO KNOW THIS GUY (UL)

Aloof   *keeping a distance*

Banal   *unoriginal and boring*

Belligerent   *hostile, warlike (bell)*

Browbeat   *to intimidate*

Choleric   *irritable*

Garrulous   *overly talkative (ous)*

Incompetent   *not able to do something properly (in)*

Insipid   *lacking interest, dull, boring (in)*

Ostentatious   *showy, pretentious (ous)*

Pedantic   *overly scholarly, boring*

Pugnacious   *hostile (ous)*

Ravenous   *extremely hungry (ous)*

Sanctimonious   *acting morally superior, holier-than-thou (ous)*

A BAD SCENE

Abyss — *a deep narrow pit*

Barrage — *a flood*

Brig — *the prison of a ship*

Hovel — *a shack*

Indictment — *the situation of having been charged with a crime (dic)*

Quiver — *a portable container for arrows; to tremble*

Plight — *a bad situation, a predicament*

Rue — *to regret*

A BAD SCENE (UL)

Adverse — *unfavorable, opposed, going against (ad + verse)*

Aggravate — *to make worse*

Assailable — *vulnerable (able)*

Corpulent — *excessively overweight*

Founder — *to sink (a boat "founders"); someone who starts something*

Impasse — *a deadlock, a point at which one can go no further (im)*

Incumbent — *someone who is currently holding a political position*

Insinuation — *a sneaky suggestion of something bad*

Mar — *to spoil, to mark*

Null — *zero value ("null and void")*

Repudiate — *to put down, to renounce*

Ruse — *a clever trick*

Sedate — *to calm, especially by use of a drug*

Slander — *a false and mean-spirited statement meant to injure someone*

Superfluous — *more than what is required or needed (super + ous)*

SIMPLY PERFECT

Benign   *harmless (bene)*

Exquisite   *beautifully made or designed*

Immaculate   *perfectly clean, free from dirt or stain (im)*

Robust   *healthy*

TIME TO MAKE A SPEECH

Illuminate   *to light up or make clear (lum)*

Imply   *to express indirectly*

Lament   *to express grief for, mourn*

Reminiscence *a memory, the act of recalling the past (re)*

SIMPLY PERFECT (UL)

Clarity   *clearness*

Deft   *skillful*

Meticulous   *careful, paying attention to details (ous)*

Pious   *deeply religious (ous)*

JUST UNDER THE SURFACE

Dormant   *temporarily inactive, asleep*

Eradicate   *to erase or get rid of*

Excavate   *to dig up (ex)*

Fundamental   *an essential part, basic*

Innate   *possessed at birth, not learned (in + nat)*

Merge   *to blend together*

HARDWORKING

Adept	*very skilled*
Facet	*an aspect of something*
Ingenuity	*innovation, creativity (in + gen + ity)*
Inscribe	*to write or etch words on or into a surface (in + scrib)*
Novice	*a beginner (nov)*
Procure	*to obtain*
Tenacious	*holding firmly, especially to a belief, stubborn (ten + ac + ous)*
Toil	*hard work, or to work hard*
Vend	*to sell*
Vigor	*strength, energy*
Wane	*to decrease in size or strength*

NICE ATTITUDE

Admiring	*regarding with approval or respect*
Ambivalent	*having opposing or mixed feelings (such as love and hate)*
Analytical	*intending to understand the nature of something (ical)*
Biased	*favoring one side or opinion over another*
Brash	*bold*
Cautious	*careful (ous)*
Dubious	*doubtful (ous)*
Ironic	*the use of words to express an unintended or contradictory meaning*
Jubilant	*overly joyful*
Objective	*not influenced by personal opinion, just the facts*
Sarcastic	*the use of witty language used to insult or show displeasure*
Skeptical	*doubtful (ical)*
Somber	*serious, dark, or gloomy*
Subjective	*influenced by personal opinion, biased*
Temperament	*your usual mood or behavior*

THE BACK-FOR-MORE LIST

The following list contains words that are at the fifth- through eleventh-grade levels and could likely appear on the SSAT, ISEE, and other equivalent standardized tests. Just as with the Hit Parade list, Lower Level and Middle Level students do not have to know the words marked "UL," but there is no harm in learning them as well. Upper Level students should know all of the words in this list.

Some words are followed by relevant roots, prefixes, and/or suffixes or by a more familiar variant of the word; these are provided in parentheses for you to use on your flash cards.

How to Use This List

This list of words is a supplement for those students who are either getting started on their preparations ten weeks or more in advance or for those students who have already learned all the words on the Hit Parade.

Go through the Back-for-More list with one hand covering the definitions, trying to define each word. Write each word you don't know or can't really define on a flash card. If you already know the word and its definition, you don't need to put it on a flash card.

Popular Secondary Definitions

We bet you've seen these words before, but you probably don't know that they have secondary definitions that are used more often on these tests than their primary definitions.

Pedestrian   *ordinary, dull*

Uniform   *all the same, common*

Sage   *wise*

Flag   *to decrease or diminish*

Refrain   *to hold back, abstain, or restrain*

WOE IS ME

Abominable   *horrible or unpleasant (able)*

Arid   *very dry*

Delusion   *a false opinion or idea*

Despair   *a feeling of absolute hopelessness, or to lose hope*

Dread   *overwhelming fear or to be very afraid*

Exasperate   *to make very angry or impatient*

Gaunt   *very thin and bony*

Impediment   *an obstacle, something in the way (im)*

Laden   *weighed down with a heavy load, burdened*

Parch   *to make very thirsty*

Pungent   *a sharp, biting smell or taste*

Rancid   *having a nasty smell or taste, rotting*

Repugnant   *highly disgusting, offensive*

Revile   *to criticize with abusive language*

Scorn   *to abuse or treat with no respect, or a strong feeling of dislike*

WOE IS ME (UL)

Abhor   *to hate or detest*

Deleterious   *harmful to one's health (ous)*

Disparage   *to criticize or speak badly of (dis)*

Penurious   *extremely stingy or miserly (ous)*

Quandary   *a state of uncertainty*

Recuperate   *to heal or return to good health (re)*

Salve   *something used to heal or soothe*

OLD SCHOOL

Authentic   *genuine and true, not fake*

Era   *a period of time (usually in the past)*

Extinct   *no longer existing (ex)*

Hackneyed   *over used and old-fashioned*

Hoary   *very old, or gray from old age*

Obsolete   *out of date, no longer useful (ob)*

Posterity   *all of a person's descendents (post + ity)*

Premise   *an essential fact that others are based on*

Retrospect   *the review of past events, hindsight (spec)*

SAY YOU'RE SORRY

Absolved   *freed from guilt or blame (ab)*

Concede   *to give in or surrender*

Contrition   *deep regret for doing something wrong*

Implore   *to beg or ask earnestly*

Indignant   *feeling angry or insulted from an injustice or wrongdoing (in)*

Obdurate   *stubborn (ob)*

Obstinate   *stubborn (ob)*

Pardoned   *forgiven*

Penitent   *feeling or expressing remorse for a wrongdoing*

Placate   *to please, or make less angry (plac)*

Revere   *to deeply respect or admire*

FROM THE INSTITUTIONS OF HIGHER LEARNING

Abridge   *to shorten in length or duration (a + bridge)*

Academic   *having to do with school or education*

Adage   *an old saying usually considered to be true*

Assert   *to state a viewpoint*

Cumulative   *increasing through successive addition*

Genre   *a specific style of art or literature*

Oration   *a formal speech*

Preamble   *an introduction to a formal document (pre)*

THINGS FALL APART

Ail   *to suffer from sickness*

Bewilder   *to confuse*

Confound   *to puzzle or confuse*

Crevice   *a narrow crack, especially in a rock*

Decompose   *to rot or decay (de + com)*

Deteriorate   *to get worse (de)*

Dilute   *to weaken, especially by adding water to a solution (di)*

Distort   *to bend or twist something out of its normal shape (dis)*

Quibble   *to complain about little things*

Rift   *a narrow break*

Squalid   *appearing dirty and wretched*

THINGS FALL APART (UL)

Cacophony   *jarring and unpleasing sounds (phon)*

Evanescence   *something that lasts for a short time, an event that fades away gradually (esce)*

Mercurial   *characterized by rapid and unpredictable changes, fickle*

Volatile   *easily changeable, quick to explode*

HEAD FOR THE HILLS

Circulate   *to move around freely, to spread widely (circ)*

Evacuate   *to leave or withdraw, as from a dangerous area*

Exclusion   *not being allowed to enter or join (ex + clu)*

Exile   *to banish someone from their native country (ex)*

Fluctuate   *to shift back and forth without regularity*

Linger   *to delay or be slow in leaving*

Ramble   *to move or speak without direction (amb)*

Recede   *to move away or become smaller (re)*

Rout   *an overwhelming defeat or to defeat*

ART APPRECIATION

Audible   *able to be heard (able)*

Dingy   *dirty, dull, or shabby*

Elaborate   *very detailed or to explain something in greater detail*

Elongate   *to lengthen*

Embroider   *to decorate an object with needlework*

Emulate   *to copy or imitate*

Fringe   *the edge or outer portion*

Hue   *the color or shade of an object*

Livid   *discolored, bruised, or very angry*

Lush   *juicy and tender or covered with plant life*

Opulent   *rich, characterized by wealth*

Plumage   *the feathers on a bird*

Stark   *bare, without decoration*

Sublime   *without equal, awe-inspiring*

Tome   *a book, especially a large and scholarly one*

Translucent   *almost transparent, able to be seen through clearly (trans + luc)*

Virtuoso   *a person with great skill, especially a musician*

Vivid   *very distinct and sharp, realistic*

BEHAVE YOURSELF

Adamant   *stubborn and persistent*

Condescend   *to act as if you are better than someone*

Contradict   *to disagree*

Egotist   *a self-centered or conceited person (big ego)*

Glutton   *one who eats and drinks too much, greedy*

Imperious   *arrogant, behaving like royalty (ous)*

Plunder   *to steal*

Shun   *to avoid deliberately*

Timid   *shy*

Wily   *cunning and crafty*

ON THE DOWN LOW

Candor   *honesty, openness*

Clandestine   *secret*

Correlation   *connection between facts or events*

Fathom   *to understand*

Frank   *honest and open*

Keen   *sharp-witted and intelligent*

Plausible   *possible or believable (able)*

Presume   *to take for granted or to assume something to be true (pre)*

Prophetic   *predicting the future (pro)*

Shrewd   *very clever and smart, tricky*

Stifle   *to hold back or smother*

Tryst   *a secret meeting*

BEHAVE YOURSELF (UL)

Abstinence   *act or practice of refraining from indulging, especially in alcohol*

Capricious   *unpredictable and impulsive (ous)*

Contemptuous   *expressing disdain or extreme dislike (ous)*

Contentious   *inclined to fight or argue (ous)*

Feral   *wild and untamed*

Rancorous   *showing hatred or ill-will (ous)*

Staid   *straightlaced and serious*

COOL, CALM, AND COLLECTED

Impervious *unable to pass or enter, unable to upset or disturb (im + ous)*

Indifferent *having no feelings or not caring one way or another (in)*

Languid *slow-moving*

Mirth *happiness and good cheer*

Nimble *agile and flexible*

Nonchalant *without concern, calm and cool*

Tepid *neither hot nor cold*

THANKS FOR THE COMPLIMENT

Burly *very stocky and muscled*

Dexterity *mental skill or quickness (ity)*

Exuberant *overflowing with joy or happiness*

Felicity *joy and happiness (ity)*

Frugal *not wasteful or extravagant*

Idiosyncratic *a characteristic peculiar to an individual, a quirk*

Integrity *a person's moral character, honesty and truthfulness (ity)*

Paramount *having superior power and influence*

Prosperous *wealthy or fortunate (ous)*

Prudent *sensible and wise*

Thrifty *able to handle money wisely, not extravagant*

Venerate *to regard with deep respect*

Whimsical *determined by chance or fancy instead of reason; impulsive*

Word Parts Index

The meaning of each word part listed is a much-abbreviated version of a long historical chain of meanings. For more information about any of these roots, consult a Latin- and Greek-root dictionary.

Suffixes

X-able	adjective	"able to be Xed"
X-archy	noun	"rulership by X"
X-ical	adjective	"characterized by X"
X-ity	noun	"condition or state of being X"
X-less	adjective	"without X"
X-ness	noun	"quality of being X"
X-ology	noun	"doctrine or theory of X" (originally "word of X")
X-ous	adjective	"having the quality of X"

Prefixes and Roots

a	without		derm	skin
ab/abs	away from, against		di	apart, through, away
ac/acr	sharp		dic	to say, to tell
ad/at	to, toward		dign/dain	worth
am	to love		dis	apart, away from, not
amb	to go, to walk		dys	faulty, bad
anim	life, spirit		epi	upon
ante	before		equi/equ	equal
anthr/andr	mankind, man		esce	to become
anti	against, opposite		eu	good, pleasing
apt/ept	skill, ability, fit		ex/ej	out, put out
bell	war		extr	outside, beyond
bene	good		fac	to make, to do
bi	two		fic/fig	to make, to do
carn	flesh		fid	faith, trust
chron	time		gen	birth, creation, kind
circ/circum	around		gyn	woman
cis	to cut		her/hes	to stick
cli	to lean		hetero	different, other
clu/clo/cla	to close, shut		homo	same
co/com/con	with, together		hyper	over
cred	believe		hypo	under
culp	blame		in/il/im/ir	not
cur/cour	to run (a course)		in/en/im/em	into
de	away from, the opposite of		inter	between, among
dem	people		intra	within, inside

loc/loq/log	to speak	pro	forward, supporting
luc/lum	light	pun/pen	to pay, compensate, punish
magna	great, big	re	again, back
mal	bad	sci	knowledge, to know
man	hand	scrib/script	to write
mis	wrong, bad	sed/sid	to sit, be still
mit/mis	to send	sequ/secu	to follow
morph	shape, form	spec	to look, appear
mut	change	sub	under, less than
nat/nas/nai	to be born	super	over, greater than
neo/nov	new	tact	touch
nom/nym	name	techn	tools, art, skill
ob	against, in front of, toward	ten	to hold
omni	all, every	tens/ten	to stretch
pan	all, everywhere	terr	earth
par	equal	tract	to drag, pull, draw
path	feeling	trans	across
phil	love of	un/non	not
phobe	fear of	uni	one
phon	sound	us/ut	to use
plac	to please	ven/vent	to come
pon/pos	place, put	vers/vert	to turn
port	to carry	vi/viv	life
post	after	vid/vis	to see
pot	power, ability	voc	to call
pre	before	vor	to eat

Chapter 2
Fundamental Math Skills
for the SSAT & ISEE

INTRODUCTION

Whether you are taking the Lower Level ISEE or the Upper Level SSAT, there are some basic math skills that are at the heart of many of the questions on your test. For students taking the Lower Level exams, the content in this section may be something you learned recently or are learning right now. You should go through this chapter very carefully and slowly. If you are having trouble understanding any of the content, you should ask your parents or teachers for help by having them explain it more thoroughly to you. For students taking the Middle and Upper Level tests, this chapter may serve more as a chance to review some things you have forgotten or that you need to practice a little. Even the most difficult questions on the Upper Level exams are built on testing your knowledge of these same skills. Make sure you read the explanations and do all of the drills before going on to either the SSAT or ISEE math chapter. Answers to these drills are provided in Chapter 3.

A Note to Lower and Middle Level Students

This section has been designed to give all students a comprehensive review of the math found on the tests. There are four sections: "The Building Blocks," "Algebra," "Geometry," and "Word Problems." At the beginnings and ends of some of these sections you will notice information about what material you should review and what material is only for Upper Level (UL) students. Be aware that you may not be familiar with all the topics on which you will be working. If you are having difficulty understanding a topic, bring this book to your teachers or parents and ask them for additional help.

Lose Your Calculator!

You will *not* be allowed to use a calculator on the SSAT or the ISEE. If you have developed a habit of reaching for your calculator whenever you need to add or multiply a couple of numbers, follow our advice: Put your calculator away now and take it out again after the test is behind you. Do your math homework assignments without it, and complete the practice sections of this book without it. Trust us, you'll be glad you did.

Write It Down

Write It Down; Get It Right!
You don't get points for doing the math in your head, so don't!

Do not try to do math in your head. You are allowed to write in your test booklet. You *should* write in your test booklet. Even when you are adding just a few numbers together, write them down and do the work on paper. Writing down things not only helps eliminate careless errors but also gives you something to refer back to if you need to double-check your work.

THE BUILDING BLOCKS

Math Vocabulary

Term	Definition	Examples
Integer	Any number that does not contain either a fraction or a decimal. Can be positive, negative, or zero.	14, 3, 0, –3
Whole number	Positive integers and zero	0, 1, 17
Positive number	Any number greater than zero	$\frac{1}{2}$, 1, 104.7
Negative number	Any number less than zero	$-\frac{1}{2}$, –1, –104.7
Even number	Any number that is evenly divisible by two. **Note:** Zero is an even number!	104, 16, 2, 0, –2, –104
Odd number	Any number that is not evenly divisible by two	115, 11, 1, –1, –11, –115
Prime number	Any number that is divisible by only 1 and itself. **Note:** One is **not** a prime number, but two **is**.	2, 3, 5, 7, 13, 131
Digit	The numbers from 0 through 9	0, 2, 3, 7. The number 237 has digits 2, 7, and 3.
Units digit	The digit in the one's place	For 281, 1 is in the units place.
Consecutive numbers	Any series of numbers listed in the order they appear on the number line	3, 4, 5 or –1, 0, 1, 2
Distinct numbers	Numbers that are different from one another	2, 7, and 19 are three distinct numbers; 4 and 4 are not distinct because they are the same number.
Divisible by	A number that can be evenly divided by another	12 is divisible by 1, 2, 3, 4, 6, 12.
Sum	The result of addition	The sum of 6 and 2 is 8 because $6 + 2 = 8$.
Difference	The result of subtraction	The difference between 6 and 2 is 4 because $6 - 2 = 4$.
Product	The result of multiplication	The product of 6 and 2 is 12 because $6 \times 2 = 12$.
Quotient	The result of division	The quotient when 6 is divided by 2 is 3 because $6 \div 2 = 3$.
Remainder	The amount left over when dividing	$17 \div 5$ leaves a remainder of 2.
Factor	Any numbers or symbols that can be multiplied together to form a product	8 and 5 are factors of 40 because $8 \times 5 = 40$.

The Rules of Zero

Zero has some funny rules. Make sure you understand and remember these rules.

- Zero is neither positive nor negative.
- Zero is even.
- Zero is an integer.
- Zero multiplied by any number is zero.
- Zero divided by any number is zero.
- You cannot divide by zero $(9 \div 0 = undefined)$.

The Times Table

Make sure you are comfortable with your multiplication tables up to 12. If you are having trouble with these, write some on flash cards. On one side of the card write down the multiplication problem, and on the other write down the answer. Now quiz yourself. You may also want to copy the table shown below so you can practice. For handy tips on using flash cards effectively, turn to the vocabulary chapter and read the section on flash cards.

	1	2	3	4	5	6	7	8	9	10	11	12
1	1	2	3	4	5	6	7	8	9	10	11	12
2	2	4	6	8	10	12	14	16	18	20	22	24
3	3	6	9	12	15	18	21	24	27	30	33	36
4	4	8	12	16	20	24	28	32	36	40	44	48
5	5	10	15	20	25	30	35	40	45	50	55	60
6	6	12	18	24	30	36	42	48	54	60	66	72
7	7	14	21	28	35	42	49	56	63	70	77	84
8	8	16	24	32	40	48	56	64	72	80	88	96
9	9	18	27	36	45	54	63	72	81	90	99	108
10	10	20	30	40	50	60	70	80	90	100	110	120
11	11	22	33	44	55	66	77	88	99	110	121	132
12	12	24	36	48	60	72	84	96	108	120	132	144

PRACTICE DRILL 1—MATH VOCABULARY

1. How many integers are there between –1 and 6 ? _____

2. List three consecutive odd integers: _____

3. How many odd integers are there between 1 and 9 ? _____

4. What is the tens digit in the number 182.09 ? _____

5. The product of any number and the smallest positive integer is: _____

6. What is the product of 5, 6, and 3 ? _____

7. What is the sum of 3, 11, and 16 ? _____

8. What is the difference between your answer to number 6 and your answer to number 7? _____

9. List three consecutive negative even integers: _____

10. Is 11 a prime number? _____

11. What is the sum of the digits in the number 5,647 ? _____

12. What is the remainder when 58 is divided by 13 ? _____

13. 55 is divisible by what numbers? _____

14. The sum of the digits in 589 is how much greater than the sum of the digits in 1,207 ? _____

15. Is 21 divisible by the remainder of 19 ÷ 5 ? _____

16. What are the prime factors of 156 ? _____

17. What is the sum of the odd prime factors of 156 ? _____

18. 12 multiplied by 3 is the same as 4 multiplied by what number? _____

19. What are the factors of 72 ? _____

20. How many factors of 72 are even? _____
    How many are odd? _____

When You Are Done
Check your answers in Chapter 3.

Working with Negative Numbers

It is helpful to think of numbers as having two component parts: the number itself and the sign in front of it (to the left of the number). Numbers that don't have signs immediately to the left of them are positive. So +7 can be, and usually is, written as 7.

Adding

If the signs to the left of the numbers are the same, you add the two numbers and keep the same sign. For example:

$$2 + 5 = (+2) + (+5) = +7 \text{ or just plain } 7$$

$$(-2) + (-5) = -7$$

If the signs to the left of the numbers are different, you subtract the numbers and the answer takes the sign of the larger number. For example:

$$5 + (-2) = 5 - 2 = 3, \text{ and because 5 is greater than 2, the answer is } +3 \text{ or just plain } 3.$$

$$(-2) + 5 = 5 - 2 = 3, \text{ and because 5 is greater than 2, the answer is } +3 \text{ or just plain } 3.$$

$$(-5) + 2 = 5 - 2 = 3, \text{ and because 5 is greater than 2, you use its sign and the answer is } -3.$$

Subtracting

All subtraction problems can be converted to addition problems. This is because subtracting is the same as adding the opposite. "Huh?" you say—well, let's test this out on something simple that you know. We know that $7 - 3 = 4$, so let's turn it into an addition problem and see if we get the same answer.

$$7 - 3 = (+7) - (+3)$$

Okay, so now we reverse only the operation sign and the sign of the number we are subtracting (the second number). The first number stays the same because that's our starting point.

$$(+7) + (-3)$$

Now use the rules for addition to solve this problem. Because the signs to the left are different, we subtract the two numbers $7 - 3 = 4$, and the sign is positive because 7 is greater than 3.

We have just proven that subtraction problems are really just the opposite of addition problems. Now let's see how this works in a variety of examples.

$3 - 7 = (+3) - (+7) = (+3) + (-7) = 7 - 3 = 4$ and, because 7 is greater than 3, the answer is -4.

$-9 - 3 = (-9) - (+3) = (-9) + (-3) = -12$

$13 - (-5) = (+13) - (-5) = (+13) + (+5) = +18$

$(-5) - (-8) = (-5) + (+8) = +3$

PRACTICE DRILL 2—ADDING AND SUBTRACTING NEGATIVE NUMBERS

1. $6 + (-14) =$

2. $13 - 27 =$

3. $(-17) + 13 =$

4. $12 - (-15) =$

5. $16 + 5 =$

6. $34 - (+30) =$

7. $(-7) + (-15) =$

8. $(-42) + 13 =$

9. $-13 - (-7) =$

10. $151 + (-61) =$

11. $(-42) - (-42) =$

12. $5 - (-24) =$

13. $14 + 10 =$

14. $(-5) + (-25) =$

15. $11 - 25 =$

When You Are Done
Check your answers in
Chapter 3.

Multiplying and Dividing

The rules for multiplying and dividing positive and negative integers are so much easier to learn and use than the rules for adding and subtracting them. You simply multiply or divide as normal, then determine the sign using the rules below.

Positive ($\div$ or $\times$) Positive = Positive

Negative ($\div$ or $\times$) Negative = Positive

Positive ($\div$ or $\times$) Negative = Negative

Negative ($\div$ or $\times$) Positive = Negative

Here are some examples.

$$6 \div 2 = 3 \qquad\qquad 2 \times 6 = 12$$

$$(-6) \div (-2) = 3 \qquad\qquad (-2) \times (-6) = 12$$

$$6 \div (-2) = -3 \qquad\qquad 2 \times (-6) = -12$$

$$(-6) \div 2 = -3 \qquad\qquad (-2) \times 6 = -12$$

If you are multiplying more than two numbers, simply work from left to right and deal with the numbers two at a time.

$$2 \times (-5) \times (-10) = 2 \times (-5) = -10 \text{ and now } (-10) \times (-10) = +100$$

Helpful Rule of Thumb
When multiplying numbers, simply count the number of negative signs. An even number of negative signs (-6×-3) means that the product must be a positive number. An odd number of negative signs (2×-5) means that the product must be negative.

PRACTICE DRILL 3—MULTIPLYING AND DIVIDING NEGATIVE NUMBERS

1. $20 \div (-5) =$

2. $(-12) \times 3 =$

3. $(-13) \times (-5) =$

4. $(-44) \div (-4) =$

5. $7 \times 9 =$

6. $(-65) \div 5 =$

7. $(-7) \times (-12) =$

8. $(-10) \div 2 =$

9. $81 \div 9 =$

10. $32 \div (-4) =$

11. $25 \times (-3) =$

12. $(-24) \times (-3) =$

13. $64 \div (-16) =$

14. $(-17) \times (-2) =$

When You Are Done
Check your answers in
Chapter 3.

15. $(-55) \div 5 =$

ORDER OF OPERATIONS

How would you attack this problem?

$$16 - 45 \div (2 + 1)2 \times 4 + 5 =$$

To solve a problem like this, you need to know which mathematical operation to do first. The way to remember the order of operations is to use PEMDAS.

Done at the same time from left to right $\left\{ \begin{array}{l} \text{Parentheses} \\ \text{Exponents} \\ \text{Multiplication} \\ \text{Division} \end{array} \right.$

$\left. \begin{array}{l} \text{Addition} \\ \text{Subtraction} \end{array} \right\}$ Done at the same time from left to right

You can remember the order of operations by using the phrase below:

"Please Excuse My Dear Aunt Sally."

Now, let's give it a try.

$$16 - 45 \div (2 + 1)2 \times 4 + 5 =$$

1. **Parentheses:**

   $$16 - 45 \div \underline{(2 + 1)^2} \times 4 + 5 =$$

   $$16 - 45 \div (3)^2 \times 4 + 5 =$$

2. **Exponents:**

   $$16 - 45 \div \underline{(3)^2} \times 4 + 5 =$$

   $$16 - 45 \div 9 \times 4 + 5 =$$

3. Multiplication and division (from left to right):

$$16 - \underline{45 \div 9} \times 4 + 5 =$$

$$16 - \underline{5 \times 4} + 5 =$$

$$16 - 20 + 5 =$$

4. Addition and subtraction (from left to right):

$$\underline{16 - 20} + 5 =$$

$$-4 + 5 = \boxed{1}$$

Just take it one step at a time and the math is easy!

PRACTICE DRILL 4—ORDER OF OPERATIONS

1. $10 - 3 + 2 =$

2. $15 + (7 - 3) - 3 =$

3. $3 \times 2 + 3 \div 3 =$

4. $2 \times (4 + 6) \div 4 =$

5. $420 \div (10 + 5 \times 12) =$

6. $20 \times 5 \div 10 + 20 =$

7. $3 + 5 \times 10 \times (7 - 6) \div 2 - 4 =$

8. $10 \times (8 + 1) \times (3 + 1) \div (8 - 2) =$

9. $12 + (5 \times 2) - 33 \div 3 =$

10. $200 - 150 \div 3 \times 2 =$

When You Are Done
Check your answers in
Chapter 3.

Factors

Factors are all the numbers that divide evenly into your original number. For example, two is a factor of ten; it goes in five times. Three is not a factor of ten because ten divided by three does not produce an integer quotient (and therefore does not "go in evenly"). When asked to find the factors of a number, just make a list.

> The factors of 16 are
> 1 and 16   (always start with 1 and the original number)
> 2 and 8
> 4 and 4
> The factors of 18 are
> 1 and 18
> 2 and 9
> 3 and 6

Knowing some rules of divisibility can save you some time.

A number is divisible by	If...
2	it ends in 0, 2, 4, 6, or 8
3	the sum of the digits is divisible by 3
5	it ends in 0 or 5
9	the sum of the digits is divisible by 9
10	it ends in 0

Factor Trees

To find the prime factors of a number, draw a factor tree.

Start by writing down the number and then drawing two branches from the number. Write down any pair of factors of that number. Now if one (or both) of the factors is not prime, draw another set of branches from the factor and write down a pair of factors for that number. Continue until you have only prime numbers at the end of your branches. Each branch end is a prime factor. Remember, 1 is NOT prime!

What are the distinct prime factors of 56? Well, let's start with the factor tree.

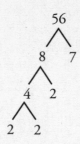

So the prime factors of 56 are 2, 2, 2, and 7. Because the question asked for only the distinct prime factors, we have to eliminate the numbers that repeat, so we cross out two of the twos. The distinct prime factors of 56 are 2 and 7.

Multiples

Multiples are the results when you multiply your number by any integer. Fifteen is a multiple of five because five times three equals fifteen. Eighteen is a multiple of three, but not a multiple of five. Another way to think about multiples is to consider them "counting by a number."

The first seven positive multiples of 7 are

7	(7 × 1)
14	(7 × 2)
21	(7 × 3)
28	(7 × 4)
35	(7 × 5)
42	(7 × 6)
49	(7 × 7)

Factors Are Small; Multiples Are Large
The factors of a number are always equal to or less than that number. The multiples of a number are always equal to or greater than that number. Be sure not to confuse the two!

PRACTICE DRILL 5—FACTORS AND MULTIPLES

1. List the first five multiples of

    2 _____

    4 _____

    5 _____

    11 _____

2. Is 15 divisible by 3 ?

3. Is 81 divisible by 3 ?

4. Is 77 divisible by 3 ?

5. Is 23 prime?

6. Is 123 divisible by 3 ?

7. Is 123 divisible by 9 ?

8. Is 250 divisible by 2 ?

9. Is 250 divisible by 5 ?

10. Is 250 divisible by 10 ?

11. Is 10 a multiple of 2 ?

12. Is 11 a multiple of 3 ?

13. Is 2 a multiple of 8 ?

14. Is 24 a multiple of 4 ?

15. Is 27 a multiple of 6 ?

16. Is 27 a multiple of 9 ?

17. How many numbers between 1 and 50 are multiples of 6 ?

18. How many even multiples of 3 are there between 1 and 50 ?

19. How many numbers between 1 and 100 are multiples of both 3 and 4 ?

20. What is the greatest multiple of 3 less than 50 ?

When You Are Done
Check your answers in
Chapter 3.

Fractions

A fraction really just tells you to divide. For instance, $\frac{5}{8}$ actually means five divided by eight (which equals 0.625 as a decimal).

Another way to think of this is to imagine a pie cut into eight pieces. $\frac{5}{8}$ represents five of those eight pieces of pie.

The parts of a fraction are called the numerator and the denominator. The numerator is the number on top of the fraction. It refers to the portion of the pie, while the denominator is on the bottom of the fraction and tells you how many pieces there are in the entire pie.

$$\frac{\text{numerator}}{\text{denominator}} = \frac{\text{part}}{\text{whole}}$$

Reducing Fractions

Imagine a pie cut into two big pieces. You eat one of the pieces. That means that you have eaten $\frac{1}{2}$ of the pie. Now imagine the same pie cut into four pieces; you eat two. That's $\frac{2}{4}$ this time. But look: The two fractions are equivalent!

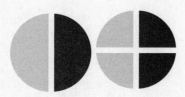

To reduce fractions, just divide the top number and the bottom number by the same amount. Start out with small numbers like 2, 3, 5, or 10 and reduce again if you need to.

$$\frac{12}{24} \, \frac{\div 2}{\div 2} = \frac{6}{12} \, \frac{\div 2}{\div 2} = \frac{3}{6} \, \frac{\div 3}{\div 3} = \frac{1}{2}$$

In this example, if you happened to see that both 12 and 24 are divisible by 12, then you could have saved two steps. However, don't spend very much time looking for the largest number possible by which to reduce a fraction. Start out with a small number; doing one extra reduction doesn't take very much time and will definitely help prevent careless errors.

PRACTICE DRILL 6—REDUCING FRACTIONS

1. $\dfrac{6}{8} =$

2. $\dfrac{12}{60} =$

3. $\dfrac{20}{30} =$

4. $\dfrac{36}{96} =$

5. $\dfrac{24}{32} =$

6. $\dfrac{16}{56} =$

7. $\dfrac{1,056}{1,056} =$

8. $\dfrac{154}{126} =$

When You Are Done
Check your answers in
Chapter 3.

9. What does it mean when the number on top is larger than the one on the bottom?

Improper Fractions and Mixed Numbers

Changing from Improper Fractions to Mixed Numbers

If you knew the answer to number 9 in the last drill or if you looked it up, you now know that when the number on top is greater than the number on the bottom, the fraction is greater than 1. That makes sense, because we also know that a fraction bar is really just another way of telling us to divide. So, $\frac{10}{2}$ is the same as $10 \div 2$, which equals 5, and which is much greater than 1!

A fraction that has a greater numerator than denominator is called an *improper fraction*. You may be asked to change an improper fraction to a mixed number. A *mixed number* is an improper fraction that has been converted into a whole number and a proper fraction. To do this, let's use $\frac{10}{8}$ as the improper fraction that we are going to convert to a mixed number.

First, divide 10 by 8. This gives us our whole number. 8 goes into 10 once.

Now, take the remainder, 2, and put it over the original fraction's denominator: $\frac{2}{8}$.

So the mixed number is $1\frac{2}{8}$, or $1\frac{1}{4}$.

> **Put Away That Calculator!**
> Remember that a remainder is just the number left over after you do long division; it is not the decimal that a calculator gives you.

PRACTICE DRILL 7—CHANGING IMPROPER FRACTIONS TO MIXED NUMBERS

1. $\dfrac{45}{9}$

2. $\dfrac{72}{42}$

3. $\dfrac{16}{3}$

4. $\dfrac{5}{2}$

5. $\dfrac{8}{3}$

6. $\dfrac{62}{9}$

7. $\dfrac{15}{10}$

8. $\dfrac{22}{11}$

9. $\dfrac{83}{7}$

10. $\dfrac{63}{6}$

When You Are Done
Check your answers in
Chapter 3.

Changing from Mixed Numbers to Improper Fractions

It's important to know how to change a mixed number into an improper fraction because it is easier to add, subtract, multiply, or divide a fraction if there is no whole number in the way. To do this, multiply the denominator by the whole number and then add the result to the numerator. Then put this sum on top of the original denominator. For example:

$$1\frac{1}{2}$$

Multiply the denominator by the whole number: $2 \times 1 = 2$

Add this to the numerator: $2 + 1 = 3$

Put this result over the original denominator: $\dfrac{3}{2}$

$$1\frac{1}{2} = \frac{3}{2}$$

PRACTICE DRILL 8—CHANGING MIXED NUMBERS TO IMPROPER FRACTIONS

1. $6\dfrac{3}{7}$

2. $2\dfrac{5}{9}$

3. $23\dfrac{2}{3}$

4. $6\dfrac{2}{3}$

5. $7\dfrac{3}{8}$

6. $7\dfrac{2}{5}$

7. $10\dfrac{1}{16}$

8. $5\dfrac{12}{13}$

9. $4\dfrac{5}{9}$

10. $33\dfrac{21}{22}$

When You Are Done
Check your answers in Chapter 3.

Adding and Subtracting Fractions with a Common Denominator

To add or subtract fractions with a common denominator, just add or subtract the top numbers and leave the bottom numbers alone.

$$\frac{5}{7} + \frac{1}{7} = \frac{6}{7}$$

$$\frac{5}{7} - \frac{1}{7} = \frac{4}{7}$$

Adding and Subtracting Fractions When the Denominators Are Different

In the past, you have probably tried to find common denominators so that you could just add or subtract straight across. There is an easier way; it is called the *Bowtie*.

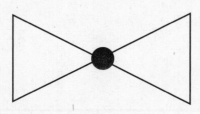

This diagram may make the Bowtie look complicated. It's not. There are three simple steps to adding and subtracting fractions.

Step 1: Multiply diagonally going up.
First **B × C**. Write the product next to **C**.
Then **D × A**. Write the product next to **A**.

Step 2: Multiply straight across the bottom, **B × D**.
Write the product as the denominator in your answer.

Step 3: To add, add the numbers written next to **A** and **C**.
Write the sum as the numerator in your answer.
To subtract, subtract the numbers written next to A and C. Write the difference as the numerator in your answer.

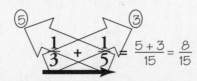

No More "Least Common Denominators"
Using the Bowtie to add and subtract fractions eliminates the need for the least common denominator, but you may need to reduce the result.

PRACTICE DRILL 9—ADDING AND SUBTRACTING FRACTIONS

1. $\dfrac{3}{8} + \dfrac{2}{3} =$

2. $\dfrac{1}{3} + \dfrac{3}{8} =$

3. $\dfrac{4}{7} + \dfrac{2}{7} =$

4. $\dfrac{3}{4} - \dfrac{2}{3} =$

5. $\dfrac{7}{9} + \dfrac{5}{4} =$

6. $\dfrac{2}{5} - \dfrac{3}{4} =$

7. $\dfrac{10}{12} + \dfrac{7}{2} =$

8. $\dfrac{17}{27} - \dfrac{11}{27} =$

9. $\dfrac{3}{20} + \dfrac{2}{3} =$

(Upper Level)

When You Are Done
Check your answers in
Chapter 3.

10. $\dfrac{x}{3} + \dfrac{4x}{6} =$

Multiplying Fractions

Multiplying is the easiest thing to do with fractions. All you need to do is multiply straight across the tops and bottoms.

$$\frac{3}{7} \times \frac{4}{5} = \frac{3 \times 4}{7 \times 5} = \frac{12}{35}$$

Dividing Fractions

Dividing fractions is almost as simple as multiplying. You just have to flip the second fraction and then multiply.

$$\frac{3}{8} \div \frac{2}{5} = \frac{3}{8} \times \frac{5}{2} = \frac{15}{16}$$

When dividing, don't ask why; just flip the second fraction and multiply!

PRACTICE DRILL 10—MULTIPLYING AND DIVIDING FRACTIONS

1. $\dfrac{2}{3} \times \dfrac{1}{2} =$

2. $\dfrac{5}{8} \div \dfrac{1}{2} =$

3. $\dfrac{4}{5} \times \dfrac{3}{10} =$

4. $\dfrac{24}{15} \times \dfrac{10}{16} =$

5. $\dfrac{16}{25} \div \dfrac{4}{5} =$

Remember Reciprocals?

A reciprocal results when you flip a fraction—that is, exchange the numerator and the denominator. So the reciprocal of $\frac{2}{3}$ is what? Yep, that's right, $\frac{3}{2}$.

When You Are Done
Check your answers in Chapter 3.

Decimals

Remember, decimals and fractions are just two different ways of writing the same thing. To change a fraction into a decimal, you just divide the bottom number into the top number.

Be sure you know the names of all the decimal places. Here's a quick reminder.

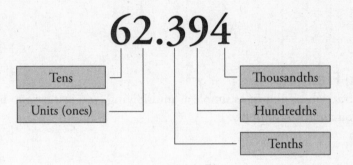

Adding Decimals

To add decimals, just line up the decimal places and add.

$$
\begin{array}{r}
48.02 \\
+\ 19.12 \\
\hline
67.14
\end{array}
$$

Subtracting Decimals

To subtract, do the same thing. Line up the decimal places and subtract.

$$
\begin{array}{r}
67.14 \\
-\ 48.02 \\
\hline
19.12
\end{array}
$$

Multiplying Decimals

To multiply decimals, first count the number of digits to the right of the decimal point in the numbers you are multiplying. Then, just multiply and move the decimal point in your answer from right to left by the same number of spaces.

$$
\begin{array}{r}
0.5 \\
\times\ 4.2 \\
\hline
2.10
\end{array}
$$
(two digits to the right of the decimal point)

Dividing Decimals

To divide, move the decimal points in both numbers the same number of spaces to the right until you are working only with integers.

$$12.5 \div 0.25 = 0.25\overline{)12.5}$$

Now move both decimals over two places and solve the problem.

$$25\overline{)1250} = 50$$

And you're done! Remember that you do not put the decimals back into the problem.

PRACTICE DRILL 11—DECIMALS

1. $1.43 + 17.27 =$

2. $2.49 + 1.7 =$

3. $7 - 2.038 =$

4. $4.25 \times 2.5 =$

5. $0.02 \times 0.90 =$

6. $180 \div 0.03 =$

7. $0.10 \div 0.02 =$

When You Are Done
Check your answers in Chapter 3.

Converting Fractions to Decimals and Back Again

From Fractions to Decimals

As we learned when we introduced fractions a little earlier, a fraction bar is really just a division sign.

$$\frac{10}{2} \text{ is the same as } 10 \div 2 \text{ or } 5$$

In the same sense,

$$\frac{1}{2} = 1 \div 2 \text{ or } 0.5$$

In fact, we can convert any fraction to its decimal equivalent by dividing the top number by the bottom number:

$$\frac{11}{2} = 11 \div 2 = 5.5$$

From Decimals to Fractions

To change a decimal to a fraction, look at the digit farthest to the right. Determine what place that digit is in (e.g., tenths, hundredths, and so on) and then put the decimal (without the decimal point) over that number (e.g., 10, 100, and so on). Let's change 0.5 into a fraction.

5 is in the tenths place so we put it over 10.

$$\frac{5}{10} \text{ reduces to } \frac{1}{2}.$$

PRACTICE DRILL 12—FRACTIONS AS DECIMALS

Fill in the table below by converting the fractions to decimals and vice versa. The fractions and decimals in this table are those most often tested on the SSAT and ISEE, so memorize them now and save yourself time later.

Fraction	Decimal
$\frac{1}{2}$	0.5
$\frac{1}{3}$	
$\frac{2}{3}$	
	0.25
	0.75
$\frac{1}{5}$	
	0.4
	0.6
$\frac{4}{5}$	
	0.125

When You Are Done
Check your answers in Chapter 3.

Percents

Percentages are really just an extension of fractions. Let's go back to that pie we were talking about in the section on fractions. Let's say we had a pie that was cut into four equal pieces. If you ate one piece of the pie, then we could say that the *fractional part* of the pie that you have eaten is

$$\frac{1}{4} \qquad \frac{\text{(the number of pieces you ate)}}{\text{(the total number of pieces in the pie)}} \qquad \frac{\text{part}}{\text{whole}}$$

Now let's find out what percentage of the pie you have eaten. Percent literally means "out of 100." When we find a percent, we are really trying to see how many times out of 100 something happens. To figure the percent you simply take the fractional part and multiply it by 100.

$$\frac{1}{4} \times 100 = \frac{100}{4} = 25\%$$

You've probably seen percents as grades on your tests in school. What does it mean to get 100% on a test? It means you got every question correct. Let's say you got 25 questions right out of a total of 25. So we put the number of questions you got right over the total number of questions and multiply by 100.

$$\frac{25}{25} = 1 \times 100 = 100\%$$

Let's says that your friend didn't do as well on this same test. He answered 20 questions correctly. Let's figure what percentage of the questions he got right.

$$\frac{20}{25} = \frac{4}{5} \times 100 = 80\%$$

What percentage did he get wrong?

$$\frac{5}{25} = \frac{1}{5} = 20\%$$

Notice that the percentage of questions he got right (80%) plus the percentage of questions he got wrong (20%) equals 100%.

PRACTICE DRILL 13—PERCENTS

1. A bag of candies contains 15 butterscotches, 20 caramels, 5 pepper-
    mints, and 10 toffees.

    The butterscotches make up what percentage of the candies?_____

    The caramels?_____

    The peppermints?_____

    The toffees?_____

2. A student answered 75% of the questions on a test correctly and left
    7% of the questions blank. What percentage of the questions did the
    student answer incorrectly?_____

3. Stephanie's closet contains 40 pairs of shoes. She has 8 sneakers, 12
    sandals, 16 boots, and the rest are high heels.

    What percentage of the shoes are sneakers? _____

    Sandals?_____

    Boots?_____

    High heels?_____

    How many high heels does Stephanie own? _____

4. A recipe for fruit punch calls for 4 cups of apple juice, 2 cups of cran-
    berry juice, 3 cups of grape juice, and 1 cup of seltzer. What percent-
    age of the punch is juice?_____

5. Five friends are chipping in for a birthday gift for their teacher. David
    and Jakob each contribute $13. Stephanie, Kate, and Janice each
    contribute $8.

    What percentage of the total did the girls contribute?_____

    The boys?_____

When You Are Done
Check your answers in
Chapter 3.

More Percents

Another place you may have seen percents is at the shopping mall. Stores offer special discounts on their merchandise to entice shoppers to buy more stuff. Most of these stores discount their merchandise by a certain percentage. For example, you may see a $16 CD that is marked 25 percent off the regular price. What does that mean?

Percents are not "real" numbers. In the above scenario, the CD was not $25 less than the regular price (then they'd have to pay you money!), but 25 percent less. So how do we figure out how much that CD really costs and how much money we are saving?

To find how much a percent really is in "real" numbers, you need to *first take the percent and change it to a fraction.*

Because percent means "out of 100," to change a percent to a fraction, simply put the percent over 100.

$$25\% = \frac{25}{100} = \frac{1}{4}$$

Now let's get back to that CD. Multiply the regular price of the CD, $16, by the fraction.

$$\$16 \times \frac{1}{4} = \$4$$

This means 25% of 16 is $4. You get $4 off the original price of the CD. If you subtract that from the original price, you find that the new sale price is $12.

Guess what percentage the sale price is of the regular price? If you said 75 percent, you'd be right!

Tip: Changing a decimal to a percent is the same as changing a fraction to a percent. Multiply the decimal by 100 (move the decimal two spaces to the right). So 0.25 as a percent is $0.25 \times 100 = 25\%$.

PRACTICE DRILL 14—MORE PERCENTS

Fill in the missing information in the table below.

Fraction	Decimal	Percent
$\frac{1}{2}$	0.5	50%
$\frac{1}{3}$		
	$0.6\overline{6}$	
		25%
	0.75	
$\frac{1}{5}$		
		40%
	0.6	
$\frac{4}{5}$		
		12.5%

1. 25% of 84 =

2. $33\frac{1}{3}$% of 27 =

3. 20% of 75 =

Tip:
The word *of* in word problems means multiply!

4.   17% of 300 =

5.   16% of 10% of 500 =

6.   A dress is marked down 15% from its regular price. If the regular price is $120, what is the sale price of the dress? The sale price is what percentage of the regular price of the dress?

7.   Steve goes to school 80% of the 365 days of the year. How many days does Steve go to school?

8.   Jennifer answered all 36 questions on her history test. If she got 25% of the questions wrong, how many questions did she get right?

When You Are Done
Check your answers in Chapter 3.

9.   During a special one-day sale, the price of a television was marked down 20% from its original price of $100. Later that day, the television was marked down an additional 10%. What was the final sale price?

Exponents

Exponents are just another way to indicate multiplication. For instance, 3^2 simply means to multiply three by itself two times, so $3^2 = 3 \times 3 = 9$. Even higher exponents aren't very complicated. For example:

$$2^5 = 2 \times 2 \times 2 \times 2 \times 2 = 32$$

When in Doubt, Write It Out!
Don't try to compute exponents in your head. Write them out and multiply!

The questions on the SSAT don't generally use exponents higher than four or five, so this is likely to be as complicated as it gets.

The rule for exponents is simple: When in doubt, write it out! Don't try to figure out two times two times two times two times two in your head (just look at how silly it looks written down using words!). Instead, write it as a math problem and just work through it one step at a time.

What would you do if you were asked to solve this problem?

$$Q^3 \times Q^2 =$$

Let's look at this one carefully. Q^3 means $Q \times Q \times Q$ and Q^2 means $Q \times Q$. Put them together and you've got:

$$(Q \times Q \times Q) \times (Q \times Q) =$$

How many Q's is that? Count them. Five! The answer is Q^5. Be careful when multiplying exponents like this that you don't get confused and multiply the actual exponents, which would give you Q^6. If you are ever unsure, don't spend a second worrying; just write out the exponent and count the number of things you are multiplying.

Square Roots

A square root is just the opposite of squaring a number. $2^2 = 2 \times 2$ or 4, so the square root of 4 is 2.

You will see square roots written this way on a test: $\sqrt{4}$.

PRACTICE DRILL 15—EXPONENTS AND SQUARE ROOTS

1. $2^3 =$

2. $2^4 =$

3. $3^3 =$

4. $4^3 =$

5. $2^6 - 5^2 =$

6. $\sqrt{81}$

7. $\sqrt{100}$

8. $\sqrt{49}$

9. $\sqrt{64}$

10. $\sqrt{9}$

When You Are Done
Check your answers in Chapter 3.

More Exponents—Upper Level Only

Multiplying and Dividing Exponents with the Same Base

You can multiply and divide exponents *with the same base* without having to expand out and calculate the value of each exponent. The bottom number, the one you are multiplying, is called the base. (However, note that to multiply $2^3 \times 5^2$ you must calculate the value of each exponent separately and then multiply the results.)

To multiply, add the exponents.

$$2^3 \times 2^4 = 2^7$$

To divide, subtract the exponents.

$$2^8 \div 2^5 = 2^3$$

To take an exponent to another power, multiply the exponents.

$$(2^3)^3 = 2^9$$

For exponents, with the same base remember MADSPM:
When you *Multiply* with exponents, *Add* them. When you *Divide* with exponents, *Subtract.* When you see *Powers* with exponents, *Multiply.*

PRACTICE DRILL 16—MORE EXPONENTS

1. $3^5 \times 3^3 =$

2. $7^2 \times 7^7 =$

3. $5^3 \times 5^4 =$

4. $15^{23} \div 15^{20} =$

5. $4^{13} \div 4^4 =$

6. $10^{10} \div 10^6 =$

7. $(5^3)^6 =$

8. $(8^{12})^3 =$

9. $(9^5)^5 =$

10. $(2^2)^{14} =$

When You Are Done
Check your answers in Chapter 3.

REVIEW DRILL 1—THE BUILDING BLOCKS

1. Is 1 a prime number?

2. How many factors does 100 have?

3. $-10 + (-20) =$

4. $100 + 50 \div 5 \times 4 =$

5. $\dfrac{3}{7} - \dfrac{1}{3} =$

6. $\dfrac{4}{5} \div \dfrac{5}{3} =$

7. $1.2 \times 3.4 =$

8. $\dfrac{x}{100} \cdot 30 = 6$

9. $1^5 =$

10. $\sqrt{16} =$

11. What are the first 10 perfect squares?

ALGEBRA

An Introduction

If you're a Lower Level or Middle Level student you may not yet have begun learning about algebra in school, but don't let that throw you. If you know how to add, subtract, multiply, and divide, you can solve an algebraic equation. Lower Level students only need to understand the section below titled "Solving Simple Equations." Middle Level ISEE students should complete all of the "Solving Simple Equations" drills and as much of the Upper Level material as possible. Upper Level students need to go through the entire Algebra section carefully to make sure they can solve each of the question types.

Solving Simple Equations

Algebraic equations involve the same basic operations that we've dealt with throughout this chapter, but instead of using only numbers, these equations use a combination of numbers and letters. These letters are called *variables*. Here are some basic rules about working with variables that you need to understand.

- A variable (usually x, y, or z) replaces an unknown number in an algebraic equation.
- It is usually your job to figure out what that unknown number is.
- If a variable appears more than once in an equation, that variable is always replacing the same number.
- When a variable is directly to the right of a number, with no sign in between them, the operation that is holding them together is multiplication (e.g., $3y = 3 \times y$).
- You can add and subtract like variables (e.g., $2z + 5z = 7z$).
- You cannot add or subtract unlike variables (e.g., $2z + 3y$ cannot be combined).

To solve simple algebraic equations you need to think abstractly about the equation. Let's try one.

$$2 + x = 7$$

What does x equal?

Well, what number plus 2 gives you 7? If you said 5, you were right and $x = 5$.

$$2y = 16$$

What does y equal?

Now you need to ask what multiplied by 2 gives you 16. If you said 8, you were right and $y = 8$.

Tip: You can check to see if you found the right number for the variable by replacing the variable with the number you found in the equation. So in the last problem, if we replace y with 8 and rewrite the problem, we get $2 \times 8 = 16$. And that's true, so we got it right!

PRACTICE DRILL 17—SOLVING SIMPLE EQUATIONS

1. If $35 - x = 23$, then $x =$

2. If $y + 12 = 27$, then $y =$

3. If $z - 7 = 21$, then $z =$

4. If $5x = 25$, then $x =$

5. If $18 \div x = 6$, then $x =$

6. If $3x = 33$, then $x =$

7. If $65 \div y = 13$, then $y =$

8. If $14 = 17 - z$, then $z =$

9. If $\frac{1}{2}y = 24$, then $y =$

10. If $136 + z = 207$, then $z =$

11. If $7x = 84$, then $x =$

12. If $y \div 2 = 6$, then $y =$

13. If $z \div 3 = 15$, then $z =$

14. If $14 + x = 32$, then $x =$

When You Are Done
Check your answers in
Chapter 3.

15. If $53 - y = 24$, then $y =$

Note:
- Lower Level ISEE students should stop here. The next section you will work on is Geometry.
- All SSAT students and Middle and Upper Level ISEE students should continue.

Manipulating an Equation—All SSAT and Middle and Upper Level ISEE Only

To solve an equation, your goal is to isolate the variable, meaning that you want to get the variable on one side of the equation and everything else on the other side.

$$3x + 5 = 17$$

To solve this equation, follow these two steps.

Step 1: Move elements around using addition and subtraction. Get variables on one side and numbers on the other. Simplify.

Step 2: Divide both sides of the equation by the *coefficient*, the number in front of the variable. If that number is a fraction, multiply everything by the denominator.

For example

$$3x + 5 = 17$$
$$\underline{\quad -5 \quad -5 \quad}$$ Subtract 5 from both sides to get rid of the numbers on the left side.
$$3x \quad = 12$$
$$\div 3 \qquad \div 3$$ Divide both sides by 3 to get rid of the 3 on the left side.
$$x \quad = \quad 4$$

Remember: Whatever you do to one side, you must also do to the other.

Equal Rights for Equations!
You can do anything you want to one side of the equation, as long as you make sure to do exactly the same thing to the other side.

PRACTICE DRILL 18—MANIPULATING AN EQUATION

1. If $8 = 11 - x$, then $x =$

2. If $4x = 20$, then $x =$

3. If $5x - 20 = 10$, then $x =$

4. If $4x + 3 = 31$, then $x =$

5. If $m + 5 = 3m - 3$, then $m =$

6. If $2.5x = 20$, then $x =$

7. If $0.2x + 2 = 3.6$, then $x =$

8. If $6 = 8x + 4$, then $x =$

9. If $3(x + y) = 21$, then $x + y =$

10. If $3x + 3y = 21$, then $x + y =$

When You Are Done
Check your answers in
Chapter 3.

11. If $100 - 5y = 65$, then $y =$

Manipulating Inequalities—Upper Level SSAT and Middle and Upper Level ISEE Only

Manipulating an inequality is just like manipulating an equation that has an equal sign, except for one rule: If you multiply or divide by a negative number, flip the inequality sign.

Let's try an example.

$$-3x < 6$$

Divide both sides by −3 and then flip the inequality sign.

$$x > -2$$

Helpful Trick
Think of the inequality sign as an alligator, and the alligator always eats the bigger meal.

PRACTICE DRILL 19—MANIPULATING INEQUALITIES

Solve for x.

1. $4x > 16$

2. $13 - x > 15$

3. $15x - 20x < 25$

4. $12 + 2x > 24 - x$

5. $7 < -14 - 3x$

When You Are Done
Check your answers in Chapter 3.

Solving Percent Questions with Algebra— All SSAT and Middle and Upper Level ISEE Only

Percentages

Learn a Foreign Language

"Percent language" is easy to learn because there are only four words you need to remember!

Solving percent problems is easy when you know how to translate them from "percent language" into "math language." Once you've done the translation, you guessed it—just manipulate the equation!

Whenever you see words from the following table, just translate them into math language and go to work on the equation!

Percent Language	Math Language
% or "percent"	out of 100 ($\frac{x}{100}$)
of	times (as in multiplication) ($\times$)
what	your favorite variable (p)
is, are, were, was, did	equals ($=$)

"What percent" is represented by $\frac{x}{100}$

For example:

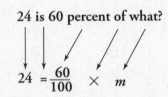

$$24 \text{ is } 60 \text{ percent of what?}$$

$$24 = \frac{60}{100} \times m$$

PRACTICE DRILL 20—TRANSLATING AND SOLVING PERCENT QUESTIONS

1. 30 is what percent of 250 ?

2. What is 12% of 200 ?

3. What is 25% of 10% of 200 ?

4. 75% of 20% of what number is 12 ?

5. 16% of what number is 25% of 80 ?

6. What percent is equal to $\dfrac{3}{5}$?

7. 30 is what percent of 75 ?

8. What is 11% of 24 ?

9. What percent of 24 is equal to 48 ?

10. 60% of what percent of 500 is equal to 6 ?

When You Are Done
Check your answers in Chapter 3.

GEOMETRY

An Introduction

Just as in the previous Algebra section, this Geometry section contains some material that is above the level tested on the Lower and Middle Level Exams. Lower and Middle Level students should read through the topics entitled "Perimeter," "Angles," "Squares and Rectangles," and "Triangles." Upper Level students should continue with the topics titled "The Pythagorean Theorem" and "Circles."

Perimeter

The perimeter is the distance around the outside of any figure. To find the perimeter of a figure, just add up the lengths of all the sides.

What are the perimeters of these figures?

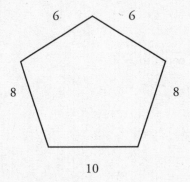

Perimeter = 6 + 6 + 8 + 8 + 10 = 38

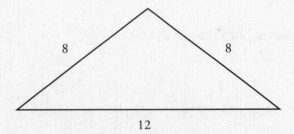

Perimeter = 8 + 8 + 12 = 28

Angles

Straight Lines

Angles that form a straight line always total 180°.

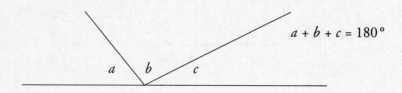

$$a + b + c = 180°$$

Triangles

All the angles in a triangle add up to 180°.

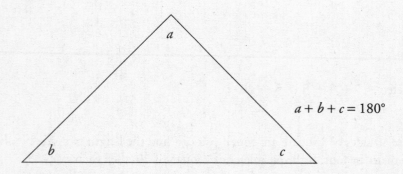

$$a + b + c = 180°$$

The Rule of 180°
There are 180 degrees in a straight line and in a triangle.

Four-Sided Figures

The angles in a square, rectangle, or any other four-sided figure always add up to 360°.

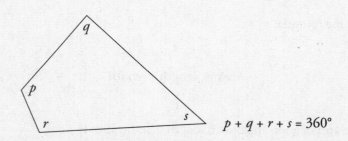

$$p + q + r + s = 360°$$

The Rule of 360°
There are 360 degrees in a four-sided figure and in a circle.

Squares and Rectangles

A *rectangle* is a four-sided figure with four right (90°) angles. Opposite sides are equal in a rectangle. The perimeter is equal to the sum of the sides.

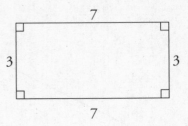

Perimeter

P = side + side + side...until you run out of sides.

Perimeter = 3 + 3 + 7 + 7 = 20

A *square* is a special type of rectangle where all the sides are equal.

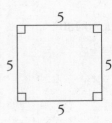

Perimeter = 5 + 5 + 5 + 5 = 20

Because all sides of a square are equal, you can find the length of a side by dividing its perimeter by four. If the perimeter of a square is 20, then each side is 5.

Area

Area is the amount of space taken up by a two-dimensional figure. An easy way to think about area is as the amount of paper that a figure covers. The larger the area, the more paper the figure takes up.

To determine the area of a square or rectangle, multiply the length by the width.

Area of a Rectangle

A = *lw*

Remember the formula:

$$\text{Area} = \text{length} \times \text{width}$$

What is the area of a rectangle with length 9 and width 4?

In this case the length is 9 and the width is 4, so 9 × 4 = 36. Now look at another example.

Area of rectangle $ABCD = 6 \times 8 = 48$

The area of squares and rectangles is given in *square feet,* square inches, and so on.

To find the area of a square you multiply two sides, and because the sides are equal, you're really finding the square of the sides. You can find the length of a side of a square by taking the square root of the area. So if a square has an area of 25, one side of the square is 5.

Area of a Square
$A = s^2$

Volume

Volume is very similar to area, except it takes into account a third dimension. To compute the volume of a figure, you simply find the area and multiply by a third dimension.

For instance, to find the volume of a rectangular object, you would multiply the length by the width (a.k.a. the area) by the height (the third dimension). So to find the volume of a rectangular solid (as a box), the only kind of figure you are likely to see in a volume question, you just use the formula below.

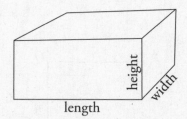

length × width × height = volume

For example:

What is the volume of a rectangular fish tank with the following specifications?
length: 6 inches
height: 6 inches
width: 10 inches

Volume of a Rectangular Solid
$V = lwh$

There isn't much to it. Just stick the numbers into the formula.
length × width × height = volume
$6 \times 10 \times 6 = 360$

PRACTICE DRILL 21—SQUARES, RECTANGLES, AND ANGLES

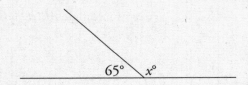

1. What is the value of x ?

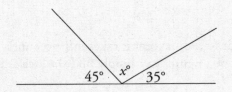

2. What is the value of x ?

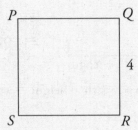

3. PQRS is a square. What is its perimeter? Area?

4. *ABCD* is a rectangle with length 7 and width 3. What is its perimeter? Area?

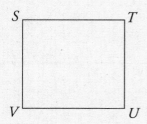

5. *STUV* is a square. Its perimeter is 12. What is its area?

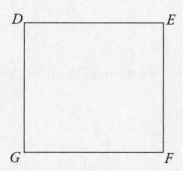

6. *DEFG* is a square. Its area is 81. What is its perimeter?

7. *JKLM* is a rectangle. If its width is 4, and its perimeter is 20, what is its area?

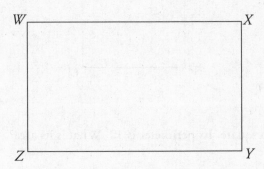

8. *WXYZ* is a rectangle. If its length is 6 and its area is 30, what is its perimeter?

When You Are Done

Check your answers in Chapter 3.

9. What is the volume of a rectangular solid with height 3, width 4, and length 2 ?

Triangles

Isosceles Triangles

Any triangle with two equal sides is an isosceles triangle.

If two sides of a triangle are equal, the angles opposite those sides are always equal.

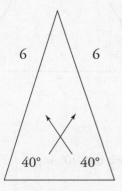

This particular isosceles triangle has two equal sides (of length 6) and therefore two equal angles (40° in this case).

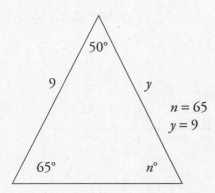

If you already know that the above triangle is isosceles, then you also know that y must equal one of the other sides and n must equal one of the other angles. If $n = 65$, then y must equal 9.

Equilateral Triangles

An equilateral triangle is a triangle with three equal sides. If all the sides are equal, then all the angles must be equal. Each angle in an equilateral triangle equals 60°.

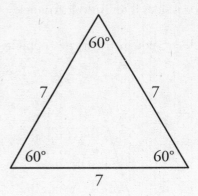

Right Triangles

A right triangle is a triangle with one 90° angle.

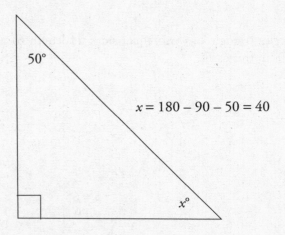

$$x = 180 - 90 - 50 = 40$$

This is a right triangle.
It is also an isosceles triangle.
What does that tell you?

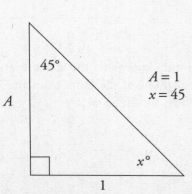

$A = 1$
$x = 45$

Area

To find the area of a triangle, you multiply $\frac{1}{2}$ times the length of the base times the length of the triangle's height, or $\frac{1}{2}b \times h$.

Don't Forget!

$A = \frac{1}{2}\,bh$

Remember the base and the height must form a 90-degree angle.

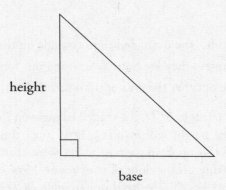

What is the area of a triangle with base 6 and height 3 ?

(A) 3
(B) 6
(C) 9
(D) 12
(E) 18

Just put the values you are given into the formula and do the math. That's all there is to it!

$$\frac{1}{2}b \times h = \text{area}$$

$$(\frac{1}{2})(6) \times 3 = \text{area}$$

$$3 \times 3 = 9$$

So, (C) is the correct answer.

The only tricky point you may run into when finding the area of a triangle is when the triangle is not a right triangle. In this case, it becomes slightly more difficult to find the height, which is easiest to think of as the distance to the point of the triangle from the base. Here's an illustration to help.

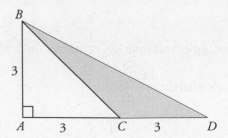

First look at triangle *BAC*, the unshaded right triangle on the left side. Finding its base and height is simple—they are both 3. So using our formula for the area of a triangle, we can figure out that the area of triangle *BAC* is $4\frac{1}{2}$.

Now let's think about triangle *BCD*, the shaded triangle on the right. It isn't a right triangle, so finding the height will involve a little more thought. Remember the question, though: How far up from the base is the point of triangle *BCD*? Think of the shaded triangle sitting on the floor of your room. How far up would its point stick up from the floor? Yes, 3! The height of triangle *BCD* is exactly the same as the height of triangle *BAC*. Don't worry about drawing lines inside the shaded triangle or anything like that, just figure out how high its point is from the ground.

Okay, so just to finish up, to find the base of triangle *BCD* (the shaded one) you will use the same area formula, and just plug in 3 for the base and 3 for the height.

$$\frac{1}{2}b \times h = \text{area}$$
$$(\frac{1}{2})(3) \times 3 = \text{area}$$

And once you do the math, you'll see that the area of triangle *BCD* is $4\frac{1}{2}$.

Not quite convinced? Let's look at the question a little differently. The base of the entire figure (triangle *DAB*) is 6, and the height is 3. Using your trusty area formula, you can determine that the area of triangle *DAB* is 9. You know the area of the unshaded triangle is $4\frac{1}{2}$, so what's left for the shaded part? You guessed it, $4\frac{1}{2}$.

Similar Triangles

Similar triangles are triangles that have the same angles but sides of different lengths. The ratio of any two corresponding sides will be the same as the ratio of any other two corresponding sides. For example, a triangle with sides 3, 4, and 5 is similar to a triangle with sides of 6, 8, and 10, because the ratio of the corresponding sides (6:12 or 7:14 or 9:18) all reduces to 1:2.

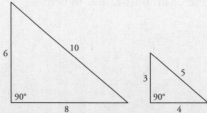

PRACTICE DRILL 22—TRIANGLES

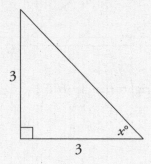

1. What is the value of x?

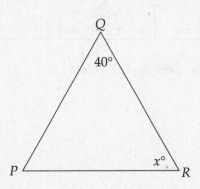

2. Triangle PQR is an isosceles triangle. $PQ = QR$. What is the value of x?

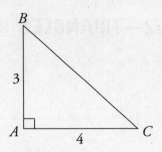

3.   What is the area of right triangle *ABC* ?

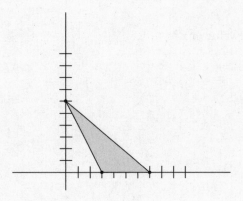

4.   What is the area of the shaded region?

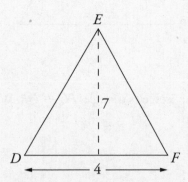

5.   What is the area of triangle *DEF* ?

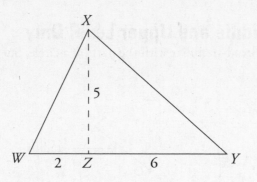

6. What is the area of triangle *WXZ* ? Triangle *ZXY* ? Triangle *WXY* ?

When You Are Done
Check your answers in Chapter 3.

Note:
*   Lower Level students should stop here. The next section you will work on is Word Problems.
*   Middle and Upper Level students should continue.

The Pythagorean Theorem—Middle and Upper Level Only

For all right triangles, $a^2 + b^2 = c^2$, where *a*, *b*, and *c* are the lengths of the triangle's sides.

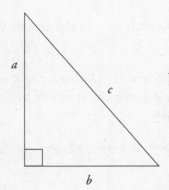

Always remember that *c* represents the *hypotenuse*, the longest side of the triangle, which is always opposite the right angle.

Try It!
Test your knowledge of triangles with the problems that follow Circles. If the question describes a figure that isn't shown, make sure you draw the figure yourself!

Circles—Middle and Upper Level Only

You are probably already familiar with the parts of a circle, but let's review.

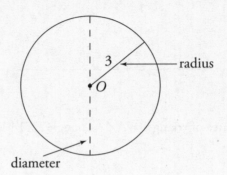

Any line drawn from the origin (the center of the circle) to its edge is called a radius.

Shorthand

Diameter: $d = 2r$

Circumference: $C = \pi d$

Area: $A = \pi r^2$

Any line that passes through the origin is called the **diameter.** The diameter is two times the length of the radius.

Area and Circumference

Circumference of a circle (which is written as C) is really just its perimeter. To find the circumference of a circle, use the formula $2\pi r$ (r stands for the radius) or πd (d stands for diameter). We can find the circumference of the circle above by taking its radius, 3, and multiplying it by 2π. The circumference is 6π.

The area of a circle is found by using the formula πr^2. So the area of the circle above is $3^2\pi$ or 9π.

You can find a circle's radius from its circumference by getting rid of π and dividing the number by 2. You can also find a circle's radius from its area by getting rid of π and taking the square root of the number.

So if a circle has an area of 81π, its radius is 9. If a circle has a circumference of 16π, its radius is 8.

What's up with π?

The Greek letter π is spelled "pi" and pronounced "pie." It is a symbol used with circles. Written as a number, π is a nonrepeating, nonending decimal (3.1415927…). We use pi to determine the true length of circles. However, on the ISEE and SSAT, we simply leave π as the Greek letter. When figuring out area or circumference, simply tack π on at the end.

PRACTICE DRILL 23—CIRCLES AND TRIANGLES

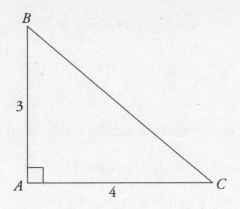

More Review
For additional math review, check out *Math Smart Junior.*

1.   What is the length of side *BC* ?

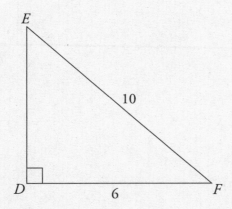

2.   What is the length of side *DE* ?

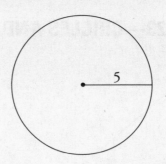

3. What is the circumference of the above circle? What is the area?

4. What is the area of a circle with radius 4 ?

5. What is the area of a circle with diameter 8 ?

6. What is the radius of a circle with area 9π ?

7. What is the diameter of a circle with area 9π ?

When You Are Done
Check your answers in
Chapter 3.

8. What is the circumference of a circle with area 25π ?

WORD PROBLEMS

Many arithmetic and algebra problems are written in paragraph form with many words. The hard part is usually not the arithmetic or the algebra; the hard part is translating the words into math. So let's focus on **translating**.

Key Words and Phrases to Translate

Specific words and phrases show up repeatedly in word problems. You should be familiar with all of the ones on this page.

What You Read in English	What You Do in Math
and, more than, the sum of, plus	+
less than, the difference between, take away from	−
of, the product of, as much as	×
goes into, divided by, the quotient	÷
is, are, was, were, the result will be, has, have, earns, equals, is the same as	=
what, what number, a certain number	variable (x, y, z)
half of a number	$\dfrac{1}{2}x$
twice as much as, twice as old as	$2x$
% (percent)	$\dfrac{}{100}$
how many times greater	divide the two numbers

Proportions

Proportions show relationships between two sets of information. For example, if you wanted to make cookies and you had a recipe for a dozen cookies but wanted to make two dozen cookies, you would have to double all of the ingredients. That's a proportion. Here's how we'd look at it in equation form.

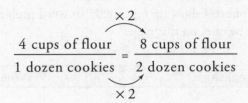

$$\frac{4 \text{ cups of flour}}{1 \text{ dozen cookies}} = \frac{8 \text{ cups of flour}}{2 \text{ dozen cookies}}$$

Whenever a question gives you one set of data and part of another set, it will ask you for the missing part of the second set of data. To find the missing information, set up the information in a fraction like the one shown above. Be careful to put the same information in the same place. In our example, we have flour on top and cookies on the bottom. Make sure both fractions have the flour over the cookies. Once we have our fraction set up, we can see what the relationship is between the two elements (in this case, flour and cookies). Whatever that relationship is, it's the same as the relationship between the other two things.

PRACTICE DRILL 24—WORD PROBLEMS

1. There are 32 ounces in 1 quart. 128 ounces equals how many quarts? How many ounces are there in 7 quarts?

2. A car travels at a rate of 50 miles per hour. How long will it take to travel 300 miles?

3. Betty is twice as old as her daughter Fiona. Fiona is twice as old as her dog Rufus. If Rufus is 11, how old is Betty?

4. A clothing store sold 1,250 pairs of socks this year. Last year it sold 250 pairs of socks. This year's sales are how many times greater than last year's sales?

5. There are 500 students at Eisenhower High School. $\frac{2}{5}$ of the total students are freshmen. $\frac{3}{5}$ of all the freshmen are girls. How many freshman girls are there?

When You Are Done
Check your answers in Chapter 3.

REVIEW DRILL 2 —THE BUILDING BLOCKS

1. If one-third of b is 15, then what is b ?

2. If $7x - 7 = 49$, then what is x ?

3. If $4(y - 5) = 20$, then what is y ?

4. $8x + 1 < 65$. Solve for x.

5. 16 is what percent of 10 ?

6. What percent of 32 is 24 ?

7. What is the area of a triangle with base 7 and height 6 ?

(Middle & Upper Level)

8. What is the diameter of a circle with an area of 9π?

9. What is the radius of a circle with a circumference 12π?

When You Are Done
Check your answers in
Chapter 3.

10. What is the area of a circle with a diameter of 10 ?

Chapter 3
Answer Key to Fundamental Math Drills

The Building Blocks

Practice Drill 1—Math Vocabulary

1.   6   0, 1, 2, 3, 4, 5

2.   1, 3, 5   Many sets of integers would answer this question correctly.

3.   3   3, 5, and 7

4.   8

5.   That number   The smallest positive integer is 1, and any number times 1 is equal to itself.

6.   90 $5 \times 6 \times 3 = 90$

7.   30 $3 + 11 + 16 = 30$

8.   60 $90 - 30 = 60$

9.   –2, –4, –6   2, 4, and 6 are consecutive integers and the question wants negative. Other sets of consecutive integers would also answer the question correctly.

10.   Yes

11.   22 $5 + 6 + 4 + 7 = 22$

12.   6   13 goes into 58, 4 times. $4 \times 13 = 52$ and $58 - 52 = 6$.

13.   1, 5, 11, 55

14.   12 $5 + 8 + 9 = 22$ and $1 + 2 + 0 + 7 = 10$. $22 - 10 = 12$

15.   No   The remainder of $19 \div 5$ is 4. And 21 is not divisible by 4.

16.   2, 2, 3, 13   Draw a factor tree.

17.   16 $3 + 13 = 16$

18.   9 $12 \times 3 = 36$ and $9 \times 4 = 36$.

19.   1, 2, 3, 4, 6, 8, 9, 12, 18, 24, 36, 72

20.   There are 9 even factors and 3 odd factors.

Practice Drill 2—Adding and Subtracting Negative Numbers

1. −8
2. −14
3. −4
4. 27
5. 21
6. 4
7. −22
8. −29
9. −6
10. 90
11. 0
12. 29
13. 24
14. −30
15. −14

Practice Drill 3—Multiplying and Dividing Negative Numbers

1. −4
2. −36
3. 65
4. 11
5. 63
6. −13
7. 84
8. −5
9. 9
10. −8
11. −75
12. 72
13. −4
14. 34
15. −11

Practice Drill 4—Order of Operations

1. 9
2. 16
3. 7
4. 5
5. 6
6. 30
7. 24
8. 60
9. 11
10. 100

Practice Drill 5—Factors and Multiples

1. 2, 4, 6, 8, 10
   4, 8, 12, 16, 20
   5, 10, 15, 20, 25
   11, 22, 33, 44, 55
2. Yes
3. Yes
4. No
5. Yes
6. Yes   Use the divisibility rule for 3. $1 + 2 + 3 = 6$ and 6 is divisible by 3.
7. No
8. Yes
9. Yes
10. Yes
11. Yes
12. No
13. No   2 is a factor of 8.
14. Yes
15. No
16. Yes
17. 8   6, 12, 18, 24, 30, 36, 42, 48
18. 8   Even multiples of 3 are really just multiples of 6.
19. 8   Multiples of both 3 and 4 are also multiples of 12.
    12, 24, 36, 48, 60, 72, 84, 96
20. 48

Practice Drill 6—Reducing Fractions

1. $\dfrac{3}{4}$

2. $\dfrac{1}{5}$

3. $\dfrac{2}{3}$

4. $\dfrac{3}{8}$

5. $\dfrac{3}{4}$

6. $\dfrac{2}{7}$

7. 1

8. $\dfrac{11}{9}$

9. If the number on top is larger than the number on the bottom, the fraction is greater than 1.

Practice Drill 7—Changing Improper Fractions to Mixed Numbers

1. 5

2. $1\dfrac{5}{7}$

3. $5\dfrac{1}{3}$

4. $2\dfrac{1}{2}$

5. $2\dfrac{2}{3}$

6. $6\dfrac{8}{9}$

7. $1\dfrac{1}{2}$

8. 2

9. $11\dfrac{6}{7}$

10. $10\dfrac{1}{2}$

Practice Drill 8—Changing Mixed Numbers to Improper Fractions

1. $\dfrac{45}{7}$

2. $\dfrac{23}{9}$

3. $\dfrac{71}{3}$

4. $\dfrac{20}{3}$

5. $\dfrac{59}{8}$

6. $\dfrac{37}{5}$

7. $\dfrac{161}{16}$

8. $\dfrac{77}{13}$

9. $\dfrac{41}{9}$

10. $\dfrac{747}{22}$

Practice Drill 9—Adding and Subtracting Fractions

1. $1\dfrac{1}{24}$ or $\dfrac{25}{24}$

2. $\dfrac{17}{24}$

3. $\dfrac{6}{7}$ Did you use the Bowtie? You didn't need to because there was already a common denominator there!

4. $\dfrac{1}{12}$

5. $2\dfrac{1}{36}$ or $\dfrac{73}{36}$

6. $-\dfrac{7}{20}$

7. $4\dfrac{1}{3}$ or $\dfrac{13}{3}$

8. $\dfrac{2}{9}$

9. $\dfrac{49}{60}$

10. $\dfrac{18x}{18} = x$

Practice Drill 10—Multiplying and Dividing Fractions

1. $\dfrac{1}{3}$

2. $1\dfrac{1}{4}$ or $\dfrac{5}{4}$

3. $\dfrac{6}{25}$

4. 1

5. $\dfrac{4}{5}$

Practice Drill 11—Decimals

1. 18.7
2. 4.19
3. 4.962
4. 10.625
5. 0.018
6. 6,000
7. 5

Practice Drill 12—Fractions as Decimals

Fraction	Decimal
$\dfrac{1}{2}$	0.5
$\dfrac{1}{3}$	$0.3\overline{3}$
$\dfrac{2}{3}$	$0.6\overline{6}$
$\dfrac{1}{4}$	0.25
$\dfrac{3}{4}$	0.75
$\dfrac{1}{5}$	0.2
$\dfrac{2}{5}$	0.4
$\dfrac{3}{5}$	0.6
$\dfrac{4}{5}$	0.8
$\dfrac{1}{8}$	0.125

Practice Drill 13—Percents

1. The butterscotches are 30% of the candy.
   The caramels are 40% of the candy.
   The peppermints are 10% of the candy.
   The toffees are 20% of the candy.

2. 18%   100% = 72% + 8% + percentage
   of questions answered incorrectly

3. The sneakers make up 20% of the shoes.
   The sandals make up 30% of the shoes.
   The boots make up 40% of the shoes.
   The high heels make up 10% of the shoes.
   There are 4 pairs of high heel shoes.

4. 90%   9 out of the 10 cups are juice.

5. The girls contributed 48%, and the boys
   contributed 52%.

Practice Drill 14—More Percents

Fraction	Decimal	Percent
$\frac{1}{2}$	0.5	50%
$\frac{1}{3}$	$0.3\overline{3}$	$33\frac{1}{3}\%$
$\frac{2}{3}$	$0.6\overline{6}$	$66\frac{2}{3}\%$
$\frac{1}{4}$	0.25	25%
$\frac{3}{4}$	0.75	75%
$\frac{1}{5}$	0.2	20%
$\frac{2}{5}$	0.4	40%
$\frac{3}{5}$	0.6	60%
$\frac{4}{5}$	0.8	80%
$\frac{1}{8}$	0.125	12.5%

1. 21
2. 9
3. 15
4. 51
5. 8
6. The sale price is $102 (15% of 120 = 18).
   The sale price is 85% of the regular price.
7. 292
8. 27
9. $72

Practice Drill 15—Exponents and Square Roots

1. 8
2. 16
3. 27
4. 64
5. 39
6. 9
7. 10
8. 7
9. 8
10. 3

Practice Drill 16—More Exponents

1. 3^8
2. 7^9
3. 5^7
4. 15^3
5. 4^9
6. 10^4
7. 5^{18}
8. 8^{36}
9. 9^{25}
10. 2^{28}

Review Drill 1—The Building Blocks

1. No
2. 9   1, 2, 4, 5, 10, 20, 25, 50, 100
3. −30
4. 140
5. $\dfrac{2}{21}$
6. $\dfrac{12}{25}$
7. 4.08
8. 20% $\dfrac{6}{30} = \dfrac{1}{5} = \dfrac{20}{100}$
9. 1
10. 4
11. 1, 4, 9, 16, 25, 36, 49, 64, 81, 100

Algebra

Practice Drill 17—Solving Simple Equations

1. $x = 12$
2. $y = 15$
3. $z = 28$
4. $x = 5$
5. $x = 3$
6. $x = 11$
7. $y = 5$
8. $z = 3$
9. $y = 48$
10. $z = 71$
11. $x = 12$
12. $y = 12$
13. $z = 45$
14. $x = 18$
15. $y = 29$

Practice Drill 18—Manipulating an Equation

1. 3
2. 5
3. 6
4. 7
5. 4
6. 8
7. 8
8. $\frac{1}{4}$
9. 7
10. 7   Numbers 9 and 10 are really the same equation. Did you see it?
11. 7

Practice Drill 19—Manipulating an Inequality

1. $x > 4$
2. $x < -2$
3. $x > -5$
4. $x > 4$
5. $x < -7$

Practice Drill 20—Translating and Solving Percent Questions

1. 12
2. 24
3. 5
4. 80
5. 125
6. 60
7. 40
8. 2.64 or $2\frac{16}{25}$ or $\frac{66}{25}$
9. 200
10. 2

Geometry

Practice Drill 21—Squares, Rectangles, and Angles

1. 115°

2. 100°

3. The perimeter of *PQRS* is 16. Its area is also 16.

4. The perimeter of *ABCD* is 20. Its area is 21.

5. The area of *STUV* is 9. One side of the square is 3.

6. The perimeter of *DEFG* is 36. One side of the square is 9.

7. The area of *JKLM* is 24. The other side of the rectangle is 6.

8. The perimeter of *WXYZ* is 22. The other side of the rectangle is 5.

9. 24

Practice Drill 22—Triangles

1. 45°

2. 70°

3. 6

4. 12

5. 14

6. *WXZ* = 5
   ZXY = 15
   WXY = 20

Practice Drill 23—Circles and Triangles

1. *BC* = 5
2. *DE* = 8
3. Circumference = 10π. Area = 25π.
4. 16π
5. 16π
6. 3
7. 6
8. 10π

Word Problems

Practice Drill 24—Word Problems

1. 128 ounces = 4 quarts. There are 224 ounces in 7 quarts.

2. 6 hours

3. 44

4. 5

5. 120

Review Drill 2—Building Blocks

1. 45
2. 8
3. 10
4. $x < 8$
5. 160
6. 75
7. 21
8. 6
9. 6
10. 25π

Chapter 4
Writing the Essay

What Is the Essay?

Both the SSAT and ISEE contain a Writing Sample section. How important is it to your score? *It doesn't affect it one bit.* Neither the SSAT people nor the ISEE people score your writing sample. They do, however, copy it and send it to schools along with each of your score reports. Keep in mind that although it does not matter what the SSAT or ISEE people think of the essay that you write, you are writing it for the admissions officers at the schools to which you are applying.

The ISEE gives you 30 minutes to write an essay on an assigned topic. The SSAT gives you 25 minutes to complete it.

Flash Card Alert
What exactly is a *proverb*?

The SSAT Topic

The topic is often a saying or cliché. You need to agree or disagree. Here are two examples:

> No pain, no gain.
> Actions speak louder than words.

The ISEE Topic

The topic often asks you to comment on some aspect of society. Here are two examples:

> Can heroes still exist today?
> How would you change your community?

Interpreting the Topic

These topics can be answered in many ways, and there is no right answer. Your job is to be thoughtful and likable—and to express yourself well!

Keep Using Reasons and Examples

Once you see your topic, don't start writing yet. You must spend four to five minutes coming up with **reasons** for your answer to the prompt or **examples** that support your prompt. Jot down some thoughts and decide which ones are the easiest to write about. One or two good, well-planned examples will take you far. Also, once you have organized your thoughts, the essay is much easier to write—and write well.

Here are two possible examples for "No pain, no gain":

- An athlete training for the Olympics
- You studying hard for a difficult final in a course you dislike

Here are two possible examples for "Can heroes still exist today?":

- A soldier who was injured trying to save others
- My teacher, who works hard every day to make sure everyone understands the material

Your turn.

Come up with two more examples for "No pain, no gain" (SSAT) or "Can heroes still exist today?" (ISEE).

_____

_____

Come up with two examples for "Actions speak louder than words" (SSAT) or "How would you change your community?" (ISEE).

_____

_____

Organize Your Essay

Opening Paragraph: Introduction

- Put the topic in your own words. Show them you understand it (sentence 1).
- State your opinion (sentence 2).
- Introduce your examples (sentence 3).

Body Paragraph: First Example

- State your first example, and explain how it supports your opinion (2 or 3 sentences).

Body Paragraph: Second Example

- State your second example, and explain how it supports your opinion, or state another way in which your first example supports your opinion (2 or 3 sentences).

Final Paragraph: Conclusion

- Paraphrase your opinion (1 sentence).
- End with "The Kicker," a final sentence that shows the wider significance of your opinion (1 sentence—optional).

This looks very familiar, right? You've probably been writing the four-paragraph essay or some variant thereof for many years. You may be way beyond it now, but for this timed essay, it's the best way to be sure you've got a reliable structure. If you practice getting all of the above elements into your essay, and you also have examples planned, then you've left very little to chance. You know everything you're going to write, except the topic.

The "kicker" in your conclusion is something that relates the topic of the essay to more than just the examples you've used. It shows how the topic applies to life, society, the world—the bigger picture. Look at Sample Essay 2 to see a typical "kicker." Even if you don't have a way to show how the position you took relates to the grand scheme of things, you must wrap up with some sort of conclusion, even if it only restates your opinion.

Let's practice writing some of these paragraphs.

Introduction

Write an opening paragraph for one of the essays using your own examples that you just outlined. Show that you understand the topic, state your opinion, and introduce your examples. Spend five minutes on each. Remember, the introduction is where the reader gets his first impression of you, so be extra careful here with spelling, punctuation, and grammar.

Some words you can use if you're agreeing with the topic: *sustain, support, advocate, uphold, endorse, espouse, maintain, bolster, strengthen, fortify,* and *align with.*

Some words you can use if you're disagreeing with the topic: *refute, counter, oppose, controvert, contest, dispute,* and *differ.*

If you want to use one of these words but it is unfamiliar to you, look it up and try using it. Then ask a parent or teacher to read your sentence or paragraph and tell you if you've used it correctly.

_____

_____

_____

_____

_____

_____

_____

_____

_____

_____

_____

Body

The body of your essay will consist of paragraphs that explain how your examples support your opinion. As we've written, details help you make a strong case. They allow you to give the reader concrete information and description, and that helps the reader understand what it is in your example that bolsters your case.

The example of the athlete training for the Olympics works nicely, but it needs more detail. The author of this essay should be answering these questions:

- Which athlete?
- What sport?
- What was the training like?
- What was the pain?
- What was the gain?

These sorts of details make for a powerful essay.

Explaining your examples is the most important thing you must do while writing the body paragraphs. Assume the burden of responsibility for making your points clear to the reader.

Something else to think about while writing these paragraphs is how you and your reader get from one paragraph to another. You want the reader to see a smooth transition from one paragraph to the next, so she knows she's still reading the same essay. Thus, if you are switching from the athlete to the final you studied for, you might say something like "I have also learned that pain can lead to gain in my own life."

Now reread your introduction on page 141, and then write the two body paragraphs using your examples. Go ahead and write your paragraphs below.

Get a Second Opinion
Get as many people as possible to read your practice essays and tell you if there are parts that are not clear or points that could be developed better. Make sure they know you have only 30 minutes to write.

_____

_____

_____

_____

_____

_____

_____

_____

_____

_____

_____

_____

_____

_____

_____

Conclusion

Write a quick closing paragraph for each of the five topics we've been using. Paraphrase the opinion expressed in your introduction (don't use the same words you used in your introduction), and try writing a "kicker" that broadens the essay outward and makes it more meaningful. If you can't come up with a "kicker," don't worry—just write something that wraps up the essay. Try to spend just three to five minutes on each conclusion.

Some words you can use to show you're concluding your essay: *therefore, in sum, clearly, consequently, thus,* or *in conclusion.*

Kicker
Need an example of a kicker? Look at the last paragraph of Sample Essay 2 on page 147.

_____

_____

_____

_____

_____

_____

_____

_____

The Basics

Here are basic things to keep in mind.

- Write legibly. Practice handwriting essays in pen. Nothing turns a reader off more quickly than an essay that's messy or difficult to decipher. Think about how many essays a school admissions officer has to read!
- If you need to delete words, draw one neat line through them.
- Indent your paragraphs substantially, so the reader can see at a glance that you've organized your essay.
- Stay within the lines and margins.
- Stick to the assigned topic.
- Keep your sentences easy to understand. If you see you've written a long, complicated sentence, think about breaking it up. You want the reader to be able to understand your points.
- Use some big vocabulary words if you're sure you really know them.
- Watch for the punctuation and grammar mistakes that you've made in the past and still tend to make. (If you're not sure which mistakes you make, ask your English teacher!)
- If you're not sure how to spell a word, think of another one you can use.
- Try to leave a minute or two to read over your essay when you're done. Catch any careless errors, and neatly correct them.

Now let's look at some sample essays. As you read them, decide which one follows the assignment and our guidelines better.

Sample Essay 1

Topic: No pain, no gain.
Prompt: Do you agree or disagree with the topic statement? Support your position with specific examples from personal experience, the experience of others, current events, history, or literature.

Get Feedback
Ask a parent or teacher to read your introduction, body paragraphs, and conclusion.

I agree with the statement "No pain, no gain." In this competitive society, an individual cannot expect to accomplish all of his or her goals without suffering first. This suffering provides a person with the incentive to learn from his or her mistakes and try harder to obtain what he or she desires. The following examples will help to make this idea clearer.

An athlete must always keep his body in top form. If the person doesn't, then his competitors will knock him out of the sport with ease. The athlete must practice many hours per day by pushing himself beyond his limits. For example, the weightlifter must lift weights that start out light and get heavier as he progresses. When the weightlifter can lift a certain amount with ease, he is forced to try a heavier amount, which may hurt at first. However, in the long run the weightlifter will be stronger than before.

In American Colonial days, colonists were in some ways tortured by the mother country, England. The Stamp Acts, tea taxes, Quartering Acts, etc., imposed by England angered the people colonists because they hurt their trade, causing the colonists to become more dependent on England. In the long run, however, these actions by England helped the colonists to win their independence. Each time England imposed another law, the colonists grew more angry. Finally, the people got up the courage to rebel. Thus, they gained their independence.

What Do You Think of Sample Essay 1?

Use these questions to evaluate Sample Essay 1.

- Is the essay legible?
- Does the essay have an introduction that is a separate paragraph?
- Does the author understand the topic?
- Is the author's opinion stated clearly?
- Does the author use examples to support his or her opinion?
- How many examples? What kind? How convincing are they?
- Does the author explain how the examples support his or her opinion?
- Has the author moved smoothly from one paragraph to the next?
- Is the essay organized? Does each example have a paragraph?
- Are the paragraphs well indented?
- Has the author stayed neatly within the lines?
- Has the author used impressive vocabulary correctly?
- Does the essay have a conclusion that is a separate paragraph?
- Does the conclusion summarize the points in the essay without repeating the introduction word for word?

For Those Who Can Help You
You can show these questions to people who read your practice essays, and ask them to answer the questions as they apply to your essays, too.

Sample Essay 2

It is absolutely true that one cannot accomplish anything without bearing some sort of pain, whether it is physical or emotional. This has been true throughout history, and remains true in our world today. One example of this is drug testing, during which animals must be hurt or killed so that new, lifesaving drugs may be developed. Another example is the Civil Rights movement, during which many people had to sacrifice a great deal for the greater good.

Before a new medicine or drug can be used on human beings, it must undergo a tremendous amount of testing on animals, to ensure that it is safe and effective. During this process, most of the animals die or are hurt so badly that they must be killed. Many people protest that it is not fair to harm all these animals, but I think this is a very good example of "no pain, no gain." Animals' pain is an unfortunate but necessary step in our making medical gains.

During the American Civil Rights movement, such people as Rosa Parks and Martin Luther King, Jr. had to undergo tremendous physical and emotional pain in order to move the country toward racial equality. Rosa Parks knew that she would be arrested for sitting in the "whites only" part of the bus, but she did it anyway, knowing that it was necessary to pay the price for advancing civil rights. She was not only arrested, but she and her whole family were harassed, receiving death threats for a long time. She did not let these dangers stop her from continuing to protest, boycott, and speak for the movement. Martin Luther King, Jr. also made many sacrifices to work for racial equality, and he died striving to further the cause, but his life and death resulted in great gains.

In summary, nothing positive can happen without some pain. We must learn to take the good with the bad and realize that we cannot gain the former without accepting the latter. It is only through this realization that we can continue to advance as individuals, citizens, and human beings.

What Do You Think of Sample Essay 2?

Use these questions to evaluate Sample Essay 2.

- Is the essay legible?
- Does the essay have an introduction that is a separate paragraph?
- Does the author understand the topic?
- Is the author's opinion stated clearly?
- Does the author use examples to support his or her opinion?
- How many examples? What kind? How convincing are they?
- Does the author explain how the examples support his or her opinion?
- Has the author moved smoothly from one paragraph to the next?
- Is the essay organized? Does each example have a paragraph?
- Are the paragraphs well indented?
- Has the author stayed neatly within the lines?
- Has the author used impressive vocabulary correctly?
- Does the essay have a conclusion that is a separate paragraph?
- Does the conclusion summarize the points in the essay without being just a word-for-word repeat of the intro?

Which writing sample was better? _____

Take a look at the Answer Key at the end of this chapter for our evaluations of these essays.

Review—The Essay Plan

The First Three Minutes

How do I spend the first three minutes?

_____

_____

Writing the Essay

Opening Paragraph: _____

What do I include here? _____

_____

Body Paragraphs: _____

What do I include here? _____

_____

Final Paragraph: _____

What do I include here? _____

_____

When I've only got three minutes left, what must I be sure to do?

_____

If you have any trouble answering these questions, reread this chapter before going further.

PRACTICE DRILL 1—ESSAY

Write an essay on the other topic for which you created examples. Ask a parent or teacher to read it. Be sure to think before you write.

_____

_____

_____

_____

_____

_____

_____

_____

_____

_____

_____

_____

_____

_____

_____

_____

_____

_____

PRACTICE DRILL 2—ESSAYS

Time yourself for each of the essays on the pages that follow. When you're done with each, ask yourself the same questions you used to evaluate the sample "No pain, no gain" essay.

Ask a parent or teacher to read one also, but be sure to let them know that what they're reading is a timed 30-minute essay, so they should read primarily for content and organization. Ask them not to grade it, but to tell you what you did well and what you could do better.

If your grammar, spelling, or punctuation is such that your reader has a hard time understanding the essay, you should pick up a basic handbook so you can identify your weak points and work on them. However, don't be concerned about a few minor errors. If you have solid examples that support your main idea, and you've organized them well and written clearly and legibly, then you've covered the most important areas. Developing your writing style by learning to vary the length of your sentences or by reviewing the basics of grammar, usage, spelling, and punctuation can be useful also and will make your essay more polished. However, only if you have plenty of preparation time should you check out handbooks of style and usage.

Lower Level ISEE Test Takers: Practice Essays
The very last essay topic (page 158) is for you.

_____

_____

_____

_____

_____

_____

_____

_____

_____

_____

_____

_____

_____

_____

_____

_____

_____

_____

_____

_____

SSAT Topic: You get what you pay for.

_____

_____

_____

_____

_____

_____

_____

_____

_____

_____

_____

_____

_____

_____

_____

_____

_____

_____

_____

_____

_____

_____

_____

_____

_____

_____

_____

_____

_____

_____

_____

_____

_____

_____

_____

_____

_____

_____

_____

Lower Level ISEE Topic: What person do you most admire?

_____

_____

_____

_____

_____

_____

_____

_____

_____

_____

_____

_____

_____

_____

_____

_____

_____

_____

ESSAY EVALUATION

Sample Essay 1 Evaluation

Sample 1 has several good points: It is legible, has a separate introduction that clearly states the author's opinion and shows that he or she understands the topic, and has two examples to support his opinion. However, the examples are weak and not fully developed. The first example is a generalized statement of which the author does not even claim to have personal experience, and the second example needs to be explained a little further. There are separate paragraphs, showing that the ideas are organized, but there are no transitions from paragraph to paragraph. There are a few errors, but this essay's biggest problem is its lack of any conclusion for the essay as a whole. Sample 1 is an essay that is a little below average.

Sample Essay 2 Evaluation

Sample 2 is a slightly longer essay that is also legible, with only a few spelling errors. It has a separate introduction that states the author's opinion, shows that he or she understands the topic, and introduces the examples that will support his or her opinion. In this essay, the author used two strong examples. One is a current event, and the other is historical. They are both explained so that the reader knows some details about each and gains some understanding of the pains and gains involved in each. Transitions between sections could be smoother, but the essay is organized and the reader can quickly see that by looking at the indentations. Finally, the reader is left with a conclusion that both summarizes the author's opinion and also broadens the essay outward, showing the importance of the topic. Sample 2 is an above average essay and could be made even better with additional details and a smoother style.

The Essay Plan

During the first three minutes, I note some examples that I could use to agree or disagree with the topic. Then I choose a side. OR, if my essay prompt is more open-ended, then I brainstorm some ideas for what I want to write and decide the order in which I'll write them.

Opening Paragraph: Introduction

I include:

- The topic (in my own words)
- My opinion
- My examples (briefly introducing them)

Body Paragraphs: Examples

I include:

- Each example
- How each example supports my opinion

Final Paragraph: Conclusion

I include:

- My opinion (in different words from how I said it in the introduction)
- The kicker

When I've got only three minutes left, I must make sure to write a conclusion.

Part II
The SSAT

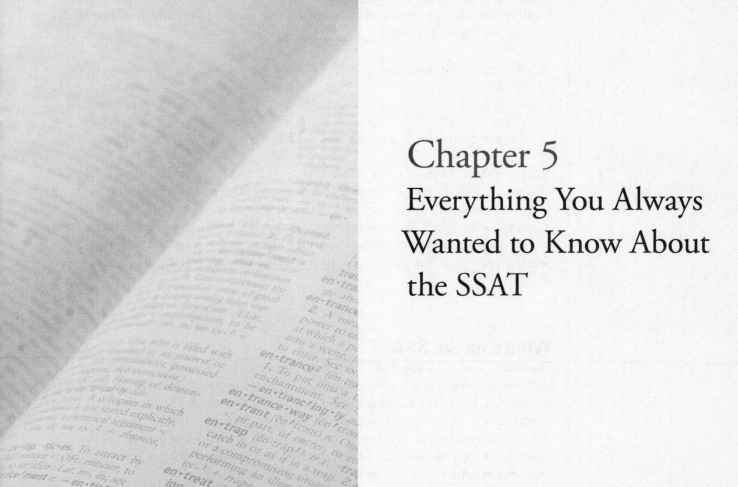

Chapter 5
Everything You Always
Wanted to Know About
the SSAT

WHAT IS THE SSAT?

The Secondary School Admission Test (SSAT) is a standardized test made up of a writing sample, which is not scored but is sent along with each score report, and a series of multiple-choice questions divided into Quantitative (Math), Verbal, and Reading sections. The entire test lasts about 155 minutes, during which you will work on five different sections.

Writing Sample (ungraded)	1 essay topic	25 minutes
Quantitative	25 questions	30 minutes
Reading	40 questions	40 minutes
Verbal	60 questions	30 minutes
Quantitative (a second section)	25 questions	30 minutes

There are three different types of sections on the SSAT: Verbal, Reading, and Quantitative (Math). You will receive four scores on the test, however. In addition to listing a score for each of these three sections, your score report will also show an overall score, which is a combination of your verbal, reading, and quantitative scores. You will also receive a percentile score of between 1 percent and 99 percent that compares your test scores with those of other test takers from the previous three years.

What's on the SSAT?

The Verbal section of the SSAT tests your knowledge of vocabulary using two different question types: synonyms and analogies. There are no sentence completions on the SSAT. The Reading section tests your ability to read and understand short passages. These reading passages include both fiction (including poetry and folklore) and nonfiction. The Math sections test your knowledge of general mathematical concepts, including arithmetic, algebra, and geometry. There are no quantitative comparison questions on the Math sections of the SSAT.

Upper Level Versus Lower Level

There are two different versions of the SSAT. The Lower Level test is taken by students who are, at the time of testing, in the fifth, sixth, and seventh grades. The Upper Level test is for students who take the test during the eighth, ninth, tenth, and eleventh grades.

One difference between the Upper and Lower Level tests is their scale. The Upper Level test gives a student four scaled scores ranging from 500 on the low end to 800 at the top. Scores on the Lower Level test range from 440 to 710 (704 for Quantitative). There are also some small differences in content; for instance, vocabulary on the Lower Level test is less challenging than it is on the Upper Level test. In Math, you will see similar general concepts tested (arithmetic, algebra, geometry, charts, and graphs) on both tests, but naturally, the Lower Level test will ask slightly easier questions than the Upper Level test. However, many of the questions are exactly the same on each level.

As you work through this book, you will notice that sets of practice problems do not distinguish between Upper and Lower Level questions. Instead, you will find practice sets that generally increase in difficulty as you move from earlier to later questions. Therefore, if you are taking the Lower Level test, don't worry if you have trouble with questions at the ends of the practice sets. **Students should stop each practice set at the point where they have reached vocabulary or math concepts with which they are unfamiliar.** This point will be different for every student.

Because the Lower Level SSAT tests fifth, sixth, and seventh graders and the Upper Level SSAT tests eighth, ninth, tenth, and eleventh graders, there is content on the tests that students testing at the lower end of each of the groups will have difficulty answering. Younger students' scaled scores and percentiles will not be harmed by this fact. Both sets of scores take into consideration a student's age and gender. However, younger students may feel intimidated by this. **If you are at the lower end of your test's age group, there will be questions you are not supposed to be able to answer, and that's perfectly all right.**

Likewise, the material in this book follows the content of the two tests without breaking it down further into age groups or grades. Content that will appear only on the Upper Level test has been labeled as Upper Level only. Students taking the Lower Level test do not need to work on the Upper Level content. Nevertheless, younger students may have not yet seen some of the material included in the Lower Level review. Parents are advised to help younger students with their work in this book and seek a teacher's advice or instruction if necessary.

Chapter 6
General Test-Taking
Techniques for the SSAT

PACING

Most people believe that to do well on a test, it is important to answer every question. While this is true of most of the tests you take in school, it is not true of many standardized tests, including the SSAT. On this test, it is very possible to score well without answering all of the questions; in fact, many students can improve their scores by answering fewer questions.

"Wait a second. I can get a better score by answering *fewer* questions?" Yes. You will be penalized only for the questions you answer incorrectly, not for skipping. Because all of the questions are worth the same amount of points, it's just as good to get an easy question right as a hard one. So for the most part, you'll give your attention to problems you think you can answer, and decide which questions are too thorny to waste time on. This test-taking approach is just as important to score improvement as knowledge of vocabulary and math rules!

In general, all math and verbal questions on the SSAT gradually increase in difficulty from first to last. (The one exception is the Reading section, where question difficulty is mixed.) This means that for most students, the longest and hardest problems are at the end of each section. For this reason, all students should focus the majority of their attention on the easiest and medium problems. Why rush through these and make careless errors, when you could spend time and get all of them right? Worry about the hard ones last, if you have time.

The reason that this approach to pacing can actually *increase* scores is that skipped questions gain you zero points, whereas incorrect answers each reduce your raw score by a quarter-point. Because your raw score will decrease only if you answer a question incorrectly, skipping is the best strategy for a problem that has you completely stumped. Ideally, you will either get a question right or skip it (with some exceptions when you can guess intelligently and aggressively).

Skipping will be a major tool mostly for the hardest of questions. Guessing will be part of the whole test, so let's look at how guessing and skipping work together.

GUESSING

When should you guess? Whenever you can eliminate even one wrong answer with certainty. Yes, really. We'll get to why in a minute. Eliminate four and you have the right answer by process of elimination. So eliminate definitely wrong answers and guess! Be aggressive.

Over the course of the whole test, this strategy will increase your score. How? Well, let's look again at how SSAT questions are scored, right answers rewarded and wrong answers penalized.

Correct answers: +1 point

Wrong answers: $-\dfrac{1}{4}$ point

Blank answers: 0 points

Suppose we asked you to place a bet on five flips of a coin. There's only one chance in five that it will come up heads, but if it does, you get a dollar. There's a four in five chance of tails; when it's tails, you pay us 25¢. Would you do it? Maybe yes, maybe no. If it came up heads once and tails four times, you'd get a dollar and then pay 25¢ four times, ending up with nothing. You wouldn't lose money, but you wouldn't win any, either. Similarly, there are five answer choices on every SSAT question, but only one right answer. So if you just guess randomly without eliminating anything first, you will be right about one time and wrong about four times for every five questions you do. That means that the one time you were right, you would get one full raw point (yay!), and you would lose a quarter-point four times (boo!). All this would get you right back to where you started.

$$1 - 4\left(\frac{1}{4}\right) = 0$$

So random guessing will pretty much keep your score flat. Here is where our guessing strategy comes in. What if, instead of a one-in-five chance of getting heads, the odds were one in four? This time, if four flips usually turned up one head ($1 for you) and three tails (pay out 75¢), you'd make a little money and come out on top. On an SSAT question, if you can eliminate one answer choice out of the five, you're in the same situation. You now have only four possible answers, and you will be right about once for every *three* times you are wrong. Now the penalty for wrong answers will have less impact. If you narrow down to three choices, you'll get about one right for every two times you're wrong. Good odds? You bet. That's like making a dollar and losing 50¢. If you can do this throughout the test, you will increase your score gradually. That's why it pays to spend time eliminating definitely wrong answers and to guess aggressively.

$$1 - 3\left(\frac{1}{4}\right) = \frac{1}{4}$$

Want to use what you've just learned to improve your score? You've come to the right place. Guessing well is one of the most important skills this book can teach you. Strategic guessing and skipping, as simple as they seem, are very powerful score-boosters on standardized tests like the SSAT. Now, let's discuss one more major test-taking approach that should be a part of your game plan.

PROCESS OF ELIMINATION

Here's a question you will not see on the SSAT, but which will show you how powerful Process of Elimination (POE) can be.

Should I Guess?
Random guessing will not improve your SSAT score. Educated guessing, however, is always a good idea.

What is the capital of Malawi?

(A) New York
(B) Paris
(C) London
(D) Lilongwe
(E) Washington, D.C.

There are two ways to get this question right. First, you can know that the capital of Malawi is Lilongwe. If you do, good for you! The second is to know that the capital of Malawi is not New York, Paris, London, or Washington, D.C. You don't get more points for knowing the right answer from the start, so one way is just as good as the other. Try to get in the habit of looking at a question and asking, "What are the wrong answers?" instead of "What is the right answer?"

By using POE this way, you will eliminate wrong answers and have fewer answers from which to pick. The result is that you will pick right answers more often. In the example above, you're not even really guessing. You *know* that the other four answers are wrong, and that's as good as knowing the right answer. In fact, now you *do* know the capital of Malawi. That's the great thing about guessing on a standardized test like the SSAT—when you have trouble finding the correct answer, you can often eliminate the wrong ones and come out on top. Now let's look at the same idea in practice in another problem.

Which of the following cities is the capital of Samoa?

(A) Vila
(B) Boston
(C) Apia
(D) Chicago
(E) Los Angeles

You may not know the right answer off the top of your head, but which cities are not the capital of Samoa? You probably know enough about the locations of (B), (D), and (E) to know that Boston, Chicago, and Los Angeles are not the capital of Samoa.

So, what's a good answer to this question? (A) or (C).

What's the right answer? That is not the right question here. The better question is: Should I guess? And the answer is absolutely yes. Yes, yes, yes. You've done a great job of narrowing the answer down to just two choices. On any question where you've done this, you'll have a 50-50 chance. In other words, on average you'll get these questions right about half the time (+1 point) and wrong the other half $(-\frac{1}{4}$ point). So chances are that you'll gain about three-quarters of a point per question whenever you can narrow questions down to two answer choices and guess. Even though you'll get some (about half) of these wrong, your score will go up overall. Always use POE and guess aggressively. Remember that you should skip the question if you can't eliminate anything at all.

A QUICK SUMMARY

These points about the SSAT are important enough that we want to mention them again. Make sure you understand them before you go any farther in this book.

- You do not have to answer every question on the test. Slow down!
- You will not immediately know the correct answer to every question. Instead, look for wrong answers that you can eliminate.
- Random guessing will not improve your score on the SSAT. However, educated guessing, which means that you eliminate even just one out of the five choices, is a good thing and will improve your score. As a general rule of thumb, if you invest enough time to read and think about the answer to a question, you should be able to eliminate at least one choice and take a good guess!

Chapter 7
SSAT Math

INTRODUCTION

This section will provide you with a review of all the math that you need to know to do well on the SSAT. When you get started, you may feel that the material is too easy. Don't worry. The SSAT measures your basic math skills, so although you may feel a little frustrated reviewing things you have already learned, this type of basic review is the best way to improve your score.

We recommend that you work through these math sections in order, reading each section and then doing each set of drills. If you have trouble with one section, mark the page so you can come back later to go over it again. Keep in mind that you shouldn't breeze over pages or sections just because they look familiar. Take the time to read over all the Math sections, so you'll be sure to know all the math you'll need!

Lose Your Calculator!

You will *not* be allowed to use a calculator on the SSAT. If you have developed a habit of reaching for your calculator whenever you need to add or multiply a couple of numbers, follow our advice: Put your calculator away now and take it out again after the test is behind you. Do your math homework assignments without it, and complete the practice sections in this book without it. Trust us, you'll be glad you did.

Write It Down

Do not try to do math in your head. You are allowed to write in your test booklet. You *should* write in your test booklet. Even when you are just adding a few numbers together, write them down and do the work on paper. Writing things down will not only help eliminate careless errors but also give you something to refer to if you need to check over your work.

One Pass, Two Pass

Within any Math section you will find three types of questions:

- Those you can answer easily without spending too much time
- Those that, if you had all the time in the world, you could do
- Some questions that you have absolutely no idea how to tackle

Don't Get Stuck
Make sure you don't spend too much time working on one tough question; there might be easier questions left in the section.

When you work on a Math section, start out with the first question. If you think you can do it without too much trouble, go ahead. If not, save it for later. Move on to the second question and decide whether or not to do that one. In general, the questions in each Math section are in a very rough order of difficulty. This means that earlier questions tend to be somewhat easier than later ones. You will likely find yourself answering more questions toward the beginning of the sections and leaving more questions blank toward the end.

Once you've made it all the way through the section, working slowly and carefully to do all the questions that come easily to you, then go back and try some of the ones that you think you can do but will take a little longer. You should pace yourself so that time will run out while you're working on the second pass through the section. Working this way, you'll know that you answered all the questions that were easy for you. Using a two-pass system is good, smart test-taking.

Guesstimating

Sometimes accuracy is important. Sometimes it isn't.

Which of the following fractions is less than $\frac{1}{4}$?

(A) $\frac{4}{18}$

(B) $\frac{4}{12}$

(C) $\frac{7}{7}$

(D) $\frac{10}{9}$

(E) $\frac{12}{5}$

Without doing a bit of calculation, think about this question. It asks you to find a fraction smaller than $\frac{1}{4}$. Even if you're not sure which one is actually smaller, you can certainly eliminate some wrong answers.

Start simple: $\frac{1}{4}$ is less than 1, right? Are there any fractions in the answer choices that are greater than 1? Get rid of (D) and (E).

Some Things Are Easier Than They Seem
Guesstimating, or finding approximate answers, can help you eliminate wrong answers and save lots of time.

Look at answer choice (C). $\frac{7}{7}$ equals 1. Can it be less than $\frac{1}{4}$? Eliminate (C). Already, without doing any math, you have a 50 percent chance of guessing the right answer.

Here's another good example.

> A group of three men buys a one-dollar raffle ticket that wins $400. If the one dollar that they paid for the ticket is subtracted and the remainder of the prize money is divided equally among the men, how much will each man receive?
>
> (A) $62.50
> (B) $75.00
> (C) $100.00
> (D) $133.00
> (E) $200.00

This isn't a terribly difficult question. To solve it mathematically, you would take $400, subtract $1, and then divide the remainder by three. But by using a little bit of logic, you don't have to do any of that.

The raffle ticket won $400. If there were four men, each one would have won about $100 (actually slightly less because the problem tells you to subtract the $1 price of the ticket, but you get the idea). So far so good?

However, there weren't four men; there were only three. This means fewer men among whom to divide the winnings, so each one should get more than $100, right? Look at the answer choices. Eliminate (A), (B), and (C).

Two choices left. Answer choice (E) is $200, half of the amount of the winning ticket. If there were three men, could each one get half? Unfortunately not. Eliminate (E). What's left? The right answer!

Guesstimating also works very well with some geometry questions, but just to give you something you can look forward to, we'll save that for the Geometry chapter.

WORKING WITH ANSWER CHOICES

In Chapter 2, "Fundamental Math Skills for the SSAT & ISEE," we reviewed the concepts that will be tested on the Lower and Upper Level SSAT tests. However, the questions in the practice drills were slightly different from the ones that you will see on your exam. The ones on the exam are going to give you five answers to choose from. There are many benefits to working with multiple-choice questions.

For one, if you really mess up calculating the question, chances are your answer choice will not be among the ones given. Now you have a chance to go back and try that problem again more carefully. Another benefit is that you may be able to use the information in the answer choices to help you solve the problems (don't worry; we'll tell you how soon).

We are now going to introduce to you the type of multiple-choice questions you will see on the SSAT. Each one of the following questions will test some skill that we covered in the Fundamental Math Skills chapter. If you don't see how to solve the question, take a look back at Chapter 2 for help.

A Tip About Answer Choices
Notice that the answer choices are often in numerical order.

Math Vocabulary

1. Which of the following is the greatest even integer less than 25 ?

   (A) 26
   (B) 24.5
   (C) 22
   (D) 21
   (E) 0

The first and most important thing you need to do on this and every problem is to read and understand the question. What important vocabulary words did you see in the question? There is "even" and "integer." You should always underline the important words in the questions. This way you will make sure to pay attention to them and avoid careless errors.

Now that we understand that the question is looking for an even integer, we can eliminate any answers that are not even or an integer. Cross out (B) and (D). We can also eliminate (A) because 26 is greater than 25 and we want a number less than 25. Now all we have to do is ask which is greater—0 or 22. (C) is the right answer.

Try it again.

Set A = {All multiples of 7}

Set B = {All odd numbers}

2. All of the following are members of both set A and
    set B above EXCEPT
    (A)   7
    (B) 21
    (C) 49
    (D) 59
    (E) 77

Did you underline the words *multiples of 7* and *odd*? Because all the answer choices are odd, you can't eliminate any that would not be in Set B, but only (D) is not
a multiple of 7. So (D) is the right answer.

The Rules of Zero

**Remember the
Rules of Zero**
Zero is even. It's neither
positive nor negative,
and anything multiplied
by $0 = 0$.

3. x, y, and z stand for three distinct numbers, where
    $xy = 0$ and $yz = 15$. Which of the following must be
    true?
    (A) $y = 0$
    (B) $x = 0$
    (C) $z = 0$
    (D) $xyz = 15$
    (E) It cannot be determined from the information
         above.

Because x times y is equal to zero, and x, y, and z are different numbers, we know
that either x or y is equal to zero. If y was equal to zero, then y times z should also
be equal to zero. Because it is not, we know that it must be x that equals zero. Answer choice (B) is correct.

The Multiplication Table

4. Which of the following is equal to $6 \times 5 \times 2$?

    (A) $60 \div 3$

    (B) 14×7

    (C) $2 \times 2 \times 15$

    (D) 12×10

    (E) $3 \times 3 \times 3 \times 9$

$6 \times 5 \times 2 = 60$ and so does $2 \times 2 \times 15$. Answer choice (C) is correct.

Working with Negative Numbers

5. $7 - 9$ is the same as

    (A) $7 - (-9)$

    (B) $9 - 7$

    (C) $7 + (-9)$

    (D) $-7 - 9$

    (E) $-9 - 7$

Remember that subtracting a number is the same as adding its opposite. Answer choice (C) is correct.

Order of Operations

6. $9 + 6 \times 2 \div 3 =$

    (A)   7

    (B)   9

    (C)   10

    (D)   13

    (E)   17

Remember your PEMDAS rules? The multiplication comes first, followed by division. The correct answer is (D).

Don't Do More Work Than You Have To
When looking at answer choices, start with what's easy; only work through the hard ones when you have eliminated the others.

Factors and Multiples

Factors Are Small; Multiples Are Large

The factors of a number are always equal to or less than that number. The multiples of a number are always equal to or greater than that number. Be sure not to confuse the two!

7. What is the sum of the prime factors of 42 ?

(A) 18
(B) 13
(C) 12
(D) 10
(E) 7

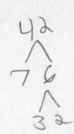

How do we find the prime factors? The best way is to draw a factor tree. Then we see that the prime factors of 42 are 2, 3, and 7. Add them up and we get 12, answer choice (C).

Fractions

8. Which of the following is less than $\frac{4}{6}$?

(A) $\frac{3}{5}$

(B) $\frac{4}{6}$

(C) $\frac{5}{7}$

(D) $\frac{7}{8}$

(E) $\frac{9}{7}$

When comparing fractions, you have three choices. You can find a common denominator and then compare the fractions (such as when you add or subtract fractions). You can also change the fractions to decimals. If you have memorized the fraction-to-decimal chart in the Fundamentals chapter, you probably found the right answer without too much difficulty. It's answer choice (A). Or, if you remember the bowtie method, you can compare that way too!

Percents

9. Thom's CD collection contains 15 jazz CDs, 45
   rap albums, 30 funk CDs, and 60 pop albums.
   What percent of Thom's CD collection is funk?

   (A) 10%
   (B) 20%
   (C) 25%
   (D) 30%
   (E) 40%

First we need to find the fractional part that represents Thom's funk CDs. He

has 30 out of a total of 150. We can reduce $\dfrac{30}{150}$ to $\dfrac{1}{5}$. As a percent, $\dfrac{1}{5}$ is 20%,

answer choice (B).

Exponents

10. $2^6 =$

    (A) 2^3
    (B) 3^2
    (C) 4^2
    (D) 4^4
    (E) 8^2

Expand 2^6 out and we can multiply to find that it equals 64. Answer choice (E) is
correct.

Square Roots

11. The square root of 75 falls between what two
    integers?

    (A) 5 and 6
    (B) 6 and 7
    (C) 7 and 8
    (D) 8 and 9
    (E) 9 and 10

If you have trouble with this one, try using the answer choices and work backward. As we discussed in the Fundamentals chapter, a square root is just the opposite of squaring a number. So let's square the answer choices. Then we find that
75 falls between 8^2 (64) and 9^2 (81). Answer choice (D) is correct.

Simple Algebraic Equations

12. $11x = 121$. What does $x = $?

    (A) 2

    (B) 8

    (C) 10

    (D) 11

    (E) 12

Remember, if you get stuck, use the answer choices and work backward. Each one provides you with a possible value for x. Start with the middle answer choice and replace x with it. $11 \times 10 = 110$. That's too small. Now we know that not only is (C) incorrect, but also that (A) and (B) are incorrect because they are smaller than (C). The correct answer choice is (D).

The Case of the Mysteriously Missing Sign

If there is no operation sign between a number and a variable (letter), the operation is multiplication.

Solve for *X*

13. If $3y + 17 = 25 - y$, then $y =$

    (A) 1

    (B) 2

    (C) 3

    (D) 4

    (E) 5

Just as above, if you get stuck, use the answer choices. The correct answer is (B).

Percent Algebra

Percent

Percent means "out of 100," and the word *of* in a word problem tells you to multiply.

14. 25% of 30% of what is equal to 18 ?

    (A)   1

    (B)   36

    (C)   120

    (D)   240

    (E)   540

If you don't remember the math conversion table, look it up in the Fundamentals chapter. You can also use the answer choices and work backward. Start with answer choice (C) and find out what 25% of 30% of 120 is. The correct answer is (D).

Geometry

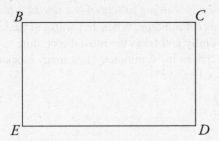

15. *BCDE* is a rectangle with a perimeter of 44. If the length of *BC* is 15, what is the area of *BCDE*?

    (A)   105
    (B)   15
    (C)   17
    (D)   14
    (E)   It cannot be determined.

From the perimeter, we can find that the sides of the rectangle are 7 and 15. So the area is 105, answer choice (A).

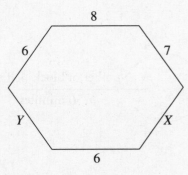

16. If the perimeter of this polygon is 37, what is the value of $X + Y$?

    (A)   5
    (B)   9
    (C)   10
    (D)   16
    (E)   20

$X + Y$ is equal to the perimeter of the polygon minus the lengths of the sides we know. Answer choice (C) is correct.

Word Problems

17. Emily is walking to school at a rate of 3 blocks every 14 minutes. When Jeff walks at the same rate as Emily and takes the most direct route to school, he arrives in 56 minutes. How many blocks away does Jeff live?

    (A) 3
    (B) 5
    (C) 6
    (D) 9
    (E) 12

This is a proportion question because we have two sets of data that we are comparing. Set up your fraction.

$$\frac{3 \text{ blocks}}{14 \text{ minutes}} = \frac{\text{Number of blocks Jeff walks}}{56 \text{ minutes}}$$

We know that we must do the same thing to the top and bottom of the first fraction to get the second fraction. Notice that the denominator of the second fraction (56) is 4 times the denominator of the first fraction (14). Therefore, the numerator of the second fraction must be 4 times the numerator of the first fraction (3).

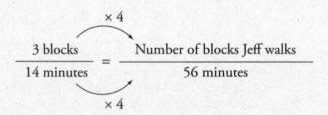

So Jeff walks 12 blocks in 56 minutes. Answer choice (E) is correct.

18. Half of the 30 students in Mrs. Whipple's first-grade class got sick on the bus on the way back from the zoo. Of these students, $\frac{2}{3}$ of them were sick because they ate too much cotton candy. The rest were sick because they sat next to the students who ate too much cotton candy. How many students were sick because they sat next to the wrong student?

    (A) 5
    (B) 10
    (C) 15
    (D) 20
    (E) 25

This is a really gooey fraction problem. Because we've seen the word *of* we know we have to multiply. First we need to multiply $\frac{1}{2}$ by 30, the number of students in the class. This gives us 15, the number of students who got sick. Now we have another *of* so we must multiply the fraction of students who ate too much cotton candy, $\frac{2}{3}$, by the number of students who got sick, 15. This gives us 10. So then the remainder, those who were unlucky in the seating plan, is 15 – 10 or 5, answer choice (A).

19. A piece of rope is 18 inches long. It is cut into 2 unequal pieces. The longer piece is twice as long as the shorter piece. How long is the shorter piece?

    (A) 2
    (B) 6
    (C) 9
    (D) 12
    (E) 18

Again, if you are stuck for a place to start, go to the answer choices. Because we are looking for the length of the shorter rope, we can eliminate any answer choice that gives us a piece equal to or longer than half the rope. That gets rid of (C), (D), and (E). Now if we take one of the pieces, we can subtract it from the total length of the rope to get the length of the longer piece. For answer choice (B), if 6 is the length of the shorter piece, we can subtract that from 18 and know that the length of the longer piece must be 12. 12 is twice 6, so we have the right answer.

PRACTICE DRILL 1—MULTIPLE CHOICE

When you are done, check your answers in Chapter 10.

1. The sum of five consecutive positive integers is 30. What is the square of the largest of the five positive integers?

    (A) 25
    (B) 36
    (C) 49
    (D) 64
    (E) 81

$$n+(n+1) + n+$$

$$5n + 10 = 30$$

$$45678$$

$$20$$

$$4$$

2. How many factors does the number 24 have?

    (A) 2
    (B) 4
    (C) 6
    (D) 8
    (E) 10

$$1\ 2\ 3\ 4\ 6\ 8\ 12\ 24$$

3. If 12 is a factor of a certain number, what must also be factors of that number?

    (A) 2 and 6 only
    (B) 3 and 4 only
    (C) 12 only
    (D) 1, 2, 3, 4, and 6
    (E) 1, 2, 3, 4, 6, and 24

4. What is the smallest number that can be added to the number 1,024 to produce a result divisible by 9 ?

    (A) 1
    (B) 2
    (C) 3
    (D) 4
    (E) 6

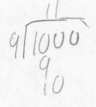

5. Which of the following is a multiple of 3 ?

    (A) 2
    (B) 6
    (C) 10
    (D) 14
    (E) 16

6. Which of the following is NOT a multiple of 6 ?

   (A) 12
   (B) 18
   (C) 23
   (D) 24
   (E) 42

7. Which of the following is a multiple of both 3 and 5 ?

   (A) 10
   (B) 20
   (C) 25
   (D) 45
   (E) 50

8. A company's profit was $75,000 in 1972. In 1992, its profit was $450,000. The profit in 1992 was how many times as great as the profit in 1972?

   (A) 2
   (B) 4
   (C) 6
   (D) 10
   (E) 60

9. Joanna owns one-third of the pieces of furniture in the apartment she shares with her friends. If there are a total of 12 pieces of furniture in the apartment, how many pieces does Joanna own?

   (A) 2
   (B) 4
   (C) 6
   (D) 8
   (E) 12

10. A tank of oil is one-third full. When full, the tank holds 90 gallons. How many gallons of oil are in the tank now?

    (A) 10
    (B) 20
    (C) 30
    (D) 40
    (E) 50

11. Tigger the Cat sleeps three-fourths of every day. In a four-day period, he sleeps the equivalent of how many full days?

(A) $\frac{1}{4}$

(B) $\frac{3}{4}$

(C) 1

(D) 3

(E) 4

12. Which of the following is the greatest?

(A) $\frac{1}{4}+\frac{2}{3}$

(B) $\frac{3}{4}-\frac{1}{3}$

(C) $\frac{1}{12}\div\frac{1}{3}$

(D) $\frac{3}{4}\times\frac{1}{3}$

(E) $\frac{1}{12}\times 2$

13. $\frac{1}{2}+\frac{2}{3}+\frac{3}{4}+\frac{1}{2}+\frac{1}{3}+\frac{1}{4}=$

(A) $\frac{3}{4}$

(B) 1

(C) 6

(D) 3

(E) 12

14. The product of 0.34 and 1,000 is approximately

   (A)   3.50
   (B)   35
   (C)   65
   (D)   350
   (E)   650

(handwritten: 1000, 34, 4000, 30000, 34000)

15. 2.398 =

   (A) $2 \times \dfrac{9}{100} \times \dfrac{3}{10} \times \dfrac{8}{1000}$

   (B) $2 + \dfrac{3}{10} + \dfrac{9}{1000} + \dfrac{8}{100}$

   (C) $2 + \dfrac{9}{100} + \dfrac{8}{1000} + \dfrac{3}{10}$

   (D) $\dfrac{3}{10} + \dfrac{9}{100} + \dfrac{8}{1000}$

   (E)   None of the above

HOW DID YOU DO?

That was a good sample of the kinds of questions you'll see on the SSAT. Now there are a few things to check other than your answers. Remember that taking the test involves much more than just getting answers right. It's also about guessing wisely, using your time well, and figuring out where you're likely to make mistakes. Once you've checked to see what you've gotten right and wrong, you should then consider the points that follow to improve your score.

Time and Pacing

How long did it take you to do the 15 questions? It's okay if you went a minute or two over. However, if you finished very quickly (in fewer than 10 minutes) or slowly (more than 20 minutes), look at any problems that may have affected your speed. Which questions seriously slowed you down? Did you answer some quickly but not correctly? Your answers to these questions will help you plan which and how many questions to answer on the SSAT.

Question Recognition and Selection

Did you use your time wisely? Did you do the questions in an order that worked well for you? Which kinds of questions were hardest for you? Remember that every question on the SSAT, whether easy or hard, is worth one point, and that you don't have to answer all the questions to get a good score. In fact, because of the guessing penalty, skipping questions can actually raise your score. So depending on your personal speed, you should concentrate most on getting as many easy and medium questions right as possible, and worry about harder problems later. Keep in mind that in Math sections, the questions generally go from easiest to hardest throughout. Getting the easy and medium questions right takes time, but you know you can—so give yourself that time!

POE and Guessing

Did you actively look for wrong answers to eliminate, instead of just looking for the right answer? (You should.) Did you physically cross off wrong answers to keep track of your POE? Was there a pattern to when guessing worked (more often when you could eliminate one wrong answer, and less often when you picked simpler-looking over harder-looking answers)?

Be Careful

Did you work problems out in the book? Did you move too quickly or skip steps on problems you found easier? Did you always double-check what the question was asking? Often students miss questions that they know how to do! Why? It's simple—they work out problems in their heads or don't read carefully. Work out every SSAT math problem on the page. Consider it a double-check because your handwritten notes confirm what you've worked out in your head.

PRACTICE DRILL 2—MULTIPLE CHOICE—UPPER LEVEL ONLY

While doing the next drill, keep in mind the general test-taking techniques we've talked about: guessing, POE, order of difficulty, pacing, and working on the page and not in your head. At the end of the section, check your answers. But don't stop there: Investigate the drill thoroughly to see how and why you got your answers wrong. And check your time. You should be spending about one minute per question on this drill. When you are done, check your answers in Chapter 10.

1. How many numbers between 1 and 100 are multiples of both 2 and 7 ?

   (A) 6
   (B) 7
   (C) 8
   (D) 9
   (E) 10

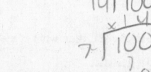

2. What is the smallest multiple of 7 that is greater than 50 ?

   (A) 7
   (B) 49
   (C) 51
   (D) 56
   (E) 63

3. $2^3 \times 2^3 \times 2^2 =$

   (A) 64
   (B) 2^8
   (C) 2^{10}
   (D) 2^{16}
   (E) 2^{18}

4. For what integer value of m does $2m + 4 = m^3$?

   (A) 1
   (B) 2
   (C) 3
   (D) 4
   (E) 5

5. One-fifth of the students in a class chose recycling as the topic for their science projects. If four students chose recycling, how many students are in the class?

   (A) 4
   (B) 10
   (C) 16
   (D) 20
   (E) 24

6. If $6x - 4 = 38$, then $x + 10 =$

   (A) 7
   (B) 10
   (C) 16
   (D) 17
   (E) 19

7. If $3x - 6 = 21$, then what is $x \div 9$?

   (A) 0
   (B) 1
   (C) 3
   (D) 6
   (E) 9

8. Only one-fifth of the chairs in a classroom are in working order. If three extra chairs are brought in, there are 19 working seats available. How many chairs were originally in the room?

   (A) 16
   (B) 19
   (C) 22
   (D) 80
   (E) 95

9. If a harvest yielded 60 bushels of corn, 20 bushels of wheat, and 40 bushels of soybeans, what percent of the total harvest was corn?

   (A) 50%
   (B) 40%
   (C) 33%
   (D) 30%
   (E) 25%

10. At a local store, an item that usually sells for $45 is currently on sale for $30. What discount does that represent?

(A) 10%
(B) 25%
(C) 33%
(D) 50%
(E) 66%

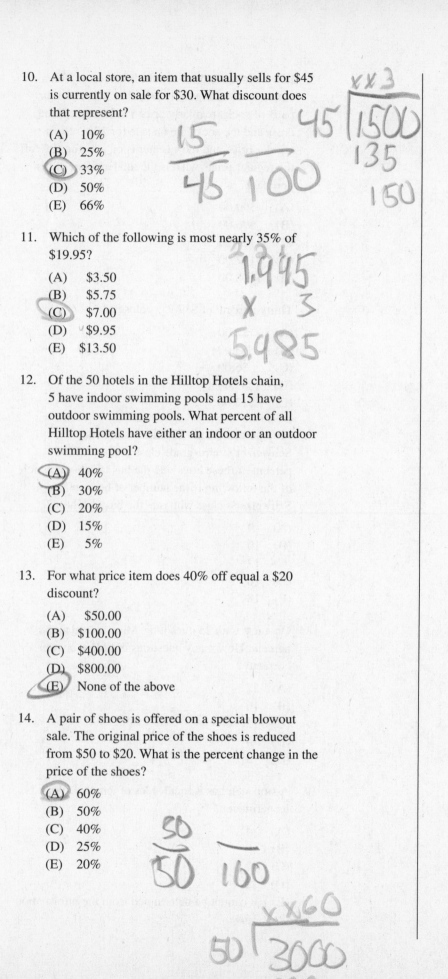

11. Which of the following is most nearly 35% of $19.95?

(A) $3.50
(B) $5.75
(C) $7.00
(D) $9.95
(E) $13.50

12. Of the 50 hotels in the Hilltop Hotels chain, 5 have indoor swimming pools and 15 have outdoor swimming pools. What percent of all Hilltop Hotels have either an indoor or an outdoor swimming pool?

(A) 40%
(B) 30%
(C) 20%
(D) 15%
(E) 5%

13. For what price item does 40% off equal a $20 discount?

(A) $50.00
(B) $100.00
(C) $400.00
(D) $800.00
(E) None of the above

14. A pair of shoes is offered on a special blowout sale. The original price of the shoes is reduced from $50 to $20. What is the percent change in the price of the shoes?

(A) 60%
(B) 50%
(C) 40%
(D) 25%
(E) 20%

15. Lisa buys a silk dress regularly priced at $60, a cotton sweater regularly priced at $40, and four pairs of socks regularly priced at $5 each. If the dress and the socks are on sale for 20% off the regular price and the sweater is on sale for 10% off the regular price, what is the total amount of her purchase?

    (A) $90.00
    (B) $96.00
    (C) $100.00
    (D) $102.00
    (E) $108.00

16. Thirty percent of $17.95 is closest to

    (A) $2.00
    (B) $3.00
    (C) $6.00
    (D) $9.00
    (E) $12.00

17. Fifty percent of the 20 students in Mrs. Schweizer's third-grade class are boys. If 90 percent of these boys ride the bus to school, which of the following is the number of boys in Mrs. Schweizer's class who ride the bus to school?

    (A) 9
    (B) 10
    (C) 12
    (D) 16
    (E) 18

18. On a test with 25 questions, Marc scored an 88 percent. How many questions did Marc answer correctly?

    (A) 22
    (B) 16
    (C) 12
    (D) 4
    (E) 3

19. A stop sign has 8 equal sides of length 4. What is its perimeter?

    (A) 4
    (B) 8
    (C) 12
    (D) 32
    (E) It cannot be determined from the information given.

20. If the perimeter of a square is 56, what is the length of each side?

   (A)   4
   (B)   7
   (C)   14
   (D)   28
   (E)   112

21. The perimeter of a square with a side of length 4 is how much less than the perimeter of a rectangle with sides of length 4 and width 6 ?

   (A)   0
   (B)   2
   (C)   4
   (D)   6
   (E)   8

22. What is the perimeter of an equilateral triangle, one side of which measures 4 inches?

   (A)   12 inches
   (B)   8 inches
   (C)   6 inches
   (D)   4 inches
   (E)   It cannot be determined from the information given.

23. $x =$

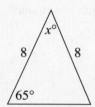

   (A)   8
   (B)   30
   (C)   50
   (D)   65
   (E)   180

24. If $b = 45$, then $v^2 =$

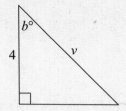

(A) 32
(B) 25
(C) 16
(D) 5
(E) It cannot be determined from the information given.

25. One-half of the difference between the number of degrees in a square and the number of degrees in a triangle is

(A) 45
(B) 90
(C) 180
(D) 240
(E) 360

26. If the area of a square is equal to its perimeter, what is the length of one side?

(A) 1
(B) 2
(C) 4
(D) 8
(E) 10

27. The area of a rectangle with width 4 and length 3 is equal to the area of a triangle with a base of 6 and a height of

(A) 1
(B) 2
(C) 3
(D) 4
(E) 12

28. Two cardboard boxes have equal volume. The dimensions of one box are $3 \times 4 \times 10$. If the length of the other box is 6 and the width is 4, what is the height of the second box?

(A) 2
(B) 5
(C) 10
(D) 12
(E) 24

29. If the area of a square is $64p^2$, what is the length of one side of the square?

(A) $64p^2$
(B) $64p$
(C) $8p^2$
(D) $8p$
(E 8

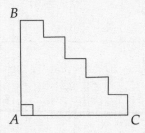

30. If $AB = 10$ and $AC = 15$, what is the perimeter of the figure above?

(A) 25
(B) 35
(C) 40
(D) 50
(E) It cannot be determined from the information given.

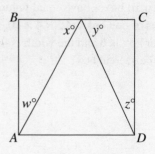

31. If *ABCD*, shown above, is a rectangle, what is the value of $w + x + y + z$?

(A) 90
(B) 150
(C) 180
(D) 190
(E) 210

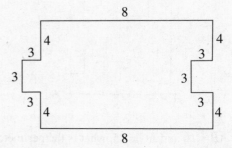

32. What is the area of the figure above if all the angles shown are right angles?

(A) 38
(B) 42
(C) 50
(D) 88
(E) 96

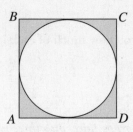

33. In the figure above, the length of side *AB* of square *ABCD* is equal to 4 and the circle has a radius of 2. What is the area of the shaded region?

   (A) $4 - \pi$
   (B) $16 - 4\pi$
   (C) $8 + 4\pi$
   (D) 4π
   (E) 8π

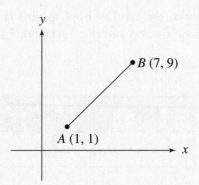

34. The distance between points *A* and *B* in the coordinate plane above is

   (A) 5
   (B) 6
   (C) 8
   (D) 9
   (E) 10

Ratios

A ratio is like a recipe. It tells you how much of each ingredient goes into a mixture.

For example:

To make punch, mix two parts grape juice with three parts orange juice.

This ratio tells you that for every two units of grape juice, you will need to add three units of orange juice. It doesn't matter what the units are; if you were working with ounces, you would mix two ounces of grape juice with three ounces of orange juice to get five ounces of punch. If you were working with gallons, you would mix two gallons of grape juice with three gallons of orange juice. How much punch would you have? Five gallons.

To work through a ratio question, first you need to organize the information you are given. Do this using the Ratio Box.

In a club with 35 members, the ratio of boys to girls is 3:2. To complete your Ratio Box, fill in the ratio at the top and the "real world" at the bottom.

	Boys	Girls	Total
Ratio	3	+ 2	= 5
Multiplier			
Real Value			35

Then look for a "magic number" that you can multiply by the ratio to get to the real world. In this case, the magic number is 7. That's all there is to it!

	Boys	Girls	Total
Ratio	3	+ 2	= 5
Multiplier	× 7	× 7	× 7
Real Value	21	14	35

PRACTICE DRILL 3—RATIOS

1. In a jar of lollipops, the ratio of red lollipops to blue lollipops is 3:5. If only red lollipops and blue lollipops are in the jar and if the total number of lollipops in the jar is 56, how many blue lollipops are in the jar?

   (A) 35
   (B) 28
   (C) 21
   (D) 8
   (E) 5

2. At Jed's Country Hotel, there are three types of rooms: singles, doubles, and triples. If the ratio of singles to doubles to triples is 3:4:5, and the total number of rooms is 36, how many doubles are there?

   (A) 4
   (B) 9
   (C) 12
   (D) 24
   (E) 36

3. Matt's Oak Superstore has exactly three times as many large oak desks as small oak desks in its inventory. If the store only sells these two types of desks, which could be the total number of desks in stock?

   (A) 10
   (B) 13
   (C) 16
   (D) 18
   (E) 25

4. In Janice's tennis club, 8 of the 12 players are right-handed. What is the ratio of right-handed to left-handed players in Janice's club?

   (A) 1:2
   (B) 1:6
   (C) 2:1
   (D) 2:3
   (E) 3:4

5. One-half of the 400 students at Booth Junior High School are girls. Of the girls at the school, the ratio of those who ride a school bus to those who walk is 7:3. What is the total number of girls who walk to school?

(A) 10
(B) 30
(C) 60
(D) 120
(E) 140

6. A pet goat eats 2 pounds of goat food and 1 pound of grass each day. When the goat has eaten a total of 15 pounds, how many pounds of grass will it have eaten?

(A) 3
(B) 4
(C) 5
(D) 15
(E) 30

When You Are Done
Check your answers in
Chapter 10.

Averages

There are three parts to every average problem: total, number, and average. Most SSAT problems will give you two of the three pieces and ask you to find the third. To help organize the information you are given, use the Average Pie.

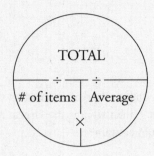

The Average Pie organizes all of your information visually. It is easy to see all of the relationships between pieces of the pie.

- TOTAL =   (*# of items*) $\times$ (*Average*)

- # of items = $\dfrac{Total}{Average}$

- Average = $\dfrac{Total}{\# \ of \ items}$

For example, if your friend went bowling and bowled three games, scoring 71, 90, and 100, here's how you would compute her average score using the Average Pie.

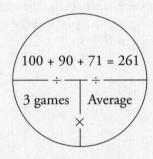

To find the average, you would simply write a fraction that represents $\dfrac{Total}{\# \ of \ items}$, in this case $\dfrac{261}{3}$.

The math becomes simple. $261 \div 3 = 87$. Your friend bowled an average of 87.

Get used to working with the Average Pie by using it to solve these problems.

PRACTICE DRILL 4—AVERAGES

1. The average of 3 numbers is 18. What is 2 times the sum of the 3 numbers?

   (A) 108
   (B) 54
   (C) 36
   (D) 18
   (E) 6

2. If Set M contains 4 positive integers whose average is 7, then what is the largest number that Set M could contain?

   (A) 6
   (B) 7
   (C) 18
   (D) 25
   (E) 28

3. An art club of 4 boys and 5 girls makes craft projects. If the boys average 2 projects each and the girls average 3 projects each, what is the total number of projects produced by the club?

   (A) 14
   (B) 23
   (C) 26
   (D) 54
   (E) 100

4. If a class of 6 students has an average grade of 72 before a seventh student joins the class, then what must the seventh student's grade be to raise the class average to 76 ?

   (A) 100
   (B) 92
   (C) 88
   (D) 80
   (E) 76

5. Catherine scores an 84, 85, and 88 on her first three exams. What must she score on her fourth exam to raise her average to an 89 ?

   (A) 99
   (B) 97
   (C) 93
   (D) 91
   (E) 89

When You Are Done
Check your answers in Chapter 10.

Percent Change—Upper Level Only

There is one special kind of percent question that shows up on the SSAT: percent change. This type of question asks you to find what percent something has increased or decreased. Instead of taking the part and dividing it by the whole, you will take the difference between the two numbers and divide it by the original number. Then, to turn the fraction to a percent, divide the numerator by the denominator and multiply by 100.

For example:

> The number of people who watched *American Idol* last year was 3,600,000. This year, only 3,000,000 are watching the show. By approximately what percent has the audience decreased?

$$\frac{\text{The difference}}{\text{The original}} = \frac{600,000}{3,600,000} \quad \text{(The difference is } 3,600,000 - 3,000,000.)$$

The fraction reduces to $\frac{1}{6}$, and $\frac{1}{6}$ as a percent is 16%.

PRACTICE DRILL 5—PERCENT CHANGE

$$\% \text{ change} = \frac{\text{difference}}{\text{original}} \times 100$$

1. During a severe winter in Ontario, the temperature dropped suddenly to 10 degrees below zero. If the temperature in Ontario before this cold spell occurred was 10 degrees above zero, by what percent did the temperature drop?

   (A)   25%
   (B)   50%
   (C)   100%
   (D)   150%
   (E)   200%

2. Fatty's Burger wants to attract more customers by increasing the size of its patties. From now on Fatty's patties are going to be 4 ounces larger than before. If the size of its new patty is 16 ounces, by what percent has the patty increased?

   (A)   25%
   (B)   27%
   (C)   33%
   (D)   75%
   (E)   80%

When You Are Done
Check your answers in Chapter 10.

Plugging In

The SSAT will often ask you questions about real-life situations where the numbers have been replaced with variables. One of the easiest ways to tackle these questions is with a powerful technique called *Plugging In*.

Mark is two inches taller than John, who is four inches shorter than Evan. If *e* represents Evan's height in inches, then in terms of *e*, an expression for Mark's height is

   (A) $e + 6$
   (B) $e + 4$
   (C) $e + 2$
   (D) e
   (E) $e - 2$

The problem with this question is that we're not used to thinking of people's heights in terms of variables. Have you ever met someone who was *e* inches tall?

Whenever you see variables used in the question and in the answer choices, just plug in a number to replace the variable.

1. Choose a number for *e*.
2. Using that number, figure out Mark's and John's heights.
3. Put a box around Mark's height because that's what the question asked you for.
4. Plug your number for *e* into the answer choices and choose the one that gives you the number you found for Mark's height.

Here's How It Works

Mark is two inches taller than John, who is four inches shorter than Evan. If *e* represents Evan's height in inches, then ~~in terms of *e*~~, an expression for Mark's height is:

(A) *e* + 6
(B) *e* + 4
(C) *e* + 2
(D) *e*
(E) *e* − 2

> ← *Cross this out! Because you are Plugging In, you don't need to pay any attention to "in terms of" any variable.*

For Evan's height, let's pick 60 inches. This means that *e* = 60.

Remember, there is no right or wrong number to pick. 50 would work just as well.

But given that Evan is 60 inches tall, now we can figure out that, because John is four inches shorter than Evan, John's height must be (60 − 4), or 56 inches.

The other piece of information we learn from the problem is that Mark is two inches taller than John. If John's height is 56 inches, that means Mark must be 58 inches tall.

So here's what we've got.

Evan	60 inches = *e*
John	56 inches
Mark	58 inches

Take the Algebra Away, and Arithmetic Is All That's Left

When you Plug In for variables, you won't need to write equations and won't have to solve algebra problems. Doing simple arithmetic is always easier than doing algebra.

Now, the question asks for Mark's height, which is 58 inches. The last step is to go through the answer choices substituting 60 for e and choose the one that equals 58.

(A)	$e + 6$	$60 + 6 = 66$	ELIMINATE
(B)	$e + 4$	$60 + 4 = 64$	ELIMINATE
(C)	$e + 2$	$60 + 2 = 62$	ELIMINATE
(D)	e	60	ELIMINATE
(E)	$e - 2$	$60 - 2 = 58$	PICK THIS ONE!

After reading this explanation, you may be tempted to say that Plugging In takes too long. Don't be fooled. The method itself is often faster and (more important) more accurate than regular algebra. Try it out. Practice. As you become more comfortable with Plugging In, you'll get even quicker and better results. You still need to know how to do algebra, but if you do only algebra, you may have difficulty improving your SSAT score. Plugging In gives you a way to break through whenever you are stuck. You'll find that having more than one way to solve SSAT math problems puts you at a real advantage.

PRACTICE DRILL 6—PLUGGING IN

1. At a charity fund-raiser, 200 people each donated x dollars. In terms of x, what was the total number of dollars donated?

    (A) $\dfrac{x}{200}$

    (B) 200

    (C) $\dfrac{200}{x}$

    (D) $200 + x$

    (E) $200x$

2. If 10 magazines cost d dollars, then in terms of d, how many magazines can be purchased for 3 dollars?

(A) $\dfrac{3d}{10}$

(B) $30d$

(C) $\dfrac{d}{30}$

(D) $\dfrac{30}{d}$

(E) $\dfrac{10d}{3}$

3. The zoo has four times as many monkeys as lions. There are four more lions than there are zebras at the zoo. If z represents the number of zebras in the zoo, then in terms of z, how many monkeys are there in the zoo?

(A) $z + 4$
(B) $z + 8$
(C) $4z$
(D) $4z + 16$
(E) $4z + 4$

Occasionally, you may run into a Plugging In question that doesn't contain variables. These questions usually ask about a percentage or a fraction of some unknown number or price. This is the one time that you should plug in even when you don't see variables in the answer!

Also, be sure you plug in good numbers. Good doesn't mean right because there's no such thing as a right or wrong number to plug in. A good number is one that makes the problem easier to work with. If a question asks about minutes and hours, try plugging in 30 or 60, not 128. Also, whenever you see the word *percent*, plug in 100!

4. The price of a suit is reduced by half, and then the resulting price is reduced by 10%. The final price is what percent of the original price?

(A) 5%
(B) 10%
(C) 25%
(D) 40%
(E) 45%

5. On Wednesday, Miguel ate one-fourth of a pumpkin pie. On Thursday, he ate one-half of what was left of the pie. What fraction of the entire pie did Miguel eat on Wednesday and Thursday?

(A) $\dfrac{3}{8}$

(B) $\dfrac{1}{2}$

(C) $\dfrac{5}{8}$

(D) $\dfrac{3}{4}$

(E) $\dfrac{7}{8}$

6. If p pieces of candy costs c cents, then in terms of p and c, 10 pieces of candy will cost

(A) $\dfrac{pc}{10}$ cents

(B) $\dfrac{10c}{p}$ cents

(C) $10pc$ cents

(D) $\dfrac{10p}{c}$ cents

(E) $10 + p + c$ cents

7. If J is an odd integer, which of the following must be true?

(A) $(J \div 3) > 1$
(B) $(J - 2)$ is a positive integer.
(C) $2 \times J$ is an even integer.
(D) $J^2 > J$
(E) $J > 0$

8. If m is an even integer, n is an odd integer, and p is the product of m and n, which of the following is always true?

(A) p is a fraction.
(B) p is an odd integer.
(C) p is divisible by 2.
(D) p is between m and n.
(E) p is greater than zero.

When You Are Done
Check your answers in
Chapter 10.

Plugging In The Answers (PITA)

Plugging In The Answers is similar to Plugging In. When you have *variables* in the answer choices, you plug in. When you have *numbers* in the answer choices, you should generally plug in the answers. The only time this may get tricky is when you have a question that asks for a percent or fraction of some unknown number.

Plugging In The Answers works because on a multiple-choice test, the right answer is always one of the answer choices. On this type of question, you can't plug in any number you want because only one number will work. Instead, you can plug in numbers from the answer choices, one of which must be correct. Here's an example.

> Nicole baked a batch of cookies. She gave half to her friend Lisa and six to her mother. If she now has eight cookies left, how many did Nicole bake originally?
>
> (A)   8
> (B)   12
> (C)   20
> (D)   28
> (E)   32

See what we mean? It would be hard to just start making up numbers of cookies and hope that eventually you guessed correctly. However, the number of cookies that Nicole baked originally must be either 8, 12, 20, 28, or 32 (the five answer choices). So pick one—always start with (C)—and then work backward to determine whether you have the right choice.

Let's start with (C): Nicole baked 20 cookies. Now work through the events listed in the question.

She had 20 cookies—from answer choice (C)—and she gave half to Lisa. That leaves Nicole with 10 cookies.

What next? She gives 6 to her mom. Now she's got 4 left.

Keep going. The problem says that Nicole now has 8 cookies left. But if she started with 20—answer choice (C)—she would only have 4 left. So is (C) the right answer? No.

No problem. Choose another answer choice and try again. Be smart about which answer choice you pick. When we used the number in (C), Nicole ended up with fewer cookies than we wanted her to have, didn't she? So the right answer must be a number larger than 20, the number we took from (C).

The good news is that the answer choices in most Plugging In The Answers questions go in order, so it is easy to pick the next larger or smaller number—you just pick either (B) or (D), depending on which direction you've decided to go.

Back to Nicole and her cookies. We need a number larger than 20. So let's go to answer choice (D)—28.

Nicole started out with 28 cookies. The first thing she did was give half, or 14, to Lisa. That left Nicole with 14 cookies.

Then she gave 6 cookies to her mother. $14 - 6 = 8$. Nicole has 8 cookies left over. Keep going with the question. It says, "If she now has eight cookies left…" She has eight cookies left and, *voilà*—she's supposed to have 8 cookies left.

What does this mean? It means you've got the right answer! Pick (D) and move on.

If answer choice (D) had not worked, and you were still certain that you needed a number larger than answer choice (C), you also would be finished. Because you started with the middle answer choice (C), and that didn't work, and then you tried the next larger choice, (D), and that didn't work either, you could pick the only answer bigger than (C) that was left—in this case (E)—and be done.

This diagram helps illustrate the way you should move through the answer choices.

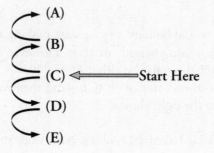

PRACTICE DRILL 7—PLUGGING IN THE ANSWERS

1. Ted can read 60 pages per hour. Naomi can read 45 pages per hour. If both Ted and Naomi read at the same time, how many minutes will it take them to read a total of 210 pages?

   (A) 36
   (B) 72
   (C) 120
   (D) 145
   (E) 180

2. If the sum of y and $y + 1$ is greater than 18, which of the following is one possible value for y?

   (A) −10
   (B) −8
   (C) 2
   (D) 8
   (E) 10

3. Kenny is 5 years older than Greg. In 5 years, Kenny will be twice as old as Greg is now. How old is Kenny now?

   (A) 5
   (B) 10
   (C) 15
   (D) 25
   (E) 35

4. Three people—Paul, Sara, and John—want to put their money together to buy a $90 radio. If Sara agrees to pay twice as much as John, and Paul agrees to pay three times as much as Sara, how much must Sara pay?

   (A) $10
   (B) $20
   (C) $30
   (D) $45
   (E) $65

5. Four less than a certain number is two-thirds of that number. What is the number?

   (A) 1
   (B) 6
   (C) 8
   (D) 12
   (E) 16

When You Are Done
Check your answers in Chapter 10.

GEOMETRY

Guesstimating: A Second Look

Guesstimating worked well back in the introduction when we were just using it to estimate or "ballpark" the size of a number, but geometry problems are undoubtedly the best place to guesstimate whenever you can.

Let's try the next problem. Remember, unless a particular question tells you otherwise, you can safely assume that figures *are* drawn to scale.

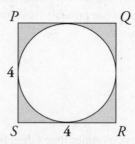

A circle is inscribed in square *PQRS*. What is the area of the shaded region?

(A) 16 – 6π
(B) 16 – 4π
(C) 16 – 3π
(D) 16 – 2π
(E) 16π

Wow, a circle inscribed in a square—that sounds tough!

It isn't. Look at the picture. What fraction of the square looks like it is shaded? Half? Three-quarters? Less than half? In fact, about one-quarter of the area of the square is shaded. You've just done most of the work necessary to solve this problem.

Now, let's just do a little math. The length of one side of the square is 4, so the area of the square is 4 × 4 or 16.

So the area of the square is 16, and we said that the shaded region was about one-fourth of the square. One-fourth of 16 is 4, right? So we're looking for an answer choice that equals about 4. Let's look at the choices.

(A) 16 – 6π
(B) 16 – 4π
(C) 16 – 3π
(D) 16 – 2π
(E) 16π

This becomes a little complicated because the answers include π. For the purposes of guesstimating, and in fact for almost any purpose on the SSAT, you should just remember that π is a little more than 3.

Let's look back at those answers.

(A)	$16 - 6\pi$	is roughly equal to	$16 - (6 \times 3) = -2$
(B)	$16 - 4\pi$	is roughly equal to	$16 - (4 \times 3) = 4$
(C)	$16 - 3\pi$	is roughly equal to	$16 - (3 \times 3) = 7$
(D)	$16 - 2\pi$	is roughly equal to	$16 - (2 \times 3) = 10$
(E)	16π	is roughly equal to	$(16 \times 3) = 48$

Now let's think about what these answers mean.

Answer choice (A) is geometrically impossible. A figure *cannot* have a negative area. Eliminate it.

Answer choice (B) means that the shaded region has an area of about 4. Sounds pretty good.

Answer choice (C) means that the shaded region has an area of about 7. The area of the entire square was 16, so that would mean that the shaded region was almost half the square. Possible, but doubtful.

Answer choice (D) means that the shaded region has an area of about 10. That's more than half the square and in fact, almost three-quarters of the entire square. No way; cross it out.

Finally, answer choice (E) means that the shaded region has an area of about 48. What? The whole square had an area of 16. Is the shaded region three times as big as the square itself? Not a chance. Eliminate (E).

At this point you are left with only (B), which we feel pretty good about, and (C), which seems a little large. What should you do?

Pick (B) and pat yourself on the back because you chose the right answer without doing a lot of unnecessary work. Also, remember how useful it was to guesstimate and make sure you do it whenever you see a geometry problem, unless the problem tells you that the figure is not drawn to scale!

Weird Shapes

Whenever the test presents you with a geometric figure that is not a square, rectangle, circle, or triangle, draw a line or lines to divide that figure into the shapes that you do know. Then you can easily work with shapes you know all about.

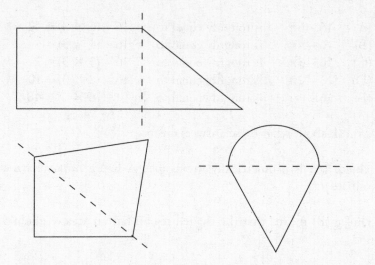

Shaded Regions

Sometimes geometry questions show you one figure inscribed in another and then ask you to find the area of a shaded region inside the larger figure and outside the smaller figure (like the problem at the beginning of this section). To find the areas of these shaded regions, find the area of the outside figure and then subtract from that the area of the figure inside. The difference is what you need.

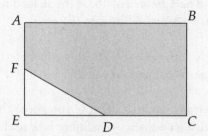

ABCE is a rectangle with a length of 10 and width of 6. Points *F* and *D* are the midpoints of *AE* and *EC*, respectively. What is the area of the shaded region?

(A) 25.5
(B) 30
(C) 45
(D) 52.5
(E) It cannot be determined from the information given.

The first step is to find the area of the rectangle. If you multiply the length by the width, you'll find the area is 60. Now we find the area of the triangle that we are removing from the rectangle. Because the height and base of the triangle are parts of the sides of the rectangle, and points D and F are half the length and width of the rectangle, we know that the height of the triangle is half the rectangle's width, or 3, and the base of the triangle is half the rectangle's length, or 5. Using the formula for area of a triangle, we find the area of the triangle is 7.5. Now we subtract the area of the triangle from the area of the rectangle. $60 - 7.5 = 52.5$. The correct answer choice is (D). Be careful not to choose (E) just because the problem looks tricky!

Functions

In a function problem, an arithmetic operation is defined and then you are asked to perform it on a number. A function is just a set of instructions written in a strange way.

$\# \, x = 3x(x + 1)$

On the left there is usually a variable with a strange symbol next to or around it.
In the middle is an equal sign.
On the right are the instructions. These tell you what to do with the variable.

$\# \, x = 3x(x + 1)$ *What does # 5 equal?*

$\# \, 5 = (3 \times 5)(5 + 1)$ *Just replace each x with a 5!*

Here, the function (indicated by the # sign) simply tells you to substitute a 5 wherever there was an x in the original set of instructions. Functions look confusing because of the strange symbols, but once you know what to do with them, they are just like manipulating an equation.

Sometimes more than one question will refer to the same function. The following drill, for example, contains two questions about one function. In cases such as this, the first question tends to be easier than the second.

PRACTICE DRILL 8—FUNCTIONS

<u>Questions 1 and 2</u> refer to the following definition.

For all real numbers n, $\$n = 10n - 10$

1. $\$7 =$
    - (A) 70
    - (B) 60
    - (C) 17
    - (D)   7
    - (E)   0

2. If $\$n = 120$, then $n =$
    - (A)   11
    - (B)   12
    - (C)   13
    - (D) 120
    - (E) 130

<u>Questions 3-5</u> refer to the following definition.

For all real numbers d and y, $d \text{ ¿ } y = (d \times y) - (d + y)$.

[Example: $3 \text{ ¿ } 2 = (3 \times 2) - (3 + 2) = 6 - 5 = 1$]

3. $10 \text{ ¿ } 2 =$
    - (A) 20
    - (B) 16
    - (C) 12
    - (D)   8
    - (E)   4

4. If $K(4 \text{ ¿ } 3) = 30$, then $K =$
    - (A) 3
    - (B) 4
    - (C) 5
    - (D) 6
    - (E) 7

5. $(2 \text{ ¿ } 4) \times (3 \text{ ¿ } 6) =$
    - (A) $(9 \text{ ¿ } 3) + 3$
    - (B) $(6 \text{ ¿ } 4) + 1$
    - (C) $(5 \text{ ¿ } 3) + 4$
    - (D) $(8 \text{ ¿ } 4) + 2$
    - (E) $(9 \text{ ¿ } 4) + 3$

When You Are Done
Check your answers in
Chapter 10.

Charts and Graphs

Charts

Chart questions are simple, but you must be careful. Follow these three steps and you'll be well on the way to mastering any chart question.

1. Read any text that accompanies the chart. It is important to know what the chart is showing and what scale the numbers are on.
2. Read the question.
3. Refer to the chart and find the specific information you need.

If there is more than one question about a single chart, the later questions will tend to be more difficult than the earlier ones. Be careful!

Here is a sample chart.

Don't Be in Too Big of a Hurry
When working with charts and graphs, make sure you take a moment to look at the chart or graph, figure out what it tells you, and then go to the questions.

Club Membership by State, 1995 and 1996		
State	1995	1996
California	300	500
Florida	225	250
Illinois	200	180
Massachusetts	150	300
Michigan	150	200
New Jersey	200	250
New York	400	600
Texas	50	100

There are many different questions that you can answer based on the information in this chart. For instance:

> What is the difference between the number of members who came from New York in 1995 and the number of members who came from Illinois in 1996?

This question asks you to look up two simple pieces of information and then do a tiny bit of math.

First, the number of members who came from New York in 1995 was 400.

Second, the number of members who came from Illinois in 1996 was 180.

Finally, look back at the question. It asks you to find the difference between these numbers. 400 − 180 = 220. Done.

> The increase in the number of members from New Jersey from 1995 to 1996 was what percent of the total number of members in New Jersey in 1995 ?

You should definitely know how to do this one! Do you remember how to translate percentage questions? If not, go back to the Fundamental Math Skills chapter.

In 1995 there were 200 club members from New Jersey. In 1996 there were 250 members from New Jersey. That represents an increase of 50 members. To determine what percent that is of the total amount in 1995, you will need to ask yourself, "50 (the increase) is what percent of 200 (the number of members in 1995)?"

Translated, this becomes

$$50 = \frac{g}{100} \times 200$$

With a little bit of simple manipulation, this equation becomes

$$50 = 2g$$

and

$$25 = g$$

So from 1995 to 1996, there was a 25% increase in the number of members from New Jersey. Good work!

> Which state had as many club members in 1996 as a combination of Illinois, Massachusetts, and Michigan had in 1995 ?

First, take a second to look up the number of members who came from Illinois, Massachusetts, and Michigan in 1995 and add them together.

$$200 + 150 + 150 = 500$$

Which state had 500 members in 1996? California. That's all there is to it!

Graphs

Some questions will ask you to interpret a graph. You should be familiar with both pie and bar graphs. These graphs are generally drawn to scale (meaning that the graphs give an accurate visual impression of the information) so you can always guess based on the figure if you need to.

The way to approach a graph question is exactly the same as the way to approach a chart question. Follow the same three steps.

1. Read any text that accompanies the graph. It is important to know what the graph is showing and what scale the numbers are on.
2. Read the question.
3. Refer back to the graph and find the specific information you need.

This is how it works.

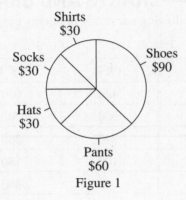

Figure 1

The graph in Figure 1 shows Emily's clothing expenditures for the month of October. On which type of clothing did she spend the most money?

(A) Shoes
(B) Shirts
(C) Socks
(D) Hats
(E) Pants

This one is easy. You can look at the pieces of the pie and identify the largest, or you can look at the amounts shown in the graph and choose the largest one. Either way, the answer is (A) because Emily spent more money on shoes than on any other clothing items in October.

Emily spent half of her clothing money on which two items?

(A) Shoes and pants
(B) Shoes and shirts
(C) Hats and socks
(D) Socks and shirts
(E) Shirts and pants

Again, you can find the answer to this question two different ways. You can look for which two items together make up half the chart, or you can add up the total amount of money Emily spent ($240) and then figure out which two items made up half (or $120) of that amount. Either way is just fine, and either way the right answer is (B), Shoes and shirts.

PRACTICE DRILL 9—CHARTS AND GRAPHS

Questions 1-3 refer to the following summary of energy costs by district.

District	1990	1991
A	400	600
B	500	700
C	200	350
D	100	150
E	600	800

(All numbers are in thousands of dollars.)

1. In 1991, which district spent twice as much on energy as district A spent in 1990 ?

    (A) A
    (B) B
    (C) C
    (D) D
    (E) E

2. Which district spent the most on energy in 1990 and 1991 combined?

    (A) A
    (B) B
    (C) D
    (D) E
    (E) It cannot be determined from the information given.

3. The total increase in energy expenditure in these districts, from 1990 to 1991, is how many dollars?

(A) $800
(B) $1,800
(C) $2,400
(D) $2,600
(E) $800,000

Questions 4 and 5 refer to Figure 2, which shows the number of compact discs owned by five students.

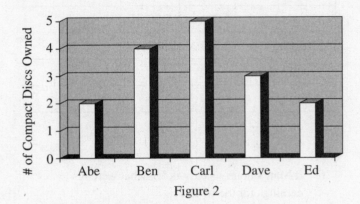

Figure 2

4. Carl owns as many CDs as which two other students combined?

(A) Abe and Ben
(B) Ben and Dave
(C) Abe and Ed
(D) Abe and Dave
(E) Ben and Ed

5. Which one student owns one-fourth of the CDs accounted for in Figure 2 ?

(A) Abe
(B) Ben
(C) Carl
(D) Dave
(E) Ed

Questions 6-8 refer to Matt's weekly time card, shown below.

Day	In	Out	Hours Worked
Monday	2:00 P.M.	5:30 P.M.	3.5
Tuesday			
Wednesday	2:00 P.M.	6:00 P.M.	4
Thursday	2:00 P.M.	5:30 P.M.	3.5
Friday	2:00 P.M.	5:00 P.M.	3
Saturday			
Sunday			

6. If Matt's hourly salary is $6, what were his earnings for the week?

(A) $6
(B) $14
(C) $21
(D) $54
(E) $84

7. What is the average number of hours Matt worked on the days he worked during this particular week?

(A) 3
(B) 3.5
(C) 4
(D) 7
(E) 14

8. The hours that Matt worked on Monday accounted for what percent of the total number of hours he worked during this week?

(A) 3.5
(B) 20
(C) 25
(D) 35
(E) 50

PRACTICE DRILL 10—UPPER LEVEL ONLY

When you are done, check your answers in Chapter 10.

1. If p is an odd integer, which of the following must be an odd integer?

   (A) $p^2 + 3$
   (B) $2p + 1$
   (C) $p \div 3$
   (D) $p - 3$
   (E) $2(p^2)$

2. If m is the sum of two positive even integers, which of the following CANNOT be true?

   (A) $m < 5$
   (B) $3m$ is odd
   (C) m is even
   (D) m^3 is even
   (E) $m \div 2$ is even

3. The product of $\frac{1}{2}b$ and a^2 can be written as

   (A) $(ab)^2$

   (B) $\dfrac{a^2}{b}$

   (C) $2a \times \dfrac{1}{2}b$

   (D) $\dfrac{a^2 b}{2}$

   (E) $\dfrac{a^2 b^2}{2}$

4. Damon has twice as many records as Graham, who has one-fourth as many records as Alex. If Damon has d records, then in terms of d, how many records do Alex and Graham have together?

   (A) $\dfrac{3d}{2}$

   (B) $\dfrac{3d}{4}$

   (C) $\dfrac{9d}{2}$

   (D) $\dfrac{5d}{2}$

   (E) $2d$

5. $x^a = (x^3)^3$

$$y^b = \frac{y^{10}}{y^2}$$

What is the value of $a \times b$?

(A) 17
(B) 30
(C) 48
(D) 45
(E) 72

6. One six-foot Italian hero serves either 12 children or 8 adults. Approximately how many sandwiches do you need to feed a party of 250, 75 of whom are children?

(A) 21
(B) 24
(C) 29
(D) 30
(E) 32

7. Liam and Noel are traveling from New York City to Dallas. If they traveled $\frac{1}{5}$ of the distance on Monday and $\frac{1}{2}$ of the distance that remained on Tuesday, what percentage of the trip do they have left to travel?

(A) 25%
(B) 30%
(C) 40%
(D) 50%
(E) 80%

8. $\frac{1}{4}$ of a bag of potato chips contains 10 grams of fat. Approximately how many grams of fat are in $\frac{1}{6}$ of that same bag of chips?

(A) 5.5
(B) 6.5
(C) 7.5
(D) 8.5
(E) 9.5

9. Students in Mr. Greenwood's history class are collecting donations for a school charity drive. If the total number of students in the class, x, donated an average of y dollars each, in terms of x and y, how much money was collected for the drive?

(A) $\dfrac{x}{y}$

(B) xy

(C) $\dfrac{xy}{x}$

(D) $\dfrac{y}{x}$

(E) $2xy$

10. Sayeeda is a point guard for her basketball team. In the last 3 games she scored 8 points once and 12 points in each of the other two games. What must she score in tonight's game to raise her average to 15 points?

(A) 28
(B) 27
(C) 26
(D) 25
(E) 15

11. What is the greatest common factor of $(3xy)^3$ and $3x^2y^5$?

(A) xy
(B) $3x^2y^5$
(C) $3x^2y^3$
(D) $27x^3y^3$
(E) $27x^5y^8$

12. The town of Mechanicville lies due east of Stillwater and due south of Half Moon Crescent. If the distance from Mechanicville to Stillwater is 30 miles, and from Mechanicville to Half Moon Crescent is 40 miles, what is the shortest distance from Stillwater to Half Moon Crescent?

(A) 10
(B) 50
(C) 70
(D) 100
(E) It cannot be determined from the information given.

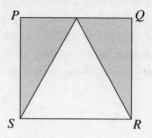

13. *PQRS* is a square with an area of 144. What is the area of the shaded region?

(A) 50
(B) 72
(C) 100
(D) 120
(E) It cannot be determined from the information given.

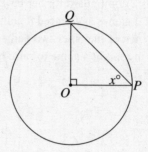

14. *PO* and *QO* are radii of the circle with center *O*. What is the value of *x* ?

(A) 30
(B) 45
(C) 60
(D) 90
(E) It cannot be determined from the information given.

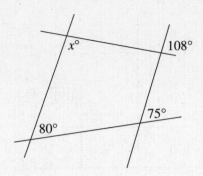

15. What is the value of *x* ?

(A)   360
(B)   100
(C)   97
(D)   67
(E)   It cannot be determined from the information
      given.

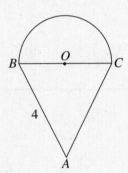

16. *ABC* is an equilateral triangle. What is the
    perimeter of this figure?

(A) $4 + 2\pi$
(B) $4 + 4\pi$
(C) $8 + 2\pi$
(D) $8 + 4\pi$
(E) $12 + 2\pi$

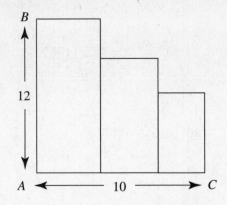

17. What is the perimeter of this figure?

(A) 120
(B)   44
(C)   40
(D)   36
(E) It cannot be determined from the information given.

MATH REVIEW

Make sure you can confidently answer all of the following questions before you take your test.

1. Is zero an integer? _____

2. Is zero positive or negative? _____

3. What operation do you perform to find a sum? _____

4. What operation do you perform to find a product?

    _____

5. What is the result called when you divide? _____

6. Is 312 divisible by 3 ? _____

    Is 312 divisible by 9 ? _____

    (Actually, dividing isn't fair—use your divisibility rules!)

7. What does the "E" in PEMDAS stand for? _____

8. Is 3 a factor of 12 ? _____

    Is 12 a factor of 3 ? _____

9. Is 3 a multiple of 12 ? _____

    Is 12 a multiple of 3 ? _____

10. What is the tens digit in the number 304.275 ? _____

11. What is the tenths digit in the number 304.275 ?

    _____

12. $2^3 =$ _____

13. In "math language" the word *percent* means _____.

14. In "math language" the word *of* means _____.

15. In a Ratio Box, the last column on the right is always the

    _____.

16. Whenever you see a problem involving averages, draw the

    _____.

17. When a problem contains variables in the question and in the

    answers, I will _____.

18. To find the perimeter of a square, I _____ the

    length(s) of _____ side(s).

19. To find the area of a square, I _____ the length(s)

    of _____ sides(s).

20. There are _____ degrees in a straight line.

21. A triangle has _____ angles, which total

    _____ degrees.

22. A four-sided figure contains _____ degrees.

23. An isosceles triangle has _____ equal sides; a(n)

    _____ triangle has three equal sides.

24. The longest side of a right triangle is called the _____

    and is located opposite the _____.

When You Are Done
Check your answers in
Chapter 10.

25. To find the area of a triangle, I use the formula _____.

Chapter 8
SSAT Verbal

INTRODUCTION

The Verbal section on the SSAT consists of:

- 30 synonym questions (questions 1 to 30)
- 30 analogy questions (questions 31 to 60)

That's 60 questions—but you only have 30 minutes! Should you try to spend 30 seconds on each question to get them all done? NO!

You Mean I Don't Have to Do All the Questions?

Nope. You'll actually improve your score by answering fewer questions, as long as you're still using all of the allotted time.

"Allotted Time"?
If you can't define *allotted*, make a flash card for it! Look in Chapter 1 for ideas on how to use flash cards to learn new words.

Remember, this test is designed for students in three or four different grade levels. There will be vocabulary in some of these questions that is aimed at students older than you, and almost no one in your grade will get those questions right. On the SSAT score report, you will be compared only with students in your own grade. The younger you are in your test level, the fewer questions you are expected to complete. Fifth graders are expected to do the least number of questions on the Lower Level test. Eighth graders are expected to do the least number of questions on the Upper Level test.

Slow and Steady
Working slowly and getting questions right is how you score well. If you haven't already, look at Chapter 6 to figure out how many questions you really need to complete.

Why rush through the questions you can get right to get to the really tough ones that almost nobody gets? That approach only ensures that you will make hasty, careless errors. Work slowly on the questions that have vocabulary that you know to make sure you get them right. Then try the ones that have some harder words in them.

Look at Chapters 6 and 13 to see how many analogies and synonyms you need to complete correctly to reach your target score. Pace yourself—you've got much more time for each question than students who think they have to get them all done.

Which Questions Should I Do?

The questions are arranged in a rough order of difficulty—the harder synonyms tend to come toward the end of the synonym section, and the harder analogies tend to come at the end of the analogy section. However, everyone is different, and some questions are harder for certain people than they are for others. You know some words that your friends don't, and vice versa.

You get as many points for an easy question as you do for a hard one. So here's the plan: Do all the questions that are easy for you first. Easy questions are those where you know the definitions of all the words involved. Then go back through and do the questions with words that sound familiar, even if you are not sure of their dictionary definitions—these are words you sort of know. As you work through these questions, you'll probably be concentrating mostly on the beginning and middle of each section, but don't be afraid to glance ahead—there may be some words you know toward the end. Remember to skip a number on the answer sheet when you skip a question.

Knowing your own vocabulary is the key to quickly deciding if you can answer a question easily.

Know Yourself

Categorize the words you see in SSAT questions into:

- Words you know
- Words you sort of know
- Words you really don't know

Be honest with yourself when it comes to deciding whether you know a word or not so you can tell which of the techniques you learn in this book works best for each question you tackle. Keep your idea of the word's meaning flexible because the test writers sometimes use the words in ways that you and I do not! (They claim to use dictionary definitions.)

The easiest way to get a verbal question right is by making sure all the words in it fall into the first category—words you know. The best way to do this is by learning new vocabulary *every day*. Check out the Vocabulary chapter (Chapter 1) for the best ways to do this.

You can raise your verbal score moderately just by using the techniques we teach in this chapter. But if you want to see a substantial rise, you need to build up your vocabulary, too.

Bubble Practice
Whenever you do a practice test, use the sample answer sheet so you get used to skipping around when you're filling in bubbles.

Eliminate Answer Choices

With math questions, there's always a correct answer; the other answers are simply wrong. With verbal questions, however, things are not that simple. Words are much more slippery than numbers. So verbal questions have *best* answers, not *correct* ones. The other answers aren't necessarily wrong, but the people who score the SSAT think they're not as good as the *best* ones. This means that your goal is to eliminate *worse* answer choices in the Verbal and Reading sections.

Cross Out the Bad Ones
Even when none of the answers looks particularly right, you can usually eliminate at least one.

Get used to looking for *worse* answers. There are many more of them than there are *best* answers, so *worse* answers are easier to find! When you find them, cross them out in the question booklet to make sure you don't spend any more time looking at them. No matter which other techniques you use to answer a question, eliminate wrong answers first instead of trying to magically pick out the best answer right away.

One thing to remember for the Verbal section: You should not eliminate answer choices that contain words you don't know. If you don't know what a word means, it could be the right answer.

What If I Can't Narrow It Down to One Answer?

Should you guess? Yes. If you can eliminate even one answer choice, you should guess from the remaining choices.

Where Do I Start?

In the Verbal section, do analogies first (questions 31 to 60)—they're easier to get right when you don't know all the words in the question.

Take two passes over each section, in the following order:

- analogies with words you know
- analogies with words you sort of know
- analogies with words you really don't know
- synonyms with words you know
- synonyms with words you sort of know

There is no need to ever try to do synonyms with words that you really don't know. You will rarely be able to eliminate answer choices in a synonym question for which you do not know the stem word.

REVIEW—THE VERBAL PLAN

Pacing and Verbal Strategy

Take a look at the test-taking techniques in Chapter 6 to answer the next two questions.

How many analogies do I need to do? _____

How many synonyms do I need to do? _____

When I start the Verbal section, with which question number do I start? _____

What's the order in which I do questions in the Verbal section?

1. _____

2. _____

3. _____

4. _____

5. _____

How many answer choices must I have eliminated to guess productively? _____

Can I eliminate answer choices that contain words I don't know? _____

If you have trouble answering any of the questions above, reread this chapter!

Knowing My Vocabulary

Look at each of the following words and decide if it's a word that you know, sort of know, or really don't know. If you know it, write down its definition.

insecticide (noun)   _____

trifle (verb)   _____

repugnant (adjective)   _____

mollify (verb)   _____

camouflage (verb)   _____

historic (adjective)   _____

When You Are Done
Check your answers in Chapter 10.

Use a dictionary to check the ones you thought you knew or sort of knew. Make flash cards for the ones you didn't know, the ones you sort of knew, and any that you thought you knew but for which you actually had the wrong definition.

ANALOGIES

What Is an Analogy?

An analogy, on the SSAT, asks you to:

1. Decide how two words are related.
2. Choose another set of words that has the same relationship.

It looks like this

A is to B as

(A) C is to D
(B) C is to D
(C) C is to D
(D) C is to D
(E) C is to D

Or like this

A is to B as C is to

(A) D
(B) D
(C) D
(D) D
(E) D

A, B, C, and D stand for words. We will call any words that are in the question part of the analogy the *stem words*. To figure out the relationship, ignore the "A is to B as C is to D" sentence that they've given you. It doesn't tell you what you need to know. Cross out "is to" and "as."

Then use the techniques that we describe on the next few pages depending on the words in the question. Get your pencil ready because you need to try this stuff out as we go along.

When You Know the Words

Make a Sentence

Here's an analogy for which you'll know all the words.

> Kitten is to cat as
>
> (A) bull is to cow
> (B) snake is to frog
> (C) squirrel is to raccoon
> (D) puppy is to dog
> (E) spider is to fly

You want to be sure you get an easy question like this one right because it's worth just as much as a hard one. Here's how to be sure you don't make a careless mistake.

Picture what the first two words ("A" and "B") stand for and how those two words are related.

> Kitten i̶s̶ ̶t̶o̶ cat a̶s̶   (Cross out "is to" and "as."
>   Just picture a kitten and a cat.)

Make a sentence to describe what you see. (We sometimes call this a "definitional" sentence.) A good sentence will do two things:

- Define one of the words using the other one.

- Stay short and simple.

> A kitten _____ cat.
> (Make a sentence.)

Now look at the answer choices and eliminate any that cannot have the same relationship as the one you've got in your sentence.

> (A) bull is to cow
> (B) snake is to frog
> (C) squirrel is to raccoon
> (D) puppy is to dog
> (E) spider is to fly

Shop Around
Try every answer choice in a verbal question to be sure you're picking the *best* answer there.

If your sentence was something like "A kitten is a young cat," you can eliminate all but (D). After all, a bull is not a young cow; a snake is not a young frog; a squirrel is not a young raccoon; and a spider is not a young fly. If you had a sentence that did not work, think about how you would define a kitten. Stay away from sentences that use the word *you*, as in "You see kittens with female cats." Also avoid sentences like "A kitten is a cat." These sentences don't give you a definition or description of one of the words. Get specific. Yes, a kitten is a cat, but what *else* do you know about it?

As you go through the answer choices, cross out the choices as you eliminate them. In the kitten analogy, you probably knew that (D) was a good fit for your sentence, but don't stop there! Always check all the answers. On the SSAT, often a so-so answer will appear before the *best* answer in the choices, and you don't want to get sidetracked by it. Try *all* the answers so you can be sure to get all the easy analogies right.

In making your sentence, you can start with either of the first two words. Try to start your sentence by defining the first word, but if that doesn't work, start by defining the second word.

Rev It Up

Use the most specific, descriptive words you can when you make a sentence. You want the sentence to define one of the words.

House is to tent as
    (Cross out "is to" and "as." Picture a house and a
    tent.)

A house _____ tent.

(Can you make a definitional sentence? Not really.)

A tent _____ house.

(Make a sentence. Now eliminate answer choices.)

House is to tent as bed is to

(A) table
(B) stool
(C) floor
(D) blanket
(E) hammock

Draw an arrow to remind yourself that you started with the second word instead of the first, as we have here. If you reverse the words in your sentence, you need to reverse them when you're trying out the answer choices, too. If you have a sentence like "A tent is a temporary house," then you can eliminate all but (E).

Write your sentence above the question, between the two words. It's a good idea to do this as you start practicing analogies, and most students find it helpful to write out their sentences all the time. If you have a tendency to change your sentence as you go through the answers, you should always write it down.

Notice that in the house analogy, they've *given* you the first word of the answer pair. Some of the analogies will be like this, but they're really no different from the others. You'll still be using the same techniques for them, and you may find them a little easier.

Make Another Sentence

Why would you ever need to change your sentence? Let's see.

> Motor is to car as
> (Cross out. Picture them. Write a sentence.
> Eliminate.)
>
> (A)   knob is to door
> (B)   shovel is to earth
> (C)   bulb is to lamp
> (D)   sail is to ship
> (E)   pond is to ocean

Did you get it down to one? If not, make your sentence more specific. You may have said "A car has a motor," in which case you can only eliminate (B) and (E). The best words to use are active verbs and descriptive adjectives. What does a motor *do* for a car? Make a more specific sentence. (Remember to draw an arrow if you start with the word *car*.)

A motor makes a car move. You could also say that a car is powered by a motor. Either sentence will help you eliminate all but (D). When your sentence eliminates some, but not all, of the choices, make it more specific.

If you have trouble picturing the relationship or making a more specific sentence, ask yourself questions that will help you get at how the two words are related.

Below are some questions to ask yourself that will help you make sentences. ("A" and "B" are the first two words in the analogy. Remember, you can start with either one.) Refer back to these questions if you get stuck when trying to make a sentence.

- What does A/B do?
- What does A/B mean?
- How does A/B work?
- What does A/B look like?
- How is A/B used?
- Where is A/B found?
- How do A and B compare?
- How are A and B associated?

If at First You Don't Succeed…
Then try the other word! You can start your sentence with the first word (A) or the second word (B).

Help!
These questions will help you come up with a sentence that defines one of the words in an analogy. Refer to them as much as you need to, until you are asking yourself these questions automatically.

PRACTICE DRILL 1—MAKING SENTENCES

Try making a sentence for each of these analogies for which you know both words. Use the questions above to guide you if you have trouble. Avoid using "A is B" or "A is the opposite of B." Instead, try using "has" or "lacks," or you can use "with" or "without." Use active verbs. Check your sentences in the Answer Key before you move on to the next practice set.

1. Chapter is to book as _____ *is a section of a* _____

2. Scale is to weight as _____

3. Striped is to lines as _____

4. Anger is to rage as _____

5. Rehearsal is to performance as _____

6. Mechanic is to car as _____

7. Traitor is to country as _____

8. Aggravate is to problem as _____

9. Trout is to fish as _____

10. General is to army as _____

11. Law is to crime as _____

12. Buckle is to belt as _____

13. Truculent is to fight as _____

14. Cure is to illness as _____

15. Toxic is to poison as _____

16. Mountain is to pinnacle as _____

17. Perilous is to safety as _____

18. Humanitarian is to philanthropy as _____

19. Notorious is to reputation as _____

20. Miser is to generosity as _____

When You Are Done
Check your answers in Chapter 10. Make flash cards for the words you sort of know or don't know at all.

PRACTICE DRILL 2—EASY ANALOGY TECHNIQUES

For each analogy that has words you know:

- Make a sentence.
- Try out your sentence on the answer choices.
- Eliminate the choices that don't fit.
- If you need to, make your sentence more specific and eliminate again.
- If there are words you don't know or just sort of know in a question, skip it.
- If there are words you don't know or just sort of know in an answer choice, do not eliminate it. Just narrow your choices down as far as you can.
- As always, look up the words you can't define and write them down on flash cards.

When you're done, check your answers in Chapter 10.

1. Chapter is to book as

   (A) glass is to water
   (B) lamp is to light
   (C) scene is to play
   (D) stew is to meat
   (E) elevator is to building

2. Refrigerator is to cool as furnace is to

   (A) radiator
   (B) house
   (C) oil
   (D) heat
   (E) furniture

3. Fish is to fin as

   (A) fruit is to stem
   (B) bird is to wing
   (C) insect is to shell
   (D) cod is to school
   (E) dog is to tail

4. Driver is to car as

   (A) pilot is to airplane
   (B) police officer is to highway
   (C) secretary is to letter
   (D) baker is to cake
   (E) carpenter is to house

5. Clock is to time as thermometer is to
   - (A) air
   - (B) pressure
   - (C) wind
   - (D) ice
   - (E) temperature

6. Envelope is to letter as
   - (A) suitcase is to clothes
   - (B) pen is to paper
   - (C) box is to cardboard
   - (D) table is to wood
   - (E) frame is to picture

7. Librarian is to library as curator is to
   - (A) museum
   - (B) studio
   - (C) mall
   - (D) workshop
   - (E) garden

8. Pen is to write as
   - (A) pencil is to point
   - (B) actor is to perform
   - (C) knife is to cut
   - (D) desk is to sit
   - (E) ink is to stain

9. Hurricane is to breeze as
   - (A) storm is to tempest
   - (B) fire is to flame
   - (C) tidal wave is to ripple
   - (D) cloud is to sunlight
   - (E) temperature is to weather

10. Circle is to ball as
   - (A) square is to cube
   - (B) pyramid is to triangle
   - (C) point is to line
   - (D) side is to rectangle
   - (E) hexagon is to polygon

11. Egg is to shell as banana is to
   - (A) fruit
   - (B) tree
   - (C) bunch
   - (D) peel
   - (E) seed

4 cup make a quart

12. Cup is to quart as

(A) week is to time
(B) minute is to hour
(C) liter is to metric
(D) coin is to dollar
(E) spoon is to measure

13. Coach is to team as

(A) captain is to platoon
(B) singer is to chorus
(C) batter is to baseball
(D) teacher is to homework
(E) king is to queen

14. Bat is to mammal as

(A) boar is to hog
(B) porpoise is to shark
(C) butterfly is to insect
(D) whale is to fish
(E) reptile is to lizard

15. Famished is to hungry as

(A) clean is to dirty
(B) destitute is to poor
(C) worried is to lonely
(D) misdirected is to lost
(E) worried is to scared

16. Sterilize is to germ as

(A) cut is to surgeon
(B) sneeze is to dust
(C) scour is to grime
(D) inject is to virus
(E) rinse is to mouth

17. Director is to actors as conductor is to

(A) writers
(B) dancers
(C) painters
(D) musicians
(E) playwrights

18. Applicant is to hire as

(A) judge is to jury
(B) candidate is to elect
(C) cashier is to work
(D) student is to study
(E) writer is to research

19. Stale is to bread as

    (A) American is to cheese
    (B) rancid is to meat
    (C) thick is to milk
    (D) dry is to rice
    (E) pulpy is to juice

20. Prejudice is to unbiased as worry is to

    (A) adamant
    (B) active
    (C) blithe
    (D) concerned
    (E) occupied

When a Sentence Doesn't Work, Go Vertical

There are some weird analogies on the SSAT, and they usually contain words you know. The problem with the weird analogies is that the words don't have a nice, normal, definitional relationship—at least not in a horizontal sense. Often, weird analogies have vertical relationships.

Let's look at the question below:

Racket is to bat as

    (A) puck is to hockey
    (B) rifle is to duck
    (C) hammer is to nail
    (D) goalie is to soccer
    (E) tennis is to baseball

You definitely know the words *racket* and *bat*. So you try making a sentence. You can't make a definitional sentence with these two words, even though you know them. Your next step is to look for a vertical relationship: Most weird analogies are vertical—and even these are not common—but there may be one or two analogies that are just plain odd. If you see one, do your best to figure it out quickly and then move on. See if *racket* is related to any of the words that are in the "C" position. Is *racket* related to *puck*? No. *Rifle*? No. *Hammer*? No. *Goalie*? No. *Tennis*? Maybe. A racket is used to hit the ball in tennis. Does that sentence work for *bat* and *baseball*? Sure. Bingo.

PRACTICE DRILL 3—WEIRD ANALOGY TECHNIQUES

1. Sad is to interested as

    (A) friendly is to ebullient
    (B) pleased is to unhappy
    (C) despair is to obsession
    (D) angry is to neutral
    (E) talkative is to anxious

2. Possible is to required as can is to

    (A) might
    (B) could
    (C) reading
    (D) may
    (E) must

3. Grape is to tree as

    (A) water is to pesticide
    (B) wine is to paper
    (C) fruit is to vegetable
    (D) olive is to oil
    (E) spruce is to pine

4. August is to November as

    (A) February is to April
    (B) March is to June
    (C) July is to May
    (D) January is to December
    (E) September is to November

When You Are Done
Check your answers in Chapter 10.

When You Know Only One of the Words

Working Backward

If you know only one of the words, go straight to the answer choices. Make a sentence with each answer choice. Keep your sentence as definitional as possible. If your sentence uses *can* or *might* or *could*, or if you find yourself really reaching to try to make up a sentence, then the relationship is not a strong definitional one and that answer is probably not right. Eliminate it. Each time you can create a good sentence with an answer choice, you should then try the sentence with the stem words. If you don't know a word in an answer choice, do not eliminate it.

Cygnet is to swan as

(A)	chicken is to egg	*a chicken lays eggs—a cygnet lays swans?*
(B)	frog is to snake	*a snake can eat a frog—not strong*
(C)	turtle is to raccoon	*no sentence—not strong*
(D)	puppy is to dog	*a puppy is a young dog—a cygnet is a young swan?*
(E)	spider is to fly	*some spiders eat flies—not strong*

Pick the *best* or most likely relationship for *cygnet* and *swan*. Which relationship is most like a definition?

Cross out (C), because we couldn't make a sentence at all. (B) and (E) are not great because snakes and spiders eat other things, too, and their definitions are not based on what they eat. Eliminate them. Now look at (A) and (D). Try their sentences on the stem words. Could something lay a swan? Probably not! Could something be a young swan? Sure, there could be a word that means *baby swan*. Sure enough, *cygnet* is exactly that.

Try Working Backward with these analogies.

Kinesiology is to motion as

(A)   numerology is to progress   _____

(B)   navigation is to ocean   _____

(C)   astronomy is to weather   _____

(D)   criminology is to perversion   _____

(E)   psychology is to mind   _____

Only (B) and (E) allow you to make strong sentences. Navigation is how you get around on the ocean. Psychology is the study of the mind. So try those sentences: Could kinesiology be how you get around on the motion? No. Could kinesiology be the study of human motion? Yep. We got it down to (E).

Apiary is to bees as

(A)   stable is to horses   _____

(B)   jar is to honey   _____

(C)   florist is to flowers   _____

(D)   dirt is to ants   _____

(E)   leash is to dog   _____

Eliminate (B), (D), and (E) because the word relationships are not strong. A stable is a place where horses are kept. A florist is someone who works with flowers. Now, do you think that an apiary is a place where bees are kept? Possibly. Do you think an apiary is someone who works with bees? Also possible. Take a guess between (A) and (C). Look up *apiary* and make a flash card for it.

Remember that the answer will *probably* be a relationship based on a definitional sentence that can be made with (A) and (B), but keep in mind that it could also be a relationship between (A) and (C).

PRACTICE DRILL 4—WORKING BACKWARD

We've hidden one of the words in the stem pair, so you can't know it. But you'll still be able to take a good guess at the answer. Work backward.

- Make sentences with the answer choices.
- Eliminate the sentences that don't show a strong, definitional relationship.
- Try out each definitional sentence on the stem words.
- If it helps, say "something" when you have to insert the unknown word.
- Does it seem possible that the unknown word has that definition? If not, eliminate it.
- Don't eliminate any answer choices that contain words you don't know.
- Get as far as you can, and then guess.

1. Island is to ??????? as
   (A) castle is to moat
   (B) star is to galaxy
   (C) river is to delta
   (D) bay is to peninsula
   (E) earth is to hemisphere

2. ??????? is to king as
   (A) legality is to lawyer
   (B) monarchy is to sovereign
   (C) hierarchy is to heir
   (D) feudalism is to farmer
   (E) duplicity is to thief

3. ??????? is to enthusiasm as submissive is to
   (A) solitude
   (B) defiance
   (C) conviction
   (D) admiration
   (E) withdrawn

4. ??????? is to jury as
   (A) eradicate is to problem
   (B) quarantine is to patient
   (C) elect is to politician
   (D) liquidate is to opponent
   (E) evacuate is to city

5. ??????? is to shape as
   (A) amorous is to trust
   (B) temporal is to patience
   (C) enticing is to guile
   (D) bland is to zest
   (E) classical is to harmony

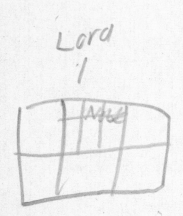

When You Sort of Know the Words

Use "Side of the Fence"

If you can't make a definitional sentence because you're not sure what the words mean, but you've got some idea from having seen the words before, determine whether the words are on the same side of the fence or different sides. That is, are they similar enough to be grouped together, or are they different enough that you'd say they're on different sides of a fence? If they are similar in meaning, write "S" next to the pair. If their meanings are more like opposites, write "D." So cat and kitten would get an "S," while black and white would get a "D."

Because the answer pair has to have the same relationship as that of the stem words, you can eliminate any answers that don't match. If your words are similar, you can eliminate any answers that are different. If your words are different, you can eliminate any answers that are similar.

PRACTICE DRILL 5—JUDGING "SIDE OF THE FENCE"

Mark the following pairs of words as "S" (similar) or "D" (different).

1. healthy is to ailing   _D_
2. limitless is to end   _D_
3. rapture is to happiness   _S_
4. humane is to brutality   _D_
5. obscure is to sight   _D_
6. incendiary is to flame   _____

7. apathetic is to passion   _____
8. boast is to vain   _____
9. tactful is to diplomacy   _____
10. innocent is to guile   _____
11. miser is to greedy   _S_
12. frivolous is to serious   _____

When You Are Done
Check your answers in Chapter 10.

Now we can try a whole analogy.

Lurid is to horror as

(A) comical is to amusement
(B) illegal is to law
(C) cowardly is to fear
(D) ghastly is to serenity
(E) humane is to treatment

Don't try to make a sentence—just decide if *lurid* and *horror* are similar or different. Then make the same decision for all the answer choices. You should wind up with a question that looks as follows:

Lurid is to horror as	S
(A) comical is to amusement	S
(B) illegal is to law	D
(C) cowardly is to fear	S
(D) ghastly is to serenity	D
(E) humane is to treatment	nice phrase, but it's not a relationship

Now you can guess from just two answers—you've increased your odds considerably! Remember to mark up your test booklet as you eliminate, and guess even if you've eliminated only one choice. If you're not sure of the definition of *lurid*, or any other word on this page, make a flash card for it!

PRACTICE DRILL 6—USING "SIDE OF THE FENCE"

In these analogies, we've taken out the stem words but told you whether they're similar or different. Eliminate the answers that you know are definitely wrong because you've written a letter next to them that doesn't match the letter next to the stem words. Remember, you can't eliminate answers that contain words you don't know!

1. (SIMILAR WORDS)

    (A) miserly is to greed
    (B) gentle is to harm
    (C) famous is to privacy
    (D) objective is to opinion
    (E) fanciful is to theory

2. (SIMILAR WORDS)

    (A) athletic is to shapely
    (B) darkened is to light
    (C) free is to liberated
    (D) brave is to cowardly
    (E) normal is to unusual

3. (DIFFERENT WORDS)

    (A) refurbish is to worn
    (B) repaint is to beautiful
    (C) shining is to new
    (D) revive is to tired
    (E) cultivate is to fertile

4. (SIMILAR WORDS)

    (A) humid is to moisture
    (B) displeased is to anger
    (C) silent is to discourse
    (D) pointless is to relevance
    (E) guilty is to neutral

5. (DIFFERENT WORDS)

    (A) flourish is to revive
    (B) wilt is to deaden
    (C) protect is to harm
    (D) heal is to injure
    (E) discuss is to debate

6. (DIFFERENT WORDS)

    (A) modify is to vary
    (B) mutter is to speak
    (C) vacillate is to stand
    (D) rectify is to fix
    (E) verify is to discover

7. (DIFFERENT WORDS)

    (A) charitable is to selfish
    (B) favorable is to despised
    (C) productive is to arid
    (D) predictable is to ordinary
    (E) verbose is to tacit

8. (SIMILAR WORDS)

    (A) anticipate is to hope
    (B) alleviate is to lessen
    (C) innovate is to predict
    (D) disseminate is to gather
    (E) elucidate is to muddle

9. (SIMILAR WORDS)

    (A) slander is to libel
    (B) avenge is to forgive
    (C) provoke is to calm
    (D) quibble is to argue
    (E) satiate is to fill

10. (SIMILAR WORDS)

    (A) supreme is to zenith
    (B) infallible is to certain
    (C) prevalent is to vacant
    (D) listless is to energetic
    (E) pessimistic is to negative

Work Backward

You can use this technique for words you just sort of know, in addition to using it on analogies where you just know one of the words. Try it on this one. *Patent* is a word we all sort of know.

Patent is to inventor as

(A)   advertisement is to merchant   _____

(B)   money is to consumer   _____

(C)   monopoly is to customer   _____

(D)   copyright is to author   _____

(E)   novelty is to journalist   _____

Choices (C) and (E) should be crossed out for sure—the words are not strongly related. You've made sentences with the other answer choices. Which sentence works best with *patent* and *inventor*? (D).

When You Really Don't Know Either of the Words

If you have never seen the stem words before, you're better off putting a circle around the question number in the test booklet and skipping the question. If you have time to go back to the ones you've circled and skipped, then try this.

Work Backward as Much as You Can

Go straight to the answer choices, and make sentences with them. Now, you can't try the sentences with the stem words because you don't know the stem words, right? So just look at the sentences you have. Which ones are not likely to be correct? The ones that are not like definitions. Eliminate those answer choices—the ones in which the words are not related in such a way that you need one to define the other.

Look at these possible answer choices and decide if they're definitional or if you should eliminate them on a question for which you do not know the stem words. Write a sentence for the answers you'd keep.

PRACTICE DRILL 7—WORKING BACKWARD AS MUCH AS YOU CAN

1. tooth is to chewing _____

2. hammer is to wood _____

3. archipelago is to islands _____

4. engine is to smoke _____

5. angry is to violence _____

6. jest is to humorous _____

7. wind is to season _____

When You Are Done

Check your answers in Chapter 10.

Remember that you're not trying to answer all the questions. There are bound to be words on the test that you do not know. Don't sweat it. Check your Pacing Chart to see how many analogies you need to complete. To reach their target scores, most students don't need to do analogies with words they don't know at all.

Review—The Analogies Plan

If I Know the Words

If I know the words, then I

_____

_____

_____

A sentence is good if it's _____ and _____ .

If my sentence eliminates some, but not all, answer choices, I can

_____

_____

A specific, definitional sentence uses words that are _____

Some questions that can help me make a sentence are

_____   _____

_____   _____

_____   _____

If I know the words but can't make a sentence, then I ask myself

_____

_____

_____

_____

_____

And finally, if none of these questions works with A and B (the first two words in the analogy), then I ask myself

_____

If I Know One of the Words
If I know one of the words, then I _____

which means that I _____

and then I _____

If I Sort of Know the Words
If I sort of know the words, then I _____

I can also _____

If I Don't Know the Words
If I don't know the words, I _____

If I have time left, then I go back and _____

If you have trouble with any of the questions above, go back and reread the appropriate part of this chapter.

When You Are Done
Check your answers in Chapter 10.

PRACTICE DRILL 8—ALL ANALOGIES TECHNIQUES

1. Chocolate is to candy as

    (A) fish is to mammal
    (B) meat is to animal
    (C) cat is to animal
    (D) brick is to house
    (E) fire is to forest

2. Pound is to weight as

    (A) decibel is to sound
    (B) inch is to foot
    (C) quart is to liter
    (D) fathom is to height
    (E) length is to distance

3. Class is to student as

    (A) cast is to actor
    (B) teacher is to staff
    (C) conductor is to band
    (D) director is to play
    (E) musician is to band

4. Composer is to symphony as

    (A) mechanic is to auto
    (B) major is to troops
    (C) architect is to building
    (D) tycoon is to wealth
    (E) writer is to paragraph

5. Link is to chain as

    (A) obstacle is to course
    (B) group is to member
    (C) sidewalk is to path
    (D) mural is to museum
    (E) word is to sentence

6. Tadpole is to frog as caterpillar is to

    (A) worm
    (B) cocoon
    (C) crawl
    (D) larvae
    (E) butterfly

7. Cuff is to wrist as

(A) string is to hood
(B) buckle is to waist
(C) cap is to hat
(D) vest is to body
(E) collar is to neck

8. Congregation is to worshippers as

(A) galaxy is to stars
(B) party is to politics
(C) mine is to gems
(D) job is to employers
(E) pottery is to shards

9. Tactile is to touch as

(A) delectable is to drink
(B) audible is to sound
(C) potable is to food
(D) servile is to obey
(E) nutritious is to meal

10. Conviction is to opinion as

(A) report is to story
(B) reverence is to admiration
(C) debate is to argument
(D) appeal is to affectation
(E) ascend is to precipice

11. Caricature is to drawing as

(A) joke is to punch line
(B) watercolor is to painting
(C) hyperbole is to statement
(D) star is to feature
(E) dynamite is to blast

12. Clap is to stomp as

(A) snap is to shout
(B) hand is to foot
(C) map is to ramp
(D) door is to wall
(E) finger is to chicken

13. Deceleration is to speed as

   (A) adulation is to praise
   (B) descent is to altitude
   (C) tyranny is to leader
   (D) hydration is to water
   (E) fear is to hatred

14. Dull is to insipid as diverting
    is to

   (A) expecting
   (B) feeling
   (C) astounding
   (D) entertaining
   (E) surprising

15. Voracious is to food as

   (A) greedy is to money
   (B) gluttonous is to obesity
   (C) clarity is to water
   (D) generosity is to object
   (E) veracity is to truth

16. Adroit is to motion as

   (A) bridled is to emotion
   (B) unfettered is to restraint
   (C) superior is to skill
   (D) ubiquitous is to presence
   (E) articulate is to speech

17. Anesthetic is to pain as

   (A) lamp is to light
   (B) mnemonic is to memory
   (C) exercise is to diet
   (D) understanding is to comprehension
   (E) muffler is to noise

18. Oven is to kiln as baker is to

   (A) potter
   (B) ceramics
   (C) bread
   (D) miner
   (E) shepherd

19. Impeccable is to adequate as

    (A)   impressionable is to eager
    (B)   inexhaustible is to sufficient
    (C)   impossible is to prepared
    (D)   intangible is to popular
    (E)   impractical is to sensible

20. Symmetrical is to amorphous as

    (A)   metric is to moronic
    (B)   shapely is to muscled
    (C)   balanced is to unshaped
    (D)   flowing is to lined
    (E)   external is to internal

SYNONYMS

What Is a Synonym?

On the SSAT, a synonym question asks you to choose the answer choice that comes closest in meaning to the stem word (the word in capitals). Often the best answer won't mean the exact same thing as the stem word, but it will be closer than any of the other choices.

Just like with analogies, you need to decide which vocabulary category the synonym stem word falls into for you, so you know which technique to use. First, do all the synonyms for which you know the stem word, and then go back and do the ones with stem words you sort of know.

When You Know the Stem Word

Write Down Your Own Definition

Come up with a simple definition—a word or a phrase. Write it next to the stem word. Then look at the answers, eliminate the ones that are farthest from your definition, and choose the closest one.

It's very simple. Don't let the test writers put words in your mouth. Make sure you're armed with your own definition before you look at their answer choices. They often like to put in a word that is a close second to the best answer, and if you've got your own synonym ready, you'll be able to make the distinction.

If you need to, cover the answers with your hand, so you can think of your definition before looking. Eventually you may not have to write down your definitions, but you should start out that way.

As you compare the choices with your definition, cross out the ones that are definitely not right. Crossing out answer choices is something you should *always* do— it saves you time because you don't go back to choices you've already decided were not the best.

As always, don't eliminate words you don't know.

Try this one. Write your definition of WITHER before you look at the answer choices.

WITHER: _____ (definition)

(A) play
(B) spoil
(C) greatly improve
(D) wilt
(E) give freely

The stem word means *shrivel* or *dry up*. Which answer is closest? (D). You may have been considering (B), but (D) is closer.

PRACTICE DRILL 9—WRITE YOUR OWN DEFINITION

Write your definition—just a word or two—for each of these stem words.

1. BIZARRE: _____Strange_____

2. PREFACE: _____begining_____

3. GENEROUS: _____Giving_____

4. MORAL: _____the main idea_____

5. ALTER: _____

6. REVOLVE: _____

7. HOPEFUL: _____full of Hop_____

8. LINGER: _____

9. ASSIST: _____

10. CONSTRUCT: _____

11. STOOP: _____

12. CANDID: _____

13. TAUNT: _____

14. COARSE: _____

15. VAIN: _____

16. SERENE: _____

17. UTILIZE: _____

18. VIGOROUS: _____

19. PROLONG: _____

20. BENEFIT: _____

When You Are Done
Check your answers in Chapter 10.

Write Another Definition

Why would you ever need to change your definition? Let's see.

MANEUVER:

(A) avoidance
(B) deviation
(C) find
(D) contrivance
(E) invent

Your definition may be something like *move* or *control* if you know the word from hearing it applied to cars. But that definition isn't in the answer choices. The problem is that you're thinking about *maneuver* as a verb. However, *maneuver* can also be a noun. It means *a plan, scheme, or trick*. Now go back and eliminate. The answer is (D).

The SSAT sometimes uses secondary definitions, which can be the same part of speech or a different part of speech from the primary definition. Just stay flexible in your definitions, and you'll be fine.

Parts of Speech?
If you need to, go back and review parts of speech in the "Word Parts" section of Chapter 1.

PRACTICE DRILL 10—WRITE ANOTHER DEFINITION

Write down as many definitions as you can think of for the following words. Your definitions may be the same part of speech or different. If you have a hard time thinking of different meanings, look the word up.

1. POINT: _____

2. INDUSTRY: _____

3. FLAG: _____

4. FLUID: _____

5. CHAMPION: _____

6. TABLE: _____

When You Are Done

Check your answers in Chapter 10.

7. SERVICE: _____

PRACTICE DRILL 11—EASY SYNONYM TECHNIQUES

Try these synonyms.

- Use the definition for the stem word that you wrote down before.
- Look at the answer choices and eliminate the ones that are farthest from your definition.

1. BIZARRE:

(A) lonely
(B) unable
(C) odd
(D) found
(E) able

2. PREFACE:

(A) introduce
(B) state
(C) propose
(D) jumble
(E) make able

3. GENEROUS:

(A) skimpy
(B) faulty
(C) ample
(D) unusual
(E) cold

4. MORAL:
   (A) imitation
   (B) full
   (C) real
   (D) upright
   (E) sure

5. ALTER:
   (A) sew
   (B) make up
   (C) react
   (D) total
   (E) change

6. REVOLVE:
   (A) push against
   (B) go forward
   (C) leave behind
   (D) turn around
   (E) move past

7. HOPEFUL:
   (A) discouraging
   (B) promising
   (C) fulfilling
   (D) deceiving
   (E) frustrating

8. LINGER:
   (A) hurry
   (B) abate
   (C) dawdle
   (D) attempt
   (E) enter

9. ASSIST:
   (A) work
   (B) discourage
   (C) appeal
   (D) hinder
   (E) help

10. CONSTRUCT:
   (A) build
   (B) type
   (C) live in
   (D) engage
   (E) enable

11. STOOP:

(A) raise
(B) elevate
(C) condescend
(D) realize
(E) imagine

12. CANDID:

(A) picture
(B) honest
(C) prepared
(D) unfocused
(E) rehearsed

13. TAUNT:

(A) delay
(B) stand
(C) show
(D) horrify
(E) tease

14. COARSE:

(A) smooth
(B) crude
(C) polite
(D) furious
(E) emotional

15. VAIN:

(A) conceited
(B) beautiful
(C) talented
(D) unattractive
(E) helpless

16. SERENE:

(A) helpful
(B) normal
(C) calm
(D) disastrous
(E) floating

17. UTILIZE:

(A) pass on
(B) break down
(C) resort to
(D) rely on
(E) make use of

18. VIGOROUS:

    (A) slothful

    (B) aimless

    (C) energetic

    (D) glorious

    (E) victorious

19. PROLONG:

    (A) affirmative

    (B) lengthen

    (C) exceed

    (D) assert

    (E) resolve

20. BENEFIT:

    (A) cooperate

    (B) struggle

    (C) assist

    (D) deny

    (E) appeal

More Review!
For further verbal review, check out
The Princeton Review's *Grammar Start Junior* and *Word Smart Junior*.

When You Sort of Know the Stem Word

Why Should You Do Synonyms Last? Why Are They Harder Than Analogies?

Synonyms are harder to beat than analogies because the SSAT gives you no context with which to figure out words that you sort of know. But that doesn't mean you should only do the easy synonyms. You can get the medium ones, too. You just need to create your own context to figure out words you don't know very well.

Keep in mind that your goal is to eliminate the worst answers, to make an educated guess. You'll be able to do this for every synonym that you sort of know, and even if you just eliminate one choice, *guess*. You'll gain points overall.

Make Your Own Context

You can create your own context for the word by figuring out how you've heard it used before. Think of the other words you've heard used with the stem word. Is there a certain phrase that comes to mind? What does that phrase mean?

If you still can't come up with a definition for the stem word, just use the context in which you've heard the word to eliminate answers that wouldn't fit at all in that same context.

How about this stem word:

ABOMINABLE

Where have you heard *abominable*? The Abominable Snowman, of course. Think about it—you know it's a monster-like creature. Which answer choices can you eliminate?

ABOMINABLE:

(A)	enormous	the enormous snowman? maybe
(B)	terrible	the terrible snowman? sure
(C)	rude	the rude snowman? probably not
(D)	showy	the showy snowman? nope
(E)	talkative	the talkative snowman? only Frosty!

You can throw out everything but (A) and (B). Now you can guess, with a much better shot at getting the answer right than guessing from five choices. Or you can think about where else you've heard the stem word. Have you ever heard something called an *abomination*? Was it something terrible or was it something enormous? (B) is the answer.

Try this one. Where have you heard this stem word? Try the answers in that context.

SURROGATE:

(A) friendly
(B) requested
(C) paranoid
(D) numerous
(E) substitute

Have you heard the stem word in *surrogate mother*? If you have, you can definitely eliminate (B), (C), and (D), and (A) isn't great either. A surrogate mother is a substitute mother.

Try one more.

ENDANGER:

(A) rescue
(B) frighten
(C) confuse
(D) threaten
(E) isolate

Everyone's associations are different, but you've probably heard of *endangered species* or *endangered lives*. Use either of those phrases to eliminate answer choices that can't fit into it. Rescued species? Frightened species? Confused species? Threatened species? Isolated species? (D) works best.

PRACTICE DRILL 12—MAKING YOUR OWN CONTEXT

Write down the phrase in which you've heard each word.

1. COMMON: _____

2. COMPETENT: _____

3. ABRIDGE : _____

4. UNTIMELY: _____

5. HOMOGENIZE: _____

6. DELINQUENT: _____

7. INALIENABLE: _____

8. PALTRY:_____

9. AUSPICIOUS: _____

10. PRODIGAL: _____

When You Are Done
Check your answers in Chapter 10.

PRACTICE DRILL 13—USING YOUR OWN CONTEXT

1. COMMON:

   (A) beautiful
   (B) novel
   (C) typical
   (D) constant
   (E) similar

2. COMPETENT:

   (A) angry
   (B) peaceful
   (C) well-written
   (D) capable
   (E) possible

3. ABRIDGE:

   (A) complete
   (B) span
   (C) reach
   (D) shorten
   (E) retain

4. UNTIMELY:

   (A) late
   (B) punctual
   (C) dependent
   (D) inappropriate
   (E) continuous

5. HOMOGENIZE:

   (A) make the same
   (B) send away
   (C) isolate
   (D) enfold
   (E) purify quickly

6. DELINQUENT:

   (A) underage
   (B) negligent
   (C) superior
   (D) advanced
   (E) independent

7. INALIENABLE:

   (A) misplaced
   (B) universal
   (C) assured
   (D) democratic
   (E) changeable

8. PALTRY:

   (A) meager
   (B) colored
   (C) thick
   (D) abundant
   (E) indistinguishable

9. AUSPICIOUS:

   (A) supple
   (B) minor
   (C) doubtful
   (D) favorable
   (E) ominous

10. PRODIGAL:

    (A) wasteful
    (B) amusing
    (C) disadvantaged
    (D) lazy
    (E) virtuous

Use Word Parts to Piece Together a Definition

Prefixes, roots, and suffixes can help you figure out what a word means. You should use this technique in addition to (not instead of) word association, because not all word parts retain their original meanings.

You may have never seen this stem word before, but if you've been working on your Vocabulary chapter, you know that the root *pac* or *peac* means peace. You can see the same root in *Pacific*, *pacifier*, and the word *peace* itself. So what's the answer to this synonym?

PACIFIST:

   (A) innocent person
   (B) person opposed to war
   (C) warmonger
   (D) wanderer of lands
   (E) journeyman

The answer is (B).

In the following stem word, we see *cred*, a word part that means "belief" or "faith." You can see this word part in *incredible*, *credit*, and *credibility*. The answer is now simple.

CREDIBLE:

(A) obsolete
(B) believable
(C) fabulous
(D) mundane
(E) superficial

Choice (B) again. What are the word parts in the following stem word?

MONOTONOUS:

(A) lively
(B) educational
(C) nutritious
(D) repetitious
(E) helpful

Mono means "one." *Tone* has to do with sound. If something keeps striking one sound, how would you describe it? (D) is the answer.

The only way you'll be able to use word parts is if you know them. Get cracking on the Vocabulary chapter!

Use "Positive/Negative"

Another way to use what you sort of know about a stem word is by asking yourself if it is positive or negative. Then, decide if each of the answers is positive or negative. Eliminate any answers that do not match. If the stem word is positive, then the answer must be positive. If the stem word is negative, then so must be the answer. Write "+" or "−" or "neither" next to each word as you make your decisions.

If someone said you were belligerent, would you be happy? No, because *belligerent* is a negative word. You might know that from hearing the word, but you might also know what the word part *bell* means. Now, decide whether each answer choice is positive or negative.

BELLIGERENT: –

(A) frisky +
(B) messy –
(C) friendly +
(D) antagonistic –
(E) persuasive +

You can eliminate (A), (C), and (E) because you're looking for a synonym, so if the stem is negative, then the answer must also be negative. *Bell* has to do with war, so the answer is (D).

Try this one.

ZENITH:

(A) distance
(B) failure
(C) high point
(D) complaint
(E) proximity

How do you know *zenith* is positive? Probably because it's the brand name of a television set, and brand names will generally be positive words. The only really positive answer choice here is (C), and that's the answer.

PRACTICE DRILL 14—DECIDE POSITIVE/NEGATIVE

1. LUGUBRIOUS: _____   6. HARMONIOUS: _____

2. DISDAIN: _____   7. INCORRIGIBLE: _____

3. CACOPHONOUS: _____   8. ELOQUENT: _____

4. COMPASSIONATE: _____   9. AGILE: _____

5. SLANDER: _____   10. TOIL: _____

When You Are Done
Check your answers in Chapter 10.

PRACTICE DRILL 15—USE POSITIVE/NEGATIVE

In these synonyms, you know only that the stem word is positive or negative. Eliminate as many answers as you can, based on what you know.

1. GOOD WORD:

   (A) harmful
   (B) helpful
   (C) unusual
   (D) horrid
   (E) therapeutic

2. GOOD WORD:

   (A) useful
   (B) handy
   (C) difficult
   (D) regular
   (E) vigorous

3. BAD WORD:

   (A) disgusting
   (B) reliable
   (C) furious
   (D) sturdy
   (E) stabilized

4. BAD WORD:

   (A) beneficial
   (B) placid
   (C) coarse
   (D) noisy
   (E) sluggish

5. BAD WORD:

   (A) faulty
   (B) vague
   (C) grateful
   (D) angry
   (E) indolent

6. GOOD WORD:

   (A) malignant
   (B) unhealthy
   (C) friendly
   (D) forward thinking
   (E) negligent

7. GOOD WORD:

   (A) incapable
   (B) useful
   (C) ferocious
   (D) flavorful
   (E) overzealous

8. BAD WORD:

   (A) assistant
   (B) culprit
   (C) patron
   (D) rival
   (E) acolyte

9. GOOD WORD:

   (A) diverse
   (B) winning
   (C) ruined
   (D) infrequent
   (E) meticulous

10. GOOD WORD:

   (A) honorable
   (B) despicable
   (C) elite
   (D) unsurpassed
   (E) dormant

11. BAD WORD:

   (A) dangerous
   (B) illegal
   (C) sophisticated
   (D) delicious
   (E) venerated

12. BAD WORD:

   (A) rascal
   (B) vermin
   (C) benefactor
   (D) addict
   (E) ally

13. GOOD WORD:

   (A) slovenly
   (B) gluttonous
   (C) envious
   (D) beatific
   (E) mercenary

14. GOOD WORD:

   (A) visionary
   (B) despot
   (C) malefactor
   (D) ingrate
   (E) jingoist

15. GOOD WORD:

   (A) significant
   (B) mediocre
   (C) provincial
   (D) opulent
   (E) vehement

16. BAD WORD:

   (A) apathetic
   (B) assertive
   (C) committed
   (D) insipid
   (E) robust

17. BAD WORD:

   (A) banal
   (B) unrealistic
   (C) vague
   (D) decisive
   (E) impartial

18. BAD WORD:

   (A) tyrant
   (B) rebel
   (C) leader
   (D) participant
   (E) misanthrope

19. GOOD WORD:

   (A) quack
   (B) expert
   (C) narrator
   (D) reporter
   (E) skeptic

20. GOOD WORD:

   (A) turmoil
   (B) amity
   (C) benign
   (D) virulent
   (E) supercilious

Eliminate Wrong Parts of Speech

Eliminate answers that cannot be the same part of speech as the stem word, even if they're close in meaning. You should keep in mind that many words can be more than one part of speech. In the model below, we've written in the parts of speech instead of the actual words:

ADJECTIVE

(A) adjective
(B) noun
(C) adjective or verb
(D) verb or noun

In the synonym above, you can eliminate (B) and (E) because they cannot be adjectives, and you know that the "best" answer is an adjective here because that's what the stem word is.

Remember, suffixes can be very helpful in telling you what part of speech a word is. Look in Chapter 1 for some helpful suffixes.

PRACTICE DRILL 16—IDENTIFYING PARTS OF SPEECH

What parts of speech are the following words? (Some of them can be more than one.)

1. mirror _____

2. flattery _____

3. cover _____

4. emaciated _____

5. adversity _____

6. malleable _____

When You Are Done
Check your answers in Chapter 10.

Words You Really Don't Know

Don't spend time on words you've never seen if you don't know any of their word parts. Check Chapter 6 to see how many synonyms you need to do.

Review—The Synonyms Plan

Words I Know

When I know the stem word, I _____

If I don't see a definition close to mine, I _____

Words I Sort of Know

When I sort of know the stem word, I can use the following techniques:

_____

_____

_____

_____

Words I Really Don't Know

If I've never seen the stem word before, I _____

When You Are Done

Check your answers in Chapter 10.

Can I eliminate answers that contain words I don't know? _____

If you have trouble with any of these questions, reread the appropriate part of this chapter.

PRACTICE DRILL 17—ALL SYNONYMS TECHNIQUES

1. PRINCIPLE:

    (A) leader
    (B) standard
    (C) theory
    (D) game
    (E) chief

2. CAPTURE:

    (A) secure
    (B) lose
    (C) steal
    (D) halt
    (E) release

3. BEFRIEND:

    (A) sever ties
    (B) close down
    (C) approach
    (D) enjoy
    (E) ignore

4. AUTOMATIC:

    (A) involuntary
    (B) enjoyable
    (C) forceful
    (D) hapless
    (E) independent

5. APTITUDE:

    (A) difficulty
    (B) reason
    (C) mistake
    (D) ability
    (E) demeanor

6. CAPITAL:

    (A) primary
    (B) regressive
    (C) capable
    (D) false
    (E) building

7. REPRESS:

    (A) defy
    (B) faithful
    (C) ruling
    (D) outside
    (E) prevent

8. ENDURE:

    (A) take in
    (B) stick with
    (C) add to
    (D) run from
    (E) push out

9. TRANSMIT:

    (A) eliminate
    (B) watch
    (C) send
    (D) symbol
    (E) retrieve

10. DIALOGUE:

    (A) speak
    (B) conversation
    (C) monologue
    (D) sermon
    (E) reading

11. EULOGY:

    (A) attack
    (B) tribute
    (C) complement
    (D) criticism
    (E) encouragement

12. BAN:

    (A) remove
    (B) imposing
    (C) forbid
    (D) specify
    (E) resign

13. APATHY:

    (A) involvement
    (B) compassion
    (C) contempt
    (D) indifference
    (E) honesty

14. OMNISCIENT:

    (A) agile
    (B) logical
    (C) knowledgeable
    (D) capable
    (E) invulnerable

15. TRANSGRESS:

    (A) transport
    (B) eradicate
    (C) include
    (D) attend
    (E) violate

16. VIVACIOUS:

    (A) nimble
    (B) lively
    (C) easily amused
    (D) direct
    (E) constantly aware

17. HYPERBOLE:

    (A) isolation
    (B) identification
    (C) exaggeration
    (D) sharp curve
    (E) qualification

18. CONGENITAL:

    (A) innocent
    (B) inborn
    (C) graceful
    (D) credible
    (E) acquired

19. SUCCINCT:

    (A) subterranean
    (B) confusing
    (C) blatant
    (D) direct
    (E) common

20. CRAFTY:

    (A) apt
    (B) sly
    (C) agile
    (D) wicked
    (E) wayward

21. FLUENT:

    (A) spoken
    (B) quiet
    (C) flowing
    (D) illness
    (E) real

22. IDENTICAL:

    (A) broken
    (B) duplicate
    (C) foolish
    (D) related
    (E) major

23. POPULAR:

    (A) rude
    (B) accepted
    (C) understood
    (D) ultimate
    (E) respected

24. WHARF:

    (A) beach
    (B) raft
    (C) flat ship
    (D) carrier
    (E) dock

25. FAITHFUL:

    (A) hopeful
    (B) unrealistic
    (C) truthful
    (D) pleasant
    (E) devoted

26. OBSTACLE:

    (A) path
    (B) great distance
    (C) ditch
    (D) impediment
    (E) ravine

27. CONVOLUTED:

    (A) interesting
    (B) expensive
    (C) twisted
    (D) forged
    (E) cheap

28. ALIGN:

   (A) repair
   (B) command
   (C) straighten
   (D) replace
   (E) intervene

29. VETO:

   (A) shorten
   (B) discuss
   (C) define
   (D) reject
   (E) submit

30. MANGLE:

   (A) shine
   (B) wear
   (C) torture
   (D) disarm
   (E) mutilate

31. FEEBLE:

   (A) fair
   (B) ineffective
   (C) tough
   (D) hardened
   (E) sickness

32. SLUGGISH:

   (A) aggressive
   (B) slow
   (C) inconsiderate
   (D) wicked
   (E) needy

33. REDUNDANT:

   (A) poor
   (B) superfluous
   (C) abundant
   (D) fancy
   (E) austere

34. LAMPOON:

   (A) article
   (B) biography
   (C) journey
   (D) satire
   (E) presentation

35. TREPIDATION:

   (A) boldness
   (B) irony
   (C) rashness
   (D) comfort
   (E) fear

36. ASSESS:

   (A) deny
   (B) accept
   (C) size up
   (D) dismiss
   (E) portray

37. GHASTLY:

   (A) responsible
   (B) erroneous
   (C) horrible
   (D) favorable
   (E) plausible

38. CENSURE:

   (A) edit
   (B) understanding
   (C) approval
   (D) disapproval
   (E) hate-mongering

39. DISMANTLE:

   (A) discourse with
   (B) break down
   (C) yield to
   (D) drive away
   (E) strip from

40. CACOPHONY:

   (A) melody
   (B) harmony
   (C) musical
   (D) rhythm
   (E) dissonance

Chapter 9
SSAT Reading

WHAT'S READING ALL ABOUT ON THE SSAT?

You have to read the SSAT reading passages differently from the way you read anything else because the passages the test writers use are packed with information.

Generally, when you read a textbook or any other book, you notice one or two phrases you want to remember in each paragraph. You can underline those phrases so you can easily find them later.

On the SSAT, however, the passages are chosen precisely because there is a lot of information in only a few paragraphs; it's all bunched in together. So if you read the way you normally read, here's what happens: you read the first sentence and try to remember it. You read the second sentence and try to remember it. You read the third sentence, and as you try to remember it, you forget the first two.

You have to read with a different goal in mind for the SSAT. This may sound crazy, but *don't* try to learn or remember anything. *You don't get any points for reading the passage well!*

Read Quickly, Answer Slowly

Your goal is to spend more time answering questions (and less time reading the passage).

What do you get points for? Answering questions correctly. On the questions and answers, you need to slow down and make sure you're checking each answer carefully before eliminating it. Don't worry about finishing the section, especially if you're in one of the lower grades taking that test. Let's take our example from before: An eighth-grade girl takes the Upper Level test and does better than 92 percent of the eighth-graders in reading. How many reading questions does she get right out of 40? 31. She probably never even read the last passage, and she's in the top 8 percent of the students with whom she's being compared. Even fewer students finish the Reading section than finish the Verbal or Quantitative sections, and those who do are hurting their scores with careless errors. Don't try to finish!

THE PASSAGES

What Are the Passages Like?

There are six to eight passages in the Reading section. The first two passages are the easiest—definitely do them.

After the first two, you can choose which to do. The Reading section purposely has far more passages and questions than most students can complete in 40 minutes—6 to 8 passages and 40 questions. Don't let the test writers choose which ones you'll finish. Choose for yourself by flipping through them and going with the types you do best. You'll do better on topics that interest you.

On which types of passages do you do better? Investigate this as you do practice questions and the practice SSAT.

Passage Types

Actual historical document • Speech • Newspaper article • Eyewitness account	These are called "primary sources" because they are written during the time they describe. The SSAT doesn't usually tell you when or where they're from.
History • A person • A group • An event • A scientific idea • A discovery or an invention	These are "secondary sources" because they are written after the events they describe, usually based on primary sources. Your history textbook is a secondary source.
Science	These are not historical. Instead, they talk about current scientific explanations.
Opinion • Comparing • Contrasting • Judging	These are written by an author stating his or her opinion. You can practice reading these in the op-ed pages of a newspaper.
Story • Entire story • Part of a story	Sometimes you get the whole story; sometimes you are dropped down in the middle of one.
Poem	See if you do well on poems in practice tests.

History and science passages are like parts of textbooks—they tend to be factual and objective. An actual historical document or a part of a story can be disorienting because often you will get no warning as to who is speaking or writing or what time or place you've been dropped into. You need to get as much of that information as possible from the clues in the passage. Of course, poems are open to even more interpretation than the other types—make sure you do well on practice poem passages if you plan on doing them on the test.

How Do I Read the Passages?

Quickly! Don't try to remember the details in the passage. Your goal is to read the passage quickly to get the main idea.

The SSAT Reading section is an open-book test—you can look back at the passage to answer questions about the details.

Label the Paragraphs

After you read each paragraph, ask yourself what you just read. Put it in your own words—just a couple of words—and label the side of the paragraph with your summary. This way you'll have something to guide you back to the relevant part of the passage when you answer a question.

Imagine your grandparents are coming to visit, and they're staying in your room. Your parents tell you to clean up your room and get all that junk off the floor. Now, that junk is important to you. Okay, so maybe you don't need your Rollerblades every day, or all those old notes from your best friend, but you do need to be able to get to them. So you get a bunch of boxes, and you throw your Rollerblades, dress shoes, and ice skates in one box. In another, you throw all your old notes, letters, cards, and schoolwork. In another, you throw all your handheld videogames, CDs, computer software, and floppy disks. Before you put the boxes in the closet, what must you do to be sure you don't have to go through every one of them the next time you want to play Tetris? You need to label them. "Shoes," "papers," and "computer/CDs" should do it.

The same thing is true of the paragraphs you read on the SSAT. You need to be able to go back to the passage and find the answer to a question quickly—you don't want to have to look through every paragraph to find it! The key to labeling the paragraphs is practice—you need to do it quickly, coming up with one or two words that accurately remind you of what's in the paragraph.

If the passage has only one paragraph, try stopping every few sentences to label them with a word or two. Poems do not need to be labeled.

State the Main Idea

After you have read the entire passage, ask yourself the following two questions:

- "What?" What is the passage about?
- "So what?" What's the author's point about this topic?

The answers to these questions will show you the main idea of the passage. Scribble down this main idea in just a few words. The answer to "What?" is the thing that was being talked about—"bees" or "weather forecasting." The answer to "So what?" gives you the rest of the sentence—"Bees do little dances that tell other bees where to go for pollen," or "Weather forecasting is complicated by many problems."

Don't assume you will find the main idea in the first sentence. While often the main idea is in the beginning of the passage, it is not *always* in the first sentence or even the first paragraph. The beginning may just be a lead-in to the main point.

PRACTICE DRILL 18—GETTING THROUGH THE PASSAGE

As you quickly read each paragraph, label it. When you finish the passage, answer "What?" and "So what?" to get the main idea.

Contrary to popular belief, the first European known to lay eyes on America was not Christopher Columbus or Amerigo Vespucci but a little-known Viking by the name of Bjarni Herjolfsson. In the summer of 986, Bjarni sailed from Norway to Iceland, heading for the Viking settlement where his father "Heriulf" resided.

When he arrived in Iceland, Bjarni discovered that his father had already sold his land and estates and set out for the latest Viking settlement on the subarctic island called Greenland. Discovered by a notorious murderer and criminal named Eric the Red, Greenland lay at the limit of the known world. Dismayed, Bjarni set out for this new colony.

Because the Vikings traveled without chart or compass, it was not uncommon for them to lose their way in the unpredictable northern seas. Beset by fog, the crew lost their bearings. When the fog finally cleared, they found themselves before a land that was level and covered with woods.

They traveled farther up the coast, finding more flat, wooded country. Farther north, the landscape revealed glaciers and rocky mountains. Though Bjarni realized this was an unknown land, he was no intrepid explorer. Rather, he was a practical man who had simply set out to find his father. Refusing his crew's request to go ashore, he promptly turned his bow back out to sea. After four days' sailing, Bjarni landed at Herjolfsnes on the southwestern tip of Greenland, the exact place he had been seeking all along.

"What" is this passage about? _____

"So what?" What's the author's point? _____

What type of passage is this? _____

Check your answers to be sure you're on the right track.

When You Are Done
Check your answers in Chapter 10.

THE QUESTIONS

Now, we're getting to the important part of the Reading section. This is where you need to spend time in order to avoid careless errors. After reading a passage, you'll have a group of questions that are in no particular order. The first thing you need to decide is whether the question you're answering is general or specific.

General Questions

General questions are about the passage as a whole. There are five types.

Main idea
- Which of the following best expresses the main point?
- The passage is primarily about
- The main idea of the passage is
- The best title for this passage would be

Tone/attitude
- The author's tone is
- The attitude of the author is one of

General interpretation
- The author's tone/attitude indicates
- The author would most likely agree with
- This passage deals with X by
- The passage implies that
- Which of the following words best describes the passage?
- It can be inferred from the passage that
- The style of the passage is most like
- Where would you be likely to find this passage?
- What is the author's opinion of X?
- The passage is best described as a

Purpose
- The purpose of the passage is
- The author wrote this passage to

Prediction
- Which is likely to happen next?
- The author will most likely discuss next

Notice that these questions all require you to know the main idea, but the ones at the beginning of the list don't require anything else, and the ones toward the end require you to interpret a little more.

Answering a General Question

Keep your answers to "What?" and "So what?" in mind. The answer to a general question will concern the main idea. If you need more, go back to your paragraph labels. The labels will allow you to look at the passage again without getting bogged down in the details.

- For a straight **main idea** question, just ask yourself, "What was the 'What? So what?' for this passage?"
- For a **tone/attitude** question, ask yourself, "How did the author feel about the subject?" Think about tone as you would a text message. Would you say the author feels ☺ or ☹ or :\ ? These three signs can help you with process of elimination.
- For a **general interpretation** question, ask yourself, "Which answer stays closest to what the author said and how he said it?"
- For a **general purpose** question, ask yourself, "Why did the author write this?"
- For a **prediction** question, ask yourself, "How was the passage arranged?" Take a look at your paragraph labels, and reread the last sentence.

Answer the question in your own words before looking at the answer choices. As always, you want to arm yourself with your own answer before looking at the SSAT's tricky answers.

PRACTICE DRILL 19—ANSWERING A GENERAL QUESTION

Use the passage about Vikings that you just read and labeled. Reread your main idea and answer the following questions. Use the questions on the previous page to help you paraphrase your own answer before looking at the choices.

What was the answer to "What?" and "So what?" for this passage?

1. This passage is primarily about
   (A) the Vikings and their civilization
   (B) the waves of Viking immigration
   (C) sailing techniques of Bjarni Herjolfsson
   (D) one Viking's glimpse of the New World
   (E) the hazards of Viking travel

Which answer is closest to what the author said overall?

2. With which of the following statements about Viking explorers would the author most probably agree?
   (A) Greenland and Iceland were the Vikings' final discoveries.
   (B) Viking explorers were cruel and savage.
   (C) The Vikings' most startling discovery was an accidental one.
   (D) Bjarni Herjolfsson was the first settler of America.
   (E) All Viking explorers were fearless.

Why did the author write this passage? Think about the main idea.

3. What was the author's purpose in writing this passage?
   (A) To turn the reader against Italian adventurers
   (B) To show his disdain for Eric the Red
   (C) To demonstrate the Vikings' nautical skills
   (D) To correct a common misconception about the European discovery of America
   (E) To prove the Vikings were far more advanced than previously thought

When You Are Done
Check your answers in Chapter 10.

Specific Questions

Specific questions are about a detail or section of the passage. There are four main types.

Fact

- According to the passage/author
- The author states that
- Which of these questions is answered by the passage?
- All of the following are mentioned EXCEPT

Definition in context

- What does the passage mean by X?
- X probably represents/means
- Which word best replaces the word X without changing the meaning?
- As it is used in X, _____ most nearly means

Specific interpretation

- The author implies in line X
- It can be inferred from paragraph X
- The most likely interpretation of X is

Purpose

- The author uses X to
- Why does the author say X?

Again, the questions above range from flat-out requests for information found in the passage (just like the straight "main idea" general questions) to questions that require some interpretation of what you find in the passage (like the general questions that ask with what the author is "likely to agree").

Answering a Specific Question

For specific questions, always reread the part of the passage concerned. Remember, this is an open-book test!

Of course, you don't want to have to reread the entire passage. What part is the question focusing on? To find the relevant part

- Use your **paragraph labels** to go straight to the information you need.
- Use the **line or paragraph reference**, if there is one, but be careful. With a line reference ("In line 10…"), be sure to read the whole surrounding paragraph, not just the line. If the question says, "In line 10…," then you need to read lines 5 through 15 to actually find the answer.

- Use words that stand out in the question and passage. Names, places, and long words will be easy to find back in the passage. We call these **lead words** because they lead you back to the right place in the passage.

Once you're in the right area, answer the question in your own words. Then look at the answer choices and eliminate any that aren't like your answer.

Answering Special Specific Questions

Definition-in-context questions

Creating your own answer before looking at the choices makes definition-in-context questions especially easy. Remember, they want to know how the word or phrase is being used *in context*, so come up with your own word that fits in the sentence before looking at the answer choices. Try one.

> In line 15, the word "spot" most closely means

Cross out the word they're asking about, and replace it with your own.

> A raptor must also have a sharp, often hooked beak so that it may tear the flesh of its prey. Because they hunt from the sky, these birds must have extremely sharp eyesight, which allows them to *spot* potential prey from a great distance.

Now, look at the answer choices, and eliminate the ones that are not at all like yours.

(A) taint
(B) mark
(C) hunt
(D) detect
(E) circle

You probably came up with something like "see." The closest answer to "see" is (D). Notice that "taint" and "mark" are possible meanings of "spot," but they don't work in this context. Those answer choices are there to catch students who do not go back to the passage to see how the word is used and to replace it with their own.

Definition-in-context questions are so quick that if you only have a few minutes left, you should definitely do them first.

I, II, III questions The questions that have three Roman numerals are confusing and time-consuming. They look like this:

According to the passage, which of the following is true?

> I.   The sky is blue.
>
> II.   Nothing rhymes with "orange."
>
> III. Smoking cigarettes increases lung capacity.
>
> (A) I only
> (B) II only
> (C) III only
> (D) I and II only
> (E) I, II, and III

On the SSAT, you will need to look up each of the three statements in the passage. This will always be time-consuming, but you can make them less confusing by making sure you look up just one statement at a time.

For instance, in the question above, say you look back at the passage and see that the passage says statement I is true. Write a big "T" next to it. What can you eliminate now? (B) and (C). Now you check out II and you find that sure enough, the passage says that, too. So II gets a big "T" and you cross off (A). Next, looking in the paragraph you labeled "Smoking is bad," you find that the passage actually says that smoking decreases lung capacity. What can you eliminate? (E).

You may want to skip a I, II, III question because it will be time-consuming, especially if you're on your last passage and there are other questions you can do instead.

EXCEPT/LEAST/NOT questions This is another confusing type of question. The test writers are reversing what you need to look for, asking you which answer is false.

> All of the following can be inferred from the
> passage EXCEPT

Before you go any further, cross out the "EXCEPT." Now, you have a much more positive question to answer. Of course, as always, you will go through *all* the answer choices, but for this type of question you will put a little "T" or "F" next to the answers as you check them out. Let's say we've checked out these answers:

> (A) Americans are patriotic.   **T**
> (B) Americans have great ingenuity.   **T**
> (C) Americans love war.   **F**
> (D) Americans do what they can to help
>   one another.   **T**
> (E) Americans are brave in times of war.   **T**

Which one stands out? The one with the "F." That's your answer. You made a confusing question much simpler than the test writers wanted it to be. If you don't go through all the choices and mark them, you run the risk of accidentally picking one of the choices that you know is true because that's what you usually look for on reading questions.

You should skip an EXCEPT/LEAST/NOT question if you're on your last passage and there are other questions you can do instead.

PRACTICE DRILL 20—ANSWERING A SPECIFIC QUESTION

Use the passage about Vikings that you just read and labeled. Use your paragraph labels and the lead words in each question to get to the part of the passage you need, and then put the answer in your own words before going back to the answer choices.

1. According to the passage, Bjarni Herjolfsson left Norway to

   (A) found a new colony
   (B) open trading lanes
   (C) visit a relative
   (D) map the North Sea
   (E) settle in Greenland

What's the lead word here? *Norway.* Norway should also be in one of your labels.

2. Bjarni's reaction upon landing in Iceland can best be described as

   (A) disappointed
   (B) satisfied
   (C) amused
   (D) indifferent
   (E) fascinated

What's the lead word here? *Iceland.* Again, this should be in one of your labels.

3. "The crew lost their bearings," in the third paragraph, probably means that

   (A) the ship was damaged beyond repair
   (B) the crew became disoriented
   (C) the crew decided to mutiny
   (D) the crew went insane
   (E) the ship's compass broke

For a paragraph reference, just go back and read that paragraph. Replace the words they've quoted with your own.

4. It can be inferred from the passage that prior to Bjarni Herjolfsson's voyage, Greenland

   (A) was covered in grass and shrubs
   (B) was overrun with Vikings
   (C) was rich in fish and game
   (D) was populated by criminals
   (E) was as far west as the Vikings had traveled

What's the lead word here? *Greenland.* Is it in one of your labels? What does that part of the passage say about Greenland? Paraphrase before looking at the answers!

When You Are Done
Check your answers in Chapter 10.

THE ANSWERS

Before you ever look at an answer choice, you've come up with your own answer, in your own words. What do you do next?

Well, you're looking for the closest answer to yours, but it's a lot easier to eliminate answers than to try to magically zone in on the best one. Work through the answers using Process of Elimination. As soon as you eliminate an answer, cross off the letter in your test booklet so that you no longer think of that choice as a possibility.

How Do I Eliminate Answer Choices?

On a General Question

Eliminate an answer that is:

- Too small. The passage may mention it, but it's only a detail—not a main idea.
- Not mentioned in the passage.
- In contradiction to the passage—it says the opposite of what you read.
- Too big. The answer tries to say that more was discussed than really was.
- Too extreme. An extreme answer is too negative or too positive, or it uses absolute words like *all, every, never,* or *always*. Eliminating extreme answers makes tone/attitude questions especially easy and quick.
- Against common sense. The passage is not likely to back up answers that just don't make sense at all.

On a Specific Question

Eliminate an answer that is:

- Too extreme
- In contradiction to passage details
- Not mentioned in the passage
- Against common sense

If you look back at the questions you did for the Viking passage, you'll see that many of the wrong answer choices fit into the categories above.

What Kinds of Answers Do I Keep?

Best answers are likely to be:

- Paraphrases of the words in the passage
- Traditional and conservative in their outlook
- Moderate, using words like *may, can,* and *often*

PRACTICE DRILL 21—ELIMINATING ANSWERS

The following phrases are answer choices. You haven't read the passage, or even the question, that goes with each of them. However, you *can* decide if each one is a *possible* correct answer or if you can eliminate it, based on the criteria we've just listed. Cross out any that you can eliminate.

Flash Card Alert
What's the definition of *criteria*?

For a general question

(A)   The author refutes each argument exhaustively.

(B)   The author admires the courage of most Americans.

(C)   Creativity finds full expression in a state of anarchy.

(D)   The passage criticizes Western society for not allowing freedom of expression to artists.

(E)   The ancient Egyptians were barbaric.

(F)   The author proves that Native American writing does not have a multicultural perspective.

(G)   The author emphasizes the significance of diversity in the United States.

(H)   The passage reports the record cold temperatures in Boston in 1816.

For a general tone/attitude question (these often have one-word answers, describing the author's tone)

For Extra Practice
Remember the smiley faces? See if you can assign them to this list, I through T.

(I)   respectful

(J)   confused

(K)   angry condemnation

(L)   admiring

(M)   mournful

(N)   objective

(O)   thrilled optimism

(P)   exaggeration

(Q)   disgusted

(R)   neutral

(S)   condescending

(T)   indifferent

For a specific question

(U)   They were always in danger of being deprived of their power.

(V)   Voters were easily misled by mudslinging campaigns.

(W)   One-celled organisms could be expected to act in fairly predictable ways.

(X)   Only a show of athletic ability can excite an audience.

(Y)   Economic events can have political repercussions.

When You Are Done
Check your answers in Chapter 10.

When You've Got It Down to Two

If you've eliminated all but two answers, don't get stuck and waste time. Keep the main idea in the back of your mind and step back.

- Reread the question.
- Look at what makes the two answers different.
- Go back to the passage.
- Which answer is worse? Eliminate it.

REVIEW—THE READING PLAN

The Passages

After I read each paragraph, I _____ it.

After I read an entire passage, I ask myself: _____ ? _____ ?

I am better at doing the following types of passages:

_____

_____

_____

_____

The Questions

The five main types of general questions, and the questions I can ask myself to answer them, are:

_____   _____

_____   _____

_____   _____

_____   _____

_____   _____

To find the answer to a specific question, I can use the following three clues:

_____

_____

_____

If the question says, "In line 22," where do I begin reading for the answer?

_____

The Answers

On a general question, I eliminate answers that are

_____

_____

_____

_____

_____

On a specific question, I eliminate answers that are

_____

_____

_____

_____

When I've got it down to two possible answers, I

_____

_____

_____

If you have trouble with any of these questions, be sure to reread this chapter before moving on.

When You Are Done
Check your answers in Chapter 10.

PRACTICE DRILL 22—ALL READING TECHNIQUES— LOWER LEVEL

The term "tides" has come to represent the cyclical rising and falling of ocean waters, most notably evident along the shoreline as the border between land and sea moves in and out with the passing of the day. The primary reason for this constant redefinition of the boundaries of the sea is the gravitational force of the moon.

This force of lunar gravity is not as strong as Earth's own gravitational pull, which keeps our bodies and our homes from being pulled off the ground, through the sky, and into space toward the moon. It is a strong enough force, however, to exert a certain gravitational pull as the moon passes over Earth's surface. This pull causes the water level to rise (as the water is literally pulled, ever so slightly, toward the moon) in those parts of the ocean that are exposed to the moon and its gravitational forces. When the water level in one part of the ocean rises, it must naturally fall in another, and this is what causes water levels to change, dramatically at times, along any given piece of coastline.

1. Which one of the following is the most obvious effect of the tides?

    (A) A part of the beach that was once dry is now under water.
    (B) Floods cause great damage during heavy rainstorms.
    (C) The moon is not visible.
    (D) Water falls.
    (E) The ocean rises.

2. The word "lunar" in the beginning of the second paragraph most nearly means

    (A) weak
    (B) strong
    (C) destructive
    (D) related to the moon
    (E) foolish

3. It can be inferred from the passage that if one were to travel to the moon

   (A) that water would be found on its surface
   (B) that an object, if dropped, would float away from the surface of the moon
   (C) that other planets besides the moon have an influence on the tides of Earth's oceans
   (D) that tides are more dramatic during the day than during the night
   (E) that an object, if dropped, would fall to the moon's surface

4. The author's primary purpose in writing this passage is to

   (A) prove the existence of water on the moon
   (B) refute claims that tides are caused by the moon
   (C) explain the main cause of the ocean's tides
   (D) argue that humans should not interfere with the processes of nature
   (E) convince students to study astrophysics

When You Are Done
Check your answers in Chapter 10.

PRACTICE DRILL 23—ALL READING TECHNIQUES— LOWER LEVEL

The Brooklyn Bridge in New York has been featured in movies, photographs, and media for over a hundred years, but the bridge is much more than just a pretty sight. It opened on May 24, 1883, and, at 3,460 feet, it was the longest suspension bridge in the world, measuring 50% longer than any previously built. The Brooklyn Bridge was a symbol of American strength and vitality, but its completion followed years of toil and sacrifice.

John Augustus Roebling, a German immigrant, envisioned the bridge that would link Manhattan to Brooklyn over the East River. While in preparations for building, however, John Roebling was injured when a ferry pinned his foot to a pylon, and he died weeks later of tetanus. This first setback to the building of the bridge was indicative of the problems that would plague its construction as well as the harrowing tenacity that led to its completion.

Washington Roebling took over the project upon his father's death. Washington persevered through many hurdles in the building of the bridge including fires, accidents, industrial corruption, and loss of public support. He continued, however, in his push to complete the bridge. In fact, it is said that he worked harder and longer than any worker he employed in even the most dangerous circumstances. While working in the caissons, underwater chambers that supported the bridge, he was stricken by the decompression sickness that led to his paralysis. Nothing could stop him, though, and he continued construction by sending messages to the site through his wife, Emily.

Fourteen years after construction began, the Brooklyn Bridge celebrated its grand opening. The total cost to build the bridge was fifteen million dollars, and 27 people died in its construction, but it stood as a tribute to American invention and industry.

1. The primary purpose of the passage is to
   (A) convince the reader that the Brooklyn Bridge is the longest suspension bridge in the world
   (B) describe Washington Roebling's rise to success
   (C) show that Americans have an inborn talent for inventiveness
   (D) describe how the Brooklyn Bridge was a great success despite the hardships faced in building it
   (E) describe the dangers of tetanus

2. It can be inferred from the third paragraph that Washington Roebling

    (A) was injured by a ferry

    (B) was determined to build the bridge despite many setbacks

    (C) suffered from depression after his injury

    (D) had a son who completed the building of the bridge

    (E) was happy not to have to go back to the construction site after his injury

3. Which one of the following is given as a difficulty faced in building the Brooklyn Bridge?

    (A) An excessive number of pylons in the East River.

    (B) An outbreak of tetanus among the workers.

    (C) An increase in public support.

    (D) A lack of funds to keep building.

    (E) The death of the man who envisioned the bridge.

4. Washington Roebling can best be described as

    (A) persistent

    (B) weak

    (C) clumsy

    (D) dangerous

    (E) cautious

5. Which of the following is NOT stated about the Brooklyn Bridge?

    (A) It was a sign of American power.

    (B) It cost millions of dollars to build.

    (C) It was not worth the money lost in building it.

    (D) It has been seen in the movies.

    (E) It has been around for over a hundred years.

When You Are Done
Check your answers in Chapter 10.

PRACTICE DRILL 24—ALL READING TECHNIQUES—ALL LEVELS

Immediately following the dramatic end of World War II came a realization that the United States now had to turn its attention inward. Years of fighting battles around the globe had drained the country of important resources. Many industries (such as housing) suffered, as both materials and workers were used elsewhere in the war effort. Once the soldiers began returning, it became clear that new jobs and new homes were among their biggest needs. The homes needed to be affordable, since few people had had the time or ability to save much during the war.

It was in this situation that many house developers saw a business opportunity. Amid such a pressing demand for new homes, developer William Levitt realized the need for a new method of building. He sought a way to build homes cheaper and faster than ever before.

He wasn't the only developer to realize this, but he was one of the best in making it happen. He applied the same ideas to homes that Henry Ford had used 50 years earlier in making cars. Levitt did not build a factory with an assembly line of fully formed homes rolling out of some giant machine. Instead, he adapted the assembly line formula into a system in which the workers, rather than the product, moved for a streamlined, efficient building process.

Previously, a developer who completed four homes a year had been moving at a good pace. Levitt planned to do that many each week, and succeeded. He created specialized teams that focused on only one job each and moved up and down the streets of new homes. Teams of foundation-builders, carpenters, roofers, and painters worked faster by sticking to just one task as they moved, factory-style, from house to house. The time and money saved allowed Levitt to build cheap homes of good value.

With this new approach, Levitt oversaw the building of some of the first towns that would eventually be called suburbs—planned communities outside the city. Some critics blame developers like Levitt for turning farmland into monotonous, characterless towns. However, most agree that his contribution to the country following a bitter war was mostly positive. He did vary the style of home from street to street, and his work on simpler home features was influenced by the work of architecture great Frank Lloyd Wright.

In the end, Levitt's success speaks for itself. After his first success—building thousands of homes in Long Island, New York—he went on to found several more "Levittowns" in Pennsylvania, New Jersey, and elsewhere. Levitt gave home buyers what they wanted: nice pieces of land with nice homes on top. In a way, by creating houses that so many families could afford, William Levitt made the American dream a more affordable reality.

1. The author's main purpose for writing the passage is to

   (A) discuss the events that occurred during the final days of World War II
   (B) question the opinion that suburban housing is unaffordable
   (C) describe one person's significant contributions to an industry
   (D) compare the economic forces affecting Americans both during World War II and after
   (E) provide a complete biography of William Levitt

2. The author would most likely agree with which of the following statements about William Levitt?

   (A) He invented the word "suburb."
   (B) He was unconcerned with the style of the homes he built.
   (C) His homes were built in factories.
   (D) His ultimate business goal was to make cars as Henry Ford did.
   (E) His efficient methods helped make homes more affordable.

3. Which of the following best describes William Levitt?

   (A) Courageous patriot
   (B) Strict businessman
   (C) Ground-breaking entrepreneur
   (D) Financial mastermind
   (E) Automotive specialist

4. It is most reasonable to infer from the passage that

   (A) William Levitt was the only developer working in New York following World War II
   (B) William Levitt and Henry Ford created homes the same way
   (C) Frank Lloyd Wright designed Levittown
   (D) Other developers did not know how to use the concept of assembly line construction
   (E) Levitt built homes much faster than was customary before World War II

5. The author suggests all of the following as reasons for the post–World War II suburban housing shortage EXCEPT:

    (A) Many American homes had been destroyed during the war.
    (B) The war affected people's ability to accumulate savings.
    (C) Most returning soldiers were seeking new jobs and new homes.
    (D) Affordability was a major issue for post-war Americans.
    (E) Housing materials and home builders were mostly used elsewhere during the war.

6. It can be inferred that a potential drawback to "assembly-line style" houses is that they

    (A) are harder to sell
    (B) are not as sturdy
    (C) may all seem to be the same
    (D) make farming impossible
    (E) are available only in selected areas

When You Are Done
Check your answers in Chapter 10.

PRACTICE DRILL 25—ALL READING TECHNIQUES— ALL LEVELS

Etymology, the study of words and word roots, may sound like the kind of thing done by boring librarians in small, dusty rooms. Yet etymologists actually have a uniquely interesting job. They are in many ways just like archaeologists digging up the physical history of people and events. The special aspect of etymology is that it digs up history, so to speak, through the words and phrases that are left behind.

The English language, in particular, is a great arena in which to explore history through words. As a language, English has an extraordinary number of words. This is in part due to its ability to adapt foreign words so readily. For example, "English" words such as *kindergarten* (from German), *croissant* (from French), and *cheetah* (from Hindi) have become part of the language with little or no change from their original sounds and spellings. So English-language etymologists have a vast world of words to explore.

Another enjoyable element of etymology for most word experts is solving word mysteries. No, etymologists do not go around solving murders, cloaked in intrigue like the great fictional detective Sherlock Holmes. What these word experts solve are mysteries surrounding the origins of some of our most common words.

One of the biggest questions English language experts have pursued is how English came to have the phrase *OK*. Though it is one of the most commonly used slang expressions, its exact beginning is a puzzle even to this day. Even its spelling is not entirely consistent—unless you spell it *okay*, it's hard even to call it a word.

Etymologists have been able to narrow *OK*'s origin down to a likely, although not certain, source. It became widely used around the time of Martin Van Buren's run for president in 1840. His nickname was Old Kinderhook. What troubles word experts about this explanation is that the phrase appeared in some newspapers before Van Buren became well known. As a result, it's unlikely that Van Buren could be called its primary source. Like bloodhounds following a faint scent, etymologists will doubtless keep searching for the initial source. However, it is clear that *OK*'s popularity and fame have exceeded those of the American president to whom it has been most clearly linked.

1. In the second paragraph, etymologists are compared with which of the following?

    (A) Librarians in a dark room
    (B) Explorers of an immense world
    (C) Expert drivers
    (D) Talented teachers
    (E) Respected scientists

2. The author uses the words "kindergarten," "croissant," and "cheetah" to illustrate

   (A) words with unknown origins
   (B) examples of difficult English vocabulary
   (C) words similarly spelled or spoken in two languages
   (D) areas of dispute among etymologists
   (E) words rarely used in English

3. Which of the following best describes an etymologist?

   (A) Pursuer of the source of words
   (B) Lover of vocabulary words
   (C) Scientist of the five senses
   (D) Archaeologist of extinct language
   (E) Creator of dictionaries

4. The author uses the example "OK" to illustrate

   (A) another non-English word
   (B) a troublesome definition
   (C) an interesting aspect of etymology
   (D) a common American phrase
   (E) a legacy of Martin Van Buren

5. This passage is primarily about

   (A) the history of the English language
   (B) enjoyable aspects of the study of words
   (C) the use of language in the American presidency
   (D) the origin of the phrase "OK"
   (E) ways to distinguish English and non-English words

When You Are Done
Check your answers in Chapter 10.

PRACTICE DRILL 26—ALL READING TECHNIQUES—UPPER LEVEL

Bob Dylan was born on May 24, 1941 in Duluth, Minnesota, but his name wasn't Dylan. He was born Robert Allen Zimmerman, one of two sons born to Abraham and Betty Zimmerman. Nineteen years later, he moved to New York City with his new name and a passion to pursue his dream of becoming a music legend.

Bob Dylan's career began like those of many musicians. He began to play in New York City at various clubs around Greenwich Village. He began to gain public recognition as a singer/songwriter and was even reviewed by the *New York Times* his first year in New York. He signed his first record deal with Columbia Records a mere ten months after moving to New York. From that point on, his career skyrocketed.

What is unique about Bob Dylan, given his huge success, is his vocal quality. Dylan's singing voice was untrained and had an unusual edge to it. Because of this, many of his most famous early songs first reached the public through versions by other performers who were more immediately palatable. Joan Baez was one of these musicians who performed many of Dylan's early songs. She furthered Dylan's already rising performance career by inviting him onstage during her concerts, and many credit her with bringing Dylan to his vast level of national and international prominence.

In his career, which spans more than four decades, Dylan has produced 500 songs and more than 40 albums. This king of songs has thirteen songs on *Rolling Stone* magazine's Top 500 Songs of All Time, including his most famous song, "Like a Rolling Stone," which tops the list. In 2004, Bob Dylan was ranked second in *Rolling Stone* magazine's 100 Greatest Artists of All Time, surpassed only by the Beatles.

In a recent television interview, Bob Dylan was asked why he became a musician. He replied that from a very early age, he knew it was his destiny to become a music legend. Certainly, that destiny has been realized!

1. Which of the following best states the main idea of the passage?

   (A) The beginning of Bob Dylan's music career is similar to the beginnings of the careers of most other musicians.

   (B) It is extremely important to follow your dreams.

   (C) Bob Dylan never really knew what he wanted to be in life.

   (D) Bob Dylan had great success despite his unusual style of singing.

   (E) People hated hearing Bob Dylan sing his own songs.

2. The word "prominence" at the end of the third paragraph most nearly means

   (A) perception
   (B) status
   (C) obviousness
   (D) protrusion
   (E) failure

3. The passage most strongly supports which of the following statements about Joan Baez?

   (A) She was jealous of Bob Dylan's superior vocal training.
   (B) She grew up in Minnesota.
   (C) She has performed more of Bob Dylan's songs than of her own.
   (D) She was destined to become a music legend.
   (E) She was a struggling, undiscovered artist.

4. The phrase "king of songs" near the beginning of the fourth paragraph refers to

   (A) Bob Dylan's prolific nature as a singer/songwriter
   (B) Bob Dylan's ownership of *Rolling Stone* magazine
   (C) how most musicians regarded Bob Dylan as a king
   (D) Bob Dylan's perception of himself
   (E) how no other artist has ever made so many songs

5. Which of the following is best supported by the passage?

   (A) Bob Dylan has two brothers.
   (B) Bob Dylan was reviewed by Columbia Records his first year in New York.
   (C) "Like a Rolling Stone" is considered by some to be the best song of all time.
   (D) Without Joan Baez, Bob Dylan would never have succeeded.
   (E) Bob Dylan beat the Beatles to become the greatest artist of all time.

When You Are Done
Check your answers in Chapter 10.

PRACTICE DRILL 27—ALL READING TECHNIQUES—UPPER LEVEL

It is easy to lose patience with science today. The questions are pressing: How dangerous is dioxin? What about low-level radiation? When will that monstrous earthquake strike California? And why can't we predict weather better? But the evidence is often described as "inconclusive," forcing scientists to base their points of view almost as much on intuition as on science.

When historians and philosophers of science listen to these questions, some conclude that science may be incapable of solving all these problems any time soon. Many questions seem to defy the scientific method, an approach that works best when it examines straightforward relationships: If something is done to variable A, what happens to variable B? Such procedures can, of course, be very difficult in their own ways, but for experiments, they are effective.

With the aid of Newton's laws of gravitational attraction, for instance, ground controllers can predict the path of a planetary probe—or satellite—with incredible accuracy. They do this by calculating the gravitational tugs from each of the passing planets until the probe speeds beyond the edge of the solar system. A much more difficult task is to calculate what happens when two or three such tugs pull on the probe at the same time. The unknowns can grow into riddles that are impossible to solve. Because of the turbulent and changing state of the earth's atmosphere, for instance, scientists have struggled for centuries to predict the weather with precision.

This spectrum of questions—from simple problems to those impossibly complex—has resulted in nicknames for various fields of study. "Hard" sciences, such as astronomy and chemistry, are said to yield precise answers, whereas "soft" sciences, such as sociology and economics, admit a great degree of uncertainty.

1. Which of the following best tells what this passage is about?

    (A) How the large variety of factors scientists deal with makes absolute scientific accuracy impossible

    (B) How Newton solved the problem of accuracy and science

    (C) How "hard" science is more important than "soft" science

    (D) Why historians do not study astronomy

    (E) Why science now uses less and less conclusive evidence

2. According to the passage, it can be inferred that the scientific method would work best in which of the following situations?

(A) Predicting public reactions to a set of policy decisions

(B) Identifying the factors that will predict a California earthquake

(C) Predicting the amount of corn that an acre will yield when a particular type of fertilizer is used

(D) Determining the dangers of low-level radiation

(E) Calculating how much a cubic centimeter of water will weigh when cooled under controlled conditions

3. The author suggests that accurately predicting the path of a planetary probe is **more** difficult than

(A) forecasting the weather

(B) determining when an earthquake will occur

(C) predicting economic behavior

(D) explaining why people behave the way they do

(E) determining the gravitational influence of one planet

4. According to the passage, "hard" science can be distinguished from "soft" science by which of the following characteristics?

(A) Seeking precise answers to its questions

(B) Identifying important questions that need answers

(C) Making significant contributions to human welfare

(D) Creating debates about unresolved issues

(E) Formulating theories to explain certain phenomena

5. The author implies that when confronted with complex questions, scientists base their opinions

(A) on theoretical foundations

(B) more on intuition than on science

(C) on science and intuition, in varying degrees

(D) on observations and past experience

(E) on experimental procedures

When You Are Done
Check your answers in Chapter 10.

Chapter 10
Answer Key to
SSAT Drills

SSAT MATH

Practice Drill 1—Multiple Choice

1. D
2. D
3. D
4. B
5. B
6. C
7. D
8. C
9. B
10. C
11. D
12. A
13. D Did you use the Bowtie? If so, look for an easier way to combine: $\frac{1}{2}+\frac{1}{2}=1$, and $\frac{2}{3}+\frac{1}{3}=1$, etc.
14. D
15. C

Practice Drill 2—Multiple Choice—Upper Level Only

1. B
2. D
3. B
4. B
5. D
6. D Be careful. Answer (A) is a partial answer. Read carefully.
7. B Be careful of choosing answer choice (E).
8. D
9. A
10. C
11. C
12. A
13. A
14. A
15. C
16. C
17. A
18. A
19. D
20. C
21. C
22. A
23. C
24. A
25. B
26. C Try to use the answer choices and work backward.
27. D
28. B
29. D
30. D Break up the small sides so they add up to 10 and 15. Add it all up to get 50. (E) is a trap!
31. C You can put in values for w, x, y, and z, as long as the sum of the angles of each triangle is 180.
32. D If you move the piece on the left back into the empty space on the right, you get a complete rectangle. The length is 8 and the width is 11, so the area is $8 \times 11 = 88$.
33. B The area of the shaded region is the area of the square minus the area of the circle, or $16 - 4\pi$.
34. E Make a right triangle. Then use the Pythagorean theorem to solve: $6^2 + 8^2 = 10^2$.

Practice Drill 3—Ratios

1. A
2. C
3. C
4. C
5. C
6. C

Practice Drill 4—Averages

1. A   Be careful of choosing answer choice (B).
2. D
3. B
4. A
5. A

Practice Drill 5—Percent Change

1. E
2. C

Practice Drill 6—Plugging In

1. E
2. D
3. D
4. E
5. C   Try drawing a pie with 8 slices and crossing them off as Miguel eats them.
6. B
7. C
8. C

Practice Drill 7—Plugging In the Answers

1. C
2. E
3. C
4. B
5. D

Practice Drill 8—Functions

1. B
2. C
3. D
4. D
5. A

Practice Drill 9—Charts and Graphs

1. E
2. D
3. E   Did you choose (A)? Be careful. The numbers in the chart are in the thousands.
4. D
5. B
6. E
7. B
8. C

Practice Drill 10—Upper Level Only

1. B
2. B
3. D
4. D
5. E
6. C
7. C
8. B
9. B
10. A
11. C
12. B
13. B
14. B
15. D
16. C
17. B

Math Review

1. Yes

2. It is neither positive nor negative

3. Addition

4. Multiplication

5. The quotient

6. Yes; No

7. Exponents

8. Yes; No

9. No; Yes

10. Zero

11. Two

12. $2 \times 2 \times 2 = 8$

13. Over 100 ($\frac{x}{100}$)

14. Multiplication

15. Total

16. Average pie

17. Plug in a number

18. Add; all four

19. Multiply; two (or square one side, since the sides of a square are the same)

20. 180

21. 3; 180

22. 360

23. 2; equilateral

24. Hypotenuse; right angle

25. Area (of a triangle) = $\frac{1}{2}$ base × height

SSAT VERBAL

Review—The Verbal Plan

Pacing and Verbal Strategy

Your answers should be similar to the following:

(Answers will vary. Look at Chapter 6 to answer the first question.)

(Answers will vary. Look at Chapter 6 to answer the second question.)

I will start on question number 31, so that I begin with analogies.

I will do the verbal questions in the following order:

1. Analogies with words I know
2. Analogies with words I sort of know
3. Synonyms with words I know
4. Synonyms with words I sort of know
5. Analogies with words I don't know

I only need to eliminate *one* answer to guess.

No, I cannot eliminate answer choices that contain words I do not know.

Analogies

Practice Drill 1—Making Sentences

You can abbreviate your sentences as we have done below, using one letter to stand for each stem word. Your sentences should be similar to these.

1. A chapter is a section of a book.
2. A scale is used to measure weight.
3. Striped means having lines.
4. Rage is a very strong anger.
5. Rehearsal is practice for a performance.
6. A mechanic fixes a car.
7. A traitor betrays a country.
8. Aggravate means to make a problem worse.
9. A trout is a type of fish.
10. A general leads an army.
11. Crime occurs when someone breaks the law.
12. A buckle fastens a belt.
13. Truculent means prone to a fight.
14. A cure gets rid of illness.
15. A poison is something toxic.
16. A pinnacle is the top of a mountain.
17. Perilous means lacking safety.
18. A humanitarian practices philanthropy.
19. Notorious means having a bad reputation.
20. A miser is a person without generosity.

Practice Drill 2—Easy Analogy Techniques

1. C A chapter is a section of a book.
2. D A refrigerator is used to cool.
3. B A fish uses a fin to move itself. (Get specific!)
4. A A driver operates/steers a car. (Picture it. Get specific!)
5. E A clock is used to measure time.
6. A An envelope contains/transports a letter. (Watch out for answer E; it's close but not the best.)
7. A A librarian is the person in charge of a library.
8. C A pen is used to write.
9. C A hurricane is a very, very strong breeze.
10. A A ball is a three-dimensional circle. (Answer B is wrong because the words are reversed.)
11. D A shell is on the outside of an egg.
12. B A cup is a smaller unit of measure than a quart.
13. A A coach leads a team.
14. C A bat is a type of flying mammal. (Get specific!)
15. B Famished means very hungry.
16. C To sterilize means to get rid of germs.
17. D A director directs/leads actors.
18. B An applicant wants to be hired. An applicant wants someone to hire him or her. (Think about who's doing what!)
19. B Stale is what bread becomes when it gets old.
20. C Unbiased means without prejudice.

Practice Drill 3—Weird Analogy Techniques

1. C Despair happens when someone is very sad, and obsession occurs when someone is very interested.
2. E Can means something is possible, and must means something is required.
3. B Wine is made from grapes, and paper is made from trees.
4. B There are two months between August and November.

Practice Drill 4—Working Backward

1. A or B because a castle is surrounded by a moat and a galaxy is a group of stars
2. B because a monarchy is ruled by a sovereign (Answer E is okay, but do thieves always practice duplicity? Not really—just thievery.)
3. B because submissive means lacking defiance
4. B or C because quarantine means to isolate a patient and elect means to choose a politician
5. D because bland means lacking zest

Practice Drill 5—Judging "Side of the Fence"

1. D
2. D
3. S
4. D
5. D
6. S
7. D
8. S
9. S
10. D
11. S
12. D

Practice Drill 6—Using "Side of the Fence"

1. A
2. A or C
3. A or D
4. A or B
5. C or D
6. B, C, or E
7. A, B, C, or E
8. A or B
9. A, D, or E
10. A, B, or E

Practice Drill 7—Working Backward as Much as You Can

1. A tooth is used for chewing.
2. Eliminate
3. An archipelago is a group of islands.
4. Eliminate
5. Eliminate
6. To jest means to try to be humorous.
7. Eliminate

Review—The Analogies Plan

Your answers should be similar to the following:

If I know the words, then I make a sentence.

A sentence is good if it's specific and definitional.

If my sentence eliminates some but not all answer choices, I can make another, more specific, sentence.

A specific, definitional sentence uses words that are descriptive.

Some questions that can help me make a sentence are as follows:

- What does A/B do?
- What does A/B mean?
- How does A/B work?
- What does A/B look like?
- How is A/B used?
- Where is A/B found?
- How do A and B compare?
- How are A and B associated?

(A and B are the first two words in the analogy.)

If I know the words but can't make a sentence, then I ask myself the following:

- Are A and B synonyms?
- Do A and B have something in common?
- Are A and B members of the same group?
- What kind of sequence or pattern are A and B in?
- Do A and B rhyme?
- Do A and B have rearranged letters?

And finally, if none of these questions works with A and B (the first two words in the analogy), then I ask myself the following:

- Can I make a definitional sentence with A and C? (C is the third word in the analogy.)

If I know one of the words, then I work backward, which means that I make a sentence with each answer choice, and then I try using that sentence with the stem words (the first two words in the analogy).

If I sort of know the words, then I use "Side of the Fence."

I can also work backward.

If I don't know the words, I circle the question in the test booklet and skip it.

If I have time left, then I go back and work backward as much as I can.

Practice Drill 8—All Analogies Techniques

1. C Chocolate is a type of candy.
2. A A pound is a unit that measures weight.
3. A A class is made up of students.
4. C A composer creates a symphony. (Answer E is not as good because a writer creates a paragraph, but a paragraph is not a large, complete work.)
5. E Many links make up a chain.
6. E A tadpole is a young form of a frog.
7. E A cuff is the part of a shirt that is at the wrist. (B and D are close but not specific!)
8. A A congregation consists of worshippers.
9. B Tactile means sensed by touch.
10. B A conviction is a strong opinion.
11. C A caricature is an exaggerated drawing. (Answer B is not as good because it is not as specific.)
12. B A clap is a sound made by a hand, and a stomp is a sound made by a foot (A:C/B:D definitional relationship).
13. B Deceleration means that speed is decreasing.
14. D Dull and insipid mean the same thing, and diverting and entertaining mean the same thing (synonyms).
15. A Voracious means wanting a lot of food.
16. E Adroit means deft of/skilled in motion. (Answer C is close, but answer E is better.)
17. E An anesthetic dulls pain.
18. A An oven is used by a baker, and a kiln is used by a potter (A:C/B:D definitional relationship).
19. B Impeccable means far beyond adequate.
20. C Symmetrical means balanced, and amorphous means unshaped. (A:C/B:D synonyms)

SYNONYMS

Practice Drill 9—Write Your Own Definition

Possible definitions

1. Weird
2. Introduction
3. Giving
4. Doing the right thing
5. Change
6. Circle around
7. Optimistic
8. Stick around
9. Help
10. Build
11. Bend down
12. Honest
13. Tease
14. Rough
15. Self-centered
16. Calm
17. Use
18. Full of life
19. Stretch out
20. Help

Practice Drill 10—Write Another Definition

Look up these seven words in a dictionary to see how many different meanings they can have.

Practice Drill 11—Easy Synonym Techniques

1. C
2. A
3. C
4. D
5. E
6. D
7. B
8. C
9. E
10. A

11. C
12. B
13. E
14. B
15. A
16. C
17. E
18. C
19. B
20. C

Practice Drill 12—Making Your Own Context

Answers will vary. Possible contexts:

1. Common cold; common man
2. Competent to stand trial
3. Abridged dictionary
4. Untimely demise; untimely remark
5. Homogenized milk

6. Juvenile delinquent; delinquent payments
7. Inalienable rights
8. Paltry sum
9. Auspicious beginning; auspicious occasion
10. Prodigal son

Practice Drill 13—Using Your Own Context

1. C
2. D
3. D
4. D
5. A

6. B
7. C
8. A
9. D
10. A

Practice Drill 14—Decide Positive/Negative

1. –
2. –
3. –
4. +
5. –

6. +
7. –
8. +
9. +
10. –

Practice Drill 15—Use Positive/Negative

Answers remaining should be

1. B E
2. A B E
3. A C
4. C D E
5. A B D E
6. C D
7. B D
8. B D
9. B E
10. A C D
11. A B
12. A B D
13. D
14. A
15. A D
16. A D
17. A B C
18. A B E
19. B C D
20. B C

You should have more answers remaining than are listed above if you encountered words you did not know in the answer choices. Don't eliminate those!

Practice Drill 16—Identifying Parts of Speech

1. Noun or verb
2. Noun
3. Noun or verb
4. Adjective
5. Noun
6. Adjective

Review—The Synonyms Plan

Your answers should be similar to the following:

When I know the stem word, I write down my own definition.

If I don't see a definition close to mine, I write another definition.

When I sort of know the stem word, I can use the following techniques:

- Use my own context.
- Use word parts to put together a definition.
- Use "positive/negative."
- Eliminate wrong parts of speech.

If I've never seen the stem word before, I don't spend time on the question.

No, I cannot eliminate answers that contain words I do not know.

Practice Drill 17—All Synonyms Techniques

1. B		21. C	
2. A		22. B	
3. C		23. B	
4. A		24. E	
5. D		25. E	
6. A		26. D	
7. E		27. C	
8. B		28. C	
9. C		29. D	
10. B		30. E	
11. B		31. B	
12. C		32. B	
13. D		33. B	
14. C		34. D	
15. E		35. E	
16. B		36. C	
17. C		37. C	
18. B		38. D	
19. D		39. B	
20. B		40. E	

READING

Practice Drill 18—Getting Through the Passage

You should have brief labels like the following:

Label for 1st paragraph: Norway → Iceland
Label for 2nd paragraph: Iceland → Greenland
Label for 3rd paragraph: lost
Label for 4th paragraph: saw America; landed Greenland
What? a Viking
So what? found America early
Passage type? history of an event

Practice Drill 19—Answering a General Question

1. D
2. C
3. D

Practice Drill 20—Answering a Specific Question

1. C
2. A   Lead word: Iceland
3. B
4. E   Lead word: Greenland

Practice Drill 21—Eliminating Answers

For a general question

A   Too large—she or he can't do that in a few paragraphs
C   Extreme
D   Extreme
E   Extreme
F   Extreme
H   Too small—this is only a detail

For a general tone/attitude question

J
K
M
O   Still too extreme, even though it's positive!
P
Q
S
T   Why would anyone write about something he/she doesn't care about?

For a specific question

U   Extreme
V   Extreme
X   Extreme and against common sense

Review—The Reading Plan

Your answers should be similar to the following:

> After I read each paragraph, I label it.
> After I read an entire passage, I ask myself: What? So what?
> I am better at doing these types of passages.

(Answers will vary. You may be better at answering questions related to history passages, science passages, opinion passages, stories, or poems. You may also be better at shorter passages or passages covering topics that you like. Take note of this when you take a practice test.)

The five main types of general questions, and the questions I can ask myself to answer them, are the following:

- Main idea: What was the "What? So what?" for this passage?
- Tone/attitude: How did the author feel about the subject?
- General interpretation: Which answer stays closest to what the author said and how he said it?
- General purpose: Why did the author write this?
- Prediction: How was the passage arranged? What will come next?

To find the answer to a specific question, I can use three clues:

- Paragraph labels
- Line or paragraph reference
- Lead words

If the question says, "In line 22," then I begin reading at approximately line 17.

On a general question, I eliminate answers that are

- Too small
- Not mentioned in the passage
- In contradiction to the passage
- Too big
- Too extreme
- Against common sense

On a specific question, I eliminate answers that are

- Too extreme
- In contradiction to passage details
- Not mentioned in the passage
- Against common sense

When I've got it down to two possible answers, I

- Reread the question
- Look at what makes the two answers different
- Go back to the passage
- Eliminate the answer that is worse

Practice Drill 22—All Reading Techniques—Lower Level

What? Tides

So what? Are caused by the moon

1. A
2. D
3. E
4. C

Practice Drill 23—All Reading Techniques—Lower Level

What? Brooklyn Bridge

So what? There were problems building it

1. D
2. B
3. E
4. A
5. C

Practice Drill 24—All Reading Techniques—All Levels

What? William Levitt

So what? Built homes efficiently

1. C
2. E
3. C
4. E
5. A
6. C

Practice Drill 25—All Reading Techniques—All Levels

What? Etymology

So what? Has many words to explore

1. B
2. C
3. A
4. C
5. B

Practice Drill 26—All Reading Techniques—Upper Level

What? Bob Dylan

So what? Was destined to be a musician

1. D
2. B
3. D
4. A
5. C

Practice Drill 27—All Reading Techniques—Upper Level

What? Science

So what? Doesn't have all the answers

1. A
2. E
3. E
4. A
5. C

Part III
SSAT Practice Tests

HOW TO TAKE A PRACTICE TEST

Here are some reminders for taking your practice test.

- Find a quiet place to take the test where you won't be interrupted or distracted, and make sure you have enough time to take the entire test.

- Time yourself strictly. Use a timer, watch, or stopwatch that will ring, and do not allow yourself to go over time for any section.

- Take a practice test in one sitting, allowing yourself breaks of no more than two minutes between sections.

- Use the attached answer sheets to bubble in your answer choices.

- Each bubble you choose should be filled in thoroughly, and no other marks should be made in the answer area.

- Make sure to double-check that your bubbles are filled in correctly!

Upper Level Practice Test

Be sure each mark *completely* fills the answer space.
Start with number 1 for each new section of the test. You may find more answer spaces than you need.
If so, please leave them blank.

SECTION 1

1 Ⓐ Ⓑ Ⓒ Ⓓ Ⓔ	6 Ⓐ Ⓑ Ⓒ Ⓓ Ⓔ	11 Ⓐ Ⓑ Ⓒ Ⓓ Ⓔ	16 Ⓐ Ⓑ Ⓒ Ⓓ Ⓔ	21 Ⓐ Ⓑ Ⓒ Ⓓ Ⓔ
2 Ⓐ Ⓑ Ⓒ Ⓓ Ⓔ	7 Ⓐ Ⓑ Ⓒ Ⓓ Ⓔ	12 Ⓐ Ⓑ Ⓒ Ⓓ Ⓔ	17 Ⓐ Ⓑ Ⓒ Ⓓ Ⓔ	22 Ⓐ Ⓑ Ⓒ Ⓓ Ⓔ
3 Ⓐ Ⓑ Ⓒ Ⓓ Ⓔ	8 Ⓐ Ⓑ Ⓒ Ⓓ Ⓔ	13 Ⓐ Ⓑ Ⓒ Ⓓ Ⓔ	18 Ⓐ Ⓑ Ⓒ Ⓓ Ⓔ	23 Ⓐ Ⓑ Ⓒ Ⓓ Ⓔ
4 Ⓐ Ⓑ Ⓒ Ⓓ Ⓔ	9 Ⓐ Ⓑ Ⓒ Ⓓ Ⓔ	14 Ⓐ Ⓑ Ⓒ Ⓓ Ⓔ	19 Ⓐ Ⓑ Ⓒ Ⓓ Ⓔ	24 Ⓐ Ⓑ Ⓒ Ⓓ Ⓔ
5 Ⓐ Ⓑ Ⓒ Ⓓ Ⓔ	10 Ⓐ Ⓑ Ⓒ Ⓓ Ⓔ	15 Ⓐ Ⓑ Ⓒ Ⓓ Ⓔ	20 Ⓐ Ⓑ Ⓒ Ⓓ Ⓔ	25 Ⓐ Ⓑ Ⓒ Ⓓ Ⓔ

SECTION 2

1 Ⓐ Ⓑ Ⓒ Ⓓ Ⓔ	9 Ⓐ Ⓑ Ⓒ Ⓓ Ⓔ	17 Ⓐ Ⓑ Ⓒ Ⓓ Ⓔ	25 Ⓐ Ⓑ Ⓒ Ⓓ Ⓔ	33 Ⓐ Ⓑ Ⓒ Ⓓ Ⓔ
2 Ⓐ Ⓑ Ⓒ Ⓓ Ⓔ	10 Ⓐ Ⓑ Ⓒ Ⓓ Ⓔ	18 Ⓐ Ⓑ Ⓒ Ⓓ Ⓔ	26 Ⓐ Ⓑ Ⓒ Ⓓ Ⓔ	34 Ⓐ Ⓑ Ⓒ Ⓓ Ⓔ
3 Ⓐ Ⓑ Ⓒ Ⓓ Ⓔ	11 Ⓐ Ⓑ Ⓒ Ⓓ Ⓔ	19 Ⓐ Ⓑ Ⓒ Ⓓ Ⓔ	27 Ⓐ Ⓑ Ⓒ Ⓓ Ⓔ	35 Ⓐ Ⓑ Ⓒ Ⓓ Ⓔ
4 Ⓐ Ⓑ Ⓒ Ⓓ Ⓔ	12 Ⓐ Ⓑ Ⓒ Ⓓ Ⓔ	20 Ⓐ Ⓑ Ⓒ Ⓓ Ⓔ	28 Ⓐ Ⓑ Ⓒ Ⓓ Ⓔ	36 Ⓐ Ⓑ Ⓒ Ⓓ Ⓔ
5 Ⓐ Ⓑ Ⓒ Ⓓ Ⓔ	13 Ⓐ Ⓑ Ⓒ Ⓓ Ⓔ	21 Ⓐ Ⓑ Ⓒ Ⓓ Ⓔ	29 Ⓐ Ⓑ Ⓒ Ⓓ Ⓔ	37 Ⓐ Ⓑ Ⓒ Ⓓ Ⓔ
6 Ⓐ Ⓑ Ⓒ Ⓓ Ⓔ	14 Ⓐ Ⓑ Ⓒ Ⓓ Ⓔ	22 Ⓐ Ⓑ Ⓒ Ⓓ Ⓔ	30 Ⓐ Ⓑ Ⓒ Ⓓ Ⓔ	38 Ⓐ Ⓑ Ⓒ Ⓓ Ⓔ
7 Ⓐ Ⓑ Ⓒ Ⓓ Ⓔ	15 Ⓐ Ⓑ Ⓒ Ⓓ Ⓔ	23 Ⓐ Ⓑ Ⓒ Ⓓ Ⓔ	31 Ⓐ Ⓑ Ⓒ Ⓓ Ⓔ	39 Ⓐ Ⓑ Ⓒ Ⓓ Ⓔ
8 Ⓐ Ⓑ Ⓒ Ⓓ Ⓔ	16 Ⓐ Ⓑ Ⓒ Ⓓ Ⓔ	24 Ⓐ Ⓑ Ⓒ Ⓓ Ⓔ	32 Ⓐ Ⓑ Ⓒ Ⓓ Ⓔ	40 Ⓐ Ⓑ Ⓒ Ⓓ Ⓔ

SECTION 3

1 Ⓐ Ⓑ Ⓒ Ⓓ Ⓔ	13 Ⓐ Ⓑ Ⓒ Ⓓ Ⓔ	25 Ⓐ Ⓑ Ⓒ Ⓓ Ⓔ	37 Ⓐ Ⓑ Ⓒ Ⓓ Ⓔ	49 Ⓐ Ⓑ Ⓒ Ⓓ Ⓔ
2 Ⓐ Ⓑ Ⓒ Ⓓ Ⓔ	14 Ⓐ Ⓑ Ⓒ Ⓓ Ⓔ	26 Ⓐ Ⓑ Ⓒ Ⓓ Ⓔ	38 Ⓐ Ⓑ Ⓒ Ⓓ Ⓔ	50 Ⓐ Ⓑ Ⓒ Ⓓ Ⓔ
3 Ⓐ Ⓑ Ⓒ Ⓓ Ⓔ	15 Ⓐ Ⓑ Ⓒ Ⓓ Ⓔ	27 Ⓐ Ⓑ Ⓒ Ⓓ Ⓔ	39 Ⓐ Ⓑ Ⓒ Ⓓ Ⓔ	51 Ⓐ Ⓑ Ⓒ Ⓓ Ⓔ
4 Ⓐ Ⓑ Ⓒ Ⓓ Ⓔ	16 Ⓐ Ⓑ Ⓒ Ⓓ Ⓔ	28 Ⓐ Ⓑ Ⓒ Ⓓ Ⓔ	40 Ⓐ Ⓑ Ⓒ Ⓓ Ⓔ	52 Ⓐ Ⓑ Ⓒ Ⓓ Ⓔ
5 Ⓐ Ⓑ Ⓒ Ⓓ Ⓔ	17 Ⓐ Ⓑ Ⓒ Ⓓ Ⓔ	29 Ⓐ Ⓑ Ⓒ Ⓓ Ⓔ	41 Ⓐ Ⓑ Ⓒ Ⓓ Ⓔ	53 Ⓐ Ⓑ Ⓒ Ⓓ Ⓔ
6 Ⓐ Ⓑ Ⓒ Ⓓ Ⓔ	18 Ⓐ Ⓑ Ⓒ Ⓓ Ⓔ	30 Ⓐ Ⓑ Ⓒ Ⓓ Ⓔ	42 Ⓐ Ⓑ Ⓒ Ⓓ Ⓔ	54 Ⓐ Ⓑ Ⓒ Ⓓ Ⓔ
7 Ⓐ Ⓑ Ⓒ Ⓓ Ⓔ	19 Ⓐ Ⓑ Ⓒ Ⓓ Ⓔ	31 Ⓐ Ⓑ Ⓒ Ⓓ Ⓔ	43 Ⓐ Ⓑ Ⓒ Ⓓ Ⓔ	55 Ⓐ Ⓑ Ⓒ Ⓓ Ⓔ
8 Ⓐ Ⓑ Ⓒ Ⓓ Ⓔ	20 Ⓐ Ⓑ Ⓒ Ⓓ Ⓔ	32 Ⓐ Ⓑ Ⓒ Ⓓ Ⓔ	44 Ⓐ Ⓑ Ⓒ Ⓓ Ⓔ	56 Ⓐ Ⓑ Ⓒ Ⓓ Ⓔ
9 Ⓐ Ⓑ Ⓒ Ⓓ Ⓔ	21 Ⓐ Ⓑ Ⓒ Ⓓ Ⓔ	33 Ⓐ Ⓑ Ⓒ Ⓓ Ⓔ	45 Ⓐ Ⓑ Ⓒ Ⓓ Ⓔ	57 Ⓐ Ⓑ Ⓒ Ⓓ Ⓔ
10 Ⓐ Ⓑ Ⓒ Ⓓ Ⓔ	22 Ⓐ Ⓑ Ⓒ Ⓓ Ⓔ	34 Ⓐ Ⓑ Ⓒ Ⓓ Ⓔ	46 Ⓐ Ⓑ Ⓒ Ⓓ Ⓔ	58 Ⓐ Ⓑ Ⓒ Ⓓ Ⓔ
11 Ⓐ Ⓑ Ⓒ Ⓓ Ⓔ	23 Ⓐ Ⓑ Ⓒ Ⓓ Ⓔ	35 Ⓐ Ⓑ Ⓒ Ⓓ Ⓔ	47 Ⓐ Ⓑ Ⓒ Ⓓ Ⓔ	59 Ⓐ Ⓑ Ⓒ Ⓓ Ⓔ
12 Ⓐ Ⓑ Ⓒ Ⓓ Ⓔ	24 Ⓐ Ⓑ Ⓒ Ⓓ Ⓔ	36 Ⓐ Ⓑ Ⓒ Ⓓ Ⓔ	48 Ⓐ Ⓑ Ⓒ Ⓓ Ⓔ	60 Ⓐ Ⓑ Ⓒ Ⓓ Ⓔ

SECTION 4

1 Ⓐ Ⓑ Ⓒ Ⓓ Ⓔ	6 Ⓐ Ⓑ Ⓒ Ⓓ Ⓔ	11 Ⓐ Ⓑ Ⓒ Ⓓ Ⓔ	16 Ⓐ Ⓑ Ⓒ Ⓓ Ⓔ	21 Ⓐ Ⓑ Ⓒ Ⓓ Ⓔ
2 Ⓐ Ⓑ Ⓒ Ⓓ Ⓔ	7 Ⓐ Ⓑ Ⓒ Ⓓ Ⓔ	12 Ⓐ Ⓑ Ⓒ Ⓓ Ⓔ	17 Ⓐ Ⓑ Ⓒ Ⓓ Ⓔ	22 Ⓐ Ⓑ Ⓒ Ⓓ Ⓔ
3 Ⓐ Ⓑ Ⓒ Ⓓ Ⓔ	8 Ⓐ Ⓑ Ⓒ Ⓓ Ⓔ	13 Ⓐ Ⓑ Ⓒ Ⓓ Ⓔ	18 Ⓐ Ⓑ Ⓒ Ⓓ Ⓔ	23 Ⓐ Ⓑ Ⓒ Ⓓ Ⓔ
4 Ⓐ Ⓑ Ⓒ Ⓓ Ⓔ	9 Ⓐ Ⓑ Ⓒ Ⓓ Ⓔ	14 Ⓐ Ⓑ Ⓒ Ⓓ Ⓔ	19 Ⓐ Ⓑ Ⓒ Ⓓ Ⓔ	24 Ⓐ Ⓑ Ⓒ Ⓓ Ⓔ
5 Ⓐ Ⓑ Ⓒ Ⓓ Ⓔ	10 Ⓐ Ⓑ Ⓒ Ⓓ Ⓔ	15 Ⓐ Ⓑ Ⓒ Ⓓ Ⓔ	20 Ⓐ Ⓑ Ⓒ Ⓓ Ⓔ	25 Ⓐ Ⓑ Ⓒ Ⓓ Ⓔ

Lower Level Practice Test

Be sure each mark *completely* fills the answer space.
Start with number 1 for each new section of the test. You may find more answer spaces than you need.
If so, please leave them blank.

SECTION 1

1 Ⓐ Ⓑ Ⓒ Ⓓ Ⓔ	6 Ⓐ Ⓑ Ⓒ Ⓓ Ⓔ	11 Ⓐ Ⓑ Ⓒ Ⓓ Ⓔ	16 Ⓐ Ⓑ Ⓒ Ⓓ Ⓔ	21 Ⓐ Ⓑ Ⓒ Ⓓ Ⓔ
2 Ⓐ Ⓑ Ⓒ Ⓓ Ⓔ	7 Ⓐ Ⓑ Ⓒ Ⓓ Ⓔ	12 Ⓐ Ⓑ Ⓒ Ⓓ Ⓔ	17 Ⓐ Ⓑ Ⓒ Ⓓ Ⓔ	22 Ⓐ Ⓑ Ⓒ Ⓓ Ⓔ
3 Ⓐ Ⓑ Ⓒ Ⓓ Ⓔ	8 Ⓐ Ⓑ Ⓒ Ⓓ Ⓔ	13 Ⓐ Ⓑ Ⓒ Ⓓ Ⓔ	18 Ⓐ Ⓑ Ⓒ Ⓓ Ⓔ	23 Ⓐ Ⓑ Ⓒ Ⓓ Ⓔ
4 Ⓐ Ⓑ Ⓒ Ⓓ Ⓔ	9 Ⓐ Ⓑ Ⓒ Ⓓ Ⓔ	14 Ⓐ Ⓑ Ⓒ Ⓓ Ⓔ	19 Ⓐ Ⓑ Ⓒ Ⓓ Ⓔ	24 Ⓐ Ⓑ Ⓒ Ⓓ Ⓔ
5 Ⓐ Ⓑ Ⓒ Ⓓ Ⓔ	10 Ⓐ Ⓑ Ⓒ Ⓓ Ⓔ	15 Ⓐ Ⓑ Ⓒ Ⓓ Ⓔ	20 Ⓐ Ⓑ Ⓒ Ⓓ Ⓔ	25 Ⓐ Ⓑ Ⓒ Ⓓ Ⓔ

SECTION 2

1 Ⓐ Ⓑ Ⓒ Ⓓ Ⓔ	9 Ⓐ Ⓑ Ⓒ Ⓓ Ⓔ	17 Ⓐ Ⓑ Ⓒ Ⓓ Ⓔ	25 Ⓐ Ⓑ Ⓒ Ⓓ Ⓔ	33 Ⓐ Ⓑ Ⓒ Ⓓ Ⓔ
2 Ⓐ Ⓑ Ⓒ Ⓓ Ⓔ	10 Ⓐ Ⓑ Ⓒ Ⓓ Ⓔ	18 Ⓐ Ⓑ Ⓒ Ⓓ Ⓔ	26 Ⓐ Ⓑ Ⓒ Ⓓ Ⓔ	34 Ⓐ Ⓑ Ⓒ Ⓓ Ⓔ
3 Ⓐ Ⓑ Ⓒ Ⓓ Ⓔ	11 Ⓐ Ⓑ Ⓒ Ⓓ Ⓔ	19 Ⓐ Ⓑ Ⓒ Ⓓ Ⓔ	27 Ⓐ Ⓑ Ⓒ Ⓓ Ⓔ	35 Ⓐ Ⓑ Ⓒ Ⓓ Ⓔ
4 Ⓐ Ⓑ Ⓒ Ⓓ Ⓔ	12 Ⓐ Ⓑ Ⓒ Ⓓ Ⓔ	20 Ⓐ Ⓑ Ⓒ Ⓓ Ⓔ	28 Ⓐ Ⓑ Ⓒ Ⓓ Ⓔ	36 Ⓐ Ⓑ Ⓒ Ⓓ Ⓔ
5 Ⓐ Ⓑ Ⓒ Ⓓ Ⓔ	13 Ⓐ Ⓑ Ⓒ Ⓓ Ⓔ	21 Ⓐ Ⓑ Ⓒ Ⓓ Ⓔ	29 Ⓐ Ⓑ Ⓒ Ⓓ Ⓔ	37 Ⓐ Ⓑ Ⓒ Ⓓ Ⓔ
6 Ⓐ Ⓑ Ⓒ Ⓓ Ⓔ	14 Ⓐ Ⓑ Ⓒ Ⓓ Ⓔ	22 Ⓐ Ⓑ Ⓒ Ⓓ Ⓔ	30 Ⓐ Ⓑ Ⓒ Ⓓ Ⓔ	38 Ⓐ Ⓑ Ⓒ Ⓓ Ⓔ
7 Ⓐ Ⓑ Ⓒ Ⓓ Ⓔ	15 Ⓐ Ⓑ Ⓒ Ⓓ Ⓔ	23 Ⓐ Ⓑ Ⓒ Ⓓ Ⓔ	31 Ⓐ Ⓑ Ⓒ Ⓓ Ⓔ	39 Ⓐ Ⓑ Ⓒ Ⓓ Ⓔ
8 Ⓐ Ⓑ Ⓒ Ⓓ Ⓔ	16 Ⓐ Ⓑ Ⓒ Ⓓ Ⓔ	24 Ⓐ Ⓑ Ⓒ Ⓓ Ⓔ	32 Ⓐ Ⓑ Ⓒ Ⓓ Ⓔ	40 Ⓐ Ⓑ Ⓒ Ⓓ Ⓔ

SECTION 3

1 Ⓐ Ⓑ Ⓒ Ⓓ Ⓔ	13 Ⓐ Ⓑ Ⓒ Ⓓ Ⓔ	25 Ⓐ Ⓑ Ⓒ Ⓓ Ⓔ	37 Ⓐ Ⓑ Ⓒ Ⓓ Ⓔ	49 Ⓐ Ⓑ Ⓒ Ⓓ Ⓔ
2 Ⓐ Ⓑ Ⓒ Ⓓ Ⓔ	14 Ⓐ Ⓑ Ⓒ Ⓓ Ⓔ	26 Ⓐ Ⓑ Ⓒ Ⓓ Ⓔ	38 Ⓐ Ⓑ Ⓒ Ⓓ Ⓔ	50 Ⓐ Ⓑ Ⓒ Ⓓ Ⓔ
3 Ⓐ Ⓑ Ⓒ Ⓓ Ⓔ	15 Ⓐ Ⓑ Ⓒ Ⓓ Ⓔ	27 Ⓐ Ⓑ Ⓒ Ⓓ Ⓔ	39 Ⓐ Ⓑ Ⓒ Ⓓ Ⓔ	51 Ⓐ Ⓑ Ⓒ Ⓓ Ⓔ
4 Ⓐ Ⓑ Ⓒ Ⓓ Ⓔ	16 Ⓐ Ⓑ Ⓒ Ⓓ Ⓔ	28 Ⓐ Ⓑ Ⓒ Ⓓ Ⓔ	40 Ⓐ Ⓑ Ⓒ Ⓓ Ⓔ	52 Ⓐ Ⓑ Ⓒ Ⓓ Ⓔ
5 Ⓐ Ⓑ Ⓒ Ⓓ Ⓔ	17 Ⓐ Ⓑ Ⓒ Ⓓ Ⓔ	29 Ⓐ Ⓑ Ⓒ Ⓓ Ⓔ	41 Ⓐ Ⓑ Ⓒ Ⓓ Ⓔ	53 Ⓐ Ⓑ Ⓒ Ⓓ Ⓔ
6 Ⓐ Ⓑ Ⓒ Ⓓ Ⓔ	18 Ⓐ Ⓑ Ⓒ Ⓓ Ⓔ	30 Ⓐ Ⓑ Ⓒ Ⓓ Ⓔ	42 Ⓐ Ⓑ Ⓒ Ⓓ Ⓔ	54 Ⓐ Ⓑ Ⓒ Ⓓ Ⓔ
7 Ⓐ Ⓑ Ⓒ Ⓓ Ⓔ	19 Ⓐ Ⓑ Ⓒ Ⓓ Ⓔ	31 Ⓐ Ⓑ Ⓒ Ⓓ Ⓔ	43 Ⓐ Ⓑ Ⓒ Ⓓ Ⓔ	55 Ⓐ Ⓑ Ⓒ Ⓓ Ⓔ
8 Ⓐ Ⓑ Ⓒ Ⓓ Ⓔ	20 Ⓐ Ⓑ Ⓒ Ⓓ Ⓔ	32 Ⓐ Ⓑ Ⓒ Ⓓ Ⓔ	44 Ⓐ Ⓑ Ⓒ Ⓓ Ⓔ	56 Ⓐ Ⓑ Ⓒ Ⓓ Ⓔ
9 Ⓐ Ⓑ Ⓒ Ⓓ Ⓔ	21 Ⓐ Ⓑ Ⓒ Ⓓ Ⓔ	33 Ⓐ Ⓑ Ⓒ Ⓓ Ⓔ	45 Ⓐ Ⓑ Ⓒ Ⓓ Ⓔ	57 Ⓐ Ⓑ Ⓒ Ⓓ Ⓔ
10 Ⓐ Ⓑ Ⓒ Ⓓ Ⓔ	22 Ⓐ Ⓑ Ⓒ Ⓓ Ⓔ	34 Ⓐ Ⓑ Ⓒ Ⓓ Ⓔ	46 Ⓐ Ⓑ Ⓒ Ⓓ Ⓔ	58 Ⓐ Ⓑ Ⓒ Ⓓ Ⓔ
11 Ⓐ Ⓑ Ⓒ Ⓓ Ⓔ	23 Ⓐ Ⓑ Ⓒ Ⓓ Ⓔ	35 Ⓐ Ⓑ Ⓒ Ⓓ Ⓔ	47 Ⓐ Ⓑ Ⓒ Ⓓ Ⓔ	59 Ⓐ Ⓑ Ⓒ Ⓓ Ⓔ
12 Ⓐ Ⓑ Ⓒ Ⓓ Ⓔ	24 Ⓐ Ⓑ Ⓒ Ⓓ Ⓔ	36 Ⓐ Ⓑ Ⓒ Ⓓ Ⓔ	48 Ⓐ Ⓑ Ⓒ Ⓓ Ⓔ	60 Ⓐ Ⓑ Ⓒ Ⓓ Ⓔ

SECTION 4

1 Ⓐ Ⓑ Ⓒ Ⓓ Ⓔ	6 Ⓐ Ⓑ Ⓒ Ⓓ Ⓔ	11 Ⓐ Ⓑ Ⓒ Ⓓ Ⓔ	16 Ⓐ Ⓑ Ⓒ Ⓓ Ⓔ	21 Ⓐ Ⓑ Ⓒ Ⓓ Ⓔ
2 Ⓐ Ⓑ Ⓒ Ⓓ Ⓔ	7 Ⓐ Ⓑ Ⓒ Ⓓ Ⓔ	12 Ⓐ Ⓑ Ⓒ Ⓓ Ⓔ	17 Ⓐ Ⓑ Ⓒ Ⓓ Ⓔ	22 Ⓐ Ⓑ Ⓒ Ⓓ Ⓔ
3 Ⓐ Ⓑ Ⓒ Ⓓ Ⓔ	8 Ⓐ Ⓑ Ⓒ Ⓓ Ⓔ	13 Ⓐ Ⓑ Ⓒ Ⓓ Ⓔ	18 Ⓐ Ⓑ Ⓒ Ⓓ Ⓔ	23 Ⓐ Ⓑ Ⓒ Ⓓ Ⓔ
4 Ⓐ Ⓑ Ⓒ Ⓓ Ⓔ	9 Ⓐ Ⓑ Ⓒ Ⓓ Ⓔ	14 Ⓐ Ⓑ Ⓒ Ⓓ Ⓔ	19 Ⓐ Ⓑ Ⓒ Ⓓ Ⓔ	24 Ⓐ Ⓑ Ⓒ Ⓓ Ⓔ
5 Ⓐ Ⓑ Ⓒ Ⓓ Ⓔ	10 Ⓐ Ⓑ Ⓒ Ⓓ Ⓔ	15 Ⓐ Ⓑ Ⓒ Ⓓ Ⓔ	20 Ⓐ Ⓑ Ⓒ Ⓓ Ⓔ	25 Ⓐ Ⓑ Ⓒ Ⓓ Ⓔ

Chapter 11
Upper Level
SSAT Practice Test

Upper Level SSAT
Writing Sample

Time - 25 Minutes
1 Topic

You have 25 minutes to complete a brief writing sample. This writing exercise will not be scored but is used by admission officers to assess your writing skills.

Directions: Read the following topic carefully. Take a few minutes to think about the topic and organize your thoughts before you begin writing. Be sure that your handwriting is legible and that you stay within the lines and margins.

| **Topic:** Imagination is more important than knowledge. | **Assignment:** Do you agree or disagree with the topic statement? Support your position with one or two specific examples from personal experience, the experience of others, current events, history, or literature. |

_____

_____

_____

_____

_____

_____

_____

_____

_____

_____

_____

_____

_____

_____

_____

_____

_____

_____

_____

Upper Level SSAT
Section 1
Time - 30 Minutes
25 Questions

$\boxed{1}$

Following each problem in this section, there are five suggested answers. Work each problem in your head or in the blank space provided at the right of the page. Then look at the five suggested answers and decide which one is best.

Note: Figures that accompany problems in this section are drawn as accurately as possible EXCEPT when it is stated in a specific problem that its figure is not drawn to scale.

Sample Problem:

5,413	(A) 586
$-\underline{4,827}$	(B) 596
	(C) 696
	(D) 1,586 ● Ⓑ Ⓒ Ⓓ Ⓔ
	(E) 1,686

---

1. If $h = 2$, and h, i, and j are consecutive even integers and $h < i < j$, what is $h + i + j$?

    (A) 3
    (B) 5
    (C) 9
    (D) 10
    (E) 12

USE THIS SPACE FOR FIGURING.

---

2. If $x = \dfrac{1}{2} + \dfrac{1}{3} + \dfrac{1}{4}$ and $y = \dfrac{1}{2} + \dfrac{2}{3} + \dfrac{3}{4}$, then $x + y =$

    (A) 3
    (B) 1
    (C) $\dfrac{2}{3}$
    (D) $\dfrac{1}{24}$
    (E) $\dfrac{1}{3}$

$\dfrac{6}{12}$ $\dfrac{4}{12}$ $\dfrac{3}{12}$ $\dfrac{13}{12}$ $\dfrac{23}{12}$ $\dfrac{6}{12}$ $\dfrac{8}{12}$ $\dfrac{9}{12}$

GO ON TO THE NEXT PAGE.

3. If the product of 412.7 and 100 is rounded to the nearest hundred, the answer will be

USE THIS SPACE FOR FIGURING.

   (A) 400
   (B) 4,100
   (C) 4,127
   (D) 41,270
   (E) 41,300

412.7
100
600

4. If $\frac{4}{5}$ of a number is 28, then $\frac{1}{5}$ of that number is

   (A) 4
   (B) 7
   (C) 21
   (D) 35
   (E) 112

5. $14 + 3 \times 7 + (12 \div 2) =$

14 + 3×7 + 6
14 + 21 + 6
35

   (A) 140
   (B) 125
   (C) $65\frac{1}{2}$
   (D) 41
   (E) 20

6. The perimeter of a square with area 100 is

   (A) 10
   (B) 25
   (C) 40
   (D) 100
   (E) 1,000

GO ON TO THE NEXT PAGE.

Questions 7 and 8 refer to the following chart.

Money Raised from Candy Sale

Cost of Candy	$1.00	$5.00	$10.00	$15.00
# Sold	100	25	20	5

Figure 1

7. How much more money was raised by the $10.00 candy than by the $5.00 candy?

    (A) $32
    (B) $50
    (C) $75
    (D) $125
    (E) $200

8. The money raised by the $15.00 candy is approximately what percent of the total money raised from the candy sale?

    (A) 15%
    (B) 20%
    (C) 30%
    (D) 45%
    (E) 50%

9. An art gallery has three collections: modern art, sculpture, and photography. If the 24 items that make up the modern art collection represent 25% of the total number of items in the gallery, then the average number of items in each of the other two collections is

    (A) 8
    (B) 24
    (C) 36
    (D) 96
    (E) 288

GO ON TO THE NEXT PAGE.

10. At Calvin U. Smith Elementary School, the ratio of students to teachers is 9:1. What fractional part of the entire population at the school is teachers?

(A) $\frac{1}{10}$

(B) $\frac{1}{9}$

(C) $\frac{1}{8}$

(D) $\frac{8}{1}$

(E) $\frac{9}{1}$

11. The Ace Delivery Company employs two drivers to make deliveries on a certain Saturday. If Driver A makes d deliveries and Driver B makes $d + 2$ deliveries, then in terms of d, the average number of deliveries made by each driver is

(A) d

(B) $d + 1$

(C) $d + 2$

(D) $\frac{1}{2}d + 2$

(E) $\frac{3}{2}d$

12. Which of the following is equal to w ?

(A) $180 - v$
(B) $180 + v$
(C) 105
(D) 115
(E) $2v$

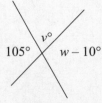

Figure 2

GO ON TO THE NEXT PAGE.

13. Tracy goes to the store and buys only candy bars and cans of soda. She buys 3 times as many candy bars as cans of soda. If she buys a total of 24 items, how many of those items are candy bars?

    (A) 3
    (B) 12
    (C) 18
    (D) 21
    (E) 24

USE THIS SPACE FOR FIGURING.

1

Questions 14-16 refer to the following definition.

For all integers x and y, $x \sim y = \dfrac{xy}{3}$

14. $10 \sim 6 =$

    (A) 4
    (B) 10
    (C) 15
    (D) 18
    (E) 20

15. If $x \sim 4$ is an integer, what is one possible value of x?

    (A) 6
    (B) 7
    (C) 8
    (D) 11
    (E) 13

$$\frac{x(4)}{3} = \cancel{78}$$

16. Which of the following produces the greatest value?

    (A) $6 \sim 4$
    (B) $8 \sim 3$
    (C) $9 \sim 2$
    (D) $-9 \sim -3$
    (E) $-9 \sim -6$

$$\frac{24}{3} \qquad \frac{24}{3} \qquad 27$$

GO ON TO THE NEXT PAGE.

17. *A*, *B*, and *C* are squares. The length of one side of square *A* is 3. The length of one side of square *B* is twice the length of a side of square *A*, and the length of one side of square *C* is twice the length of a side of square *B*. What is the average area of the three squares?

    (A) 21
    (B) 36
    (C) 63
    (D) 84
    (E) 144

USE THIS SPACE FOR FIGURING.

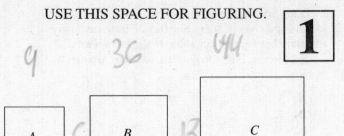

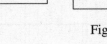

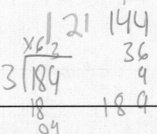

Figure 3

18. There are 12 homes on a certain street. If 4 homes are painted blue, 3 are painted red, and the remaining homes are green, what fractional part of the homes on the street are green?

    (A) 7

    (B) 5

    (C) $\frac{7}{12}$

    (D) $\frac{5}{12}$

    (E) $\frac{1}{12}$

19. Christina is twice as old as Amy, and Amy is five years younger than Kimberly. If Christina is 12, how old will Kimberly be in 15 years?

    (A) 6
    (B) 11
    (C) 15
    (D) 26
    (E) 27

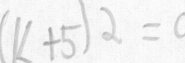

GO ON TO THE NEXT PAGE.

20. If, at a fund-raising dinner, x guests each donate $200 and y guests each donate $300, in terms of x and y, what is the total number of dollars raised?

    (A) $250(x + y)$

    (B) $200x + 300y$

    (C) $250xy$

    (D) $\dfrac{xy}{250}$

    (E) $500xy$

USE THIS SPACE FOR FIGURING.

1

21. A rectangular fish tank with dimensions 2 feet × 3 feet × 4 feet is being filled by a hose that produces 6 cubic feet of water per minute. At this rate, how many minutes will it take to fill the tank?

    (A) 24
    (B) 6
    (C) 4
    (D) 3
    (E) 2

22. With 4 days left in the Mountain Lake Critter Collection Contest, Mary has caught 15 fewer critters than Natalie. If Mary is to win the contest by collecting more critters than Natalie, at least how many critters per day must Mary catch?

    (A) 4
    (B) 5
    (C) 16
    (D) 30
    (E) 46

$x - 15 = y$

GO ON TO THE NEXT PAGE.

23. If $3x - y = 23$ and x is an integer greater than 0, which of the following is NOT a possible value for y?

(A) 9
(B) 7
(C) 4
(D) 1
(E) −2

USE THIS SPACE FOR FIGURING.

1

[handwritten work: 3x − 4 = 23, 3x − −2, 3x + 2 = −23, 3x − 1 = 23, 3x − 9 = 23, 3x − 1 = 33, 3x = 33, 3011]

24. Rectangle *PQRS* has an area of 12. What is its perimeter?

(A) 12
(B) 14
(C) 16
(D) 24
(E) It cannot be determined from the information given.

P   2   *Q*

[rectangle figure, labeled 6 on left side]

R   *S*

Figure 4

25. $30.00 is taken off the price of a dress. If the new price is now 60% of the original price, what was the original price of the dress?

(A) $75.00
(B) $60.00
(C) $50.00
(D) $45.00
(E) $30.00

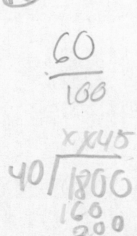

[handwritten work: 30.00 = 40%, 60/100, 60, 30, 18 00, 40 | 1800, 160, 200]

STOP

IF YOU FINISH BEFORE TIME IS CALLED,
YOU MAY CHECK YOUR WORK ON THIS SECTION ONLY.
DO NOT TURN TO ANY OTHER SECTION IN THE TEST.

GO ON TO THE NEXT PAGE.

NO TEST MATERIAL ON THIS PAGE.

Upper Level SSAT
Section 2
Time - 40 Minutes
40 Questions

Read each passage carefully and then answer the questions about it. For each question, decide on the basis of the passage which one of the choices best answers the question.

The reading passages in this test are brief excerpts or adaptations of excerpts from published material. To make the text suitable for testing purposes, we may have, in some cases, altered the style, contents, or point of view of the original.

Florence Nightingale was a woman ahead of her time. Before the nineteenth century, the profession of nursing was largely untrained. Midwives were the only practitioners who had any training at all. For the most part, sick people were looked after by the women of the house in their own homes.

Florence Nightingale began a school in London, England to set the standards for nursing. She was able to do this because she had already established a reputation for her work with soldiers during the Crimean War. She carried a lamp above her head as she walked among the wounded men, thereby earning the nickname "the lady with the lamp." It was this great lady who lit the way for nursing to become the respected profession it is today.

---

1. The passage is mainly about

    (A) the impact of nursing on the soldiers of the Crimean War
    (B) Florence Nightingale and her influence on the profession of nursing
    (C) the difference between nurses and midwives
    (D) how Florence Nightingale earned the nickname "the lady with the lamp"
    (E) why only females entered the profession of nursing

2. Which of the following was a method most people used to receive care before Florence Nightingale's time?

    (A) They would be cared for only by doctors.
    (B) They would be cared for by their children.
    (C) They were largely left uncared for.
    (D) They were cared for by midwives.
    (E) They were cared for by female relatives.

3. The style of the passage is most like that found in a(n)

    (A) personal letter to a trusted friend
    (B) anthology of short biographies of famous women
    (C) history of nineteenth-century England
    (D) textbook on medicine
    (E) editorial written for a daily paper

4. According to the author, the primary reason that Florence Nightingale was able to open a school for nursing was that

    (A) she was already famous for her work in the war
    (B) her family was willing to finance her work
    (C) she had gained notoriety as a difficult woman to challenge
    (D) she had cared for many wealthy sick people herself
    (E) she worked endless hours every night

5. According to the passage, all of the following could be said of nurses EXCEPT

    (A) prior to Florence Nightingale, only midwives were trained
    (B) Florence Nightingale raised the standards of their profession
    (C) they are well-respected professionals today
    (D) they are exceedingly well paid for their work
    (E) prior to Florence Nightingale, their work was done often by female relatives

GO ON TO THE NEXT PAGE.

2

In England during the mid-1600s, a group of poor English farmers led by Gerrard Winstanley united to form an organization known as the True Levelers. Their stated goal was to change the laws regarding real estate and ownable property so that all willing citizens would be able to support themselves through farming. At the time in England, there was great social unrest and food prices were very high. Most of the land throughout the country was strictly divided and controlled by a small number of the elite ruling class. The True Levelers believed that they could "level" the different classes of society by creating communities in which the farmable private land was owned by all and available for agrarian purposes. To fight the unequal system that only benefited the wealthy landowners, the True Levelers defiantly occupied private and public land and began farming.

Because much of farming involves plowing and planting, these groups of communal farmers became better known by the name Diggers. Their hope was that their act of rebellion would stir the sympathies of the other poor people throughout the country. The Digger philosophy was to unite all the poor and working classes behind the idea that the land should be shared. If thousands of common English folk began to claim reasonable access to the land, the powerful landowners would be unable to stop them. In practice for a brief time, Digger communities flourished as they welcomed anyone who wished to merely grow their own food and live freely.

Sadly, the landowners believed the Diggers were a threat and began to take steps to preserve their control over the farmable land. Many members of the Digger communities were harassed, threatened, and jailed. Planting vegetables was viewed as a rebellious act and dealt with as if it were a crime. The majority of land reverted back into the hands of the landowners. Ultimately, most of the Digger communities that had briefly thrived were disbanded. In their place, other political groups arose and continued to protest the various injustices of the time. The Digger name continues to the present day in some English folk songs as a reminder of their ideals.

6. The word "agrarian" is most similar to which of the following?

   (A) Testing
   (B) Private
   (C) Unequal
   (D) Farming
   (E) Aggressive

7. Which of the following can be inferred about the Diggers as described in the passage?

   (A) They had a different political philosophy than the True Levelers.
   (B) They allowed others to join them in their farming activities.
   (C) They were skilled political speakers.
   (C) They defeated the powerful landowners through military force.
   (E) They were exceptional folk singers.

8. Which of the following was the most significant point of conflict between landowners and Diggers?

   (A) The Diggers had the willingness but not the space on which to grow enough food to support themselves.
   (B) Wealthy landowners in England at the time were usually violent.
   (C) There was no agreement between Diggers and True Levelers.
   (D) The quality of vegetables grown by the Diggers was inferior to that produced on wealthy estates.
   (E) The local government did not have any authority in the dispute.

GO ON TO THE NEXT PAGE.

9. The passage is primarily about

  (A) working hard even in challenging times
  (B) social problems in England in the seventeenth century
  (C) the inhumanity of wealthy English landowners
  (D) Gerrard Winstanley's ideas
  (E) the brief history of an English community organization

10. According to the passage, what is the most significant difference between True Levelers and the Diggers?

  (A) The True Levelers believed in farming private land, while the Diggers believed in farming public land.
  (B) The True Levelers followed Gerrard Winstanley, while the Diggers had other leaders.
  (C) There is no difference between the two groups, as the names refer to the same people.
  (D) The True Levelers were accepted by landowners, while the Diggers were jailed.
  (E) The True Levelers are not remembered in folk songs, while the Diggers are.

GO ON TO THE NEXT PAGE.

2

Flax has been raised for many thousands of years, for many different reasons. Probably the two most important reasons are for the fabric made from it and the oil produced from it. The woody stem of the flax plant contains the long, strong fibers that are used to make linen. The seeds are rich in an oil important for its industrial uses.

The people of ancient Egypt, Assyria, and Mesopotamia raised flax for cloth; Egyptian mummies were wrapped in linen. Since the discovery of its drying ability, the oil from flaxseed, called linseed oil, has been used as a drying agent in paints and varnishes.

The best fiber and the best seed cannot be obtained from the same kinds of plant. Fiber flax grows tall and has few branches. It needs a short, cool growing season with plenty of rainfall evenly distributed. Otherwise, the plants become woody and the fiber is rough and dry. On the other hand, seed flax grows well in places that are too dry for fiber flax. The plants are lower to the ground and have more branches.

11. Which of the following would be the best title for the passage?

(A) "How Mummies Were Preserved"
(B) "The Many Uses of the Flax Plant"
(C) "The Difference Between Seeds and Fibers"
(D) "The Types of Plant Life Around the World"
(E) "Ancient Sources of Oil and Linen"

12. The author suggests that ancient people raised flax primarily for

(A) its oil, used to preserve wood
(B) its oil, used as a rich source of nutrient
(C) its fabric, used for their clothes
(D) its fabric, used to wrap their dead
(E) its fabric and oil, for industrial uses

13. This passage sounds as if it were an excerpt from

(A) a letter to the Egyptians
(B) a book on plant life
(C) a scientific treatise
(D) a persuasive essay from an ecologist
(E) a friendly reminder to a politician

14. Which of the following questions is answered by the passage?

(A) Can the same plant be grown for the best fabric and the best oil?
(B) How did the Egyptians wrap their mummies?
(C) What temperature is optimal for growing flax?
(D) How is flax harvested?
(E) Is it possible to produce a new type of flax for fabric and oil production?

15. Which of the following is the author most likely to discuss next?

(A) How flax is used around the world today
(B) Other types of useful plants
(C) Other sources of oil
(D) The usefulness of synthetic fabrics
(E) The advantages of pesticides and crop rotation

GO ON TO THE NEXT PAGE.

2

William, Duke of Normandy, conquered England in 1066. One of the first tasks he undertook as king was the building of a fortress in the city of London. Begun in 1066 and completed several years later by William's son, William Rufus, this structure was called the White Tower.

The Tower of London is not just one building, but an 18-acre complex of buildings. In addition to the White Tower, there are 19 other towers. The Thames River flows by one side of the complex and a large moat, or shallow ditch, surrounds it. Once filled with water, the moat was drained in 1843 and is now covered with grass.

The Tower of London is the city's most popular tourist attraction. A great deal of fascinating history has taken place within its walls. The tower has served as a fortress, royal residence, prison, royal mint, public records office, observatory, military barracks, place of execution, and city zoo.

As recently as 1941, the tower was used as a prison for Adolf Hitler's associate Rudolf Hess. Although it is no longer used as a prison, the tower still houses the crown jewels and a great deal of English history.

16. The primary purpose of this passage is to

(A) discuss the future of the Tower of London
(B) discuss the ramifications of using the Tower as a prison
(C) argue that the Tower is an improper place for crown jewels
(D) describe and discuss the history of the Tower of London
(E) debate the relative merits of the uses of the Tower in the past to the present

17. All of the following were uses for the Tower of London EXCEPT

(A) a place where money was made
(B) a palace for the royals
(C) a place where executions were held
(D) a place of religious pilgrimage
(E) a place where records were stored

18. Which of the following questions is answered by the passage?

(A) What controversy has surrounded the Tower of London?
(B) How much revenue does the Tower generate for England?
(C) In what year did construction on the Tower of London begin?
(D) What is the type of stone used in the Tower of London?
(E) Who was the most famous prisoner in the Tower?

19. When discussing the Tower of London the author's tone could best be described as

(A) bewildered
(B) objective
(C) overly emotional
(D) envious
(E) disdainful

20. Which of the following does the author imply about Rudolph Hess?

(A) He was executed at the Tower of London.
(B) He was one of the last prisoners in the Tower of London.
(C) He died an untimely death.
(D) He was a tourist attraction.
(E) He was respectful of the great Tower of London.

21. The author would most probably agree that

(A) the Tower of London is useful only as a tourist attraction
(B) the Tower of London could never be built today
(C) the Tower of London cannot generate enough revenue to justify its expenses
(D) the Tower of London has a complex history
(E) the prisoners at the Tower were relatively well treated

GO ON TO THE NEXT PAGE.

2

Most art enthusiasts agree that *Mona Lisa* by Leonardo da Vinci is the most famous painting in the world. It is the portrait of a woman, the wife of Francesco del Giocondo, a wealthy Florentine business man. The name roughly translates from Italian to mean "Madam Lisa" and is a respectful term. Anyone who has ever viewed the painting, seasoned art critic or inexperienced museum visitor, remembers well its greatest feature—Mona Lisa's smile. It is this smile that has captured the imagination of the millions of visitors who have seen the painting over the years.

There is something powerful and alluring contained in Mona Lisa's smile that intrigues all who see it. The reason for her smile has long been the subject of discussion in the art world. But perhaps it is the fact that no one knows why she smiles that makes *Mona Lisa* the most famous of all paintings. There is something so appealing and recognizably human about an unexplained smile to which everyone can relate. Furthermore, if we ever tire of analyzing why

Mona Lisa smiles, we can consider how da Vinci managed to capture the smile. What could he have been thinking while painting? A genuine smile is hard to capture even in a photograph with a modern camera, yet Leonardo da Vinci managed to capture this subtle expression in a painting. It is amazing that da Vinci was able to create for eternity a frozen picture of a smile that in reality lasts less than an instant.

The painting now hangs in the Musee du Louvre in Paris, France. Several different owners have possessed it at various times throughout history, including Louis XIV and Napoleon. It was even temporarily in the possession of a former museum employee who stole it in 1911. He was caught in 1913. It is likely that all who held the painting at one time or another wondered about the Mona Lisa smile, just as today's museum visitors do. Now the painting officially belongs to the French government. In some ways, though, it is really a painting (and a mystery) that belongs to the world.

22. Which of the following best expresses the author's attitude toward the painting?

   (A) It should be well protected so that it is not stolen again.
   (B) It is difficult to preserve such old masterpieces.
   (C) Its greatest appeal is the mystery surrounding it.
   (D) There will never be a painter as great as Leonardo da Vinci again.
   (E) Everyone should have a chance to own great art.

23. Which of the following is a fact from the passage?

   (A) A good smile lasts only a few seconds.
   (B) There is tremendous mystery surrounding which painter created *Mona Lisa*.
   (C) Napoleon donated *Mona Lisa* to the Musee du Louvre.
   (D) There has been some focus on Mona Lisa's smile in artistic communities.
   (E) All art historians agree that *Mona Lisa* is the greatest work of art in the world.

24. The author implies which of the following?

   (A) A painting can be owned, but the powerful effect of a work of art is available to everyone who sees it.
   (B) Leonardo da Vinci was hiding a secret that he wished to reveal through his painting.
   (C) *Mona Lisa* has caused much turmoil in the art world due to its peculiar details.
   (D) The Musee du Louvre does not have proper equipment in place for capturing modern criminals.
   (E) The only detail viewers of *Mona Lisa* can later recall is her smile.

25. The author's tone can best be described as

   (A) appreciative
   (B) investigative
   (C) artistic
   (D) confused
   (E) indifferent

GO ON TO THE NEXT PAGE.

2

The first old "horseless carriages" of the 1880s may have been worthy of a snicker or two, but not the cars of today. The progress that has been made over the last one hundred years has been phenomenal. In fact, much progress was made even in the first twenty years—in 1903, cars could travel at 70 miles per hour. The major change from the old cars to today is the expense. Whereas cars were once a luxury that only the very wealthy could afford, today, people of all income levels own cars.

In fact, there are so many cars that if they were to line up end to end, they would touch the moon. Cars are used for everyday transportation for millions of people, for recreation, and for work. Many people's jobs depend on cars—police officers, health care workers, and taxi drivers all rely on automobiles.

One thing that hasn't changed is how cars are powered. The first cars ran on gas and diesel fuel just as the most modern ones do. The newer cars, however, are much more fuel efficient and much research is devoted to saving fuel and finding new sources of energy for cars.

26. The "progress" mentioned in line 2 most likely refers to

   (A) the ability of a car to move forward
   (B) technological advancement
   (C) research
   (D) the new types of fuels available
   (E) the cost of the car

27. Which of the following is answered by the passage?

   (A) What are some ways people use cars?
   (B) Why did people laugh at the "horseless carriage"?
   (C) Where will the fuels of the future come from?
   (D) When will cars become even more efficient?
   (E) How much money is spent on cars today?

28. The passage is primarily concerned with

   (A) the problem of fuel consumption
   (B) the difficulty of driving
   (C) the invention of the car
   (D) the development of the car from the past to now
   (E) the future of automobiles

29. According to the passage, scientists devote much of their research today to

   (A) making cars faster
   (B) making more cars
   (C) making cars more affordable
   (D) making cars more fuel efficient
   (E) making cars that hold more people

30. When discussing the technological advances of the early car, the author's tone could best be described as

   (A) proud
   (B) hesitant
   (C) informative
   (D) pedantic
   (E) sarcastic

31. The author would most likely agree that

   (A) cars are incredibly useful to many different sorts of people
   (B) the problems we face in the future are very important
   (C) cars are more trouble than they are worth
   (D) early car owners were all snobs
   (E) we will never make the same technological advances as we did in the past

GO ON TO THE NEXT PAGE.

> By the rude bridge that arched the flood,
> Their flag to April's breeze unfurled,
> Here once the embattled farmers stood
> And fired the shot heard round the world.
> The foe long since in silence slept;
> Alike the conqueror silent sleeps;
> And Time the ruined bridge has swept
> Down the dark stream which seaward creeps.
> On this green bank, by this soft stream,
> We set to-day a votive stone;
> That memory may their deed redeem,
> When, like our sires, our sons are gone.
> Spirit, that made those heroes dare
> To die, and leave their children free,
> Bid Time and Nature gently spare
>   The shaft we raise to them and thee.
>
> —"Concord Hymn" by Ralph Waldo Emerson

2

32. The statements in lines 3-4 most likely mean

    (A) the narrator is a farmer
    (B) the place described is a battle site
    (C) a crime took place at that site
    (D) the farmers described were all killed
    (E) it is a cold day

33. In the poem, the speaker claims which of the reasons for writing this poem?

    I. To warn future generations about the horrors of war
    II. To keep the memory of the great deeds of soldiers alive
    III. To gain courage to fight himself

    (A) I only
    (B) II only
    (C) II and III only
    (D) I and III only
    (E) I, II, and III

34. The "votive stone" referred to in line 10 probably refers to

    (A) a candle
    (B) a weapon
    (C) an old stone fence
    (D) a war memorial
    (E) a natural landmark

35. With which statement would the author most strongly agree?

    (A) All war is in vain.
    (B) Farming is a difficult life.
    (C) It is important to remember the brave soldiers.
    (D) How a man fights is as important as how he lives his life.
    (E) A memorial is an insignificant way to remember the past.

GO ON TO THE NEXT PAGE.

Jose Ferrer was known as one of the most successful American film actors of his generation, but he actually began his career in theater. He was born January 8, 1909 in Puerto Rico and moved to the United States when he was six years old. His acting skills were first showcased while he attended Princeton University and performed with the Triangle Club, a student acting group whose alumni also include Jimmy Stewart and F. Scott Fitzgerald.

After graduating, Ferrer continued to perform in theater until he made his Broadway debut in 1935 in the play *Charley's Aunt*. He had many successful roles on Broadway, including a role in 1943 when he played the villain Iago in Shakespeare's play Othello. The title role of *Othello* in that production was played by the acclaimed actor Paul Robeson. With these two powerful performers, *Othello* became the longest running play in Broadway history. This record still stands. Ferrer's greatest role, though, was still to come.

In 1946, Ferrer was cast in the title role of *Cyrano de Bergerac*. He won the prestigious Tony award as Cyrano, the tragic hero who fights men with supreme courage but cowardly hides his love for the beautiful Roxanne. His success in this role led directly to his repeated performances as Cyrano in a film version (for which he won an Oscar) and a television version (for which he won an Emmy). He is the only actor to win all three of those special awards for playing the same role. This feat is all the more remarkable because Cyrano de Bergerac was known as a desirable role, one that had been played very well previously by other talented actors.

Through these roles, Ferrer earned a reputation on Broadway as an extremely flexible actor, talented enough to play many diverse roles. Eight years after his debut in professional theater, he finally started performing in movies. Once he began appearing in films, that skill translated into many great performances and memorable roles. His film career included both acting and directing opportunities and lasted nearly forty years.

36. Which of the following is the primary purpose of the passage?

(A) To discuss the success of Puerto Rican actors on Broadway
(B) To suggest that Jose Ferrer was the best actor ever to play Cyrano de Bergerac
(C) To provide a synopsis of the career of a well-regarded American actor
(D) To contrast the history of theater with the history of television
(E) To compare two great Broadway actors, Paul Robeson and Jose Ferrer

37. The author would most likely agree with which of the following?

(A) Ferrer's career was long because he was able to play many different roles.
(B) Ferrer regretted waiting years before he became a screen actor.
(C) Princeton University's Triangle Club allowed Ferrer to learn from Jimmy Stewart and F. Scott Fitzgerald.
(D) Cyrano de Bergerac is the greatest role ever written for the Broadway stage.
(E) Cyrano de Bergerac was Ferrer's favorite role to perform.

GO ON TO THE NEXT PAGE.

38. Which of the following can be inferred from the passage?

    (A) Most members of the Triangle Club have successful acting careers.
    (B) Ferrer was more honored by his Tony award than by his Emmy or Oscar.
    (C) The record-setting run of *Othello* may have been in part due to Paul Robeson.
    (D) Ferrer did not perform again on Broadway after he began performing in movies.
    (E) Ferrer's performance as Cyrano set a record that still stands today.

39. The author would most likely agree with all of the following EXCEPT

    (A) Paul Robeson was seen by some as a very talented actor.
    (B) Ferrer is somewhat responsible for the success of the longest-running Broadway play in history.
    (C) Some actors consider Cyrano de Bergerac a role they would like to perform.
    (D) It is difficult to win prestigious acting awards.
    (E) Ferrer's successful performance in Othello was his first Broadway performance.

40. Which of the following best describes the author's attitude toward Jose Ferrer?

    (A) Indifference
    (B) Envy
    (C) Friendship
    (D) Isolation
    (E) Admiration

STOP

IF YOU FINISH BEFORE TIME IS CALLED,
YOU MAY CHECK YOUR WORK ON THIS SECTION ONLY.
DO NOT TURN TO ANY OTHER SECTION IN THE TEST.

GO ON TO THE NEXT PAGE.

Upper Level SSAT
Section 3
Time - 30 Minutes
60 Questions

This section consists of two different types of questions. There are directions and a sample question for each type.

Each of the following questions consists of one word followed by five words or phrases. You are to select the one word or phrase whose meaning is closest to the word in capital letters.

Sample Question:

CHILLY:
(A) lazy
(B) nice
(C) dry
(D) cold
(E) sunny   Ⓐ Ⓑ Ⓒ ⬤ Ⓔ

---

1. CONTORT:
   (A) bend
   (B) deform
   (C) color
   (D) amuse
   (E) occupy

2. GRIM:
   (A) clean
   (B) relaxing
   (C) frown
   (D) harsh
   (E) irresponsible

3. PROHIBIT:
   (A) attempt
   (B) recount
   (C) diminish
   (D) conserve
   (E) forbid

4. VACANT:
   (A) stark
   (B) varied
   (C) dreary
   (D) rented
   (E) huge

5. AUSTERE:
   (A) plentiful
   (B) ornate
   (C) miserly
   (D) severe
   (E) empty

6. QUELL:
   (A) stifle
   (B) dissemble
   (C) articulate
   (D) rock gently
   (E) praise highly

7. FORTIFY:
   (A) emphasize
   (B) strengthen
   (C) revere
   (D) diffuse
   (E) surround

8. PROCLIVITY:
   (A) efficiency
   (B) tend
   (C) authenticity
   (D) propensity
   (E) proprietary

GO ON TO THE NEXT PAGE.

9. FORMIDABLE:
   - (A) malleable
   - (B) powerful
   - (C) talented
   - (D) fear
   - (E) trainable

10. STYMIE:
    - (A) construct
    - (B) swindle
    - (C) depress
    - (D) frustrate
    - (E) reason

11. ERRATIC:
    - (A) constant
    - (B) amiable
    - (C) innate
    - (D) inconsistent
    - (E) caustic

12. CONCILIATE:
    - (A) pacify
    - (B) replace
    - (C) inform
    - (D) expose
    - (E) surpass

13. REFRACTORY:
    - (A) stubborn
    - (B) excessive
    - (C) ironic
    - (D) inhumane
    - (E) improper

14. TRUNCATE:
    - (A) packed
    - (B) shorten
    - (C) grow
    - (D) remind
    - (E) reproach

15. MEAGER:
    - (A) gullible
    - (B) novel
    - (C) sparse
    - (D) vulnerable
    - (E) providential

16. CREDIBLE:
    - (A) obsolete
    - (B) plausible
    - (C) fabulous
    - (D) mundane
    - (E) superficial

17. CULPABLE:
    - (A) elusive
    - (B) unheralded
    - (C) esoteric
    - (D) worthy of blame
    - (E) sanctioned

18. DEPLORE:
    - (A) rejoice
    - (B) mitigate
    - (C) lament
    - (D) imply
    - (E) prevent

19. ACCLAIM:
    - (A) compliment
    - (B) feast
    - (C) assert
    - (D) blame
    - (E) compose

20. GUILE:
    - (A) vengeance
    - (B) fear
    - (C) trust
    - (D) loathing
    - (E) cunning

GO ON TO THE NEXT PAGE.

21. FALLOW:
    (A) prompt
    (B) unused
    (C) deep
    (D) secondary
    (E) recessive

22. CHAMPION:
    (A) deter
    (B) force
    (C) fight
    (D) side with
    (E) change

23. IMBUE:
    (A) renew
    (B) suffuse
    (C) dawdle
    (D) compete
    (E) impress

24. POSTHUMOUS:
    (A) in the future
    (B) post war
    (C) after death
    (D) during the age of
    (E) promptly

25. INAUSPICIOUS:
    (A) colorless
    (B) prudent
    (C) misplaced
    (D) ominous
    (E) raising intelligent questions

26. RENAISSANCE:
    (A) carnival
    (B) fortune
    (C) burial
    (D) revival
    (E) earlier time

27. DECOMPOSITION:
    (A) combustion
    (B) infiltration
    (C) perturbation
    (D) equalization
    (E) disintegration

28. AGGRANDIZEMENT:
    (A) assessment
    (B) leniency
    (C) restitution
    (D) annulment
    (E) glorification

29. GULLIBLE:
    (A) stranded
    (B) easily deceived
    (C) distant
    (D) assailable
    (E) scheduled

30. REFUTATION:
    (A) attraction
    (B) disproof
    (C) legal activity
    (D) deny
    (E) enthusiastic response

GO ON TO THE NEXT PAGE.

The following questions ask you to find relationships between words. For each question, select the answer choice that best completes the meaning of the sentence.

Sample Question:

> Kitten is to cat as
> (A) fawn is to colt
> (B) puppy is to dog
> (C) cow is to bull
> (D) wolf is to bear
> (E) hen is to rooster

Choice (B) is the best answer because a kitten is a young cat, just as a puppy is a young dog. Of all the answer choices, (B) states a relationship that is most like the relationship between <u>kitten</u> and <u>cat</u>.

31. Composer is to score as
    (A) conductor is to orchestra
    (B) operator is to telephone
    (C) teacher is to classroom
    (D) attorney is to trial
    (E) author is to book

32. Stanza is to poem as
    (A) sonnet is to play
    (B) drama is to theater
    (C) paragraph is to essay
    (D) teacher is to class
    (E) preface is to book

33. Sovereign is to monarchy as principal is to
    (A) school
    (B) administrators
    (C) workers
    (D) crew
    (E) town

34. Cylinder is to can as
    (A) circle is to square
    (B) perimeter is to area
    (C) cube is to dice
    (D) line is to angle
    (E) arc is to sphere

35. Laughter is to joke as
    (A) read is to story
    (B) question is to answer
    (C) wince is to pain
    (D) talk is to conversation
    (E) cramp is to swim

36. Massive is to weight as
    (A) gargantuan is to size
    (B) acute is to hearing
    (C) tender is to feeling
    (D) simple is to thought
    (E) foolish is to idea

37. Pint is to quart as
    (A) cup is to teaspoon
    (B) mile is to road
    (C) measure is to recipe
    (D) week is to year
    (E) temperature is to thermometer

38. Scrawl is to writing as
    (A) decipher is to code
    (B) babble is to speaking
    (C) carve is to stone
    (D) tango is to dancing
    (E) direct is to acting

GO ON TO THE NEXT PAGE.

39. Stoic is to emotion as
    (A) serious is to concern
    (B) soothe is to injury
    (C) amorphous is to shape
    (D) choke is to morsel
    (E) breathe is to life

40. Frugal is to spending as unruly is to
    (A) fractious
    (B) impossible
    (C) obedient
    (D) warmth
    (E) pride

41. Integrity is to honesty as
    (A) comprehension is to instruction
    (B) fame is to happiness
    (C) resolution is to determination
    (D) severity is to compassion
    (E) quotation is to report

42. Lily is to flower as pine is to
    (A) oak
    (B) needle
    (C) forest
    (D) winter
    (E) wood

43. Kitchen is to galley as
    (A) wheel is to car
    (B) fireplace is to heat
    (C) lobby is to apartment
    (D) house is to ship
    (E) exhibit is to museum

44. Blooming is to rose as
    (A) withered is to vine
    (B) prolific is to weed
    (C) fertile is to field
    (D) edible is to corn
    (E) ripe is to tomato

45. Mask is to face as
    (A) coat is to fabric
    (B) shoe is to foot
    (C) belt is to leather
    (D) hem is to skirt
    (E) invitation is to party

46. Agenda is to meeting as
    (A) clipboard is to paper
    (B) rule is to order
    (C) map is to car
    (D) blueprint is to building
    (E) gavel is to podium

47. Pathology is to disease as psychology is to
    (A) mind
    (B) science
    (C) doctor
    (D) anguish
    (E) hospital

48. Autobiography is to author as
    (A) autograph is to signature
    (B) self-sufficiency is to provision
    (C) automation is to worker
    (D) self-portrait is to artist
    (E) autopsy is to doctor

49. Bird is to migration as
    (A) parrot is to imitation
    (B) ranger is to conservation
    (C) bear is to hibernation
    (D) lawyer is to accusation
    (E) traveler is to location

50. Border is to country as
    (A) perimeter is to object
    (B) land is to owner
    (C) road is to street
    (D) area is to volume
    (E) capital is to state

GO ON TO THE NEXT PAGE.

3

51. Patter is to rain as
    (A) rainbow is to storm
    (B) call is to telephone
    (C) clank is to chain
    (D) volume is to radio
    (E) eruption is to volcano

52. Brazen is to tact as
    (A) lethargic is to energy
    (B) agile is to strength
    (C) humongous is to size
    (D) ancient is to time
    (E) fallen is to grace

53. Taciturn is to words as
    (A) thrifty is to money
    (B) petty is to concern
    (C) silly is to extras
    (D) startled is to surprise
    (E) trusting is to care

54. Scalpel is to razor as surgeon is to
    (A) barber
    (B) gardener
    (C) chef
    (D) patient
    (E) engineer

55. Storyteller is to listener as
    (A) accompanist is to composer
    (B) critique is to commentator
    (C) banter is to humorist
    (D) anthologist is to editor
    (E) pantomime is to viewer

56. Gully is to erosion as
    (A) drought is to precipitation
    (B) mine is to excavation
    (C) clot is to dispersion
    (D) forest is to cultivation
    (E) water is to inundation

57. Drip is to deluge as
    (A) shine is to polish
    (B) warm is to heat
    (C) yearn is to wish
    (D) smolder is to blaze
    (E) bend is to straight

58. Lax is to resolution as
    (A) hapless is to circumstance
    (B) detrimental is to destruction
    (C) deceitful is to sincerity
    (D) vulnerable is to wound
    (E) accessible is to rewarded

59. Hammer is to pound as
    (A) vase is to flowers
    (B) briefcase is to papers
    (C) nail is to wood
    (D) screwdriver is to tool
    (E) jack is to raise

60. Lexicon is to words as anthology is to
    (A) reading
    (B) library
    (C) books
    (D) works
    (E) pages

STOP

IF YOU FINISH BEFORE TIME IS CALLED,
YOU MAY CHECK YOUR WORK ON THIS SECTION ONLY.
DO NOT TURN TO ANY OTHER SECTION IN THE TEST.

GO ON TO THE NEXT PAGE.

Upper Level SSAT
Section 4
Time - 30 Minutes
25 Questions

Following each problem in this section, there are five suggested answers. Work each problem in your head or in the blank space provided at the right of the page. Then look at the five suggested answers and decide which one is best.

<u>Note:</u> Figures that accompany problems in this section are drawn as accurately as possible EXCEPT when it is stated in a specific problem that its figure is not drawn to scale.

Sample Problem:

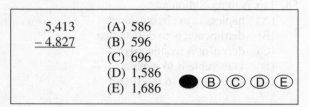

---

1. $2^4 =$

    (A) 24
    (B) 16
    (C) 8
    (D) 6
    (E) 4

USE THIS SPACE FOR FIGURING.

---

2. $x =$

    (A) 30
    (B) 60
    (C) 90
    (D) 120
    (E) 300

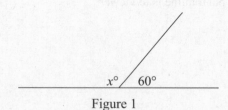

Figure 1

---

3. If $-4 < x < 2$, how many possible integer values
    for x are there?

    (A) 6
    (B) 5
    (C) 4
    (D) 3
    (E) 2

GO ON TO THE NEXT PAGE.

Questions 4-6 refer to the following graph.

Ken's Savings Account Balance, 2004–2007

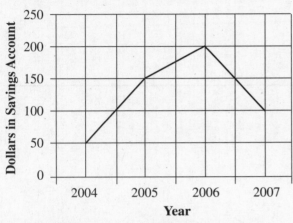

Figure 2

4. By how many dollars did Ken's savings account balance grow from 2004 to 2005?

    (A) $25.00
    (B) $50.00
    (C) $75.00
    (D) $100.00
    (E) $150.00

5. The decrease in Ken's account balance from 2006 to 2007 equals what percent of Ken's account balance at the start of 2005?

    (A) 100%

    (B) 75%

    (C) $66\frac{2}{3}$ %

    (D) 50%

    (E) 25%

6. If during 2007, Ken withdrew from his account one-half the amount he withdrew in 2006, how many dollars would be left in his account at the end of 2007?

    (A) $50
    (B) $75
    (C) $100
    (D) $150
    (E) $200

GO ON TO THE NEXT PAGE.

7. If *M* is an integer that is divisible by both 5 and 4, which of the following is a possible value for *M* ?

(A) 9
(B) 12
(C) 24
(D) 45
(E) 60

8. If $3^x = 9^4$, then $x =$

(A) 2
(B) 4
(C) 8
(D) 12
(E) 16

9. Which of the following fractions is greatest?

(A) $\dfrac{3}{4}$

(B) $\dfrac{5}{8}$

(C) $\dfrac{1}{2}$

(D) $\dfrac{3}{7}$

(E) $\dfrac{5}{9}$

10. If $x + y = z$, then $z =$

(A) 180
(B) 90
(C) 60
(D) 45
(E) 30

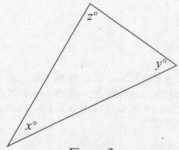

Figure 3

GO ON TO THE NEXT PAGE.

11. Anita bowled a 100, a 120, and an 88 on her first three games. What must her score be on the fourth game to raise her average for the day to a 130 ?

    (A) 80
    (B) 95
    (C) $102\frac{2}{3}$
    (D) 145
    (E) 212

USE THIS SPACE FOR FIGURING.

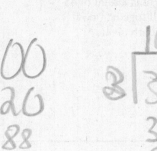

12. $\frac{5}{6}$ is closest in value to which of the following?
    (A) 0.20
    (B) 0.30
    (C) 0.60
    (D) 0.80
    (E) 0.90

13. If 10 rolls of film can be purchased for n dollars, how many rolls can be purchased for m dollars?

    (A) $\frac{10n}{m}$

    (B) $\frac{nm}{10}$

    (C) $\frac{10}{mn}$

    (D) $\frac{m}{10n}$

    (E) $\frac{10m}{n}$

14. All numbers divisible by both 6 and by 15 are also divisible by

    (A) 3
    (B) 7
    (C) 8
    (D) 9
    (E) 10

GO ON TO THE NEXT PAGE.

15. The ratio of rhubarb plants to tomato plants in Jim's garden is 4 to 5. If there is a total of 45 rhubarb and tomato plants all together, how many of these plants are rhubarb plants?

   (A) 4
   (B) 5
   (C) 9
   (D) 20
   (E) 25

USE THIS SPACE FOR FIGURING.

4

16. If m is a positive integer, and if $3 + 16 \div m$ is an integer less than 19, which of the following must be true of m?

   (A) $m = 19$
   (B) m is even
   (C) $m = 16$
   (D) m is a prime number
   (E) m is a multiple of four

17. If an item that is discounted by 20% still costs more than $28.00, the original price of the item must be

   (A) less than $3.50
   (B) less than $7.00
   (C) less than $35.00
   (D) equal to $35.00
   (E) more than $35.00

18. What is the perimeter of triangle *MNO*?

   (A) 3
   (B) 9
   (C) 18
   (D) 27
   (E) It cannot be determined from the information given.

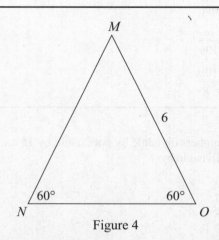

Figure 4

GO ON TO THE NEXT PAGE.

Questions 19 and 20 refer to the following definition.

USE THIS SPACE FOR FIGURING.

For all integers x, $£x = \left(\dfrac{x}{x-1}\right) + 1$

19. $£3 =$

   (A) $1\dfrac{1}{3}$

   (B) 2

   (C) $2\dfrac{1}{2}$

   (D) 4

   (E) 6

20. $\dfrac{1}{2}(£4) =$

   (A) $\dfrac{4}{3}$

   (B) $1\dfrac{1}{6}$

   (C) 2

   (D) $2\dfrac{1}{3}$

   (E) $4\dfrac{2}{3}$

GO ON TO THE NEXT PAGE.

Questions 21 and 22 refer to the following chart.

Number of Patients Seen by Four Doctors During a Certain Week

	Monday	Tuesday	Wednesday	Thursday	Friday	Total
Dr. Adams	6	12	10	0	0	28
Dr. Chou	8	8	0	8	8	32
Dr. Davis	4	0	5	3	4	16
Dr. Rosenthal	0	8	10	6	0	24
Total	18	28	25	17	12	100

Figure 5

21. The number of patients that Dr. Davis saw on Friday represents what percent of the total number of patients she saw during the entire week?

    (A) $33\frac{1}{3}\%$
    (B) 25%
    (C) 10%
    (D) 4%
    (E) It cannot be determined from the information given.

22. Over the entire week, Dr. Adams and Dr. Davis together saw what percent of the total number of patients seen by all four doctors?

    (A) 16%
    (B) 28%
    (C) 44%
    (D) 50%
    (E) 88%

USE THIS SPACE FOR FIGURING.

GO ON TO THE NEXT PAGE.

23. A store sells mints for 50¢ each or $4.80 for a case of 12 mints. The cost per mint is what percent greater when the mints are purchased separately than when purchased in a case?

    (A) 10%
    (B) 20%
    (C) 22%
    (D) 25%
    (E) 30%

USE THIS SPACE FOR FIGURING.

4

24. A certain hen house contains x hens. A farmer puts 12 new hens into the house, and later that day moves one-quarter of the hens out of the hen house. If no other hens are put into or taken from the house, then in terms of x, how many hens are left in the hen house?

    (A) $\dfrac{3x}{4} + 9$

    (B) $x + 4$

    (C) $4x + 12$

    (D) $\dfrac{x + 12}{4}$

    (E) $4x + 48$

25. If the length of one of the legs of a right triangle is decreased by 10%, and the length of the other leg is increased by 20%, then what is the approximate percent change in the area of the triangle?

    (A) 2%
    (B) 8%
    (C) 10%
    (D) 15%
    (E) 18%

STOP

IF YOU FINISH BEFORE TIME IS CALLED,
YOU MAY CHECK YOUR WORK ON THIS SECTION ONLY.
DO NOT TURN TO ANY OTHER SECTION IN THE TEST.

NO TEST MATERIAL ON THIS PAGE.

Chapter 12
Lower Level
SSAT Practice Test

Lower Level SSAT
Writing Sample

Time - 25 Minutes
1 Topic

You have 25 minutes to complete a brief writing sample. This writing exercise will not be scored but is used by admission officers to assess your writing skills.

Directions: Read the following topic carefully. Take a few minutes to think about the topic and organize your thoughts before you begin writing. Be sure that your handwriting is legible and that you stay within the lines and margins.

Topic: Out with the old, in with the new.	**Assignment:** Do you agree or disagree with the topic statement? Support your position with one or two specific examples from personal experience, the experience of others, current events, history, or literature.

_____

_____

_____

_____

_____

_____

_____

_____

_____

_____

_____

_____

_____

_____

_____

_____

_____

_____

_____

Lower Level SSAT
Section 1
Time - 30 Minutes
25 Questions

Following each problem in this section, there are five suggested answers. Work each problem in your head or in the blank space provided at the right of the page. Then look at the five suggested answers and decide which one is best.

<u>Note:</u> Figures that accompany problems in this section are drawn as accurately as possible EXCEPT when it is stated in a specific problem that its figure is not drawn to scale.

Sample Problem:

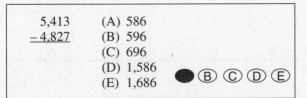

1. Which fraction equals $\frac{2}{3}$?   USE THIS SPACE FOR FIGURING.

    (A) $\frac{3}{2}$

    (B) $\frac{3}{6}$

    (C) $\frac{9}{12}$

    (D) $\frac{8}{12}$

    (E) $\frac{5}{6}$

2. Which of the following is an even positive integer
   that lies between 22 and 27 ?

    (A) 25
    (B) 24
    (C) 22
    (D) 21
    (E) 20

GO ON TO THE NEXT PAGE.

3. In the number 281, the sum of the digits is how much less than the product of the digits?

(A) 16
(B) 11
(C) 10
(D) 5
(E) 4

USE THIS SPACE FOR FIGURING.

4. $(109 - 102) \times 3 - 4^2 =$

(A) 5
(B) 0
(C) −5
(D) −7
(E) −336

5. A concert is held at a stadium that has 25,000 seats. If exactly $\frac{3}{4}$ of the seats were filled, to the nearest thousand, how many people attended the concert?

(A) 10,000
(B) 14,000
(C) 15,000
(D) 19,000
(E) 21,000

6. The perimeter of a square with an area of 81 is

(A) 81
(B) 54
(C) 36
(D) 18
(E) 9

7. If the sum of three consecutive positive integers is 9, what is the middle integer?

(A) 1
(B) 2
(C) 3
(D) 4
(E) 5

GO ON TO THE NEXT PAGE.

8. A number greater than 2 that is a factor of both 20 and 16 is also a factor of which number?
   - (A) 10
   - (B) 14
   - (C) 18
   - (D) 24
   - (E) 30

USE THIS SPACE FOR FIGURING.

1

9. $(2^3)^2 =$
   - (A) 2
   - (B) 2^5
   - (C) 2^6
   - (D) 4^5
   - (E) 4^6

10. If $\frac{1}{2}$ is greater than $\frac{M}{16}$, then M could be
   - (A) 7
   - (B) 8
   - (C) 9
   - (D) 10
   - (E) 32

11. The sum of the lengths of two sides of an equilateral triangle is 4. What is the perimeter of the triangle?
   - (A) 2
   - (B) 4
   - (C) 6
   - (D) 8
   - (E) 12

GO ON TO THE NEXT PAGE.

Questions 12-14 refer to the following chart.

Stacey's Weekly Mileage

Day	Miles Driven
MONDAY	35
TUESDAY	70
WEDNESDAY	50
THURSDAY	105
FRIDAY	35
SATURDAY	35
SUNDAY	20
Total	**350**

Figure 1

USE THIS SPACE FOR FIGURING.

12. What percentage of her total weekly mileage did Stacey drive on Monday?

    (A) 10%
    (B) 20%
    (C) 35%
    (D) 60%
    (E) 90%

13. The number of miles Stacey drove on Thursday is equal to the sum of the miles she drove on which days?

    (A) Monday and Wednesday
    (B) Saturday and Sunday
    (C) Tuesday, Wednesday, and Friday
    (D) Friday, Saturday, and Sunday
    (E) Monday, Friday, and Saturday

14. The number of miles Stacey drove on Sunday is equal to what percent of the number of miles she drove on Wednesday?

    (A) 10%
    (B) 20%
    (C) 40%
    (D) 50%
    (E) 80%

GO ON TO THE NEXT PAGE.

15. If $x = 5$, which of the following is equal to $\dfrac{1}{x}$?

    (A) 10%
    (B) 20%
    (C) 40%
    (D) 2
    (E) 3

USE THIS SPACE FOR FIGURING.

1

16. What is 20% of 25% of 80 ?

    (A) 4
    (B) 5
    (C) 10
    (D) 16
    (E) 20

17. During one week, Roy worked 3 hours on Monday, 5 hours on Tuesday, and 8 hours each day on Saturday and Sunday. The following week Roy worked a total of 40 hours. What was the average number of hours Roy worked each week?

    (A) 32
    (B) 28
    (C) 24
    (D) 12
    (E) 6

18. A box with dimensions $4 \times 8 \times 10$ is equal in volume to a box with dimensions $16 \times g \times 2$. What does g equal?

    (A) 2
    (B) 4
    (C) 8
    (D) 10
    (E) 16

GO ON TO THE NEXT PAGE.

19. Otto wants to buy two tapes that regularly sell for *b* dollars each. The store is having a sale in which the second tape costs half price. If he buys the tapes at this store, what is the overall percent he will save on the price of the two tapes?

    (A) 10%

    (B) 25%

    (C) $33\frac{1}{3}$%

    (D) 50%

    (E) 75%

USE THIS SPACE FOR FIGURING.

1

20. In a certain month Ben eats 8 dinners at Italian restaurants, 4 dinners at Chinese restaurants, and 6 dinners at steakhouses. If these dinners account for all Ben's restaurant visits during the month, what percent of Ben's restaurant meals were at steakhouses?

    (A) 75%

    (B) $66\frac{1}{2}$%

    (C) 50%

    (D) $33\frac{1}{3}$%

    (E) 10%

21. What is the area of the shaded region?

    (A) 48
    (B) 36
    (C) 24
    (D) 12
    (E) It cannot be determined from the information given.

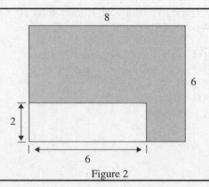

Figure 2

22. In the equation (2 + _ + 3)(2) = 16, what does the _ stand for?

    (A) 3
    (B) 8
    (C) 9
    (D) 10
    (E) 12

GO ON TO THE NEXT PAGE.

23. At Skytop Farm, the ratio of cows to pigs is 16 to 1. Which of the following could be the total number of cows and pigs at the farm?

    (A) 15
    (B) 16
    (C) 32
    (D) 68
    (E) 74

USE THIS SPACE FOR FIGURING.

1

24. Sibyl has seen four more films than Linda has seen. Linda has seen twice as many films as Joel has seen. If Sibyl has seen s films, then in terms of s, which of the following is an expression for the number of films Joel has seen?

    (A) $\dfrac{s}{2} - 2$

    (B) $\dfrac{s}{2} - 4$

    (C) $s - 2$

    (D) $s - 4$

    (E) $\dfrac{8}{s-2}$

Question 25 refers to the following definition.

For all integers x, @ $x = 2x$

25. @3 – @2 =

    (A) @4
    (B) @2
    (C) @1
    (D) @–2
    (E) @–3

STOP

IF YOU FINISH BEFORE TIME IS CALLED,
YOU MAY CHECK YOUR WORK ON THIS SECTION ONLY.
DO NOT TURN TO ANY OTHER SECTION IN THE TEST.

Lower Level SSAT
Section 2
Time - 40 Minutes
40 Questions

2

Read each passage carefully and then answer the questions about it. For each question, decide on the basis of the passage which one of the choices best answers the questions.

> The native inhabitants of the Americas arrived from Asia more than 20,000 years ago. They belonged to numerous tribes and many were skilled hunters, farmers, and fishers. Some of the most famous of the tribes of Native Americans are the Sioux, the Cheyenne, the Iroquois, and the Apache.
>
> These tribes settled and developed organized societies. The settlers to North America from Europe fought the Native Americans for land. Geronimo was the last great Native American chief to organize rebellions against the settlers. He led raids across the southwest and into Mexico. Although he eventually was captured, he later became a celebrity.
>
> After a long battle, the United States government moved the Native Americans onto reservations—special sections of land set aside for them—where many still reside today.

1. The main purpose of this passage is to

    (A) report on the current status of Native Americans
    (B) offer a solution to the problems of Native Americans
    (C) give a brief history of Native Americans
    (D) discuss ways Native Americans are able to work on reservations
    (E) give a history of different Native American tribes

2. According to the passage, the fate of Geronimo was

    (A) to live out his life in disgrace
    (B) to become a great war hero with no defeats
    (C) to become famous throughout the country
    (D) to die penniless and alone
    (E) to commit suicide

3. The author's tone in regard to the fate of Native Americans is

    (A) passionate
    (B) objective
    (C) disappointed
    (D) ambivalent
    (E) envious

4. Which of the following is the author most likely to discuss next?

    (A) Possible causes of Native American resentment
    (B) The life of the Native American in modern society
    (C) The battle that defeated Geronimo
    (D) The differences among tribes
    (E) A detailed history of the Sioux

5. The passage names all the following as skills possessed by Native Americans EXCEPT:

    (A) farming
    (B) hunting
    (C) fishing
    (D) gathering
    (E) fighting

GO ON TO THE NEXT PAGE.

Twenty percent of all the land on Earth consists of deserts. When most people think of deserts, they think of searing heat, big sand dunes, and camels. But not all deserts are huge sand piles—many are strewn with rocks and some, like those at high altitudes, may actually be quite cold.

Desert life is interesting and varied as well. Though the desert is a punishing place—it is difficult to find food and water in the desert—many animals live there. Because there is so little water, desert animals have adapted. Camels can survive for days without drinking. Other animals get their water from the insects and plants they eat.

The extreme temperatures of the desert can make life difficult as well. Many of the mammals there have thick fur to keep out the heat and the cold. Some desert animals are nocturnal, sleeping by day and hunting by night when the air is cooler. It may seem that all deserts are the same, but they are as different as the animals that inhabit them.

6. The passage is primarily about

   (A) deserts and desert wildlife
   (B) nocturnal animals
   (C) plant life of the desert
   (D) sources of water in the desert
   (E) average desert temperatures

7. Which of the following can be inferred as an example of an adaptation to desert life?

   (A) The large claws of the lizard
   (B) The heavy outer shell of the beetle
   (C) The long ears of the hedgehog that give off heat to cool the animal
   (D) The large hood of the cobra that scares off predators
   (E) The quick speed of the mongoose so that it may catch its prey

8. The style of the passage is most like that found in a(n)

   (A) scientific thesis
   (B) general book on desert life
   (C) advanced text on animal adaptations
   (D) diary of a naturalist
   (E) biography of a desert researcher

9. According to the passage, camels are well adapted to desert life because

   (A) they have long legs
   (B) they have thick fur that keeps them cool
   (C) they have large hooded eyes
   (D) they are capable of hunting at night
   (E) they can store water for many days

10. According to the passage, some deserts

   (A) are filled with lush vegetation
   (B) are home to large bodies of water
   (C) actually get a good deal of rainfall
   (D) can be in a cold climate
   (E) are home to large, thriving cities

11. The word "punishing" in line 5 most closely means

   (A) beating
   (B) harsh
   (C) unhappy
   (D) deadly
   (E) fantastic

GO ON TO THE NEXT PAGE.

The original Olympic Games started in Greece more than 2,000 years ago. These games were a religious festival, and, at their height, lasted for five days. Only men could compete, and the sports included running, wrestling, and chariot racing.

Today's Olympic Games are quite a bit different. First, there are two varieties: Winter Olympics and Summer Olympics. They each boast many men and women competing in a multitude of sports, from skiing to gymnastics. They are each held every four years, but not during the same year. They alternate so that there are Olympic Games every two years. The Olympics are no longer held only in one country. They are hosted by different cities around the world. The opening ceremony is a spectacular display, usually incorporating the traditional dances and culture of the host city.

The highlight of the opening ceremony is the lighting of the Olympic flame. Teams of runners carry the torch from Olympia, the site of the ancient Greek games. Although the games have changed greatly throughout the centuries, the spirit of competition is still alive. The flame represents that spirit.

12. The passage is primarily concerned with

(A) justifying the existence of the Olympic Games
(B) explaining all about the games in Ancient Greece
(C) discussing the differences between Winter Olympics and Summer Olympics
(D) comparing the modern Olympic Games to those in Ancient Greece
(E) explaining the process for choosing a host country

13. The author mentions "traditional dances and culture of the host city" in order to

(A) give an example of how the opening ceremony is so spectacular
(B) explain the differences among the different host cities
(C) show that Ancient Greek games were quite boring by contrast
(D) make an analogy to the life of the Ancient Greeks
(E) illustrate the complexity of the modern games

14. The author's tone in the passage can best be described as

(A) disinterested
(B) upbeat
(C) gloating
(D) depressing
(E) fatalistic

15. The lighting of the torch is meant to symbolize

(A) the destruction caused in Ancient Greece
(B) the spirit of Ancient Greek competition
(C) the rousing nature of the games
(D) the heat generated in competition
(E) an eternal flame so that the games will continue forever

16. Which of the following can be inferred from the passage?

(A) Women in ancient Greece did not want to compete in the Olympics.
(B) The Olympics were held every year.
(C) The Olympics used to be held in just one country.
(D) Ice skating is a winter event.
(E) Opening ceremonies today are more spectacular than ones in ancient Greece.

GO ON TO THE NEXT PAGE.

2

Like snakes, lizards, and crocodiles, turtles are reptiles. The earliest fossils recognized as turtles are about 200 million years old and date from the time when dinosaurs roamed Earth. Unbelievably, turtles have changed little in appearance since that time.

There are many different types of turtles in many different climates around the world. In contrast to other reptiles, whose populations are confined largely to the tropics, turtles are most abundant in southeastern North America and southeastern Asia. They live in lakes, ponds, salt marshes, rivers, forests, and even deserts. The sizes of turtles vary. Bog or mud turtles grow no larger than about 4 inches (10 centimeters) long. At the other end of the spectrum is the sea-roving leatherback turtle, which may be more than 6.5 feet (2 meters) in length and weigh more than 1,100 pounds (500 kilograms).

Turtles live longer than most other animals, but reports of turtles living more than a century are questionable. Several kinds, however, have lived more than 50 years in captivity. Even in natural environments, box turtles and slider turtles can reach ages of 20 to 30 years. The ages of some turtles can be estimated by counting the growth rings that form each year on the external bony plates of the shell.

17. The author mentions dinosaurs in the first paragraph to

    (A) illustrate the age of the turtle fossils
    (B) uncover the mystery of turtle origins
    (C) show that turtles may become extinct
    (D) give an example of the type of predator that turtles once faced
    (E) bring the life of the turtle into focus

18. Turtles are different from other reptiles because they

    (A) date back to dinosaur times
    (B) have not adapted to their environment
    (C) live in different climates
    (D) are desert dwellers
    (E) are good pets

19. When the author discusses the theory that turtles may live to be more than 100, the tone can best be described as

    (A) respectful
    (B) ridiculing
    (C) horrified
    (D) interested
    (E) skeptical

20. One of the ways to verify the age of a turtle is to

    (A) measure the turtle
    (B) count the rings on its shell
    (C) examine the physical deterioration of its shell
    (D) weigh the turtle
    (E) subtract its weight from its length

21. The author would most probably agree that

    (A) turtles are more interesting than other reptiles
    (B) there is a lot to be learned about turtles
    (C) turtles live longer than any other animal
    (D) turtles can be very dangerous
    (E) there are no bad turtles

GO ON TO THE NEXT PAGE.

2

> The summer holidays! Those magic words! The mere mention of them used to send shivers of joy rippling over my skin. All my summer holidays, from when I was four years old to when I was seventeen (1920 to 1932), were idyllic. This, I am certain, was because we always went to the same idyllic place, and that place was Norway.
>
> Except for my ancient half-sister and my not-quite-so-ancient half-brother, the rest of us were all pure Norwegian by blood. We all spoke Norwegian and all our relations lived over there. So in a way, going to Norway every summer was like going home.
>
> Even the journey was an event. Do not forget that there were no commercial aeroplanes in those times, so it took us four whole days to complete the trip out and another four days to get home again.

22. The author's goal in writing was to express

(A) his affection for Norway
(B) his dislike of his half-sister and half-brother
(C) dismay at the drudgery of the journey
(D) how different life was back then
(E) his realization that the trip was so long

23. The author uses the word "idyllic" in the first paragraph to mean

(A) scary
(B) pleasant
(C) religious
(D) cold
(E) boring

24. The author uses the analogy that "going to Norway every summer was like going home" to illustrate

(A) how much he dreaded the journey
(B) how frequently they went to Norway
(C) why his half-sister and half-brother were going along
(D) how long they stayed in Norway
(E) how happy and comfortable he was there

25. The author mentions the length of the trip in order to

(A) make the reader sympathetic to his plight
(B) make the reader understand why the trip was an adventure
(C) help the reader visualize the boredom that he faced
(D) give the reader some sympathy for the half-sister and half-brother
(E) help the reader visualize Norway

GO ON TO THE NEXT PAGE.

You may love to walk along the seashore and collect beautiful shells, but do you ever think about whose home that shell was before you found it? That's right, seashells are the home of a whole group of creatures known as shellfish. Some of the most common types of shellfish are the mussel, the clam, and the scallop.

It may surprise you to learn that the shellfish themselves make the shells. They manage to draw calcium carbonate, a mineral, from the water. They use that mineral to build the shell up layer by layer. The shell can grow larger and larger as the shellfish grows in size.

There are two main types of shells. There are those that are a single unit, like a conch's shell, and those that are in two pieces, like a clam's shell. The two-piece shell is called a bivalve, and the two pieces are hinged together, like a door, so that the shell can open and close for feeding.

26. The "home" mentioned in line 2 most likely refers to

(A) the sea
(B) the planet
(C) the places shellfish can be found
(D) the shell
(E) a shelter for fish

27. Which of the following questions is answered by the passage?

(A) How do shellfish reproduce?
(B) How much does the average shellfish weigh?
(C) What is the average life span of a shellfish?
(D) What do shellfish feed on?
(E) How do shellfish make their shells?

28. This passage is primarily concerned with

(A) how shellfish differ from other fish
(B) the life span of shellfish
(C) shellfish and their habitats
(D) a general discussion of shells
(E) the origin of shells

29. The author uses the comparison of the bivalves' hinge to a door in order to

(A) illustrate how the shell opens and closes
(B) explain why the shell is so fragile
(C) give a reason for the shells that are found open
(D) explain the mechanism for how the shells are made
(E) illustrate that shellfish are not so different from other fish

30. What is the best title of the selection?

(A) "A Conch by Any Other Name Would Shell as Sweet"
(B) "Going to the Beach"
(C) "I Can Grow My Own Home!"
(D) "The Prettiest Aquatic Life"
(E) "How to Find Shells"

31. According to the passage, the primary difference between the conch's shell and the clam's shell is that

(A) the conch shell is more valuable than the clam's shell
(B) the conch shell protects better than the clam's shell
(C) the conch shell is more beautiful than the clam's shell
(D) the clam's shell is more difficult for the clam to manufacture than the conch shell is for the conch to manufacture
(E) the conch shell has fewer pieces than the clam shell

GO ON TO THE NEXT PAGE.

2

By day the bat is cousin to the mouse;

He likes the attic of an aging house.

His fingers make a hat about his head.

His pulse-beat is so slow we think him dead.

He loops in crazy figures half the night

Among the trees that face the corner light.

But when he brushes up against a screen,

We are afraid of what our eyes have seen:

For something is amiss or out of place

When mice with wings can wear a human face.

—Theodore Roethke

32. The "hat" referred to in line 3 is meant to refer to

   (A) the attic of the house
   (B) the bat's head
   (C) the bat's wings
   (D) the death of the bat
   (E) the mouse

33. The passage uses which of the following to describe the bat?

   I. The image of a winged mouse
   II. The image of a vampire
   III. The way he flies

   (A) I only
   (B) I and II only
   (C) II and III only
   (D) I and III only
   (E) I, II, and III

34. The author mentions the "crazy figures" in line 5 to refer to

   (A) the comic notion of a mouse with wings
   (B) the pattern of the bat's flight
   (C) the shape of the house
   (D) the reason the bat appears dead
   (E) the trees in the yard

35. The author would most probably agree with which of the following statements?

   (A) Bats are useful animals.
   (B) Bats are related to mice.
   (C) Bats are feared by many.
   (D) Most people have bats in their attic.
   (E) Bats are an uninteresting phenomenon.

GO ON TO THE NEXT PAGE.

Did you ever watch a sport and admire the players' uniforms? Perhaps you play in a sport and know the thrill of putting on your team's uniform. Uniforms are important for many different reasons, whether you are playing a sport or watching one.

If you are playing a sport, you have many reasons to appreciate your uniform. You may notice how different uniforms are for different sports. That's because they are designed to make participation both safe and easy. If you participate in track and field, your uniform is designed to help you run faster and move more easily. If you participate in a sport like boxing or football, your uniform will protect you as well. You may wear special shoes, like sneakers or cleats, to help you run faster or keep you from slipping.

If you watch sports, you can appreciate uniforms as well. Imagine how difficult it would be to tell the players on a field apart without their uniforms. And of course, as sports fans all over the world do, you can show support for the team you favor by wearing the colors of the team's uniform.

36. The primary purpose of the passage is to

   (A) discuss the importance of team spirit
   (B) explain why uniforms are important for safety
   (C) give a general history of uniforms
   (D) help shed light on the controversy surrounding uniforms
   (E) give some reasons why uniforms are useful

37. The "support" mentioned in line 12 most probably means

   (A) nourishment
   (B) salary
   (C) endorsement
   (D) brace
   (E) relief

38. Which of the following best describes the author's attitude toward uniforms?

   (A) Most of them are basically the same.
   (B) They have many different purposes.
   (C) They're most useful as protection against injury.
   (D) They are fun to wear.
   (E) They don't serve any real purpose.

39. According to the passage, people need special uniforms for track and field sports to

   (A) help spectators cheer on the team
   (B) distinguish them from other athletes
   (C) protect against injury
   (D) give them freedom of movement
   (E) prevent them from losing

40. According to the passage, the primary reason that spectators like uniforms is that

   (A) they help them to distinguish teams
   (B) they have such vibrant colors
   (C) they make great souvenirs
   (D) they are collectible
   (E) they are not too expensive

STOP

IF YOU FINISH BEFORE TIME IS CALLED,
YOU MAY CHECK YOUR WORK ON THIS SECTION ONLY.
DO NOT TURN TO ANY OTHER SECTION IN THE TEST.

Lower Level SSAT
Section 3
Time - 30 Minutes
60 Questions

This section consists of two different types of questions. There are directions and a sample question for each type.

Each of the following questions consists of one word followed by five words or phrases. You are to select the one word or phrase whose meaning is closest to the word in capital letters.

Sample Question:

CHILLY:
(A) lazy
(B) nice
(C) dry
(D) cold
(E) sunny   Ⓐ Ⓑ Ⓒ ● Ⓔ

1. OBEDIENT:
   (A) amenable
   (B) excessive
   (C) ironic
   (D) inhumane
   (E) improper

2. CONTAMINATE:
   (A) deodorize
   (B) decongest
   (C) deter
   (D) taint
   (E) defoliate

3. WOEFUL:
   (A) wretched
   (B) bloated
   (C) dim
   (D) animated
   (E) reasonable

4. PRACTICAL:
   (A) difficult to learn
   (B) inferior in quality
   (C) providing great support
   (D) having great usefulness
   (E) feeling great regret

5. SCRUTINIZE:
   (A) examine carefully
   (B) announce publicly
   (C) infer correctly
   (D) decide promptly
   (E) warn swiftly

6. CONFIDE:
   (A) judge
   (B) entrust
   (C) secret
   (D) profess
   (E) confuse

7. INITIATE:
   (A) bring to an end
   (B) sign
   (C) commence
   (D) hinder
   (E) guide

8. FORTUNATE:
   (A) lucky
   (B) wealthy
   (C) intelligent
   (D) poor
   (E) downtrodden

GO ON TO THE NEXT PAGE.

9. CRUMBLE:
   (A) eat
   (B) stumble
   (C) dry out
   (D) small
   (E) deteriorate

10. DESPERATE:
    (A) hungry
    (B) frantic
    (C) delicate
    (D) adaptable
    (E) contaminated

11. FRET:
    (A) listen
    (B) provide
    (C) worry
    (D) require
    (E) stash

12. DISGUISE:
    (A) mystery
    (B) convict
    (C) present
    (D) false front
    (E) pressure

13. ASSIST:
    (A) support
    (B) bring
    (C) distrust
    (D) yearn
    (E) destroy

14. REPRIMAND:
    (A) praise
    (B) insure
    (C) liberate
    (D) chide
    (E) forgive

15. EVADE:
    (A) take from
    (B) blind
    (C) help
    (D) sidestep
    (E) successful

16. FATIGUE:
    (A) grow weary
    (B) become fluid
    (C) increase in height
    (D) recede from view
    (E) improve

17. ANTIDOTE:
    (A) foundation
    (B) vacation
    (C) poison
    (D) learning experience
    (E) antitoxin

18. PROPOSE:
    (A) speak up
    (B) marriage
    (C) fall away
    (D) suggest
    (E) lease

19. INCREDIBLE:
    (A) mundane
    (B) uncivilized
    (C) sophisticated
    (D) believable
    (E) extraordinary

20. VIGILANT:
    (A) observant
    (B) sleepy
    (C) overly anxious
    (D) brutal
    (E) moving

3

GO ON TO THE NEXT PAGE.

3

21. TATTERED:
    (A) unkempt
    (B) neat
    (C) exuberant
    (D) unruly
    (E) pressed

22. PRECEDE:
    (A) stand alongside
    (B) move toward
    (C) come before
    (D) hurl
    (E) beg

23. LAMENT:
    (A) relish
    (B) drench
    (C) moan
    (D) invent
    (E) incline

24. ENGAGE:
    (A) date
    (B) employ
    (C) train
    (D) dismiss
    (E) fear

25. COMPETENT:
    (A) disastrous
    (B) fast
    (C) cautious
    (D) able
    (E) inanimate

26. SINCERE:
    (A) new
    (B) passionate
    (C) expensive
    (D) genuine
    (E) untold

27. RICKETY:
    (A) strong
    (B) wooden
    (C) antique
    (D) beautiful
    (E) feeble

28. CONSPICUOUS:
    (A) plain as day
    (B) identity
    (C) camouflaged
    (D) shiny
    (E) cramped

29. VERSATILE:
    (A) peaceful
    (B) disruptive
    (C) adaptable
    (D) truthful
    (E) charming

30. CORROBORATION:
    (A) attraction
    (B) confirmation
    (C) legal activity
    (D) unfulfilled expectation
    (E) enthusiastic response

GO ON TO THE NEXT PAGE.

The following questions ask you to find relationships between words. For each question, select the answer choice that best completes the meaning of the sentence.

Sample Question:

> Kitten is to cat as
> (A) fawn is to colt
> (B) puppy is to dog
> (C) cow is to bull
> (D) wolf is to bear
> (E) hen is to rooster

Choice (B) is the best answer because a kitten is a young cat, just as a puppy is a young dog.
Of all the answer choices, (B) states a relationship that is most like the relationship between <u>kitten</u> and <u>cat</u>.

---

31. Fish is to water as
    (A) bird is to egg
    (B) roe is to pouch
    (C) lion is to land
    (D) flower is to pollen
    (E) bee is to honey

32. Sick is to healthy as jailed is to
    (A) convicted
    (B) free
    (C) guilty
    (D) trapped
    (E) hurt

33. Dancer is to feet as
    (A) surgeon is to heart
    (B) juggler is to hands
    (C) drummer is to drums
    (D) conductor is to voice
    (E) musician is to eyes

34. Bystander is to event as
    (A) juror is to verdict
    (B) culprit is to crime
    (C) tourist is to journey
    (D) spectator is to game
    (E) model is to portrait

35. Baker is to bread as
    (A) shop is to goods
    (B) butcher is to livestock
    (C) politician is to votes
    (D) sculptor is to statue
    (E) family is to confidence

36. Igneous is to rock as
    (A) stratum is to dig
    (B) fossil is to dinosaur
    (C) computer is to calculator
    (D) watercolor is to painting
    (E) calendar is to date

37. Delicious is to taste as melodious is to
    (A) sound
    (B) movie
    (C) ears
    (D) eyes
    (E) sight

38. Clog is to shoe as
    (A) sneaker is to run
    (B) lace is to tie
    (C) beret is to hat
    (D) shirt is to torso
    (E) sock is to foot

GO ON TO THE NEXT PAGE.

3

39. Cube is to square as
    (A) box is to cardboard
    (B) circle is to street
    (C) cylinder is to pen
    (D) line is to angle
    (E) sphere is to circle

40. Jam is to fruit as
    (A) bread is to toast
    (B) butter is to milk
    (C) crayon is to color
    (D) height is to stone
    (E) write is to pencil

41. Mile is to quart as
    (A) sky is to height
    (B) coffee is to drink
    (C) pot is to stew
    (D) floor is to ground
    (E) length is to volume

42. Biologist is to scientist as surgeon is to
    (A) doctor
    (B) scar
    (C) cut
    (D) heart
    (E) scalpel

43. Clay is to potter as
    (A) sea is to captain
    (B) magazine is to reader
    (C) marble is to sculptor
    (D) word is to teacher
    (E) bubble is to child

44. Clip is to movie as
    (A) buckle is to shoe
    (B) excerpt is to novel
    (C) jar is to liquid
    (D) room is to house
    (E) filling is to pie

45. Ruthless is to mercy as naive is to
    (A) thoughtfulness
    (B) illness
    (C) worldliness
    (D) contempt
    (E) purity

46. Glacier is to ice as
    (A) rain is to snow
    (B) bay is to sea
    (C) cloud is to storm
    (D) ocean is to water
    (E) pond is to fish

47. Glass is to window as
    (A) wood is to building
    (B) car is to motor
    (C) job is to skills
    (D) fabric is to clothing
    (E) loan is to interest

48. Buttress is to support as scissor is to
    (A) press
    (B) store
    (C) create
    (D) cool
    (E) cut

49. Sneer is to disdain as cringe is to
    (A) loneliness
    (B) bravery
    (C) intelligence
    (D) distrust
    (E) fear

50. Library is to book as
    (A) bank is to money
    (B) museum is to patron
    (C) opera is to audience
    (D) restaurant is to waiter
    (E) concert is to music

51. Famine is to food as
    (A) drought is to water
    (B) paper is to print
    (C) legend is to fantasy
    (D) debate is to issue
    (E) clause is to contract

52. Teacher is to student as
    (A) coach is to player
    (B) assistant is to executive
    (C) nurse is to doctor
    (D) patient is to dentist
    (E) theory is to technician

GO ON TO THE NEXT PAGE.

53. Muffle is to noise as
    (A) engine is to bicycle
    (B) wind is to vane
    (C) dam is to flood
    (D) aroma is to fetid
    (E) nibble is to eat

54. Rest is to exhaustion as
    (A) pack is to vacation
    (B) water is to thirst
    (C) audit is to forms
    (D) jury is to trial
    (E) tide is to ocean

55. Playwright is to script as
    (A) choreographer is to dance
    (B) mathematician is to science
    (C) philosopher is to insight
    (D) enemy is to strategy
    (E) athlete is to prowess

56. Gluttony is to food as
    (A) sheer is to wall
    (B) avarice is to money
    (C) enterprise is to earning
    (D) curiosity is to danger
    (E) mystery is to solution

57. Facile is to effort as
    (A) deception is to trick
    (B) helpful is to friend
    (C) inconsiderate is to thought
    (D) pious is to religion
    (E) incompetent is to task

58. Single-handed is to assistance as anonymous is to
    (A) praise
    (B) authorship
    (C) recognition
    (D) sincerity
    (E) ideas

59. Stable is to horse as kennel is to
    (A) farm
    (B) storage
    (C) dog
    (D) groomer
    (E) boarding

60. Tree is to knee as
    (A) pot is to cot
    (B) bam is to lamb
    (C) forest is to body
    (D) bob is to cob
    (E) seek is to leek

3

STOP

IF YOU FINISH BEFORE TIME IS CALLED,
YOU MAY CHECK YOUR WORK ON THIS SECTION ONLY.
DO NOT TURN TO ANY OTHER SECTION IN THE TEST.

GO ON TO THE NEXT PAGE.

Lower Level SSAT
Section 4
Time - 30 Minutes
25 Questions

Following each problem in this section, there are five suggested answers. Work each problem in your head or in the blank space provided at the right of the page. Then look at the five suggested answers and decide which one is best.

Note: Figures that accompany problems in this section are drawn as accurately as possible EXCEPT when it is stated in a specific problem that its figure is not drawn to scale.

Sample Problem:

5,413	(A) 586
− 4,827	(B) 596
	(C) 696
	(D) 1,586
	(E) 1,686 ● Ⓑ Ⓒ Ⓓ Ⓔ

1. Which of the following fractions is greatest?

USE THIS SPACE FOR FIGURING.

(A) $\frac{3}{4}$

(B) $\frac{5}{8}$

(C) $\frac{1}{2}$

(D) $\frac{3}{7}$

(E) $\frac{5}{9}$

2. The sum of the factors of 12 is

(A) 28
(B) 21
(C) 20
(D) 16
(E) 15

GO ON TO THE NEXT PAGE.

3. $16 + 2 \times 3 + 2 =$

   (A) 90
   (B) 56
   (C) 24
   (D) 23
   (E) 18

USE THIS SPACE FOR FIGURING.

4

4. $D + E + F + G =$

   (A) 45
   (B) 90
   (C) 180
   (D) 270
   (E) 360

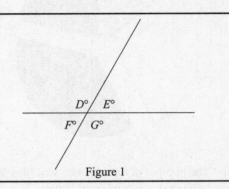

Figure 1

5. What are two different prime factors of 48 ?

   (A) 2 and 3
   (B) 3 and 4
   (C) 4 and 6
   (D) 4 and 12
   (E) 6 and 8

6. The difference between 12 and the product of 4 and 6 is

   (A) 12
   (B) 10
   (C) 2
   (D) 1
   (E) 0

7. The sum of the number of degrees in a straight line and the number of degrees in a triangle equals

   (A) 720
   (B) 540
   (C) 360
   (D) 180
   (E) 90

GO ON TO THE NEXT PAGE.

Questions 8-10 refer to the following graph.

USE THIS SPACE FOR FIGURING.

4

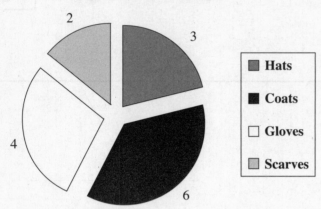

Joseph's Winter Clothing

- **Hats**
- **Coats**
- **Gloves**
- **Scarves**

8. The number of scarves Joe owns plus the number of coats he owns equals

(A) 5
(B) 7
(C) 8
(D) 9
(E) 10

9. Hats represent what percentage of the total number of garments accounted for in the graph?

(A) 10%
(B) 20%
(C) 30%
(D) 50%
(E) 80%

10. Which types of garments represent one-third of the total number of garments accounted for in the graph?

(A) Hats and coats
(B) Gloves and scarves
(C) Hats and scarves
(D) Gloves and coats
(E) Hats, gloves, and scarves

GO ON TO THE NEXT PAGE.

11. George bought five slices of pizza for $10. At this rate, how many slices of pizza could he buy with $32 ?

    (A) 16
    (B) 15
    (C) 14
    (D) 12
    (E) 10

USE THIS SPACE FOR FIGURING.

4

12. On a certain English test, the 10 students in Mrs. Bennett's class score an average of 85. On the same test, 15 students in Mrs. Grover's class score an average of 70. What is the combined average score for all the students in Mrs. Bennett's and Mrs. Grover's classes?

    (A) 80
    (B) 77.5
    (C) 76
    (D) 75
    (E) 72

13. If Mary bought e pencils, Jane bought 5 times as many pencils as Mary, and Peggy bought 2 pencils fewer than Mary, then in terms of e, how many pencils did the three girls buy all together?

    (A) $5e - 2$
    (B) 7
    (C) $7e - 2$
    (D) $8e$
    (E) $8e - 2$

14. $\dfrac{4}{1,000} + \dfrac{3}{10} + 3 =$
    (A) 4,033
    (B) 433
    (C) 334
    (D) 3.34
    (E) 3.304

GO ON TO THE NEXT PAGE.

Questions 15 and 16 refer to the following definition.

$\boxed{}$ **USE THIS SPACE FOR FIGURING.**

4

For all real numbers f, $\boxed{f} = -2f$

15. $\boxed{0}$ =

(A) 4
(B) 2
(C) 0
(D) −2
(E) −4

16. $\boxed{2} \times \boxed{3}$ =

(A) $\boxed{24}$
(B) $\boxed{2}$
(C) $\boxed{3}$
(D) $\boxed{-3}$
(E) $\boxed{-12}$

17. $2\frac{1}{4}\%$ =

(A) 0.0025
(B) 0.0225
(C) 0.225
(D) 2.025
(E) 2.25

18. The area of triangle *UVW* is

(A) $2h^2$
(B) h^2
(C) h
(D) 3
(E) 2

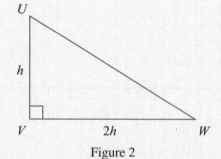

Figure 2

GO ON TO THE NEXT PAGE.

19. 9^4 is equal to which of the following?

(A) $(3) \times (3) \times (3) \times (3)$
(B) $(9) \times (3) \times (9) \times (3)$
(C) $(9) \times (4)$
(D) $(3) \times (3) \times (3) \times (3) \times (3) \times (3) \times (3) \times (3)$
(E) $(9) \times (9) + (9) \times (9)$

20. It costs h cents to make 12 handkerchiefs. At the same rate, how many cents will it cost to make 30 handkerchiefs?

(A) $30h$

(B) $\dfrac{5h}{2}$

(C) $\dfrac{2h}{5}$

(D) $\dfrac{2}{5h}$

(E) $5h$

21. A girl collects rocks. If her collection consists of 12 pieces of halite, 16 pieces of sandstone, 8 pieces of mica, and 8 pieces of galaxite, then the average number of pieces of each type of rock in her collection is

(A) 8
(B) 11
(C) 12
(D) 16
(E) 44

22. A recipe calls for 24 ounces of water for every two ounces of sugar. If 12 ounces of sugar are used, how much water should be added?

(A) 6
(B) 12
(C) 24
(D) 36
(E) 144

GO ON TO THE NEXT PAGE.

23. The number of people now employed by a certain company is 240, which is 60% of the number employed five years ago. How many more employees did the company have five years ago than it has now?

    (A) 160
    (B) 360
    (C) 400
    (D) 720
    (E) 960

$$\begin{array}{r} 1B5 \\ \times\ 15 \\ \hline 2{,}025 \end{array}$$

24. In the multiplication problem above, B represents which digit?

    (A) 1
    (B) 2
    (C) 3
    (D) 5
    (E) 7

25. If the area of each of the smaller squares that make up rectangle *ABCD* is 4, what is the perimeter of rectangle *ABCD* ?

    (A) 220
    (B) 64
    (C) 55
    (D) 32
    (E) 4

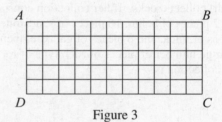

Figure 3

STOP

**IF YOU FINISH BEFORE TIME IS CALLED,
YOU MAY CHECK YOUR WORK ON THIS SECTION ONLY.
DO NOT TURN TO ANY OTHER SECTION IN THE TEST.**

Chapter 13
Answer Key to
SSAT Practice Tests

SSAT UL MATH 1

1. E	4. B	7. C	10. A	13. C	16. E	19. D	22. A	25. A
2. A	5. D	8. A	11. B	14. E	17. C	20. B	23. A
3. E	6. C	9. C	12. D	15. A	18. D	21. C	24. E

SSAT UL READING 2

1. B	5. D	9. E	13. B	17. D	21. D	25. A	29. D	33. B	37. A
2. E	6. D	10. C	14. A	18. C	22. C	26. B	30. C	34. D	38. C
3. B	7. B	11. B	15. A	19. B	23. D	27. A	31. A	35. C	39. E
4. A	8. A	12. D	16. D	20. B	24. A	28. D	32. B	36. C	40. E

SSAT UL VERBAL 3

1. A	7. B	13. A	19. A	25. D	31. E	37. D	43. D	49. C	55. E
2. D	8. D	14. B	20. E	26. D	32. C	38. B	44. E	50. A	56. B
3. E	9. B	15. C	21. B	27. E	33. A	39. C	45. B	51. C	57. D
4. A	10. D	16. B	22. D	28. E	34. C	40. C	46. D	52. A	58. C
5. D	11. D	17. D	23. B	29. B	35. C	41. C	47. A	53. A	59. E
6. A	12. A	18. C	24. C	30. B	36. A	42. E	48. D	54. A	60. D

SSAT UL MATH 4

1. B	4. D	7. E	10. B	13. E	16. B	19. C	22. C	25. B
2. D	5. C	8. C	11. E	14. A	17. E	20. B	23. D
3. B	6. A	9. A	12. D	15. D	18. C	21. B	24. A

SSAT LL MATH 1

1. D	4. A	7. C	10. A	13. E	16. A	19. B	22. A	25. C
2. B	5. D	8. D	11. C	14. C	17. A	20. D	23. D
3. D	6. C	9. C	12. A	15. B	18. D	21. B	24. A

SSAT LL READING 2

1. C	5. D	9. E	13. A	17. A	21. B	25. B	29. A	33. D	37. C
2. C	6. A	10. D	14. B	18. C	22. A	26. D	30. C	34. B	38. B
3. B	7. C	11. B	15. B	19. E	23. B	27. E	31. E	35. C	39. D
4. B	8. B	12. D	16. C	20. B	24. E	28. D	32. C	36. E	40. A

SSAT LL VERBAL 3

1. A	7. C	13. A	19. E	25. D	31. C	37. A	43. C	49. E	55. A
2. D	8. A	14. D	20. A	26. D	32. B	38. C	44. B	50. A	56. B
3. A	9. E	15. D	21. A	27. E	33. B	39. E	45. C	51. A	57. C
4. D	10. B	16. A	22. C	28. A	34. D	40. B	46. D	52. A	58. C
5. A	11. C	17. E	23. C	29. C	35. D	41. E	47. D	53. C	59. C
6. B	12. D	18. D	24. B	30. B	36. D	42. A	48. E	54. B	60. C

SSAT LL MATH 4

1. A	4. E	7. C	10. C	13. C	16. E	19. D	22. E	25. B
2. A	5. A	8. C	11. A	14. E	17. B	20. B	23. A
3. C	6. A	9. B	12. C	15. C	18. B	21. B	24. C

Chapter 14
Scoring Your
Practice SSAT

CHECK YOUR ANSWERS

Use the Answer Key to determine how many questions you answered correctly and how many you answered incorrectly. You may want to check your numbers by adding together your number of correct answers, your number of incorrect answers, and the number of questions you left blank. Make sure this total matches the total number of questions in the section.

Compute Your Raw Score

To compute your raw score, fill in the chart below. Your raw score equals the number of questions you answered correctly, minus one-fourth of the number of questions you answered incorrectly (the random-guessing penalty).

VERBAL: $\underline{}$ $-(\frac{1}{4} \times \underline{}) = \underline{}$
Right Answers   Wrong Answers   Raw Score

MATH: $\underline{}$ $-(\frac{1}{4} \times \underline{}) = \underline{}$
Right Answers   Wrong Answers   Raw Score

READING: $\underline{}$ $-(\frac{1}{4} \times \underline{}) = \underline{}$
Right Answers   Wrong Answers   Raw Score

Find Your Raw Score on the Conversion Chart

On the following pages you will find a conversion chart for both the Upper Level and Lower Level tests. Make sure you use the chart that corresponds to the test you took. Look in the appropriate column on the left to find your raw score and then read across to find your scaled score. This will give you your scaled score for each test section: Verbal, Quantitative, and Reading. (In other words, you'll have three separate scores.)

Keep in mind that these raw, scaled, and percentile scores are all rough estimates of how you will do on the actual SSAT. Actual exam scores are adjusted to account for the difficulty of each form of the test.

What About the Overall Score?

In addition to scores in each of the three sections—Verbal, Quantitative (math), and Reading—you will also receive an overall score, which is the sum of these three scores.

SSAT UPPER LEVEL SCORE CONVERSION CHART

Raw Score	Reading	Verbal	Quantitative
60	–	800	–
55	–	800	–
50	–	779	800
45	–	752	782
40	800	725	755
35	722	698	725
30	692	671	698
25	662	644	668
20	632	617	641
15	602	590	614
10	572	563	584
5	542	533	557
0	512	506	530
–5 and lower	500	500	500

SSAT LOWER LEVEL SCORE CONVERSION CHART

Raw Score	Reading	Verbal	Quantitative
60	–	710	–
55	–	710	–
50	–	710	704
45	–	698	680
40	710	674	659
35	686	650	635
30	656	626	614
25	626	602	593
20	596	578	569
15	566	554	540
10	536	530	527
5	506	506	503
0	476	482	482
–5	446	458	458
–10 and lower	440	440	440

SSAT NOTES

SSAT NOTES

SSAT NOTES

SSAT NOTES

SSAT NOTES

SSAT NOTES

Part IV
The ISEE

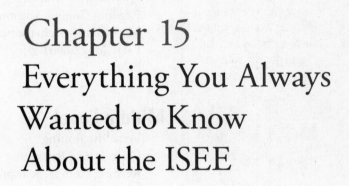

Chapter 15
Everything You Always
Wanted to Know
About the ISEE

WHAT IS THE ISEE?

The Independent School Entrance Examination (ISEE) is a standardized test made up of a series of multiple-choice questions and a writing sample. The entire test lasts a little less than three hours, during which you will work on five different sections.

Plan Ahead

Early registration will not only give you one less thing to worry about as the test approaches, but also get you your first-choice test center.

Lower Level

Verbal Reasoning	34 questions	20 minutes
Quantitative Reasoning	38 questions	35 minutes
Reading Comprehension	25 questions	25 minutes
Mathematics Achievement	30 questions	30 minutes
Essay (ungraded)	1 essay topic	30 minutes

Middle Level

Verbal Reasoning	40 questions	20 minutes
Quantitative Reasoning	37 questions	35 minutes
Reading Comprehension	36 questions	35 minutes
Mathematics Achievement	47 questions	40 minutes
Essay (ungraded)	1 essay topic	30 minutes

Prepare Wisely

Print or order "What to Expect on the ISEE" from the ERB, at www.erblearn.org.

Upper Level

Verbal Reasoning	40 questions	20 minutes
Quantitative Reasoning	37 questions	35 minutes
Reading Comprehension	36 questions	35 minutes
Mathematics Achievement	47 questions	40 minutes
Essay (ungraded)	1 essay topic	30 minutes

What's on the ISEE?

The Verbal section of the ISEE tests your knowledge of vocabulary using two different question types: synonyms and sentence completions. There are no analogies on the ISEE. The Reading Comprehension section tests your ability to read and understand short passages. These reading passages include both fiction (including poetry and folklore) and nonfiction. The Math sections test your knowledge of general mathematical concepts through two different question types: problem-solving questions and quantitative comparison questions. The quantitative comparison questions ask you to compare two columns of data. There are no quantitative comparison questions on the Lower Level ISEE.

Upper Versus Middle Versus Lower Level

There are, in effect, three different versions of the ISEE. The Lower Level test is taken by students who are, at the time of testing, in the fourth and fifth grades. Students who are in the sixth and seventh grades take the Middle Level test. Students who are in the eighth, ninth, tenth, and eleventh grades take the Upper Level test.

There are few major differences between the Lower, Middle, and Upper Level tests. There are some differences in content, however; for instance, vocabulary on the Middle Level test is less challenging than it is on the Upper Level test. The Middle and Upper Level tests cover the same general math concepts (arithmetic, algebra, geometry, charts, and graphs), but naturally, the Middle Level test will ask slightly easier questions than the Upper Level test. There are no quantitative comparison questions on the Lower Level test. The Lower Level test is 20 minutes shorter than the others.

Because the Lower Level ISEE tests both fourth and fifth graders, the Middle Level tests both sixth and seventh graders, and the Upper Level tests eighth, ninth, tenth, and eleventh graders, there are questions on the tests that students testing at the lower end of each of the groups will have difficulty answering. Younger students' scaled scores and percentiles will not be harmed by this fact. Both sets of scores take into consideration a student's age. However, younger students may feel intimidated by this. If you are at the lower end of your test's age group, there will be questions you are not supposed to be able to answer and that's perfectly all right.

Likewise, the material in this book follows the content of the two tests without breaking it down further into age groups or grades. Content that will appear only on the Upper Level test has been labeled as "Upper Level only." Students taking the Lower and Middle Level tests do not need to work on the Upper Level content. Nevertheless, younger students may not have yet seen some of the material included in the Lower and Middle Level review. Parents are advised to help younger students with their work in this book and seek teachers' advice or instruction if necessary.

Chapter 16
General Test-Taking
Techniques for the ISEE

PACING

Most people believe that to do well on a test, it is important to try to work on every question. While this is true of most of the tests you take in school, it is not true of many standardized tests, including the ISEE. On this test, it is very possible to score well without working on all of the questions. In fact, many students can improve their scores by spending their time working on fewer questions.

"Wait a second. I can get a better score by doing less work?" Yes. The reason is that in their effort to answer all the questions, many students spend very little time on easy questions and make careless errors. They then spend more of their time on harder questions that they are likely to answer incorrectly anyway. Instead, you should spend most of your time making sure you get as many points as possible from the easy and medium questions. Work on fewer questions, but get more of the questions that you do answer right. If you don't finish the test, that's fine. By working slowly and carefully you got more points than you would have by rushing to answer more questions.

As we'll explain in a moment, if you do have a little time at the end, you should pick an answer for every question on the test that you skipped and left blank, taking random guesses on the questions you did not have time to solve. This last-minute guessing can earn you quick and easy points that you would miss if you left any questions blank.

***Answer* Every Question but Don't *Do* Every Question**

There is no penalty for wrong answers on the ISEE, so it is to your advantage to choose an answer for every question. This doesn't mean that you need to rush through the test to try to solve every question. Work at a pace that will maximize correct answers, and be ready to guess at the questions you don't have time to answer. You should *answer* every question, but that does not mean you should *work on* every question.

PROCESS OF ELIMINATION

Here's a question that you won't see on the ISEE, but which shows how powerful the Process of Elimination (or POE) can be.

> What is the capital of Malawi?
>
> (A) New York
> (B) Paris
> (C) London
> (D) Lilongwe

There are two ways to get this question right. First, you might know that the capital of Malawi is Lilongwe. If you do, good for you! The second is to know that the capital of Malawi is not New York, Paris, or London. You don't get more points for knowing the right answer from the start, so one way is just as good as the other. Try to get in the habit of looking at a question and asking, "What are the wrong answers?" instead of "What is the right answer?"

By using POE this way, you will eliminate wrong answers and then have fewer answers from which to pick. The result is that you will pick right answers more often.

GUESSING

Some standardized tests, including the SSAT, include a component in their scoring that penalizes you for wrong answers. This is called a guessing penalty. *There is no guessing penalty on the ISEE.* Therefore, although you may not have time to look at or do every problem on the test, you should be certain to choose an answer for every question. For instance, if you only have time to attempt 30 out of 40 verbal questions, you should still guess an answer for each of the ten questions you did not have time to complete. We suggest that you simply choose your favorite letter—A, B, C, or D—and make that your "letter of the day," which you will fill in for every question you do not have time to answer.

In addition to this random guessing, you can also improve your score by taking educated guesses. For instance, if you encounter a verbal question to which you do not know the right answer, don't just give up. Instead, look at the answer choices and try to identify wrong answers so you can eliminate them. Eliminating some answer choices turns guessing into a way to improve your score. Will you always guess correctly? No, but the odds of guessing correctly only get better with each answer choice you eliminate, so POE is a technique you should use often. Give it a try.

> Which of the following cities is the capital of Samoa?
>
> (A) Vila
> (B) Boston
> (C) Apia
> (D) Chicago

You may not know the right answer off the top of your head, but which cities are *not* the capital of Samoa? You probably know enough about the locations of (B) and (D) to know that Boston and Chicago are not the capitals of Samoa.

So what's a good answer to this question? (A) or (C).

What's the right answer? It isn't important. You took a good guess, and that's all that matters.

A QUICK SUMMARY

These points are important enough that we want to mention them again. Make sure you understand these points about the ISEE before you go any further in this book.

- You do not have to work on every problem on the test. Slow down!
- You will not immediately know the correct answer to every question. Instead, look for wrong answers that you can eliminate.
- Set aside the last minute or two of each section to fill in a guess for each question you did not have time to answer. Don't leave anything blank!

Should I Guess?
YES! But before you just make a random guess, always try to eliminate wrong answers.

When Should I Guess?
After you answer all easy problems on your first pass, go back to answer all the ones that gave you trouble.

Chapter 17
ISEE Math

Taking the Lower Level ISEE?
You can skip the section on quantitative comparison (pages 475–487).

INTRODUCTION

This section will provide you with a review of all the math that you need to do well on the ISEE. When you get started, you may feel that the material is too easy. Don't worry. This test measures your basic math skills, so although you may feel a little frustrated reviewing things you have already learned, this type of basic review is undoubtedly the best way to improve your score.

Lose Your Calculator!

You will *not* be allowed to use a calculator on the ISEE. If you have developed a habit of reaching for your calculator whenever you need to add or multiply a couple of numbers, follow our advice: Put your calculator away now, and don't take it out again until the test is behind you. Do your homework assignments without it, and complete the practice sections of this book without it. Trust us, you'll be glad you did.

Write It Down

Do not try to do math in your head. You are allowed to write in your test booklet. You *should* write in your test booklet. Even when you are just adding a few numbers together, write them down and do the work on paper. Writing things down will not only help eliminate careless errors but also give you something to refer back to if you need to check over your work.

One Pass, Two Pass

Within any math section, you will find three types of questions:

- Those you can answer easily in a short period of time
- Those that, given enough time, you can do
- Some questions that you have absolutely no idea how to tackle

When you work on a math section, start out with the first question. If it is one of the first type and you think you can do it without too much trouble, go ahead. If not, mark it and save it for later. Move on to the second question and decide whether or not to do that one.

Once you've made it all the way through the section, working slowly and carefully to do all the questions that come easily to you, then go back and try some of those that you think you can do but will take you a little longer. You should pace yourself so that time will run out while you're working on the second pass through the section. Make sure you save the last minute to bubble in an answer for any question you didn't get to. Working this way, you'll know that you answered all the questions that were easy for you. Using a two-pass system is good, smart test-taking.

Guesstimating

Sometimes accuracy is important. Sometimes it isn't.

Some Things Are Easier Than They Seem

Guesstimating, or finding approximate answers, can help you eliminate wrong answers and save lots of time.

Which of the following fractions is less than $\frac{1}{4}$?

(A) $\frac{4}{18}$

(B) $\frac{4}{12}$

(C) $\frac{7}{7}$

(D) $\frac{12}{5}$

Without doing a bit of calculation, think about this question. It asks you to find a fraction smaller than $\frac{1}{4}$. Even if you're not sure which one is actually smaller, you can certainly eliminate some wrong answers.

Start simple: $\frac{1}{4}$ is less than 1, right? Are there any fractions in the answer choices that are greater than 1? Get rid of (D).

Look at answer choice (C). $\frac{7}{7}$ equals 1. Can it be less than $\frac{1}{4}$? Eliminate (C). Already, without doing any math, you have a 50 percent chance of guessing the right answer.

Here's another good example.

A group of three men buys a one-dollar raffle ticket that wins $400. If the one dollar that they paid for the ticket is subtracted and the remainder of the prize money is divided equally among the men, how much will each man receive?

(A) $62.50

(B) $75.00

(C) $100.00

(D) $133.00

This isn't a terribly difficult question. To solve it mathematically, you would take $400, subtract $1, and then divide the remainder by three. But by using a little logic, you don't have to do any of that.

The raffle ticket won $400. If there were four men, each one would have won about $100 (actually slightly less because the problem tells you to subtract the $1 price of the ticket, but you get the idea). So far so good? However, there weren't four men; there were only three. This means fewer men among whom to divide the winnings, so each one should get more than $100, right?

Look at the answer choices. Eliminate (A), (B), and (C). What's left? The right answer!

Guesstimating Geometry

Don't Forget to Guesstimate!
Guesstimating works best on geometry questions. Make sure you use your common sense, combined with POE, to save time and energy.

Now that you've seen a couple examples that used guesstimating in arithmetic and word problems, you will see how we can also guesstimate geometry problems.

Let's try the problem below. Remember that unless a particular question tells you that a figure is not drawn to scale, you can safely assume that the figure *is* drawn to scale.

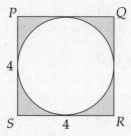

A circle is inscribed in square *PQRS*. What is the area of the shaded region?

(A) $16 - 6\pi$
(B) $16 - 4\pi$
(C) $16 - 3\pi$
(D) 16π

Wow, a circle inscribed in a square—that sounds tough!

Try these values when guesstimating:
$\pi \approx 3^+$
$\sqrt{2} = 1.4$
$\sqrt{3} = 1.7$

It isn't. Look at the picture. What fraction of the square looks like it is shaded? Half? Three-quarters? Less than half? In fact, about one-quarter of the area of the square is shaded. You've just about guesstimated the answer!

Now, let's do a tiny bit of math. The length of one side of the square is 4, so the area of the square is 4 × 4 or 16.

So the area of the square is 16 and we said that the shaded region was about one-fourth of the square. One-fourth of 16 is 4, right? So we're looking for an answer choice that equals about 4. Let's look at the choices.

(A) $16 - 6\pi$

(B) $16 - 4\pi$

(C) $16 - 3\pi$

(D) 16π

This could get a little complicated since the answers include π. However, since you're guesstimating, you should just remember that π is just a little more than 3.

Let's look back at those answers.

(A) $16 - 6\pi$ is roughly equal to $16 - (6 \times 3) = -2$

(B) $16 - 4\pi$ is roughly equal to $16 - (4 \times 3) =$ 4

(C) $16 - 3\pi$ is roughly equal to $16 - (3 \times 3) =$ 7

(D) 16π is roughly equal to (16×3) $= 48$

Now, let's think about what these answers mean.

Therefore, since we guesstimated that the shaded region's area is roughly 4, answer choice (B) must be correct….and it is! Pat yourself on the back because you chose the right answer without doing a lot of unnecessary work. Unless the problem tells you that the figure is not drawn to scale, remember how useful guesstimating on geometry problems can be!

Working with Answer Choices

In Chapter 2, "Fundamental Math Skills for the SSAT & ISEE," we reviewed the concepts that the ISEE will be testing on the Lower, Middle, and Upper Level tests. However, the questions in the practice drills were slightly different from those that you will see on your exam. The ones on the exam are going to give you four answers from which to choose. There are many benefits to working with multiple-choice questions.

For one, if you really mess up calculating the question, chances are your answer choice will not be among those given. Now you have a chance to go back and try that problem again more carefully. Another benefit, which this chapter will explore in more depth, is that you may be able to use the information in the answer choices to help you solve the problems.

We are now going to introduce you to the type of multiple-choice questions you will see on the ISEE. Each one of the questions on the pages that follow will test some skill that we covered in the Fundamental Math Skills chapter. If you don't see how to solve the question, take a look at Chapter 2 for help.

Math Vocabulary

Notice that the answer choices are often in numerical order.

1. Which of the following is the greatest even integer less than 25 ?

   (A) 26
   (B) 24.5
   (C) 22
   (D) 21

The first and most important thing you need to do on this and every problem is to read and understand the question. What important vocabulary words did you see in the question? There is *even* and *integer*. You should always underline the important words in the questions. This way, you will make sure to pay attention to them and avoid careless errors.

Now that we understand that the question is looking for an even integer, we can eliminate any answers that are not even or an integer. Cross out (B) and (D). We can also eliminate (A) because 26 is greater than 25 and we want a number less than 25. So (C) is the right answer.

Try it again.

$$\text{Set A} = \{\text{All multiples of 7}\}$$

$$\text{Set B} = \{\text{All odd numbers}\}$$

2. Which of the following is NOT a member of both set A and set B above?

   (A)   7
   (B)   21
   (C)   49
   (D)   59

Remember the Rules of Zero
Zero is even. It's neither + nor −, and anything multiplied by 0 = 0.

Did you underline the words *multiples of 7* and *odd*? Because all the answer choices are odd, you can't eliminate any that would not be in Set B, but only (D) is not a multiple of 7. So (D) is the right answer.

The Rules of Zero

3. x, y, and z stand for three distinct numbers, where $xy = 0$ and $yz = 15$. Which of the following must be true?

   (A) $y = 0$
   (B) $x = 0$
   (C) $z = 0$
   (D) $xyz = 15$

Because x times y is equal to zero, and x, y, and z are different numbers, we know that either x or y is equal to zero. If y was equal to zero, then y times z should also be equal to zero. Because it is not, we know that it must be x that equals zero. Answer choice (B) is correct.

The Multiplication Table

4. Which of the following is equal to $6 \times 5 \times 2$?

    (A) $60 \div 3$
    (B) 14×7
    (C) $2 \times 2 \times 15$
    (D) 12×10

$6 \times 5 \times 2 = 60$ and so does $2 \times 2 \times 15$. Answer choice (C) is correct.

Working with Negative Numbers

5. $7 - 9$ is the same as

    (A) $7 - (-9)$
    (B) $9 - 7$
    (C) $7 + (-9)$
    (D) $-7 - 9$

Remember that subtracting a number is the same as adding its opposite. Answer choice (C) is correct.

Order of Operations

6. $9 + 6 \times 2 \div 3 =$

    (A) 7
    (B) 9
    (C) 10
    (D) 13

Remember your PEMDAS rules? The multiplication comes first. The correct answer is (D).

Factors and Multiples

Remember!

1 is NOT a prime number.

7. What is the sum of the prime factors of 42 ?

   (A) 18
   (B) 13
   (C) 12
   (D) 10

How do we find the prime factors? The best way is to draw a factor tree. Then we see that the prime factors of 42 are 2, 3, and 7. Add them up and we get 12, answer choice (C).

Fractions

8. Which of the following is less than $\frac{4}{6}$?

   (A) $\frac{3}{5}$

   (B) $\frac{2}{3}$

   (C) $\frac{5}{7}$

   (D) $\frac{7}{8}$

When comparing fractions, you have two choices. You can find a common denominator and then compare the fractions (such as when you add or subtract them). You can also change the fractions to decimals. If you have memorized the fraction to decimal chart in the Fundamentals chapter, you probably found the right answer without too much difficulty. It's answer choice (A).

Percents

9. Thom's CD collection contains 15 jazz CDs, 45 rap albums, 30 funk CDs, and 60 pop albums. What percent of Thom's CD collection is funk?

   (A) 10%
   (B) 20%
   (C) 25%
   (D) 30%

First, we need to find the fractional part that represents Thom's funk CDs. He has 30 out of a total of 150. We can reduce $\frac{30}{150}$ to $\frac{1}{5}$; $\frac{1}{5}$ as a percent is 20%, answer choice (B).

Exponents

10. $2^6 =$

    (A) 2^3

    (B) 4^2

    (C) 3^2

    (D) 8^2

Expand 2^6 out and we can multiply to find that it equals 64. Answer choice (D) is correct.

Square Roots

11. The square root of 75 falls between what two integers?

    (A) 5 and 6

    (B) 6 and 7

    (C) 7 and 8

    (D) 8 and 9

If you have trouble with this one, use the answer choices and work backward. As we discussed in the Fundamentals chapter, a square root is just the opposite of squaring a number. So let's square the answer choices. Then we find that 75 falls between 8^2 (64) and 9^2 (81). Answer choice (D) is correct.

Basic Algebraic Equations

12. $11x = 121$. What does $x = $?

    (A)   2

    (B)   8

    (C) 10

    (D) 11

Remember, if you get stuck, use the answer choices and work backward. Each one provides you with a possible value for x. Start with the middle answer choice and replace x with it. $11 \times 10 = 110$. That's too small. Now we know not only that (C) is the incorrect answer, but also that (A) and (B) are incorrect because they are smaller than (C). The correct answer choice is (D).

Solve for X—Upper Level Only

13. $3y + 17 = 25 - y$. What does $y = $?

 (A) 1
 (B) 2
 (C) 3
 (D) 4

Just as on the previous question, if you get stuck, use the answer choices. The correct answer is (B).

Percent Algebra—Upper Level Only

Percent means *out of 100*, and the word *of* in a word problem tells you to multiply.

14. 25% of 30% of what is equal to 18 ?

 (A) 1
 (B) 36
 (C) 120
 (D) 240

If you don't remember the math conversion table, look it up in the Fundamentals chapter. You can also use the answer choices and work backward. Start with answer choice (C), and find out what 25% of 30% of 120 is. The correct answer is (D).

Geometry

15. *BCDE* is a rectangle with a perimeter of 44. If the length of *BC* is 15, what is the area of *BCDE* ?

 (A) 105
 (B) 17
 (C) 15
 (D) 14

From the perimeter, we can find that the sides of the rectangle are 7 and 15. So the area is 105, answer choice (A).

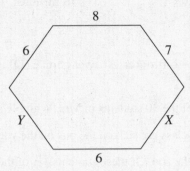

16. If the perimeter of this polygon is 37, what is the value of $x + y$?

    (A)   5
    (B)   9
    (C)   10
    (D)   16

$x + y$ is equal to the perimeter of the polygon minus the lengths of the sides we know. Answer choice (C) is correct.

Word Problems

17. Emily is walking to school at a rate of 3 blocks every 14 minutes. When Jeff walks at the same rate as Emily, and takes the most direct route to school, he arrives in 42 minutes. How many blocks away does Jeff live?

    (A)   3
    (B)   5
    (C)   6
    (D)   9

This is a proportion question because we have two sets of data we are comparing. Set up your fraction.

$$\frac{3 \text{ blocks}}{14 \text{ minutes}} = \frac{\text{Number of blocks Jeff walks}}{42 \text{ minutes}}$$

Because we know that we must do the same thing to the top and the bottom of the first fraction to get the second fraction, and because $14 \times 3 = 42$, we must multiply 3×3 to get 9.

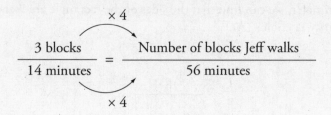

So Jeff walks 9 blocks in 42 minutes. Answer choice (D) is correct.

18. Half of the 30 students in Mrs. Whipple's first-grade class got sick on the bus on the way back from the zoo. Of these students, $\frac{2}{3}$ of them were sick because they ate too much cotton candy. The rest were sick because they sat next to the students who ate too much cotton candy. How many students were sick because they sat next to the wrong student?

(A)   5
(B)   10
(C)   15
(D)   20

This is a really gooey fraction problem. Because we've seen the word *of*, we know we have to multiply. First, we need to multiply $\frac{1}{2}$ by 30, the number of students in the class. This gives us 15, the number of students who got sick. Now we have another *of*, so we must multiply the fraction of students who ate too much cotton candy, $\frac{2}{3}$, by the number of students who got sick, 15. This gives us 10. So then the remainder, those who were unlucky in the seating plan, is 15 − 10, or 5, answer choice (A).

19. A piece of rope is 18 inches long. It is cut into 2 unequal pieces. The longer piece is twice as long as the shorter piece. How long is the shorter piece?

(A)   2
(B)   6
(C)   9
(D)   12

Again, if you are stuck for a place to start, go to the answer choices. Because we are looking for the length of the shorter rope, we can eliminate any answer choice that gives us a piece equal to or longer than half the rope. That gets rid of (C) and (D). Now, if we take one of the pieces, we can subtract it from the total length of the rope to get the length of the longer piece. In answer choice (B), if 6 is the length of the shorter piece, we can subtract it from 18 and now we know the length of the longer piece is 12. And 12 is twice the length of 6, so we have the right answer.

PRACTICE DRILL 1—LOWER LEVEL

Time yourself on this drill. When you are done, check your answers in Chapter 20.

1. How many factors does the number 24 have?

    (A) 2
    (B) 4
    (C) 6
    (D) 8

2. If 12 is a factor of a certain number, what must also be factors of that number?

    (A) 2 and 6 only
    (B) 3 and 4 only
    (C) 12 only
    (D) 1, 2, 3, 4, and 6

3. Which of the following is a multiple of 3?

    (A) 2
    (B) 6
    (C) 10
    (D) 14

4. Which of the following is NOT a multiple of 6?

    (A) 12
    (B) 18
    (C) 23
    (D) 24

5. Which of the following is a multiple of both 3 and 5?

    (A) 10
    (B) 20
    (C) 25
    (D) 45

6. What is the smallest number that can be added to the number 1,024 to produce a result divisible by 9?

   (A) 1
   (B) 2
   (C) 3
   (D) 4

7. The sum of five consecutive positive integers is 30. What is the square of the largest of the five positive integers?

   (A) 25
   (B) 36
   (C) 49
   (D) 64

8. A company's profit was $75,000 in 1972. In 1992, its profit was $450,000. The profit in 1992 was how many times as great as the profit in 1972?

   (A) 2
   (B) 4
   (C) 6
   (D) 10

9. Joanne owns one-third of the pieces of furniture in the apartment she shares with her friends. If there is a total of 12 pieces of furniture in the apartment, how many pieces does Joanne own?

   (A) 2
   (B) 4
   (C) 6
   (D) 8

10. A tank of oil is one-third full. When full, the tank holds 90 gallons. How many gallons of oil are in the tank now?

    (A) 10
    (B) 20
    (C) 30
    (D) 40

11. Ginger the dog sleeps three-fourths of every day. In a four-day period, she sleeps the equivalent of how many full days?

    (A) $\dfrac{1}{4}$

    (B) $\dfrac{3}{4}$

    (C) 1

    (D) 3

12. Which of the following is greatest?

(A) $\dfrac{1}{4} + \dfrac{2}{3}$

(B) $\dfrac{3}{4} - \dfrac{1}{3}$

(C) $\dfrac{1}{12} \div \dfrac{1}{3}$

(D) $\dfrac{3}{4} \times \dfrac{1}{3}$

13. $\dfrac{1}{2} + \dfrac{2}{3} + \dfrac{3}{4} + \dfrac{1}{2} + \dfrac{1}{3} + \dfrac{1}{4} =$

(A) $\dfrac{3}{4}$

(B) 1

(C) 3

(D) 6

14. The product of 0.34 and 1,000 is approximately

(A) 3.50
(B) 35
(C) 65
(D) 350

15. 2.398 =

(A) $2 \times \dfrac{9}{100} \times \dfrac{3}{10} \times \dfrac{8}{1000}$

(B) $2 + \dfrac{3}{10} + \dfrac{9}{1000} + \dfrac{8}{100}$

(C) $2 + \dfrac{9}{100} + \dfrac{8}{1000} + \dfrac{3}{10}$

(D) $\dfrac{3}{10} + \dfrac{9}{100} + \dfrac{8}{1000}$

Stop. Check your time for this drill: _____

How Did You Do?

That was a good sample of the kinds of questions you'll see on the ISEE. There are a few things to check other than your answers. Remember that taking the test involves much more than just getting answers right. It's also about guessing wisely, using your time well, and figuring out where you're likely to make mistakes. Once you've checked to see what you've gotten right and wrong, you should then consider the following to improve your score.

Time and Pacing

How long did it take you to do the 15 questions? It's okay if you went a minute or two over. However, if you finished very quickly (in fewer than 10 minutes) or slowly (more than 20 minutes), your pacing is off. Take a look at any problems that may have affected your speed. Were there any questions that seriously slowed you down? Did you answer some quickly but not correctly? In general, don't just look to see what you got right, but rather *how* you got it right.

Question Recognition and Selection

Did you use your time wisely? Did you do the questions in an order that worked well for you? Did you get stuck on one problem and spend too much time on it? Which kinds of questions were hardest for you? Remember that on the ISEE you must answer every question, but you don't have to *work on* every problem. Every question on the ISEE, whether easy or hard, is worth one point, and there is no penalty for wrong answers. You should concentrate most on getting all easy and medium questions right, and worry about doing harder problems later. Keep in mind that questions generally go from easiest to hardest throughout the section. Getting the easy and medium questions right takes time, but you know you can do it, so give yourself that time! If you don't have time for a question or can't guess wisely, pick a "letter of the day" (the same letter for every problem you can't do), fill it in, and move on. Because there is no penalty for wrong answers, guessing can only help your score.

POE and Guessing

Did you actively look for wrong answers to eliminate, rather than looking for the right answer? (You should.) Did you physically cross off wrong answers to keep track of your POE? Was there a pattern to when guessing worked (more often when you could eliminate one wrong answer and less often when you picked simpler-looking over harder-looking numbers)?

Write It Down

Did you work problems out in the book? Did you move too quickly or skip steps on problems you found easier? Did you always double-check what the question was asking? Often students miss questions that they know how to do! Why? It's simple—they work out problems in their heads or don't read carefully. Work out every ISEE math problem on the page. Consider it a double-check because your handwritten notes confirm what you've worked out in your head.

PRACTICE DRILL 2—MULTIPLE CHOICE—MIDDLE AND UPPER LEVEL ONLY

While doing the next drill, keep in mind the general test-taking techniques we've talked about: guessing, POE, order of difficulty, pacing, choosing a letter-of-the-day for problems that stump you, and working on the page and not in your head. At the end of the section, check your answers in Chapter 20. But don't stop there: Investigate the drill thoroughly to see how and why you got your answers wrong, and check your time. You should be spending about one minute per question on this drill.

1. How many numbers between 1 and 100, inclusive, are both prime and a multiple of 4?

   (A)   0
   (B)   12
   (C)   20
   (D)   25

2. How many factors do the integers 24 and 81 have in common?

   (A)   1
   (B)   2
   (C)   3
   (D)   4

3. If the final total of a dinner bill—after including a 25% tip—is $50, what was the cost of the dinner before including the tip?

   (A) $12.50
   (B) $25.00
   (C) $37.50
   (D) $40.00

4. How many numbers between 1 and 100 are multiples of both 2 and 7?

   (A)   6
   (B)   7
   (C)   8
   (D)   9

5. $2^3 \times 2^3 \times 2^3 =$

   (A) 2^6
   (B) 2^9
   (C) 2^{27}
   (D) 8^9

6. For what integer value of m does $2m + 4 = m^3$?

   (A) 1
   (B) 2
   (C) 3
   (D) 4

7. If $6x - 4 = 38$, then $x + 10 =$

   (A) 7
   (B) 10
   (C) 16
   (D) 17

8. What is the smallest multiple of 7 that is greater than 50?

   (A) 7
   (B) 49
   (C) 51
   (D) 56

9. One-fifth of the students in a class chose recycling as the topic for their science projects. If four students chose recycling, how many students are in the class?

   (A) 4
   (B) 10
   (C) 16
   (D) 20

10. If a harvest yielded 60 bushels of corn, 20 bushels of wheat, and 40 bushels of soybeans, what percent of the total harvest was corn?

    (A) 50%
    (B) 40%
    (C) 33%
    (D) 30%

11. At a local store, an item that usually sells for $45 is currently on sale for $30. What discount does that represent?

    (A) 10%
    (B) 25%
    (C) 33%
    (D) 50%

12. Which of the following is most nearly 35% of $19.95?

    (A) $3.50
    (B) $5.75
    (C) $7.00
    (D) $9.95

13. A pair of shoes is offered on a special blowout sale. The original price of the shoes is reduced from $50 to $20. What is the percent change in the price of the shoes?

    (A) 60%
    (B) 50%
    (C) 40%
    (D) 25%

14. If the perimeter of a square is 56, what is the length of each side?

    (A) 4
    (B) 7
    (C) 14
    (D) 28

15. What is the perimeter of an equilateral triangle, one side of which measures 4 inches?

    (A) 12 inches
    (B)   8 inches
    (C)   6 inches
    (D)   4 inches

Upper Level Only

16. If $b = 45$, then $v^2 =$

    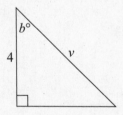

    (A) 32
    (B) 25
    (C) 16
    (D)   5

17. One-half of the difference between the number of degrees in a square and the number of degrees in a triangle is

    (A) 45
    (B) 90
    (C) 180
    (D) 240

18. If the area of a square is equal to its perimeter, what is the length of one side?

    (A) 1
    (B) 2
    (C) 4
    (D) 8

19. The area of a rectangle with width 4 and length 3 is equal to the area of a triangle with a base of 6 and a height of

    (A) 1
    (B) 2
    (C) 3
    (D) 4

20. Two cardboard boxes have equal volume. The dimensions of one box are $3 \times 4 \times 10$. If the length of the other box is 6 and the width is 4, what is the height of the second box?

    (A) 2
    (B) 5
    (C) 10
    (D) 12

21. If the area of a square is $64p^2$, what is the length of one side of the square?

    (A) $64p^2$
    (B) $8p^2$
    (C) $64p$
    (D) $8p$

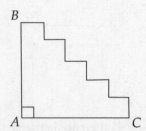

22. If $AB = 10$ and $BC = 15$, what is the perimeter of the figure above?

    (A) 25
    (B) 35
    (C) 40
    (D) 50

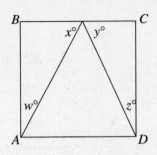

23. If *ABCD* is a rectangle, what is the value of
    $w + x + y + z$?

    (A)   90
    (B)   150
    (C)   180
    (D)   190

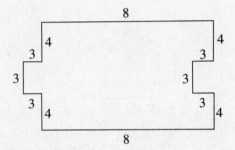

24. What is the area of the figure above if all the
    angles shown are right angles?

    (A)   38
    (B)   42
    (C)   50
    (D)   88

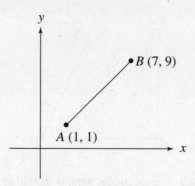

25. The distance between points *A* and *B* in the coordinate plane above is

(A)   5
(B)   6
(C)   8
(D)   10

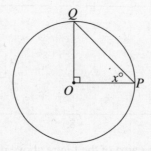

26. *PO* and *QO* are radii of the circle with center *O*. What is the value of *x* ?

(A)   30
(B)   45
(C)   60
(D)   90

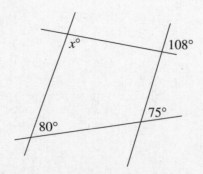

27. What is the value of *x* ?

(A)   360
(B)   100
(C)   97
(D)   67

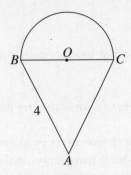

28 *ABC* is an equilateral triangle. What is the perimeter of this figure?

(A) $4 + 2\pi$
(B) $4 + 4\pi$
(C) $8 + 2\pi$
(D) $8 + 4\pi$

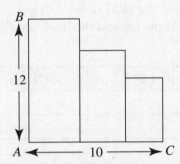

29. What is the perimeter of this figure?

(A)   120
(B)   44
(C)   40
(D)   36

Ratios

A ratio is like a recipe. It tells you how much of each ingredient goes into a mixture.

For example:

To make punch, mix two parts grape juice with three parts orange juice.

This ratio tells you that for every two units of grape juice, you will need to add three units of orange juice. It doesn't matter what the units are; if you were working with ounces, you would mix two ounces of grape juice with three ounces of orange juice to get five ounces of punch. If you were working with gallons, you would mix two gallons of grape juice with three gallons of orange juice. How much punch would you have? Five gallons.

To work through a ratio question, first you need to organize the information you are given. Do this using the Ratio Box.

In a club with 35 members, the ratio of boys to girls is 3:2. To complete your Ratio Box, fill in the ratio at the top and the "real value" at the bottom.

	BOYS	**GIRLS**	**TOTAL**
Ratio	3	+ 2	= 5
Multiplier			
Real Value			35

Then look for a "magic number" that you can multiply by the ratio to get to the real value. In this case, the magic number is 7. That's all there is to it!

	BOYS	**GIRLS**	**TOTAL**
Ratio	3	+ 2	= 5
Multiplier	×7	×7	×7
Real Value	21	14	35

PRACTICE DRILL 3—RATIOS

1. At Jed's Country Hotel, there are three types of rooms: singles, doubles, and triples. If the ratio of singles to doubles to triples is 3:4:5, and the total number of rooms is 36, how many doubles are there?

   (A)   4
   (B)   9
   (C) 12
   (D) 24

2. In Janice's tennis club, 8 of the 12 players are right-handed. What is the ratio of right-handed to left-handed players in Janice's club?

   (A) 1:2
   (B) 1:6
   (C) 2:1
   (D) 2:3

3. A pet goat eats 2 pounds of goat food and 1 pound of grass each day. When the goat has eaten a total of 15 pounds, how many pounds of grass will it have eaten?

   (A)   3
   (B)   4
   (C)   5
   (D) 15

Averages

There are three parts to every average problem: total, number, and average. Most ISEE problems will give you two of the three pieces and ask you to find the third. To help organize the information you are given, use the Average Pie.

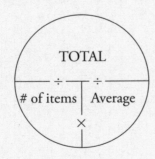

The Average Pie organizes all of your information visually. It is easy to see all of the relationships between pieces of the pie.

- TOTAL = (# of items) × (Average)

- # of items = $\dfrac{Total}{Average}$

- Average = $\dfrac{Total}{\text{# of items}}$

For example, if your friend went bowling and bowled three games, scoring 71, 90, and 100, here's how you would compute her average score using the Average Pie.

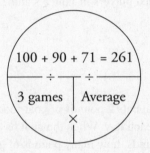

To find the average, you would simply write a fraction that represents $\dfrac{Total}{\text{# of items}}$, in this case $\dfrac{261}{3}$.

The math becomes simple. $261 \div 3 = 87$. Your friend bowled an average of 87.

Get used to working with the Average Pie by using it to solve the following problems.

PRACTICE DRILL 4—AVERAGES

1. The average of 3 numbers is 18. What is two times the sum of the 3 numbers?

   (A) 108
   (B) 54
   (C) 36
   (D) 18

2. An art club of 4 boys and 5 girls make craft projects. If the boys average 2 projects each and the girls average 3 projects each, what is the total number of projects produced by the club?

   (A) 14
   (B) 23
   (C) 26
   (D) 54

3. Catherine scores 84, 85, and 88 on her first three exams. What must she score on her fourth exam to raise her average to an 89?

   (A) 99
   (B) 97
   (C) 93
   (D) 91

4. If a class of 6 students has an average grade of 72 before a seventh student joins the class, what must the seventh student's grade be to raise the class average to 76?

   (A) 100
   (B) 92
   (C) 88
   (D) 80

More Practice: Lower Level

5. Anna ate 2 doughnuts on Monday, Wednesday, and Friday and ate 4 doughnuts on Tuesday and Thursday. She did not eat any doughnuts on Saturday or Sunday. What is the average number of doughnuts that Anna ate for the week?

   (A) 2.0
   (B) 2.5
   (C) 2.8
   (D) 3.0

6. Merry drove 350 miles from New Orleans to Houston in 7 hours. She then drove 240 miles from Houston to Dallas in 4 hours. What was her approximate average rate of speed, in miles per hour (mph), for the entire trip?

(A) 50.0 mph
(B) 53.6 mph
(C) 55.0 mph
(D) 60.0 mph

7. The ticket price to a school's spring musical production is $6. The auditorium has a seating capacity of 300. After having spent $550 on stage production and $250 on advertising, how much profit did the school make?

(A) $700
(B) $800
(C) $900
(D) $1,000

More Practice: Middle and Upper Levels

8. Michael scored an average of 24 points over his first 5 basketball games. How many points must he score in his 6th game to average 25 points over all 6 games?

(A) 24
(B) 25
(C) 30
(D) 36

9. Dwan measured a total of 245 inches of rainfall in his hometown over one week. During the same period last year in his hometown, Dwan measured a total of 196 inches. How many more inches was the average amount of rainfall this year higher than that of last year?

(A) 6
(B) 7
(C) 8
(D) 9

When You Are Done
Check your answers in Chapter 20.

Percent Change—Upper Level Only

There is one special kind of percent question that shows up on the ISEE: percent change. This type of question asks you to find what percent something has increased or decreased. Instead of taking the part and dividing it by the whole, you will take the difference between the two numbers and divide it by the original number. Then, to turn the fraction to a percent, divide the numerator by the denominator and multiply by 100.

For example:

> The number of people who watched *Who Wants to Be a Millionaire* last year was 3,600,000. This year, only 3,000,000 are watching the show. By approximately what percent has the audience decreased?

$$\frac{\text{The difference}}{\text{The original}} = \frac{600,000}{3,600,000} \quad \text{(The difference is } 3,600,000 - 3,000,000.)$$

The fraction reduces to $\frac{1}{6}$, and $\frac{1}{6}$ as a percent is 16%.

PRACTICE DRILL 5—PERCENT CHANGE

$$\% \text{ change} = \frac{\text{difference}}{\text{original}} \times 100$$

1. During a severe winter in Ontario, the temperature dropped suddenly to 10 degrees below zero. If the temperature in Ontario before this cold spell occurred was 10 degrees above zero, by what percent did the temperature drop?

   (A) 50%
   (B) 100%
   (C) 150%
   (D) 200%

2. Fatty's Burger wants to attract more customers by increasing the size of its patties. From now on Fatty's patties are going to be 4 ounces larger than before. If the size of its new patty is 16 ounces, by what percent has the patty increased?

   (A)   25%
   (B)   27%
   (C)   33%
   (D)   75%

When You Are Done
Check your answers in Chapter 20.

Plugging In

The ISEE will often ask you questions about real-life situations where the numbers have been replaced with variables. One of the easiest ways to tackle these questions is with a powerful technique called *Plugging In*.

> Mark is two inches taller than John, who is four inches shorter than Evan. If e represents Evan's height in inches, then in terms of e, an expression for Mark's height is
>
> (A) $e + 6$
> (B) $e + 4$
> (C) $e + 2$
> (D) $e - 2$

The problem with this question is that we're not used to thinking of people's heights in terms of variables. Have you ever met someone who was e inches tall?

Whenever you see variables used in the question and in the answer choices, just plug in a number to replace the variable.

1. Choose a number for e.
2. Using that number, figure out Mark's and John's heights.
3. Put a box around Mark's height, because that's what the question asked you for.
4. Plug your number for e into the answer choices and choose the one that gives you the number you found for Mark's height.

Here's How It Works

> Mark is two inches taller than John, who is four inches shorter than Evan. If e represents Evan's height in inches, then ~~in terms of e,~~ an expression for Mark's height is
>
> (A) $e + 6$
> (B) $e + 4$
> (C) $e + 2$
> (D) $e - 2$

Cross this out! Because you are Plugging In, you don't need to pay any attention to "in terms of" any variable.

For Evan's height, let's pick 60 inches. This means that $e = 60$. Remember, there is no right or wrong number to pick. 50 would work just as well.

But given that Evan is 60 inches tall, now we can figure out that, because John is four inches shorter than Evan, John's height must be $(60 - 4)$, or 56 inches.

The other piece of information we learn from the problem is that Mark is two inches taller than John. If John's height is 56 inches, that means Mark must be 58 inches tall.

So here's what we've got.

Evan   60 inches $= e$
John   56 inches
Mark $\boxed{58}$ inches

Now, the question asks for Mark's height, which is 58 inches. The last step is to go through the answer choices substituting 60 for e, and choose the one that equals 58.

(A) $e + 6$ $60 + 6 = 66$ ELIMINATE
(B) $e + 4$ $60 + 4 = 64$ ELIMINATE
(C) $e + 2$ $60 + 2 = 62$ ELIMINATE
(D) $e - 2$ $60 - 2 = 58$ PICK THIS ONE!

After reading this explanation, you may be tempted to say that Plugging In takes too long. Don't be fooled. The method itself is often faster and more accurate than regular algebra. Try it out. Practice. As you become more comfortable with Plugging In, you'll get even quicker and better results. You still need to know how to do algebra, but if you do only algebra, you may have difficulty improving your ISEE score. Plugging In gives you a way to break through whenever you are stuck. You'll find that having more than one way to solve ISEE math problems puts you at a real advantage.

PRACTICE DRILL 6—PLUGGING IN

Take the Algebra Away, and Arithmetic Is All That's Left

When you plug in for variables, you won't need to write equations and won't have to solve algebra problems. Doing simple arithmetic is always easier than doing algebra.

1. At a charity fund-raiser, 200 people each donated x dollars. In terms of x, what was the total number of dollars that was donated?

    (A) $\dfrac{x}{200}$

    (B) $200x$

    (C) $\dfrac{200}{x}$

    (D) $200 + x$

2. If 10 magazines cost d dollars, how many magazines can be purchased for 3 dollars?

    (A) $\dfrac{3d}{10}$

    (B) $30d$

    (C) $\dfrac{d}{30}$

    (D) $\dfrac{30}{d}$

3. The zoo has four times as many monkeys as lions. There are four more lions than there are zebras at the zoo. If z represents the number of zebras in the zoo, then in terms of z, how many monkeys are there in the zoo?

    (A) $4z$
    (B) $z + 4$
    (C) $4z + 16$
    (D) $4z + 4$

Occasionally, you may run into a Plugging In question that doesn't contain variables. These questions usually ask about a percentage or a fraction of some unknown number or price. This is the one time that you should plug in even when you don't see variables in the answer.

Also, be sure you plug in good numbers. Good doesn't mean right, because there's no such thing as a right or wrong number to plug in. A good number is one that makes the problem easier to work with. If a question asks about minutes and hours, try 30 or 60, not 128. Also, whenever you see the word *percent*, plug in 100!

More Practice: Lower Level

1. There were 6 pairs of earrings sold at a price of y dollars each. In terms of y, what is the total amount of money for which these earrings were sold?

   (A) $6 + y$
   (B) $6y$
   (C) 6^y
   (D) $6 + 6y$

2. If p pieces of candy costs c cents, 10 pieces of candy will cost

   (A) $\dfrac{pc}{10}$ cents

   (B) $\dfrac{10c}{p}$ cents

   (C) $\dfrac{10p}{c}$ cents

   (D) $10pc$ cents

More Practice: Middle Level

3. If J is an odd integer, which of the following must be true?

   (A) $(J \div 3) > 1$
   (B) $(J - 2)$ is a positive integer.
   (C) $2 \times J$ is an even integer.
   (D) $J > 0$

4. On Monday, Sharon ate one-half of a fruit tart. On Tuesday, Sharon then ate one-fourth of what was left of the tart. What fraction of the tart did Sharon eat on Monday and Tuesday?

   (A) $\dfrac{3}{8}$

   (B) $\dfrac{1}{2}$

   (C) $\dfrac{5}{8}$

   (D) $\dfrac{3}{4}$

More Practice: Middle and Upper Levels

5. The price of a suit is reduced by 20%, and then the resulting price is reduced by another 10%. The final price is what percent off the original price?

   (A) 20%
   (B) 25%
   (C) 28%
   (D) 30%

6. If m is an even integer, n is an odd integer, and p is the product of m and n, which of the following is always true?

   (A) p is a fraction.
   (B) p is an odd integer.
   (C) p is divisible by 2.
   (D) p is greater than zero.

More Practice: Upper Level

7. If p is an odd integer, which of the following must be an odd integer?

   (A) $p^2 + 3$
   (B) $2p + 1$
   (C) $p \div 3$
   (D) $p - 3$

8. If m is the sum of two positive even integers, which of the following CANNOT be true?

   (A) $m < 5$
   (B) $3m$ is odd.
   (C) m is even.
   (D) m^3 is even.

9. Anthony has twice as many baseball cards as Keith, who has one-third as many baseball cards as Ian. If Keith has k baseball cards, how many baseball cards do Anthony and Ian have together?

   (A) $\dfrac{3k}{2}$

   (B) $\dfrac{6k}{2}$

   (C) $\dfrac{8k}{2}$

   (D) $\dfrac{10k}{2}$

10. The product of $\frac{1}{2}b$ and a^2 can be written as

(A) $(ab)^2$

(B) $\dfrac{a^2}{b}$

(C) $2a \times \dfrac{1}{2}b$

(D) $\dfrac{a^2 b}{2}$

11. $x^a = (x^3)^3$

$$y^b = \frac{y^{10}}{y^2}$$

What is the value of $a \times b$?

(A) 17
(B) 30
(C) 48
(D) 72

12. Students in Mr. Greenwood's history class are collecting donations for a school charity drive. If the total number of students in the class, x, donated an average of y dollars each, in terms of x and y, how much money was collected for the drive?

(A) $\dfrac{x}{y}$

(B) xy

(C) $\dfrac{xy}{x}$

(D) $\dfrac{y}{x}$

13. What is the greatest common factor of $(3xy)^3$ and $3x^2y^5$?

(A) xy
(B) $3x^2y^5$
(C) $3x^2y^3$
(D) $27x^3y^3$
(D) p is greater than zero.

When You Are Done
Check your answers in Chapter 20.

Plugging In The Answers (PITA)

Plugging In The Answers is similar to Plugging In. When you have *variables* in the answer choices, you plug in. When you have *numbers* in the answer choices, you should generally plug in the answers.

Plugging In The Answers works because on a multiple-choice test, the right answer is always one of the answer choices. On this type of question, you can't plug in any number you want because only one number will work. Instead, you can plug in numbers from the answer choices, one of which must be correct. Here's an example.

> Nicole baked a batch of cookies. She gave half to her friend Lisa and six to her mother. If she now has eight cookies left, how many did Nicole bake originally?
>
> (A)   8
> (B)   12
> (C)   20
> (D)   28

See what we mean? It would be hard to just start making up numbers of cookies and hope that eventually you guessed correctly. However, the number of cookies that Nicole baked originally must be either 8, 12, 20, or 28 (the four answer choices). So pick one—start with either (B) or (C)—and then work backward to determine whether you have the right choice.

Let's start with (C): Nicole baked 20 cookies. Now work through the events listed in the question. She had 20 cookies and she gave half to Lisa. That leaves Nicole with 10 cookies. Then, she gave 6 to her mom. Now she's got 4 left.

Keep going. The problem says that Nicole now has 8 cookies left. But if she started with 20—answer choice (C)—she would only have 4 left. So is (C) the right answer? No.

No problem. Choose another answer choice and try again. Be smart about which answer choice you pick. When we used the number in (C), Nicole ended up with fewer cookies than we wanted her to have, didn't she? So the right answer must be a number larger than 20, the number we took from (C).

The good news is that the answer choices in most Plugging In The Answers questions go in order, so it is easy to pick the next larger or smaller number, depending on which direction you've decided to go. We need a number larger than 20. So let's go to answer choice (D)—28.

Nicole started out with 28 cookies. The first thing she did was give half, or 14, to Lisa. That left Nicole with 14 cookies. Then she gave 6 cookies to her mother. $14 - 6 = 8$. Nicole has 8 cookies left over. Keep going with the question. It says, "If she now has eight cookies left..." She has eight cookies left and, *voilà*—she's supposed to have 8 cookies left.

What does this mean? It means you've got the right answer!

PRACTICE DRILL 7—PLUGGING IN THE ANSWERS

1. Ted can read 60 pages per hour. Naomi can read 45 pages per hour. If both Ted and Naomi read at the same time, how many minutes will it take them to read a total of 210 pages?

   (A) 72
   (B) 120
   (C) 145
   (D) 180

2. Three people—Paul, Sara, and John—want to put their money together to buy a $90 radio. If Sara agrees to pay twice as much as John, and Paul agrees to pay three times as much as Sara, how much must Sara pay?

   (A) $10
   (B) $20
   (C) $30
   (D) $45

3. Four less than a certain number is two-thirds of that number. What is the number?

   (A)   1
   (B)   6
   (C)   8
   (D)   12

When You Are Done
Check your answers in Chapter 20.

More Practice: Lower Level

4. There are 12 more girls than boys in a classroom. If there are 30 total students in the classroom, how many girls are there in the classroom?

   (A)   9
   (B)   12
   (C)   20
   (D)   21

5. Victor, Jonathan, and Russell buy a home theater system. Victor pays twice as much as Jonathan, and Victor pays half as much Russell. If the home theater system costs $560, how much does Jonathan pay?

   (A) $60
   (B) $80
   (C) $100
   (D) $12

More Practice: Middle and Upper Levels

6. Adam is half as old as Bob and three times as old as Cindy. If the sum of their ages is 40, what is Bob's age?

(A) 6
(B) 12
(C) 18
(D) 24

7. If $70x + 33y = 4233$ and x and y are positive integers, x could be which of the following values?

(A) 42
(B) 47
(C) 55
(D) 60

8. The sum of three positive integers is 9 and their product is 24. If the smallest of the integers is 2, what is the largest?

(A) 4
(B) 6
(C) 8
(D) 9

9. Lori is 15 years older than Carol. In 10 years, Lori will be twice as old as Carol. How old is Lori now?

(A) 5
(B) 12
(C) 20
(D) 25

10. A group of people are sharing equally the $30 cost of renting a car. If an additional person joined the group, each person would owe $1 less. How many people are in the group currently?

(A) 5
(B) 6
(C) 10
(D) 12

GEOMETRY

Weird Shapes

Whenever the test presents you with a geometric figure that is not a square, rectangle, circle, or triangle, draw a line or lines to divide that figure into the shapes that you do know. Then you can easily work with shapes you know all about.

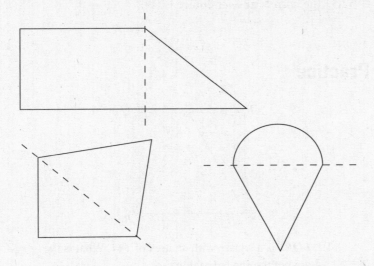

Shaded Regions—Middle and Upper Level Only

Sometimes geometry questions show you one figure inscribed in another and ask you to find the area of a shaded region inside the larger figure and outside the smaller figure (like the problem at the beginning of this section). To find the areas of these shaded regions, find the area of the outside figure and then subtract the area of the figure inside. The difference is what you need.

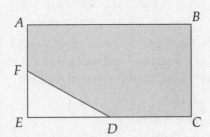

ABCE is a rectangle with a length of 10 and width of 6. Points *F* and *D* are the midpoints of *AE* and *EC*, respectively. What is the area of the shaded region?

(A) 25.5
(B) 30
(C) 45
(D) 52.5

The first step is to find the area of the rectangle. Multiply the length by the width and find that the area of the rectangle is 60. Now we find the area of the triangle that we are removing from the rectangle. Because the height and base of the triangle are parts of the sides of the rectangle, and points D and F are half the length and width of the rectangle, we know that the height of the triangle is half the rectangle's width, or 3, and the base of the triangle is half the rectangle's length, or 5. Using the formula for the area of a triangle, we find the area of the triangle is 7.5. Now we subtract the area of the triangle from the area of the rectangle. $60 - 7.5 = 52.5$. The correct answer choice is (D).

Extra Practice

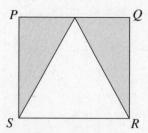

1. *PQRS* is a square with an area of 144. What is the area of the shaded region?

    (A) 50
    (B) 72
    (C) 100
    (D) 120

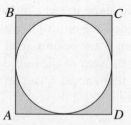

2. In the figure above, the length of side *AB* of square *ABCD* is equal to 4 and the circle has a radius of 2. What is the area of the shaded region?

    (A) $4 - \pi$
    (B) $16 - 4\pi$
    (C) $8 + 4\pi$
    (D) 4π

Functions

In a function problem, an arithmetic operation is defined, and then you are asked to perform it on a number. A function is just a set of instructions written in a strange way.

$$\# x = 3x(x + 1)$$

On the left there is usually a variable with a strange symbol next to or around it.

In the middle is an equal sign.

On the right are the instructions. These tell you what to do with the variable.

$\# x = 3x(x + 1)$ *What does # 5 equal?*

$\# 5 = (3 \times 5)(5 + 1)$ *Just replace each x with a 5!*

Here, the function (indicated by the # sign) simply tells you to substitute a 5 wherever there was an x in the original set of instructions. Functions look confusing because of the strange symbols, but once you know what to do with them, they are just like manipulating an equation.

Sometimes, more than one question will refer to the same function. The following drill, for example, contains two questions about one function. In cases such as this, the first question tends to be easier than the second.

PRACTICE DRILL 8—FUNCTIONS

<u>Questions 1 and 2</u> refer to the following definition.

For all real numbers n, $\$n = 10n - 10$

1. $\$7 =$
    (A) 70
    (B) 60
    (C) 17
    (D) 7

2. If $\$n = 120$, then $n =$
    (A) 11
    (B) 12
    (C) 13
    (D) 120

<u>Questions 3-5</u> refer to the following definition.

For all real numbers d and y, $d \, ¿ \, y = (d \times y) - (d + y)$.

[Example: $3 \, ¿ \, 2 = (3 \times 2) - (3 + 2) = 6 - 5 = 1$]

3. $10 \, ¿ \, 2 =$
    (A) 20
    (B) 16
    (C) 12
    (D)   8

4. If $K \, (4 \, ¿ \, 3) = 30$, then $K =$
    (A) 3
    (B) 4
    (C) 5
    (D) 6

5. $(2 \, ¿ \, 4) \times (3 \, ¿ \, 6) =$
    (A) $(9 \, ¿ \, 3) + 3$
    (B) $(6 \, ¿ \, 4) + 1$
    (C) $(5 \, ¿ \, 3) + 4$
    (D) $(8 \, ¿ \, 4) + 2$

When You Are Done
Check your answers in
Chapter 20.

Charts and Graphs

Charts

Chart questions usually do not involve much computation, but you must be careful. Follow these three steps and you'll be well on the way to mastering any chart question.

1. Read any text that accompanies the chart. It is important to know what the chart is showing and what scale the numbers are on.
2. Read the question.
3. Refer to the chart and find the specific information you need.

If there is more than one question about a single chart, the later questions will tend to be more difficult than the earlier ones. Be careful!

Here is a sample chart.

Club Membership by State, 1995 and 1996

State	1995	1996
California	300	500
Florida	225	250
Illinois	200	180
Massachusetts	150	300
Michigan	150	200
New Jersey	200	250
New York	400	600
Texas	50	100

There are many different questions that you can answer based on the information in this chart. For instance:

> What is the difference between the number of members who came from New York in 1995 and the number of members who came from Illinois in 1996?

This question asks you to look up two simple pieces of information and then do a tiny bit of math.

First, the number of members who came from New York in 1995 was 400.

Second, the number of members who came from Illinois in 1996 was 180.

Don't Be in Too Big a Hurry
When working with charts and graphs, make sure you take a moment to look at the chart or graph, figure out what it tells you, and then go to the questions.

Finally, look back at the question. It asks you to find the difference between these numbers. 400 − 180 = 220. Done.

> The increase in the number of members from New Jersey from 1995 to 1996 was what percent of the total number of members in New Jersey in 1995?

You should definitely know how to do this one! Do you remember how to translate percentage questions? If not, go back to Chapter 2.

In 1995 there were 200 club members from New Jersey. In 1996 there were 250 members from New Jersey. That represents an increase of 50 members. To determine what percent that is of the total amount in 1995, you need to ask yourself, "50 (the increase) is what percent of 200 (the number of members in 1995)?"

Translated, this becomes

$$50 = \frac{g}{100} \times 200$$

With a little bit of simple manipulation, this equation becomes

$$50 = 2g$$

and

$$25 = g$$

So from 1995 to 1996, there was a 25% increase in the number of members from New Jersey. Good work!

> Which state had as many club members in 1996 as a combination of Illinois, Massachusetts, and Michigan had in 1995?

First, take a second to look up the number of members who came from Illinois, Massachusetts, and Michigan in 1995 and add them together.

$$200 + 150 + 150 = 500$$

Which state had 500 members in 1996? California. That's all there is to it!

Graphs

Some questions will ask you to interpret a graph. You should be familiar with both pie and bar graphs. These graphs are generally drawn to scale (meaning that the graphs give an accurate visual impression of the information) so you can always guess based on the figure if you need to.

The way to approach a graph question is exactly the same as the way to approach a chart question. Follow the same three steps.

1. Read any text that accompanies the graph. It is important to know what the graph is showing and what scale the numbers are on.
2. Read the question.
3. Refer back to the graph and find the specific information you need.

This is how it works.

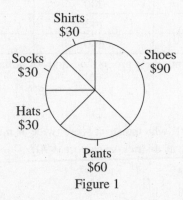

Figure 1

The graph in Figure 1 shows Emily's clothing expenditures for the month of October. On which type of clothing did she spend the most money?

(A) Shoes
(B) Shirts
(C) Socks
(D) Hats

This one is easy. You can look at the pieces of the pie and identify the largest, or you can look at the amounts shown in the graph and choose the largest one. Either way, the answer is (A) because Emily spent more money on shoes than on any other clothing items in October.

Emily spent half of her clothing money on which two items?

(A) Shoes and pants
(B) Shoes and shirts
(C) Hats and socks
(D) Socks and shirts

Again, you can find the answer to this question two different ways. You can look for which two items together make up half the chart, or you can add up the total amount of money Emily spent ($240) and then figure out which two items made up half (or $120) of that amount. Either way is just fine, and either way the right answer is (B), shoes and shirts.

PRACTICE DRILL 9—CHARTS AND GRAPHS

Questions 1-3 refer to the following summary of energy costs by district.

District	1990	1991
A	400	600
B	500	700
C	200	350
D	100	150
E	600	800

(All numbers are in thousands of dollars.)

1. In 1991, which district spent twice as much on energy as district A spent in 1990?

    (A) A
    (B) B
    (C) C
    (D) E

2. Which district spent the most on electricity in 1990 and 1991 combined?

    (A) A
    (B) B
    (C) D
    (D) E

3. The total increase in energy expenditure in these districts, from 1990 to 1991, is how many dollars?

    (A) $800
    (B) $1,800
    (C) $2,600
    (D) $800,000

Questions 4 and 5 refer to Figure 2, which shows the number of compact discs owned by five students.

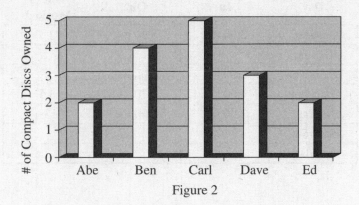

Figure 2

4. Carl owns as many CDs as which two other students combined?

    (A) Abe and Ben
    (B) Ben and Dave
    (C) Abe and Ed
    (D) Abe and Dave

5. Which one student owns one-fourth of the CDs accounted for in Figure 2?

    (A) Abe
    (B) Ben
    (C) Carl
    (D) Dave

Questions 6-8 refer to Matt's weekly time card, shown below.

Day	In	Out	Hours Worked
Monday	2:00 P.M.	5:30 P.M.	3.5
Tuesday			
Wednesday	2:00 P.M.	6:00 P.M.	4
Thursday	2:00 P.M.	5:30 P.M.	3.5
Friday	2:00 P.M.	5:00 P.M.	3
Saturday			
Sunday			

6. If Matt's hourly salary is $6, what were his earnings for the week?

   (A) $14
   (B) $21
   (C) $54
   (D) $84

7. What is the average number of hours Matt worked on the days he worked during this particular week?

   (A) 3
   (B) 3.5
   (C) 4
   (D) 7

8. The hours that Matt worked on Monday accounted for what percent of the total number of hours he worked during this week?

   (A) 3.5
   (B) 20
   (C) 25
   (D) 35

When You Are Done
Check your answers in Chapter 20.

QUANTITATIVE COMPARISON—MIDDLE AND UPPER LEVEL ONLY

Quant Comp: Same Book, Different Cover

Quantitative comparison is a type of question—one slightly different from the traditional multiple-choice questions you've seen so far—that tests exactly the same math concepts you have learned so far in this book. There is no new math for you to learn here, just a different mode of operation to answer this different type of question.

You will see a total of 17 quant comp questions in one of your ISEE Math sections.

The Rules of the Game

In answering a quant comp question your goal is very simple: Determine which column is larger and choose the appropriate answer choice. There are four possible answers.

(A)   means that Column A is always greater
(B)   means that Column B is always greater
(C)   means that Column A is always equal to Column B
(D)   means that A, B, or C are not always true

So that you can use POE in quant comp, where there are no answer choices written out for you, we suggest that you write "A B C D" next to each question. Then when you eliminate an answer, you can cross it off.

Don't Do Too Much Work

Quant comp is a strange, new question type for most students. Don't let it intimidate you, however. Always keep your goal in mind: to figure out which column is larger. Do you care how much larger one column is? We hope not.

Here's a good example.

Column A	Column B
$2 \times 4 \times 6 \times 8$	$3 \times 5 \times 7 \times 9$

Lower Level Test Takers

The ISEE's Lower Level test does not include quantitative comparison questions, so you can skip this section.

They Look Different, but the Math Is the Same

This section will introduce you to quantitative comparison, a different type of question from the "regular" multiple-choice questions you've seen so far. Don't worry—these questions test your knowledge of exactly the same math skills you have already learned in this chapter.

Test takers who don't appreciate the beauty of quant comp look at this one and immediately start multiplying. Look carefully, however, and compare the numbers in both columns.

Which is larger, 2 or 3 ?

Which is larger, 4 or 5 ?

Which is larger, 6 or 7 ?

Which is larger, 8 or 9 ?

In each case, column B contains larger numbers. Now, when you multiply larger numbers together, what happens? You guessed it—even larger numbers!

Which column is larger? Without doing a single bit of multiplication you know that (B) is the right answer. Good work!

(D) Means Different

Answer choice (D) is useful when the relationship between the columns can change. You may have to choose (D) when you have variables in a quant comp problem. For example:

Column A	Column B
$g + 12$	$h - 7$

Which column is larger here depends entirely on what g and h equal, and the problem doesn't give you that information. This is a perfect time to choose (D).

But be careful and don't be too quick to choose (D) whenever you see a variable.

Column A	Column B
$g + 12$	$g - 7$

With one small change, the answer is no longer (D). Because the variables are the same here, you can determine that no matter what number is represented by g, column A will always be larger. So in this case the answer is (A).

One valuable thing to remember is that when a quant comp question contains no variables and no unknown quantities, the answer cannot be (D).

Column A	Column B
$6 \times 3 \times 4$	$4 \times 6 \times 3$

Even if you somehow forget how to multiply (don't worry, you won't forget), someone somewhere knows how to multiply, so you can get rid of (D).

By the way, look quickly at the last example. First, you eliminate (D) because there are no variables. Do you need to multiply? Nope! The columns contain exactly the same numbers, just written in a different order. What's the answer? You got it: (C)!

PRACTICE DRILL 10—QUANT COMP—MIDDLE AND UPPER LEVEL ONLY

	Column A	Column B
1.	17×3	$17 \times 2 + 17$

	Column A	Column B
2.	$\dfrac{1}{2}$	$\dfrac{3}{8}$

	Column A	Column B
3.	$b + 80$	$b + 82$

Rob is two inches shorter than Matt.

Joel is four inches taller than Matt.

	Column A	Column B
4.	Rob's height	Joel's height

	Column A	Column B
5.	16^3	4^6

(A) means that Column A is always greater
(B) means that Column B is always greater
(C) means that Column A is always equal to Column B
(D) means that A, B, or C are not always true

Kimberly lives two miles from school.

Jennifer lives four miles from school.

When You Are Done
Check your answers in
Chapter 20.

	Column A	Column B
6.	The distance from Kimberly's house to school	The distance from Kimberly's house to Jennifer's house

Quant Comp Plugging In

Think back to the Algebra section. Plugging In helped you deal with variables, right? The same technique works on quant comp questions. There are some special rules you'll need to follow to make sure you can reap all the benefits that Plugging In has to offer you in the Quantitative Comparison section.

Column A	Column B
x	x^2

Follow these three simple steps, and you won't go wrong.

Weird Numbers
For your second Plug In,
try something weird:
Zero
One
Negative
Extreme
Fraction

Step 1: Write "A B C D" next to the problem.

Step 2: Plug In an "easy" number for x. By easy number, we mean a nice simple integer, like 3. When you Plug In 3 for x in the above example, column A is 3 and column B is 9, right? Think about the answer choices and what they mean. Column B is larger, so can the correct answer be (A)? No, eliminate it. Can the correct answer be (C)? No, you can get rid of that one, too!

Step 3: Plug In a "weird" number for x. A weird number is a little harder to define, but it is something that most test takers won't think of—for instance, zero, one, a fraction, or a negative number. In this case, try plugging in 1. Column A is 1 and column B is also 1. So the columns *can* be equal. Now look at the answer choices you have left. Answer choice (B) means that column B is always greater. Is it? No. Cross off (B) and pick (D).

Remember, if you get one result from Plugging In a number and you get a different result by Plugging In another number, you have to pick answer choice (D). But don't think too much about these questions, or you'll end up spending a lifetime looking for the perfect "weird" number. Just remember that you always have to Plug In **twice** on quant comp questions.

PRACTICE DRILL 11—QUANT COMP—MIDDLE AND UPPER LEVEL ONLY

	Column A	Column B

$$x > 1$$

1. x x^2

---

b is an integer and $-1 < b < 1$

2. $\dfrac{b}{2}$ $\dfrac{b}{8}$

---

3. p gallons m quarts

---

x is a positive integer

4. $\dfrac{x}{4}$ $\dfrac{x}{5}$

---

w is an integer less than 4

p is an integer greater than 10

5. pw w

---

6. $4c + 6$ $3c + 12$

PRACTICE DRILL 12—QUANT COMP—MIDDLE AND UPPER LEVEL ONLY

	Column A	Column B
1.	The total cost of 3 plants that cost $4 each	The total cost of 4 plants that cost $3 each

	Column A	Column B
2.	$30(1 - 2n)$	$30 - 2n$

The product of 3 integers is 48.

	Column A	Column B
3.	The smallest of the 3 integers	1

	Column A	Column B
4.	$(x + y)(x - y)$	$x^2 - y^2$

	Column A	Column B
5.	$(7 - 4) \times 3 - 3$	0

Line m is the graph of $y = x + 4$.

	Column A	Column B
6.	Slope of line m	Slope of line l that is perpendicular to line m

The price of a pair of shoes is $100. The price is increased by 20%. Nobody buys it, so the price is then reduced by another 20%.

	Column A	Column B
7.	The final price of the pair of shoes after reductions	$100

8.　$\left(-\dfrac{5}{6}\right)^3$　　　　　　　　　$\left(-\dfrac{5}{6}\right)^5$

9.　$\left(\dfrac{5}{6}\right)^4$　　　　　　　　　$\left(\dfrac{5}{6}\right)^6$

10.　$\left(-\dfrac{5}{6}\right)^2$　　　　　　　　$\left(-\dfrac{5}{6}\right)^4$

11.　$\left(\dfrac{5}{6}\right)^3$　　　　　　　　　$\left(\dfrac{5}{6}\right)^5$

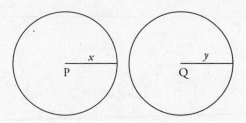

Note: Figure not drawn to scale.

12.　Circumference of Circle P　　Area of Circle Q

A 6-sided number die, numbered 1 to 6, is rolled.

13.　Probability that the number　　$\dfrac{3}{6}$
rolled is prime.

---

a and b are integers.

$$a + b = 5$$

14.　a　　　　　　　　　　　　　b

15. $\sqrt{25-9}$ $\sqrt{25}-\sqrt{9}$

Set A: {all prime numbers}

Set B: {all positive multiples of 5 less than 50}

Set C: intersection of Sets A and B

16.   Number of elements in Set C 1

---

17. $\dfrac{3}{4} \times \dfrac{3}{4}$ $\dfrac{3}{4} + \dfrac{3}{4}$

$a > 0$

$b < 0$

18. $-(ab)$ $-ab$

Set A: {1, 3, 8, 11, 15}

Set B: {2, 4, 8, 9, 10, 20}

19.   Median of Set A Median of Set B

---

20.   Sum of all consecutive
integers between 1 and
10, inclusive   5(11)

21. $2^3 + 2^3 + 2^3$ 2^9

---

22. $7(x - 3)$ $21 - 7x$

---

23. The smallest positive factor
     of 25 multiplied by biggest
     positive factor of 16   40

---

24. Probability of a fair penny   Probability of a fair
     having heads face up on   penny having heads face
     two consecutive flips   up on three consecutive flips

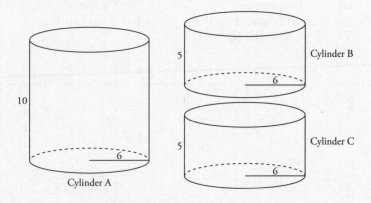

Note: Volume of a right cylinder: $V = r^2h$

25. Volume of Cylinder A   Total Volume of
                                   Cylinders B and C

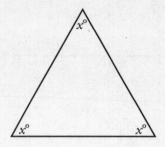

26. x 60

---

27.   The percent increase   The percent decrease
        from 1 to 2   from 2 to 1

---

28.   The average   The median of
        (arithmetic mean) of   4, 6, 8, and 10
        4, 6, 8, and 10

$$x > 0$$
$$y > 0$$

29. $\dfrac{xy}{2}$ $\sqrt{xy}$

---

30.   (567.83) (.40)   (40) (5.6783)

Meredith has 7 pairs of purple shoes, 2 pairs of red shoes,
and 1 pair of white shoes. She chooses one pair of shoes at random.

31.   Probability of <u>not</u> picking $\dfrac{8}{10}$
a red pair of shoes

---

32.   Total cost of 10 shirts at   Total cost of 20 shirts at
$8 each $4.50 each

---

33. $\dfrac{x^2 x^5}{x^4}$ x^3

---

34. $x^2 = 36$ -6

---

35.   Largest positive factor   Smallest positive multiple
of 16   of 16

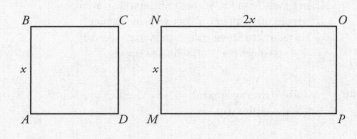

36.   Perimeter of   Perimeter of
square *ABCD*   rectangle *MNOP*

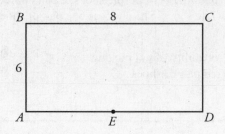

E is the midpoint of side AD.

37.   Area of $\triangle BDE$ 12

---

38. 4^{12} 64^4

A hat contains blue and red tickets.
The ratio of blue tickets to red tickets is 3:5.

39. $\dfrac{3}{5}$ The fractional part of all the
                                    tickets in the hat that are blue

---

Luke travels from Providence to Boston at an average
speed of 50 miles per hour without stopping.
He returns to Providence at an average speed of
60 miles per hours without stopping.

40.   Luke's average speed   55 miles per hour
        for the entire trip

41. The slope of the line
     $12x - 4y = 16$

The slope of the line
containing points
$(-3,\ 6)$ and $(3,\ 12)$

---

42. $\sqrt{0.81}$

$\sqrt{8.1}$

A rectangle with sides y and z has an area of 36.

43. The length of y

The length of z

---

44. The number of non-negative
     even integers less than 10

4

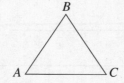

Triangle ABC is isosceles.
$BC = 2$

45. The area of triangle ABC

4

MATH REVIEW

Make sure you can confidently answer all of the following questions before you take the ISEE.

1. Is zero an integer? _____

2. Is zero positive or negative? _____

3. What operation do you perform to find a sum? _____

4. What operation do you perform to find a product? _____

5. What is the result called when you divide? _____

6. Is 312 divisible by 3 ? _____

    Is 312 divisible by 9 ? _____

    (Actually, dividing isn't fair. Use your divisibility rules!)

7. What does the "E" in PEMDAS stand for? _____

8. Is 3 a factor of 12 ? _____

    Is 12 a factor of 3 ? _____

9. Is 3 a multiple of 12 ? _____

    Is 12 a multiple of 3 ? _____

10. What is the tens digit in the number 304.275 ? _____

11. What is the tenths digit in the number 304.275 ? _____

12. 2^3 = _____

13. In "math language" the word percent means: _____.

14. In "math language" the word of means: _____.

15. In a Ratio Box, the last column on the right is always the

    _____.

16. Whenever you see a problem involving averages, draw the

_____.

17. When a problem contains variables in the question and in the

answers, I will _____.

18. To find the perimeter of a square, I _____ the

length(s) of _____ side(s).

19. To find the area of a square, I _____

the length(s) of _____ sides.

20. There are _____ degrees in a straight line.

21. A triangle has _____ angles, which total

_____ degrees.

22. A four-sided figure contains _____ degrees.

23. An isosceles triangle has _____ equal sides; a(n)

_____ triangle has three equal sides.

24. The longest side of a right triangle is called the _____

and is located opposite the _____.

25. To find the area of a triangle, I use the formula: _____.

Chapter 18
ISEE Verbal

INTRODUCTION

Take a look at the Verbal section of a practice ISEE in this book. The Verbal section on the ISEE consists of 40 questions (34 for the Lower Level), usually broken into

- 20 synonym questions (questions 1 to 20)
- 20 sentence completion questions (questions 21 to 40)

That's 40 questions—but you only have 20 minutes! Should you try to spend 30 seconds on each question to get them all done? **No!**

You Mean I Don't Have to Do All the Questions?

Nope. You'll actually improve your score by working on fewer questions, as long as you're still using all of the allotted time. Even though you shouldn't work on all of the questions, you should still answer them all with your favorite letter because there is no penalty for a wrong answer!

"Allotted Time"?
If you can't define *allotted*, make a flash card for it! Look in Chapter 1 for ideas on how to use flash cards to learn new words.

Remember, this test is designed for students in two to four different grade levels. There will be vocabulary on some of these questions that is aimed at students older than you, and almost no one in your grade will get those questions right. The ISEE score you receive will compare you only with students in your own grade. The younger you are in your test level, the fewer questions you are expected to complete. Sixth graders are expected to complete the fewest questions on the Middle Level test. Eighth graders are expected to do the fewest questions on the Upper Level test.

So, why rush through the questions you can get right to get to the really tough ones that almost nobody gets? That approach only ensures that you will make hasty, careless errors. Work slowly on the questions that have vocabulary that you know to make sure you get them right. Then try the ones that have some harder words in them.

If you pace yourself, you'll have much more time for each question than students who think they have to get them all done.

Which Questions Should I Work on?

Everybody's different. You know some words that your friends don't, and vice versa. Some verbal questions are harder for certain people than they are for others.

Guess?
Yes. Fill in an answer even for the questions you don't read. Why? Because there is no penalty for a wrong answer on the ISEE, so you've got nothing to lose (and plenty to gain when you happen to be right!).

So, here's the plan: Go through the first section, and do all the synonyms that are easy for you first. Easy questions are those where you know the definitions of the words involved. Then, go back through and do the questions with words that sound familiar, even if you are not sure of their dictionary definition—these are words you sort of know. Then, move on to sentence completions, leaving yourself more than half the time in the section. Remember to skip a number on the answer sheet when you skip a question—but do fill it in at some point!

Knowing your own vocabulary is the key to deciding if you can answer a question easily.

Know Yourself

Categorize the words you see in ISEE questions into

- Words you know
- Words you sort of know
- Words you really don't know

Be honest with yourself when it comes to deciding if you know a word or not, so you apply the techniques that are best for the questions on which you are working. Keep your idea of the word's meaning flexible, because the test writers sometimes use the words in ways that you and I do not! (They claim to use dictionary definitions.)

Of course, the easiest way to get a verbal question right is by making sure all the words in it fall into the first category—words you know. The best way to do this is by learning new vocabulary words *every day*. Check out the Vocabulary chapter (Chapter 1) for the best ways to do this.

You can raise your verbal score moderately just by using the techniques we teach in this chapter. But if you want to see a substantial rise in your score, you need to build up your vocabulary, too.

Eliminate Answer Choices

With math questions, there's always one *correct* answer. The other answers are simply wrong. In a verbal question, however, things are not that simple. Words are much more slippery than numbers. So verbal questions have *best* answers, not *correct* answers. The other answers aren't necessarily wrong, but the people who score the ISEE think they're not as good as the *best* one. This means that, even more than on the Quantitative sections, in the Verbal and Reading sections you should always try to eliminate answer choices.

Get used to looking for *worse* answers. There are many more of them than there are *best* answers, so *worse* answers are easier to find!

When you find them, cross them out in the question booklet to make sure you don't spend any more time looking at them. No matter which other techniques you use to answer a question, first eliminate wrong answers, instead of trying to magically pick out the best answer right away.

Cross Out the Bad Ones
Even when none of the answers looks particularly right, you can usually eliminate at least one.

Shop Around
Try every answer choice in a verbal question to be sure you're picking the *best* answer there.

Don't Rule It Out
Don't eliminate answers
with words you don't
know.

One thing to remember for the Verbal section: You should not eliminate answer choices that contain words you don't know. It doesn't matter that *you* don't know what a word means—it could still be the answer.

What If I Can't Narrow It Down to One Answer?

Should you guess? Yes. Even if you can't eliminate any choices, you should guess. We mentioned before that you should leave a minute or two at the end of the section to fill in an answer for any questions you did not get to. Why? *Because there's no guessing penalty on the ISEE.* Nothing is subtracted from your score for a wrong answer, and because there are four answer choices, you'll get approximately 25 percent correct of the questions on which you guess randomly.

That means that you should *never* leave a question blank. Pick a letter (A, B, C, or D) to fill in for your random guesses. It doesn't matter which letter you use, but stick with one letter-of-the-day so you don't have to think about it.

Of course, the number of questions you get right will increase if you can eliminate some answer choices before you guess, so we'll teach you techniques to do this.

Where Do I Start?

Bubble Practice
Whenever you do a
practice test, use the
sample answer sheet so
you get used to skipping
around and making sure
you're always on the same
number on the test booklet
and answer sheet.

Do synonyms first in the Verbal section, right where you find them. Get them done in less than ten minutes so you have a little more than half the time in the section for sentence completions. Sentence completions take longer to read and work through, but they have more context to help you get the question right, even if you don't know all the words involved. If you get stuck on a sentence completion, simply fill in the letter-of-the-day and move on. Don't save it for a second pass. Similarly, if you realize you simply don't know the stem word or a synonym, just fill in your guess and keep going.

You'll be doing the questions in the following order:

- Synonyms with words you know
- Synonyms with words you sort of know
- Sentence completions

REVIEW—THE VERBAL PLAN

Pacing and Verbal Strategy

What's the order in which I do questions in the Verbal section?

1. _____

2. _____

3. _____

   How long should I spend on synonyms? _____

   What's the technique I'll be using all the time, regardless of whatever

   else I'm using to answer a question? _____

   How many answer choices must I have eliminated to guess

   productively? _____

   Can I eliminate answer choices that contain words I don't know?

   _____

If you had trouble with any of these questions, just review this part of the chapter before moving on.

Knowing My Vocabulary

Look at each of the following words and decide if it's a word that you know, sort of know, or really don't know. If you know it, write down its definition.

insecticide (noun)   _____

trifle (verb)   _____

repugnant (adjective)   _____

mollify (verb)   _____

camouflage (verb)   _____

historic (adjective)   _____

Check the ones you thought you knew or sort of knew. Look them up in the dictionary and make flash cards for them.

When You Are Done
Check your answers in Chapter 20.

Be Honest
Do you really know the definition of the word? The ISEE uses dictionary definitions, and these may differ from your own sometimes. If you're not positive, you may want to use the techniques for when you sort of know the word.

SYNONYMS

What Is a Synonym?

On the ISEE, a synonym question asks you to choose the answer choice that comes closest in meaning to the stem word (the word in capital letters). Often, the best answer won't mean the exact same thing as the stem word, but it will be closer than any of the other choices.

You need to decide which vocabulary category the synonym stem word falls into for you, so you know which technique to use. First, do all the synonyms for which you know the stem word, and then go back and do the ones with stem words you sort of know.

When You Know the Stem Word

Write Down Your Own Definition

Don't Waste Time
Make sure you cross out answers you've elimi-nated, so you don't look at them again.

Come up with a simple definition—a word or a phrase. Write it next to the stem word. Then look at the answers, eliminate the ones that are furthest from your definition, and choose the closest one.

It's very simple. Don't let the test writers put words in your mouth. Make sure you're armed with your own definition before you look at their answer choices. They often like to put in a word that is a close second to the best answer; if you've got your own synonym ready, you'll be able to make the distinction.

If you need to, cover the answers with your hand so you can think of your defini-tion before looking. Eventually, you may not have to write down your definitions, but you should start out that way so that you are not influenced by the choices they give you.

As you compare the choices with your definition, cross out the wrong ones with your pencil. Crossing out answer choices is something you should *always* do—it saves you time because you don't go back to choices you've already decided were not the best.

As always, don't eliminate words you don't know. Try this one. Write your defini-tion of WITHER before you look at the answer choices.

WITHER: _____

(A)   play
(B)   spoil
(C)   greatly improve
(D)   wilt

The stem word means "shrivel" or "dry up." Which answer is closest? (D). You may have been considering (B), but (D) is closer.

PRACTICE DRILL 1—WRITE YOUR OWN DEFINITION

Write your definition—just a word or two—for each of these stem words.

1. BIZARRE: _____

2. PREFACE: _____

3. GENEROUS: _____

4. MORAL: _____

5. ALTER: _____

6. REVOLVE: _____

7. HOPEFUL: _____

8. LINGER: _____

9. ASSIST: _____

10. CONSTRUCT: _____

11. STOOP: _____

12. CANDID: _____

13. TAUNT: _____

14. COARSE: _____

15. VAIN: _____

16. SERENE: _____

17. UTILIZE: _____

18. VIGOROUS: _____

19. PROLONG: _____

20. BENEFIT: _____

When You Are Done
Check your answers in
Chapter 20.

Write Another Definition

Why would you ever need to change your definition? Let's see.

MANEUVER:

(A) avoidance
(B) deviation
(C) find
(D) contrivance

Parts of Speech?

If you need to, go back and review parts of speech in the Word Parts section of Chapter 1.

Your definition may be something like *move* or *control* if you know the word from hearing it applied to cars. But that definition isn't in the answer choices. The problem is that you're thinking about *maneuver* as a verb. However, *maneuver* can also be a noun. It means "a plan, scheme, or trick." Now go back and eliminate. The answer is (D).

The ISEE sometimes uses secondary definitions, which can be the same part of speech or a different part of speech from the primary definition. Just stay flexible in your definitions, and you'll be fine.

PRACTICE DRILL 2—WRITE ANOTHER DEFINITION

Write down as many definitions as you can think of for the following words. Your definitions may be the same part of speech or different. If you have a hard time thinking of different meanings, look up the word.

1. POINT: _____   _____

2. INDUSTRY: _____   _____

3. FLAG: _____   _____

4. FLUID: _____   _____

5. CHAMPION: _____   _____

6. TABLE: _____   _____

When You Are Done

Check your answers in Chapter 20.

7. SERVICE: _____   _____

PRACTICE DRILL 3—EASY SYNONYM TECHNIQUES

Try these synonyms.

- Use the definition for the stem word that you wrote down before.
- Look at the answer choices, and eliminate the ones that are furthest from your definition.
- If there are stem words you don't know well enough to define, just skip and mark them and come back after you've learned techniques for stem words you sort of know.

1. BIZARRE:

   (A) lonely
   (B) unable
   (C) odd
   (D) found

2. PREFACE:

   (A) introduce
   (B) state
   (C) propose
   (D) jumble

3. GENEROUS:

   (A) skimpy
   (B) faulty
   (C) ample
   (D) unusual

4. MORAL:

   (A) imitation
   (B) full
   (C) real
   (D) upright

5. ALTER:

   (A) sew
   (B) make up
   (C) react
   (D) change

6. REVOLVE:

   (A) push against
   (B) go forward
   (C) leave behind
   (D) turn around

7. HOPEFUL:

   (A) discouraging
   (B) promising
   (C) fulfilling
   (D) deceiving

8. LINGER:

   (A) hurry
   (B) abate
   (C) dawdle
   (D) attempt

9. ASSIST:

   (A) work
   (B) discourage
   (C) hinder
   (D) help

10. CONSTRUCT:

    (A) build
    (B) type
    (C) live in
    (D) engage

11. STOOP:

    (A) raise
    (B) elevate
    (C) condescend
    (D) realize

12. CANDID:

    (A) picture
    (B) honest
    (C) prepared
    (D) unfocused

13. TAUNT:

    (A) delay
    (B) stand
    (C) show
    (D) tease

14. COARSE:

    (A) smooth
    (B) crude
    (C) polite
    (D) furious

15. VAIN:

(A) conceited
(B) beautiful
(C) talented
(D) helpless

16. SERENE:

(A) helpful
(B) normal
(C) calm
(D) disastrous

17. UTILIZE:

(A) pass on
(B) resort to
(C) rely on
(D) make use of

18. VIGOROUS:

(A) slothful
(B) aimless
(C) energetic
(D) glorious

19. PROLONG:

(A) affirmative
(B) lengthen
(C) exceed
(D) assert

20. BENEFIT:

(A) cooperate
(B) struggle
(C) assist
(D) appeal

When You Sort of Know the Stem Word

Why should you do synonyms quickly? Why are they harder than sentence completions, even though you should do them faster?

Synonyms can be harder to beat than sentence completions because the ISEE gives you no context with which to figure out words that you sort of know. But that doesn't mean you're done after the easy synonyms. You can get the medium ones, too. You just need to create your own context to figure out words you don't know very well.

Also, keep in mind that your goal is to eliminate the worst answers and make educated guesses. You'll be able to do this for every synonym that you sort of know. Even if you eliminate just one choice, you've increased your chances of guessing correctly. You'll gain points overall.

Make Your Own Context

You can create your own context for the word by figuring out how you've heard it used before. Think of the other words you've heard used with the stem word. Is there a certain phrase that comes to mind? What does that phrase mean?

If you still can't come up with a definition for the stem word, just use the context in which you've heard the word to eliminate answers that wouldn't fit at all in that same context.

How about this stem word?

ABOMINABLE:

Where have you heard *abominable*? The Abominable Snowman, of course. Think about it—you know it's a monster-like creature. Which answer choices can you eliminate?

ABOMINABLE:

(A) enormous   the enormous snowman? maybe
(B) terrible   the terrible snowman? sure
(C̶) rude   the rude snowman? probably not
(D̶) talkative   the talkative snowman? only Frosty!

You can throw out everything but (A) and (B). Now you can guess, with a much better shot at getting the answer right than guessing from four choices. Or you can think about where else you've heard the stem word. Have you ever heard something called an *abomination*? Was it something terrible or was it something enormous? (B) is the answer.

Try this one. Where have you heard this stem word? Try the answers in that context.

SURROGATE:

(A) requested
(B) paranoid
(C) numerous
(D) substitute

Have you heard the stem word in *surrogate mother*? If you have, you can definitely eliminate (A), (B), and (C). A surrogate mother is a substitute mother.

Try one more.

ENDANGER:

(A) rescue
(B) frighten
(C) confuse
(D) threaten

Everyone's associations are different, but you've probably heard of *endangered species* or *endangered lives*. Use either of those phrases to eliminate answer choices that can't fit into it. Rescued species? Frightened species? Confused species? Threatened species? (D) works best.

PRACTICE DRILL 4—MAKING YOUR OWN CONTEXT
Write down the phrase in which you've heard each word.

1. COMMON: _____

2. COMPETENT: _____

3. ABRIDGE: _____

4. UNTIMELY: _____

5. HOMOGENIZE: _____

6. DELINQUENT: _____

7. INALIENABLE: _____

8. PALTRY: _____

9. AUSPICIOUS: _____

10. PRODIGAL: _____

When You Are Done
Check your answers in Chapter 20.

PRACTICE DRILL 5—USING YOUR OWN CONTEXT

1. COMMON:

   (A) beautiful
   (B) novel
   (C) typical
   (D) constant

2. COMPETENT:

   (A) angry
   (B) peaceful
   (C) well-written
   (D) capable

3. ABRIDGE:

   (A) complete
   (B) span
   (C) reach
   (D) shorten

4. UNTIMELY:

   (A) late
   (B) punctual
   (C) inappropriate
   (D) continuous

5. HOMOGENIZE:

   (A) make the same
   (B) send away
   (C) isolate
   (D) enfold

6. DELINQUENT:

   (A) underage
   (B) negligent
   (C) superior
   (D) advanced

7. INALIENABLE:

   (A) misplaced
   (B) universal
   (C) assured
   (D) democratic

8. PALTRY:

   (A) meager
   (B) colored
   (C) thick
   (D) abundant

9. AUSPICIOUS:

   (A) supple
   (B) minor
   (C) favorable
   (D) ominous

10. PRODIGAL:

   (A) wasteful
   (B) amusing
   (C) disadvantaged
   (D) lazy

Use Word Parts to Piece Together a Definition

Prefixes, roots, and suffixes can help you figure out what a word means. You should use this technique in addition to word association, because not all word parts retain their original meanings.

You may never have seen this stem word before, but if you've been working on your Vocabulary chapter, you know that the root *pac* or *peac* means peace. You can see the same root in *Pacific*, *pacifier*, and the word *peace* itself. So what's the answer to this synonym?

PACIFIST:

   (A) innocent person
   (B) person opposed to war
   (C) warmonger
   (D) wanderer of lands

It's (B). In the following stem word, we see *cred*, a word part that means "belief" or "faith." You can see this word part in *incredible*, *credit*, and *credibility*. The answer is now simple.

CREDIBLE:

   (A) obsolete
   (B) believable
   (C) fabulous
   (D) mundane

(B) again. What are the word parts in the following stem word?

MONOTONOUS:

(A) lively
(B) educational
(C) nutritious
(D) repetitious

Mono means "one." *Tone* has to do with sound. If something keeps striking one sound, how would you describe it? (D) is the answer.

The only way you'll be able to use word parts is if you know them. Get cracking on the Vocabulary chapter!

Use "Positive/Negative"

Another way to use what you sort of know about a stem word is to ask yourself whether it is positive or negative. Then, decide if each of the answer choices is positive or negative. Eliminate any answers that do not match. If the stem word is positive, then the answer must be positive. If the stem word is negative, then the answer must be as well. Write "+" or "−" or "neither" next to each word as you make your decisions.

If someone said you were belligerent, would you be happy? No, because *belligerent* is a negative word. You might know that from hearing the word, but you might also know what the word part *bell* means. Now, decide whether each answer choice is positive or negative.

BELLIGERENT: −

(A) frisky   +
(B) friendly   +
(C) antagonistic   −
(D) persuasive   +

You can eliminate (A), (B), and (D) because you're looking for a synonym, so if the stem is negative, then the answer must also be negative.

Try this one.

ZENITH:

(A) distance
(B) failure
(C) high point
(D) complaint

How do you know *zenith* is positive? Probably because it's the brand name of a television set, and brand names will generally be positive words. The only really positive answer choice here is (C), and that's the answer.

PRACTICE DRILL 6—DECIDE POSITIVE/NEGATIVE

1. LUGUBRIOUS: _____   6. HARMONIOUS: _____

2. DISDAIN: _____   7. INCORRIGIBLE: _____

3. CACOPHONOUS: _____   8. ELOQUENT: _____

4. COMPASSIONATE: _____   9. AGILE: _____

5. SLANDER: _____   10. TOIL: _____

When You Are Done
Check your answers in Chapter 20.

PRACTICE DRILL 7—USE POSITIVE/NEGATIVE

In these synonyms, you know only that the stem word is positive or negative. Eliminate as many answers as you can, based on what you know.

1. GOOD WORD:
   (A) harmful
   (B) helpful
   (C) unusual
   (D) horrid

2. GOOD WORD:
   (A) useful
   (B) handy
   (C) difficult
   (D) regular

3. BAD WORD:
   (A) disgusting
   (B) reliable
   (C) furious
   (D) sturdy

4. BAD WORD:
   (A) beneficial
   (B) placid
   (C) coarse
   (D) noisy

5. BAD WORD:

   (A) faulty
   (B) vague
   (C) grateful
   (D) angry

6. GOOD WORD:

   (A) malignant
   (B) unhealthy
   (C) friendly
   (D) forward thinking

7. GOOD WORD:

   (A) incapable
   (B) useful
   (C) ferocious
   (D) flavorful

8. BAD WORD:

   (A) assistant
   (B) culprit
   (C) patron
   (D) rival

9. GOOD WORD:

   (A) diverse
   (B) winning
   (C) ruined
   (D) infrequent

10. GOOD WORD:

   (A) honorable
   (B) despicable
   (C) elite
   (D) unsurpassed

11. BAD WORD:

   (A) dangerous
   (B) illegal
   (C) sophisticated
   (D) delicious

12. BAD WORD:

   (A) rascal
   (B) vermin
   (C) benefactor
   (D) addict

13. GOOD WORD:

   (A) slovenly
   (B) gluttonous
   (C) envious
   (D) beatific

14. GOOD WORD:

   (A) visionary
   (B) despot
   (C) malefactor
   (D) ingrate

15. GOOD WORD:

   (A) significant
   (B) mediocre
   (C) provincial
   (D) opulent

16. BAD WORD:

   (A) apathetic
   (B) assertive
   (C) committed
   (D) insipid

17. BAD WORD:

   (A) banal
   (B) unrealistic
   (C) vague
   (D) decisive

18. BAD WORD:

   (A) tyrant
   (B) rebel
   (C) leader
   (D) participant

19. GOOD WORD:

   (A) quack
   (B) expert
   (C) narrator
   (D) reporter

20. GOOD WORD:

   (A) turmoil
   (B) amity
   (C) benign
   (D) virulent

Eliminate Wrong Parts of Speech

Eliminate answers that cannot be the same part of speech as the stem word, even if they're close in meaning. You should keep in mind that many words can be more than one part of speech. In the model below, we've written in the parts of speech instead of the actual words:

ADJECTIVE

(A)   adjective
(B)   noun
(C)   adjective or verb
(D)   verb or noun

In the synonym above, you can eliminate (B) and (D) because they cannot be adjectives, and you know that the "best" answer is an adjective here because that's what the stem word is.

Remember, suffixes can be very helpful in telling you what part of speech a word is. Look in Chapter 1 for some helpful suffixes.

PRACTICE DRILL 8—IDENTIFYING PARTS OF SPEECH

What parts of speech are the following words? (Some of them can be more than one.)

1.   mirror _____

2.   flattery _____

3.   cover _____

4.   emaciated _____

5.   adversity _____

6.   malleable _____

When You Are Done
Check your answers in Chapter 20.

Words You Really Don't Know

Don't spend time on a synonym with a stem word you've never seen if you don't know any of its word parts. Simply make sure you fill in your letter-of-the-day for that question.

Review—The Synonyms Plan

Words I know

When I know the stem word, I _____

If I don't see a definition close to mine, I _____

Words I sort of know

When I sort of know the stem word, I can use the following techniques:

_____

_____

_____

Words I really don't know

If I've never seen the stem word before, I _____

Can I eliminate answers that contain words I don't know? _____

If you have trouble with any of these questions, review the appropriate part of this chapter before you move on.

When You Are Done

Check your answers in Chapter 20.

PRACTICE DRILL 9—ALL SYNONYMS TECHNIQUES

1. PRINCIPLE:
   - (A) leader
   - (B) standard
   - (C) theory
   - (D) chief

2. CAPTURE:

   (A) secure
   (B) lose
   (C) steal
   (D) halt

3. BEFRIEND:

   (A) sever ties
   (B) close down
   (C) approach
   (D) enjoy

4. AUTOMATIC:

   (A) involuntary
   (B) enjoyable
   (C) forceful
   (D) hapless

5. APTITUDE:

   (A) difficulty
   (B) reason
   (C) mistake
   (D) ability

6. CAPITAL:

   (A) primary
   (B) regressive
   (C) capable
   (D) central

7. REPRESS:

   (A) defy
   (B) faithful
   (C) ruling
   (D) prevent

8. ENDURE:

   (A) take in
   (B) stick with
   (C) add to
   (D) run from

9. TRANSMIT:

   (A) eliminate
   (B) watch
   (C) send
   (D) annoy

10. DIALOGUE:

    (A) speak
    (B) conversation
    (C) monologue
    (D) sermon

11. EULOGY:

    (A) attack
    (B) tribute
    (C) complement
    (D) encouragement

12. BAN:

    (A) remove
    (B) impose
    (C) forbid
    (D) specify

13. APATHY:

    (A) involvement
    (B) compassion
    (C) contempt
    (D) indifference

14. OMNISCIENT:

    (A) agile
    (B) logical
    (C) knowledgeable
    (D) invulnerable

15. TRANSGRESS:

    (A) transport
    (B) eradicate
    (C) include
    (D) violate

16. VIVACIOUS:

    (A) nimble
    (B) lively
    (C) easily amused
    (D) direct

17. HYPERBOLE:

    (A) isolation
    (B) identification
    (C) exaggeration
    (D) sharp curve

18. CONGENITAL:

    (A) innocent
    (B) inborn
    (C) graceful
    (D) acquired

19. SUCCINCT:

    (A) subterranean
    (B) confusing
    (C) blatant
    (D) direct

20. CRAFTY:

    (A) apt
    (B) sly
    (C) agile
    (D) wicked

21. FLUENT:

    (A) spoken
    (B) quiet
    (C) flowing
    (D) fast

22. IDENTICAL:

    (A) broken
    (B) duplicate
    (C) foolish
    (D) related

23. POPULAR:

    (A) rude
    (B) accepted
    (C) understood
    (D) respected

24. WHARF:

    (A) beach
    (B) raft
    (C) flat ship
    (D) dock

25. FAITHFUL:

    (A) hopeful
    (B) unrealistic
    (C) truthful
    (D) devoted

26. OBSTACLE:

   (A) path
   (B) great distance
   (C) ditch
   (D) impediment

27. CONVOLUTED:

   (A) interesting
   (B) expensive
   (C) twisted
   (D) forged

28. ALIGN:

   (A) repair
   (B) command
   (C) straighten
   (D) replace

29. VETO:

   (A) reject
   (B) discuss
   (C) define
   (D) submit

30. MANGLE:

   (A) shine
   (B) wear
   (C) torture
   (D) mutilate

31. FEEBLE:

   (A) fair
   (B) ineffective
   (C) tough
   (D) hardened

32. SLUGGISH:

   (A) aggressive
   (B) slow
   (C) inconsiderate
   (D) wicked

33. REDUNDANT:

   (A) poor
   (B) superfluous
   (C) abundant
   (D) fancy

34. LAMPOON:

    (A) article
    (B) biography
    (C) journey
    (D) satire

35. TREPIDATION:

    (A) boldness
    (B) irony
    (C) rashness
    (D) fear

36. ASSESS:

    (A) deny
    (B) accept
    (C) size up
    (D) dismiss

37. GHASTLY:

    (A) responsible
    (B) erroneous
    (C) horrible
    (D) favorable

38. CENSURE:

    (A) editing
    (B) understanding
    (C) approval
    (D) disapproval

39. DISMANTLE:

    (A) discourse with
    (B) break down
    (C) yield to
    (D) drive away

40. CACOPHONY:

    (A) melody
    (B) harmony
    (C) music
    (D) dissonance

SENTENCE COMPLETIONS

What Is a Sentence Completion?

On an ISEE sentence completion, you need to pick the answer that best fills the blank in the sentence they've given you. Just like with synonym problems, you have to choose the best word from the answer choices, and sometimes it's not a perfect fit. On the Upper Level test, some questions will have two blanks.

Often, however, you'll actually find more than one choice that could fit in the blank. How do you decide which is best to choose?

Just like on the synonyms, you need to make sure the ISEE test writers don't get to put words in your mouth. That's how they confuse you, especially on the medium and hard questions. You need to have your own answer ready before you look at theirs.

Come Up with Your Own Word

The easiest way to make sure you don't get caught up in the ISEE's tricky answers is to cover them with your hand until you've thought of your own word for the blank. Why waste your time plugging all their answers into the sentence, anyway? Let's look at one.

> Quite ------- conditions continue to exist in many
> mountain towns in America where houses do not
> have running water or electricity.

What word would you put in the blank? Something like *basic* or *old-fashioned* or *harsh*? Write down any words that occur to you. Which part of the sentence lets you know which words could fit? "Where houses do not have running water or electricity" gives you the clue.

Just Use the Sentence
Don't try to use outside knowledge to fill in the blank. Use only what the sentence tells you.

When you've come up with one or two words you would put in the blank, write them down. (You may not always have to write them, but during practice you should, so you can compare your answers with the answers in this book.) Then, uncover the answers.

    (A) common
    (B) primitive
    (C) orderly
    (D) lively

Which looks most like your words? (B). Any of the other words could appear in this sentence in real life, right? However, because the only context you have is the sentence itself, you have to use what the sentence gives you to get the *best* answer for the ISEE.

Use the Clue

Try this one.

> Museums are good places for students of ------.

What word did you come up with? Art? History? Science? Those words are all different! Don't worry, you will not get a sentence completion like this because there's not enough information to go on—any answer choice could be defended! There will always be a clue to tell you what can go in the blank.

> Museums that house paintings and sculptures are good places for students of -------.

What's your word? Something like "art." What told you it was art, and not history or science? Underline the part of the sentence that gave you the clue. The clue is the most important part of the sentence—the part that tells you what to put in the blank.

Try another one. Underline the clue and fill in the blank.

> The businessman was ------- because sales were down and costs were up, and his demeanor showed his unhappiness.

Recycle
Often you can use the very same word(s) you see in the clue—
or something close!

Don't be afraid to just reuse the clue in the blank—the clue is *unhappiness* and the word *unhappy* would go well in the blank! When it fits, use the clue itself. Now eliminate answers.

    (A)   despondent
    (B)   persuasive
    (C)   indifferent
    (D)   unresponsive

Even if you're not sure what *despondent* means, do the other words mean *unhappy*? No. (A) must be the answer.

Cover the answers, underline the clue, and fill in the blank before looking at the choices.

> To join the soccer team, a student absolutely had to be able to practice two hours a day; however, buying the uniform was -------.

    (A)   obligatory
    (B)   universal
    (C)   natural
    (D)   optional

Your word was probably something like "not required" or "unnecessary." (Don't worry if you're using a short phrase instead of a word—anything that expresses the meaning of what should go in the blank is fine.) But the clue was "absolutely had to," and your words are the opposite of that. What's going on?

Up until now, all the sentences we've seen have had a clue that was pretty much the same as the word in the blank. But sometimes the word in the blank is actually different from the clue—in fact, an opposite. How can you tell when this is true? Well, which word in the sentence told you? *However*. *However* let you know that the word in the blank would be the opposite of the clue (the clue was "absolutely had to").

There are many little words that can tell you if the blank is the same as the clue or different.

Use Direction Words

Direction words tell you if the blank continues in the same direction as the clue or if it changes direction.

Which of these responses do you want to hear when you've just asked someone to the prom?

I really like you, *but* _____.

I really like you, *and* _____.

Why is the first one so awful to hear? *But* lets you know that the sentence is going to suddenly change direction and not be about liking you anymore. Why is the second one so much better? *And* lets you know that the sentence is going to continue in the same direction and continue to be all about liking you. Some other direction words are below. Add any others you can think of.

Different Direction	Same Direction
but	and
however	thus
although	therefore
rather	so
instead	because
despite	in addition
yet	consequently

Now, cover the answers, underline the clue, circle the direction words, and fill in your own word.

> When people first began investigating the human brain they were unscientific in their methods, but eventually they began to develop methods that were -------.
>
> (A) objective
> (B) inconclusive
> (C) lucrative
> (D) widespread

Which choice is closest to yours? If you underlined *unscientific* and circled *but*, then you could have written *scientific* in the blank. (A) is closest.

PRACTICE DRILL 10—COMING UP WITH YOUR OWN WORD

Underline the clues, circle the direction words, and come up with one or two words for each of these sentences.

1. The leading man's rehearsals were so _____ that the director and producer were already imagining what a hit the movie would be.

2. Once very _____, computers are now found in almost every home.

3. After playing more than a dozen different concert halls, the orchestra was praised by critics for its _____ rendition of Beethoven's famous *Fifth Symphony*.

4. Although Miles had been unable to sleep the night before, he seemed remarkably _____ when he gave his presentation.

5. Julie was _____ to have been in the right place at the right time; the drama coach gave her the lead in our class play.

6. Mr. Jones is an intelligent and _____ teacher; his knowledge is matched only by his concern for his students.

7. To the casual observer, all fingerprints may appear to be _____; but in fact each individual's prints are unique.

8.   Hardly one to _____, Josh tackled every project as soon as he got it.

9.   In Charles Dickens's *A Christmas Carol*, Scrooge is a particularly _____ character, refusing to give his assistant, Bob Cratchit, a raise, despite his enormous wealth.

10. Alfred Wegener's theory that the continents are slowly drifting apart has recently been confirmed by instruments that measure very small _____ in land masses.

11. Despite their seemingly _____ architecture, the pyramids of Giza are actually intricate marvels of ancient engineering.

12. Unlike animals, which must seek sustenance in their surrounding environments, plants are able to _____ their own food.

13. Great variations in successive layers of polar ice make it possible for scientists to determine how the climate has _____ over the past millennium.

14. Because of the rigors of mountain climbing, the team needs equipment that is both _____ enough to support the members and completely reliable.

15. For a student to qualify for the foreign study program, good language skills are absolutely necessary; however, prior travel to the host country is _____.

16. The task was very _____ because certain parts needed to be carried out over and over again.

17. Because the ground there was steep and dangerous, the mountain guide told us that it was _____ to approach the edge.

18. Most members of the drama club, though reserved in real life, are quite _____ once they get on stage.

19. Physicians offer recommendations about food groups and eating habits to help their patients follow a more _____ diet.

20. Fund-raising is only effective when _____ individuals are available, showing their concern by their readiness to give.

21. Not one to be easily intimidated, the corporal remained _____ while the opposing army pressed toward his troop's position.

22. Unlike her confident companion, she tended to be _____ when she found herself among strangers.

23. Although the rest of the class laughed at her antics, the teacher was _____ by Shelly's constant interruptions.

24. To avoid being penalized for tardiness, you should be _____ with your assignments.

25. Carpentry and cabinetmaking are such difficult trades that they require great _____ with woodworking tools.

26. One of the most ecologically diverse places on Earth, the tropical rain forests of Brazil are home to an incredible _____ of insect species.

27. Higher math is a _____ discipline; it requires just as much imagination and insight as do any of the arts.

28. Many tribes in New Guinea are known for their _____ societies; all property belongs to all members of the tribe.

29. Because their roots are external and their leaf bases clasp, palm trees are rigid and upright, yet _____ enough to bend in strong winds.

30. Though some assert that all behavior is learned, there are others who hold that some behaviors are _____, existing before any learning occurs.

31. A very outgoing and _____ individual, the mayor loved to talk to her fellow citizens.

32. Staring wide eyed, the crowd was _____ by the magician's amazing feats of illusion.

When You Are Done
Check your answers in Chapter 20.

PRACTICE DRILL 11—ELIMINATING ANSWERS BASED ON YOUR WORD

Using what you wrote in the sentences above, eliminate answers that cannot fit.

1. The leading man's rehearsals were so ------- that the director and producer were already imagining what a hit the movie would be.

   (A) indignant
   (B) overacted
   (C) trite
   (D) imaginative

2. Once very -------, computers are now found in almost every home.

   (A) common
   (B) unusual
   (C) obtainable
   (D) simple

3. After playing more than a dozen different concert halls, the orchestra was praised by critics for its ------- rendition of Beethoven's famous *Fifth Symphony*.

   (A) unimaginative
   (B) typical
   (C) moving
   (D) loud

4. Although Miles had been unable to sleep the night before, he seemed remarkably ------- when he gave his presentation.

   (A) worn
   (B) tired
   (C) presentable
   (D) alert

5. Julie was ------- to have been in the right place at the right time; the drama coach gave her the lead in our class play.

   (A) fortunate
   (B) inspired
   (C) dramatic
   (D) impressive

6. Mr. Jones is an intelligent and ------- teacher; his knowledge is matched only by his concern for his students.

   (A) caring
   (B) experienced
   (C) unusual
   (D) original

7. To the casual observer, all fingerprints may appear to be -------, but in fact, each individual's prints are unique.

   (A) different
   (B) complicated
   (C) personal
   (D) similar

8. Hardly one to -------, Josh tackled every project as soon as he got it.

   (A) strive
   (B) volunteer
   (C) procrastinate
   (D) disagree

9. In Charles Dickens's *A Christmas Carol*, Scrooge is a particularly ------- character, refusing to give his assistant, Bob Cratchit, a raise, despite his enormous wealth.

   (A) circumspect
   (B) miserly
   (C) generous
   (D) demure

10. Alfred Wegener's theory that the continents are slowly drifting apart has recently been confirmed by instruments that measure very small ------- in land masses.

    (A) locomotion
    (B) adhesion
    (C) punishment
    (D) erosion

11. Despite their seemingly ------- architecture, the pyramids of Giza are actually intricate marvels of ancient engineering.

    (A) revolutionary
    (B) complex
    (C) archaic
    (D) simplistic

12. Unlike animals, which must seek sustenance in their surrounding environment, plants are able to ------- their own food.

    (A) find
    (B) digest
    (C) gather
    (D) manufacture

13. Great variations in successive layers of polar ice make it possible for scientists to determine how the climate has ------- over the past millennium.

    (A) migrated
    (B) altered
    (C) tended
    (D) petrified

14. Because of the rigors of mountain climbing, the team needs equipment that is both ------- enough to support two members and completely reliable.

    (A) weighty
    (B) consistent
    (C) sturdy
    (D) innovative

15. For a student to qualify for the foreign study program, good language skills are absolutely necessary, however, prior travel to the host country is -------.

    (A) inevitable
    (B) mandatory
    (C) plausible
    (D) optional

16. The task was very ------- because certain parts needed to be carried out over and over again.

    (A) standard
    (B) enjoyable
    (C) tiresome
    (D) common

17. Because the ground there was steep and dangerous, the mountain guide told us that it was ------- to approach the edge.

    (A) encouraged
    (B) forbidden
    (C) important
    (D) possible

18. Most members of the drama club, though reserved in real life, are quite ------- once they get on stage.

    (A) dynamic
    (B) quarrelsome
    (C) threatening
    (D) behaved

19. Physicians offer recommendations about food groups and eating habits in order to help their patients follow a more ------- diet.

    (A) total
    (B) hearty
    (C) balanced
    (D) fulfilling

20. Fund-raising is only effective when ------- individuals are available, showing their concern by their readiness to give.

    (A) popular
    (B) famous
    (C) selfless
    (D) meaningful

21. Not one to be easily intimidated, the corporal remained ------- while the opposing army pressed toward his troop's position.

    (A) commanding
    (B) composed
    (C) aggressive
    (D) communicative

22. Unlike her confident companion, she tended to be ------- when she found herself among strangers.

    (A) lively
    (B) friendly
    (C) crowded
    (D) bashful

23. Although the rest of the class laughed at her antics, the teacher was ------- by Shelly's constant interruptions.

    (A) irked
    (B) amused
    (C) consoled
    (D) confused

24. To avoid being penalized for tardiness, you should be ------- with your assignments.

   (A) original
   (B) punctual
   (C) precise
   (D) thorough

25. Carpentry and cabinetmaking are such difficult trades that they require great ------- with woodworking tools.

   (A) adeptness
   (B) alertness
   (C) awareness
   (D) assertiveness

26. One of the most ecologically diverse places on Earth, the tropical rain forests of Brazil are home to an incredible ------- of insect species.

   (A) size
   (B) collection
   (C) range
   (D) group

27. Higher math is a very ------- discipline; it requires just as much imagination and insight as do any of the arts.

   (A) logical
   (B) creative
   (C) new
   (D) surprising

28. Many tribes in New Guinea are known for their ------- societies; all property belongs to all members of the tribe.

   (A) primitive
   (B) communal
   (C) ancient
   (D) savage

29. Because their roots are external and their leaf bases clasp, palm trees are rigid and upright, yet ------- enough to bend in strong winds.

   (A) tropical
   (B) vibrant
   (C) elastic
   (D) flamboyant

30. Though some assert that all behavior is learned, there are others who hold that some behaviors are -------, existing before any learning occurs.

    (A) ostentatious
    (B) innate
    (C) durable
    (D) cultural

31. A very outgoing and ------- individual, the mayor loved to talk to her fellow citizens.

    (A) garrulous
    (B) majestic
    (C) classy
    (D) rambunctious

32. Staring wide eyed, the crowd was ------- by the magician's amazing feats of illusion.

    (A) rewarded
    (B) conjoined
    (C) stupefied
    (D) pleased

Use "Positive/Negative"

Sometimes you'll have trouble coming up with a word of your own. Don't sweat it; you can still eliminate answers.

> Gregor was a gifted violinist who was ------- about practicing, showing a dedication to his art that even surpassed his talent.

If you can't come up with an exact word, decide if it's good or bad. In the sentence above, is Gregor good about practicing or is he bad about practicing? Underline the clue that tells you, and put a little "+" sign if the word is good, and a "−" sign if the word is bad. (You can put an "n" if it's neither.) Gregor is good about practicing, so which of the following answer choices can you eliminate? We've marked whether they're positive or negative, so cross out the ones you know are wrong.

(A)	diligent	+
(B)	ornery	−
(C)	practical	+
(D)	ambivalent	n

(B) and (D) cannot fit because they don't match what we know about the word in the blank (it's positive). So between (A) and (C), which best expresses the same thing as the clue? (A). If you're not sure what *diligent* means, make an flash card for it. (And if you're not sure what to do with the flash card, get cracking on the Vocabulary chapter!)

PRACTICE DRILL 12—USING POSITIVE/NEGATIVE

Decide if the blank is positive, negative, or neutral. Try to come up with a word of your own, if you can.

1. Our manager was normally so _____ that it surprised everyone when he failed so badly on the test.

2. Frozen vegetables, though perhaps not as nutritious as fresh ones, can be a _____ way to get vitamins into a dietary plan.

3. The five-person team of adventurers almost _____ after ten grueling days in stormy weather.

4. David enjoyed the Matisse exhibit at the museum; Matisse is one of his _____ artists.

5. Petra was so _____ while giving her speech in front of the class that her stomach began to ache.

6. The Neanderthals of Krapina were _____ hunters, possessing great strength and prowess.

7. Mr. Lambert _____ the class for not studying enough for the science exam.

8. The two knights engaged in a _____ fight; it would not end until one of them lay dead on the ground.

9. If Wanda had a better sense of her accomplishments, she would stop making such _____ remarks about herself.

10. As their diet became enriched by energy-laden fat, the populations of early hunters _____ and spread throughout the plains.

When You Are Done
Check your answers in Chapter 20.

PRACTICE DRILL 13—ELIMINATING BASED ON POSITIVE/NEGATIVE

Use your judgment on the sentences below to eliminate answers that cannot fit.

1. Our manager was normally so ------- that it surprised everyone when he failed so badly on the test.

   (A) successful
   (B) conceited
   (C) hateful
   (D) spiteful

2. Frozen vegetables, though perhaps not as nutritious as fresh ones, can be a ------- way to get vitamins into a dietary plan.

   (A) poor
   (B) inadequate
   (C) convenient
   (D) lenient

3. The five-person team of adventurers almost ------- after ten grueling days in stormy weather.

   (A) struggled
   (B) perished
   (C) paused
   (D) lapsed

4. David enjoyed the Matisse exhibit at the museum; Matisse is one of his ------- artists.

   (A) unusual
   (B) respected
   (C) unknown
   (D) cherished

5. Petra was so ------- while giving her speech in front of the class that her stomach began to ache.

   (A) loud
   (B) calm
   (C) anxious
   (D) relaxed

6. The Neanderthals of Krapina were
   ------- hunters, possessing great strength and
   prowess.

   (A) formidable
   (B) unsuitable
   (C) unstable
   (D) researched

7. Mr. Lambert ------- the class for not studying
   enough for the science exam.

   (A) congratulated
   (B) warned
   (C) chastised
   (D) corrected

8. The two knights engaged in a ------- fight; it would
   not end until one of them lay dead on the ground.

   (A) divided
   (B) humiliating
   (C) tenuous
   (D) perilous

9. If Wanda had a better sense of her accomplishments,
   she would stop making such ------- remarks about
   herself.

   (A) deprecating
   (B) indelicate
   (C) rebellious
   (D) fertile

10. As their diet became enriched by energy-laden fat,
    the populations of early hunters ------- and spread
    throughout the plains.

    (A) divided
    (B) congregated
    (C) thrived
    (D) restored

When You Are Done
Check your answers in
Chapter 20.

Two-Blank Sentences—Upper Level Only

Two-blank sentences are usually longer than one-blanks. Does that mean they're harder? Nope. Actually, if you take two-blank sentences slowly, one blank at a time, they can be easier to get right! Check it out.

> Since Europe has been polluting its rivers, the
> ------- of many species of fish has been severely
> -------.

Take It Easy
As long as you do two-blank sentence completions the way we've shown you, they'll be easier because you won't need to know all the vocabulary.

Cover your answers, and look for the clues and direction words. Which blank do you do first? Whichever is easier for you, whichever you have more information for, in the form of clues and direction words. For this example, let's go with the second blank, because we know something bad has been happening to the fish. How do we know? The clues are *polluting its rivers* and *severely*, and the direction word is *Since*, which keeps everything moving in the same direction. We can at least put a "−" sign next to the second blank. Now, when you uncover the answers to check them, only uncover the words for the blank you're working on. Don't even look at the words for the first blank here! You're only going to eliminate answers based on what cannot fit in the second blank.

(A) XXXX . . augmented
(B) XXXX . . observed
(C) XXXX . . approached
(D) XXXX . . threatened

You can eliminate (B) and (C), because they're not negative enough. Cross them out so you don't look at them again. Do you know what (A) means? If not, you can't eliminate it. Never eliminate words you don't know.

Now look back at the sentence and fill in a word or two for the first blank. What is it that can be negatively affected by pollution? Once you've got a word or two, look at the choices that are left for the first blank.

(A)   acceptance . . augmented
(B)   audacity . . observed
(C)   equanimity . . approached
(D)   habitat . . threatened

Which sounds better? You may have had a word like *environment* or *survival* filled in. (D) definitely fits better than (A). Notice that if you didn't know what *augmented*, *audacity*, or *equanimity* meant, you could still get this question right. That's because on two-blank sentence completions, as soon as you eliminate an answer choice based on one of its words, the whole thing is gone—you never have to look at it again, and it doesn't matter what the other word in it is. (However, if *augmented*, *audacity*, or *equanimity* comes up in a one-blank sentence, you do need to know it to eliminate it—so make some flash cards for those words.)

Think of all the time you'd waste if you tried plugging the words for each answer choice into the sentence. You'd be reading the sentence four or five times! Plus, you'd find more than one answer choice that sounded okay, and you'd have nothing with which to compare them.

Two-blank sentence completions are your friends on the ISEE. Treat your friends right—do them one blank at a time, coming up with your own words.

PRACTICE DRILL 14—TWO-BLANK SENTENCE COMPLETIONS (UPPER LEVEL ONLY)

Cover the answers, underline the clues, circle the direction words, and come up with a word for one of the blanks. Eliminate answers based on that blank alone, and then go back up to the sentence to work on the other blank. Then, eliminate again.

1. Psychologists have long ------- the connection between violence on television and actual crime; the wealth of different ------- makes it very hard to reach a consensus.

   (A) found . . facts
   (B) debated . . opinions
   (C) agreed . . articles
   (D) argued . . criminals

2. Jason felt quite ------- about his ability to score well; he had studied ------- the night before.

   (A) frightened . . thoroughly
   (B) happy . . poorly
   (C) confident . . diligently
   (D) resistant . . lately

3. Although the pilot checked all his instruments before takeoff, the ------- of one of them almost caused the plane to -------.

   (A) malfunction . . crash
   (B) misuse . . land
   (C) safety . . abort
   (D) refusal . . fly

4. Her treatment of the subject was so ------- that the class was convinced she had only ------- the material the night before.

   (A) spotty . . skimmed
   (B) thorough . . misunderstood
   (C) partial . . memorized
   (D) confused . . learned

5. Communities need to work not -------, but
   -------; as a group, they can solve problems more
   easily.

   (A) in groups . . communally
   (B) at home . . detached
   (C) always . . constantly
   (D) in isolation . . together

6. Despite the best efforts of his coach, Josh
   remained ------- in his ------- streak.

   (A) mired . . losing
   (B) upbeat . . winning
   (C) free . . consistent
   (D) taken . . sportsman

7. Due to the author's ------- handwriting, the typist
   had a difficult time ------- the manuscript.

   (A) perfect . . transcribing
   (B) careful . . reading
   (C) illegible . . deciphering
   (D) readable . . translating

8. The maid, while appropriately ------- to the guests
   of the hotel, was ------- with her employers.

   (A) indifferent . . curt
   (B) submissive . . pleasant
   (C) obsequious . . obstinate
   (D) reliable . . obedient

9. The owner is difficult to work for, less for her
   critical and ------- nature than for her -------.

   (A) exacting . . procrastination
   (B) perfect . . assistance
   (C) meticulous . . encouragement
   (D) carefree . . complaints

10. Smithers hoped that the committee would not
    ------- a course of action that would ------- an
    already bad situation in the workplace.

    (A) relate . . assist
    (B) formulate . . amend
    (C) recommend . . exacerbate
    (D) present . . mediate

When You Are Done
Check your answers in
Chapter 20.

Text Complete Sentences—Lower Level Only

For text completions, you need to finish a sentence. This might seem hard, but it's not if you use common sense. The correct answer will follow the correct direction (same/opposite) and make sense in context. Let's try one:

Even though Peter's mom said he wouldn't have dessert if he didn't clean his room, _____.

(A) he was unable to fall asleep that night
(B) she decided it was time to go on a diet
(C) he continued playing with his toys until dinner time
(D) she prepared a delicious and healthy salad

Which answer makes sense? Choice (C) does. The "even though" tells us that Peter didn't do what he was supposed to do. While choices (B) and (D) relate to food, they have nothing to do with dessert or Peter's room. Choice (A) is just weird.

Guess Aggressively When You've Worked on a Sentence

When you've narrowed a sentence completion down to two or three answers, it's probably because you don't know the vocabulary in some of those answers. Just take a guess and move on—you're not going to be able to divine the meanings of the words (and trust us, the proctor will not let you pull out a dictionary). You've increased your chances of getting the question right by eliminating one or two choices, and there's no guessing penalty, so fill in a bubble and move on.

When to Take a Guess

What if you come across a sentence that is so confusing that you can't even decide if the blank(s) should be positive or negative, much less come up with a word of your own? Don't waste your time on it. Just make sure you fill in your letter-of-the-day and move on.

If you only have a minute left, and you're not yet done, make sure you fill in your letter-of-the-day on all remaining questions.

Which Letter Should I Use?
No matter what you may have heard, it doesn't matter which letter you use to fill in answers for questions you don't work on. ERB tries to use letters in equal amounts.

Review—The Sentence Completions Plan

One-Blank Sentence Completions

For each and every sentence completion, the first thing I do is _____ the answers.

I look for the _____, and I mark it by _____ it.

I look for any _____ words, and I _____ them.

Then I _____.

If I have trouble coming up with a word for the blank, I decide if the blank is _____ or _____ (or neither).

Then I _____ answer choices and _____.

Two-Blank Sentence Completions—Upper Level Only

For each and every sentence completion, the first thing I do is _____ the answers.

I look for the _____, and I mark it by _____ it.

I look for any _____ words, and I _____ them.

If the sentence completion has two blanks, I do them _____.

Which blank do I do first? _____

I come up with a word for one of the blanks, and when I uncover the answer choices, I only uncover _____ and I eliminate based on those.

Then I go back to the sentence and _____ for the other blank, uncover the answer choices that are left, and eliminate.

Eliminating Choices and Guessing

Can I eliminate answer choices just because they contain words I do not know?

_____

What do I do if I can only eliminate one or two answer choices? _____

_____

What do I do if the sentence or the vocabulary looks so difficult that I can't come up with a word or decide if the blank is positive or negative? _____

_____

What do I spend my last minute on? _____

_____

Why should I never leave a question unanswered, even if I did not work on that question at all? _____

If you have trouble answering any of these questions, go back and review the appropriate section of this chapter before going on.

When You Are Done
Check your answers in Chapter 20.

PRACTICE DRILL 15—ALL SENTENCE COMPLETION TECHNIQUES

Upper level test-takers should complete the entire drill. Others should stop after question 13.

1. One of the simple guidelines of public speaking is that good presentations require ------- preparation.
   (A) thorough
   (B) fretful
   (C) partial
   (D) solitary

2. Franklin D. Roosevelt was an effective -------, taking time out each week to speak to the people of the United States by radio in casual "fireside chats."
   (A) writer
   (B) warrior
   (C) communicator
   (D) legislator

3. Compared with Asia, the huge continent to its east, Europe is actually quite ------- in size, though not in its impressive and numerous cultural contributions.
   (A) mammoth
   (B) modest
   (C) irregular
   (D) predictable

4. Even though she was known to be quite outgoing, Janet could be ------- if she didn't know everyone in the room.

(A) timid
(B) extroverted
(C) diverse
(D) separate

5. Unlike the convex lens, which brings light rays together, the concave lens actually ------- light rays.

(A) merges
(B) dissolves
(C) assists
(D) spreads out

6. Usually cool and collected, the coach grew ------- when he saw his best player needlessly injured in the illegal play.

(A) indifferent
(B) furious
(C) realistic
(D) impatient

7. The ruler of the kingdom was known to be quite a -------; he was domineering and cruel to all his subjects.

(A) leader
(B) tyrant
(C) democrat
(D) highbrow

8. Most house fires can be avoided through such simple ------- as proper education and a well-placed fire extinguisher.

(A) previews
(B) presentations
(C) precautions
(D) preventions

9. The dishonest employee ------- his company, absconding with more than two thousand dollars' worth of supplies.

(A) relieved
(B) reported
(C) swindled
(D) demoted

10. Almost worse than the cast that covered it, the scar on Jennifer's leg was quite -------.

   (A) pleasant
   (B) ghastly
   (C) beneficial
   (D) ingenious

11. Theories of the origin of the universe are far from -------; after all, no one was around to witness the event.

   (A) hypothetical
   (B) plausible
   (C) credible
   (D) definitive

12. The situation called for ------- measures; the solution would not be simple and straightforward.

   (A) complex
   (B) unique
   (C) elementary
   (D) firsthand

13. The day was hardly a ------- one; everything that could possibly go wrong did.

   (A) reluctant
   (B) blithe
   (C) resistant
   (D) frenetic

14. Known for their ------- skills at goldsmithing, the Incas produced some of the most beautiful and ------- gold figurines of all time.

   (A) primitive . . expensive
   (B) early . . religious
   (C) expert . . intricate
   (D) novice . . strong

15. It is hard to imagine that so much modern machinery, from huge oil tankers, cars, and jet engines all the way down to ------- nuts, bolts, and screws, is made from ------- material: steel.

   (A) minuscule . . the same
   (B) tremendous . . the common
   (C) countless . . the perfect
   (D) flimsy . . the unique

When You Are Done
Check your answers in Chapter 20.

16. Once a common and important means of -------,
    sailing has become more of a sport and a -------
    than a primary way of getting around.

    (A) conveyance . . profession
    (B) transportation . . hobby
    (C) relaxation . . business
    (D) socialization . . vocation

17. Because he was the best at spelling, Michael was
    ------- to be our ------- at the county
    spelling bee.

    (A) assigned . . principal
    (B) picked . . treasurer
    (C) chosen . . representative
    (D) elected . . washout

18. Martha could no longer keep -------; with unusual
    -------, she spoke out passionately against the
    injustices at her school.

    (A) pace . . speed
    (B) quiet . . timidity
    (C) up . . facility
    (D) silent . . vigor

19. With a multitude of nationalities present, this
    campus is one of the most ------- and ------- in the
    whole country.

    (A) diverse . . fascinating
    (B) uniform . . tremendous
    (C) multifaceted . . bland
    (D) homogeneous . . ethnic

20. Standing on their feet and applauding, the
    audience was ------- the actor's ------- performance
    of Abe Lincoln in Illinois.

    (A) rebellious at . . fanatic
    (B) thrilled by . . weak
    (C) impressed with . . uninspired
    (D) electrified by . . marvelous

Chapter 19
ISEE Reading

WHAT'S READING ALL ABOUT ON THE ISEE?

You have to read the ISEE reading passages differently from the way you read anything else. The passages the test writers use are packed with information.

Read Quickly, Answer Slowly
Your goal is to spend more time answering questions (and less time reading the passage).

Generally, when you read a textbook or any other book, you notice one or two phrases you want to remember in each paragraph. You can underline those phrases to show that they seem important, so you can easily find them later.

On the ISEE, however, the passages are chosen precisely because there is a lot of information in only a few paragraphs. It's all bunched in together. So, if you read your normal way, here's what happens: You read the first sentence, and you try to remember it. You read the second sentence and try to remember it. You read the third sentence, and, as you try to remember it, you forget the first two.

You have to read with a different goal in mind for the ISEE. This may sound crazy, but don't try to learn or remember anything. *You don't get any points for reading the passage well!*

What do you get points for? Answering questions correctly. On the questions and answers, you need to slow down and make sure you're checking each answer carefully before eliminating it. Don't worry about finishing the section, especially if you're in one of the lower grades taking that test. Working slowly and carefully will gain you points here.

THE PASSAGES

What Are the Passages Like?

There are six passages in a Reading Comprehension section, and there are 36 questions (the Lower Level test has five passages with 25 questions). Some questions are based on science passages, and other questions are based on social studies passages.

You can choose which passages to do. The Reading Comprehension section purposely has more passages and questions than many students can complete in 35 minutes (25 for the Lower Level). Don't let the test writers choose which ones you'll get to. Choose for yourself by flipping through them and doing the ones that look easiest first. You will probably do better on topics that interest you.

Also, do you tend to do better on science passages, or do you do better on social studies passages? Investigate this as you do the practice drills and the practice ISEE. Social studies passages can be about the history of a person, a group, or an event. Science passages explain some phenomenon or theory. Both types of passages are like your school textbooks—unemotional and striving to be objective.

HOW DO I READ THE PASSAGES?

Quickly! Don't try to remember the details in the passage. Your goal is to read the passage quickly to get the main idea.

The ISEE Reading Comp section is an open-book test—you can look back at the passage to answer questions about the details.

Label the Paragraphs

As you read ISEE passages, you will find that although many of them look like one big paragraph, they can be broken up into smaller pieces. After you read a few sentences, ask yourself what you just read. Put it in your own words—just a couple of words—and label the side of the paragraph with your summary. This way you'll have something to guide you back to the relevant part of the passage when you answer a question.

Imagine your grandparents are coming to visit, and they're staying in your room. Your parents tell you to clean up your room and get all that junk off the floor. Now, that junk is important to you. Okay, so maybe you don't need your Roller-blades every day or all those old notes from your best friend, but you do need to be able to get to them. So, you get a bunch of boxes, and you throw your Roller-blades, dress shoes, and ice skates in one box. In another, you throw all your old notes, letters, cards, and schoolwork. In another, you throw all your hand-held videogames, CDs, and computer software. Before you put the boxes in the closet, what must you do to be sure you don't have to go through every one of them the next time you want to play Tetris? You need to label them. "Shoes," "papers," and "computer/CDs" should do it.

The same thing is true of the paragraphs you read on the ISEE. You need to be able to go back to the passage and find the answer to a question quickly—you don't want to have to look through the entire passage to find it! The key to labeling the paragraphs is practice—you need to do it quickly, coming up with one or two words that accurately remind you of what's in each part of the passage. You'll find that some passages really should be broken up into more paragraphs, and your labels can show you where the breaks occur.

For very short passages, you can skip right to the next step.

State the Main Idea

After you have read the entire passage, ask yourself two questions.

- **"What?"** What is the passage about?

- **"So what?"** What's the author's point about this topic?

The answers to these questions will show you the main idea of the passage. Scribble down this main idea in just a few words. The answer to "What?" is the thing that was being talked about—"bees" or "weather forecasting." The answer to "So what?" gives you the rest of the sentence; "Bees do little dances that tell other bees where to go for pollen" or "Weather forecasting is complicated by many problems."

Don't assume you will find the main idea in the first sentence. While often the main idea is in the beginning of the passage, it is not always in the first sentence. The beginning may just be a lead-in to the main point.

PRACTICE DRILL 16—GETTING THROUGH THE PASSAGE

As you quickly read each paragraph, label it. When you finish the passage, answer "What?" and "So what?" to get the main idea.

Line

1　　Contrary to popular belief, the first European known to lay
2　　eyes on America was not Christopher Columbus or Amerigo
3　　Vespucci but a little-known Viking by the name of Bjarni
4　　Herjolfsson. In the summer of 986, Bjarni sailed from Norway
5　　to Iceland, heading for the Viking settlement where his father,
6　　Heriulf, resided.
7　　　　When he arrived in Iceland, Bjarni discovered that his father
8　　had already sold his land and estates and set out for the latest
9　　Viking settlement on the subarctic island called Greenland.
10　　Discovered by a notorious murderer and criminal named
11　　Eric the Red, Greenland lay at the limit of the known world.
12　　Dismayed, Bjarni set out for this new colony.
13　　　　Because the Vikings traveled without chart or compass, it was
14　　not uncommon for them to lose their way in the unpredictable
15　　northern seas. Beset by fog, the crew lost their bearings. When
16　　the fog finally cleared, they found themselves before a land that
17　　was level and covered with woods.
18　　　　They traveled farther up the coast, finding more flat, wooded
19　　country. Farther north, the landscape revealed glaciers and rocky
20　　mountains. Though Bjarni realized this was an unknown land,
21　　he was no intrepid explorer. Rather, he was a practical man who
22　　had simply set out to find his father. Refusing his crew's request
23　　to go ashore, he promptly turned his bow back out to sea. After
24　　four days' sailing, Bjarni landed at Herjolfsnes on the
25　　southwestern tip of Greenland, the exact place he had been
26　　seeking all along.

"What" is this passage about? _____

"So what?" What's the author's point? _____

What type of passage is this? _____

Check your answers to be sure you're on the right track.

When You Are Done
Check your answers in Chapter 20.

ISEE Reading | 545

THE QUESTIONS

Now, we're getting to the important part of the Reading Comprehension section. This is where you need to spend time to avoid careless errors. After reading a passage, you'll have a group of questions that are in no particular order. The first thing you need to decide is whether the question you're answering is general or specific.

General Questions

General questions are about the passage as a whole. There are five types.

Main idea

- Which of the following best expresses the main point?

- The passage is primarily about

- The main idea of the passage is

- The best title for this passage would be

Tone/attitude

- The author's tone is

- The attitude of the author is one of

General interpretation

- The author's tone/attitude indicates

- The author would most likely agree with

- This passage deals with X by

- The passage implies that

- Which of the following words best describes the passage?

- It can be inferred from the passage that

- The style of the passage is most like

- Where would you be likely to find this passage?

- What is the author's opinion of X?

- The passage is best described as a

Purpose

- The purpose of the passage is

- The author wrote this passage to

Prediction

- Which is likely to happen next?

- The author will most likely discuss next

Notice that these questions all require you to know the main idea, but the ones at the beginning of the list don't require anything else, and the ones toward the end require you to interpret a little more.

Answering a General Question

Keep your answers to "What? So what?" in mind. The answer to a general question will concern the main idea. If you need more, go back to your paragraph labels. The labels will allow you to look at the passage again without getting bogged down in the details.

- For a straight **main idea** question, just ask yourself, "What was the 'What? So what?' for this passage?"

- For a **tone/attitude question**, ask yourself, "How did the author feel about the subject?"

- For a **general interpretation** question, ask yourself, "Which answer stays closest to what the author said and how he or she said it?"

- For a **general purpose** question, ask yourself, "Why did the author write this?"

- For a **prediction** question, ask yourself, "How was the passage arranged?" Take a look at your paragraph labels, and reread the last sentence.

Answer the question in your own words before looking at the answer choices. As always, you want to arm yourself with your own answer before looking at the ISEE's tricky answers.

PRACTICE DRILL 17—ANSWERING A GENERAL QUESTION

Use the passage about Vikings that you just read and labeled. Reread your main idea and answer the following questions. Use the questions above to help you paraphrase your own answer before looking at the choices.

What was the answer to "What? So what?" for this passage?

1. This passage is primarily about
   (A) the Vikings and their civilization
   (B) the waves of Viking immigration
   (C) sailing techniques of Bjarni Herjolfsson
   (D) one Viking's glimpse of the New World

Which answer is closest to what the author said overall?

2. With which of the following statements about Viking explorers would the author most probably agree?
   (A) Greenland and Iceland were the Vikings' final discoveries.
   (B) Viking explorers were cruel and savage.
   (C) The Vikings' most startling discovery was an accidental one.
   (D) Bjarni Herjolfsson was the first settler of America.

Why did the author write this passage? Think about the main idea.

3. What was the author's purpose in writing this passage?
   (A) To turn the reader against Italian adventurers
   (B) To show his disdain for Eric the Red
   (C) To demonstrate the Vikings' nautical skills
   (D) To correct a common misconception about the European discovery of America

When You Are Done
Check your answers in Chapter 20.

Specific Questions

Specific questions are about a detail or a section of the passage. There are four main types.

Fact

- According to the passage/author

- The author states that

- Which of these questions is answered by the passage?

- All of the following are mentioned EXCEPT

Definition in context

- What does the passage mean by X?

- X probably represents/means

- Which word best replaces the word X without changing the meaning?

Specific interpretation

- The author implies in line X

- It can be inferred from paragraph X

- The most likely interpretation of X is

Purpose

- The author uses X to

- Why does the author say X?

Again, the questions above range from flat-out requests for information found in the passage (just like the straight "main idea" general questions) to questions that require some interpretation of what you find in the passage (like the general questions that ask with what the author is "likely to agree").

Answering a Specific Question

For specific questions, always reread the part of the passage concerned. Remember, this is an open-book test!

Of course, you don't want to have to reread the entire passage. What part is the question focusing on? To find the relevant part:

- Use your **paragraph labels** to go straight to the information you need.

- Use the **line or paragraph reference**, if there is one, but be careful. With a line reference ("In line 10 . . . "), be sure to read the whole surrounding paragraph, not just the line. If the question says, "In line 10 . . . ," then you need to read lines 5 through 15 to actually find the answer.

- Use words that stand out in the question and passage. Names, places, and long words will be easy to find back in the passage. We call these **lead words** because they lead you back to the right place in the passage.

Once you're in the right area, answer the question in your own words. Then, look at the answer choices and eliminate any that aren't like yours.

Answering Special Specific Questions

Definition-in-context questions   Creating your own answer before looking at the choices makes definition-in-context questions especially easy. Remember, they want to know how the word or phrase is being used *in context*, so come up with your own word that fits in the sentence before looking at the answer choices. Try one.

> In line 15, the word "spot" most closely means

Cross out the word they're asking about, and replace it with your own.

> A raptor must also have a sharp, often hooked beak so that it may tear the flesh of its prey. Because they hunt from the sky, these birds must have extremely sharp eyesight, which allows them to *spot* potential prey from a great distance.

Now look at the answer choices and eliminate the ones that are not at all like yours.

(A) taint
(B) mark
(C) hunt
(D) detect

You probably came up with something like *see*. The closest answer to *see* is (D). Notice that *taint* and *mark* are possible meanings of *spot*, but they don't work in this context. Those answer choices are there to catch students who do not go back to the passage to see how the word is used and to replace it with their own.

Definition-in-context questions are so quick that if you only have a few minutes left, you should definitely do them first.

I, II, III questions The questions that have three Roman numerals are confusing and time consuming. They look like this.

According to the passage, which of the following is true?
I.   The sky is blue.
II. Nothing rhymes with "orange."
III. Smoking cigarettes increases lung capacity.

(A) I only
(B) II only
(C) I and II only
(D) I, II, and III

On the ISEE, you will need to look up each of the three statements in the passage. This will always be time-consuming, but you can make them less confusing by making sure you look up just one statement at a time.

For instance, in the question at the bottom of the previous page, say you look back at the passage and see that the passage says I is true. Write a big "T" next to it. What can you eliminate now? (B). Now, you check out II, and you find that sure enough, the passage says that too. II gets a big "T" and you cross off (A). Next, looking in the paragraph that you labeled "smoking is bad," you find that the passage actually says that smoking decreases lung capacity. What can you eliminate? (D).

You may want to skip a I, II, III question because it will be time-consuming, especially if you're on your last passage and there are other questions you can do instead. If you skip it, remember to fill in your letter-of-the-day.

EXCEPT/LEAST/NOT Questions   This is another confusing type of question. The test writers are reversing what you need to look for, asking you which answer is false.

> All of the following can be inferred from the passage EXCEPT

Before you go any further, cross out "EXCEPT." Now, you have a much more positive question to answer. Of course, as always, you will go through all the answer choices, but for this type of question you will put a little "T" or "F" next to the answers as you check them out. Let's say we've checked out these answers.

(A)   Americans are patriotic.   T

(B)   Americans have great ingenuity.   T

(C)   Americans love war.   F

(D)   Americans do what they can to help one another.   T

Which one stands out? The one with the "F." That's your answer. You made a confusing question much simpler than the test writers wanted it to be. If you don't go through all the choices and mark them, you run the risk of accidentally picking one of the choices that you know is true because that's what you usually look for on reading comp questions.

You should skip an EXCEPT/LEAST/NOT question if you're on your last passage and there are other questions you can do instead, and just fill in your letter-of-the-day on your answer sheet.

PRACTICE DRILL 18—ANSWERING A SPECIFIC QUESTION

Use the passage about Vikings that you just read and labeled. Use your paragraph labels and the lead words in each question to get to the part of the passage you need, and then put the answer in your own words before going back to the answer choices.

1. According to the passage, Bjarni Herjolfsson left Norway to

    (A) found a new colony
    (B) open trading lanes
    (C) visit a relative
    (D) map the North Sea

What's the lead word here? *Norway. Norway* should also be in one of your labels.

2. Bjarni's reaction upon landing in Iceland can best be described as

    (A) disappointed
    (B) satisfied
    (C) amused
    (D) indifferent

What's the lead word here? *Iceland.* Again, this should be in one of your labels. Go back and read this part.

3. "The crew lost their bearings" probably means that

    (A) the ship was damaged beyond repair
    (B) the crew became disoriented
    (C) the crew decided to mutiny
    (D) the crew went insane

Go back and read this part. Replace the words they've quoted with your own.

4. It can be inferred from the passage that, prior to Bjarni Herjolfsson's voyage, Greenland

    (A) was covered in grass and shrubs
    (B) was overrun with Vikings
    (C) was rich in fish and game
    (D) was as far west as the Vikings had traveled

What's the lead word here? *Greenland.* Is it in one of your labels? What does that part of the passage say about Greenland? Paraphrase before looking at the answers!

When You Are Done
Check your answers in Chapter 20.

THE ANSWERS

Before you ever look at an answer choice, you've come up with your own answer, in your own words. What do you do next?

Well, you're looking for the closest answer to yours, but it's much easier to eliminate answers than to try to magically zoom in on the best one. Work through the answers using Process of Elimination. As soon as you eliminate an answer, cross off the letter in your test booklet so that you no longer think of that choice as a possibility.

How Do I Eliminate Answer Choices?

On a General Question

Eliminate an answer that is:

- Too small. The passage may mention it, but it's only a detail—not a main idea.

- Not mentioned in the passage.

- In contradiction to the passage—it says the opposite of what you read.

- Too big. The answer tries to say that more was discussed than really was.

- Too extreme. An extreme answer is one that is too negative or too positive, or uses absolute words like *all*, *every*, *never*, or *always*. Eliminating extreme answers makes tone/attitude questions especially easy and quick.

- Going against common sense. The passage is not likely to back up answers that just don't make sense at all.

On a Specific Question
Eliminate an answer that is:

- Too extreme

- In contradiction to passage details

- Not mentioned in the passage

- Against common sense

If you look back at the questions you did for the Viking passage, you'll see that many of the wrong answer choices fit into the categories above.

What Kinds of Answers Do I Keep?
Best answers are likely to be:

- Paraphrases of the words in the passage

- Traditional and conservative in their outlook

- Moderate, using words like *may*, *can*, and *often*

PRACTICE DRILL 19—ELIMINATING ANSWERS

The following phrases are answer choices. You haven't read the passage, or even the question, that goes with each of them. However, you can decide if each one is a possible correct answer, or if you can eliminate it, based on the criteria above. Cross out any that you can eliminate.

For a general question

(A)   The author refutes each argument exhaustively.

(B)   The author admires the courage of most Americans.

(C)   Creativity finds full expression in a state of anarchy.

(D)   The passage criticizes Western society for not allowing freedom of expression to artists.

(E)   The ancient Egyptians were barbaric.

(F)   The author proves that Native American writing does not have a multicultural perspective.

(G)   The author emphasizes the significance of diversity in the United States.

(H)   The passage reports the record cold temperatures in Boston in 1816.

For a general tone/attitude question

(I)   respectful

(J)   confused

(K)   angry condemnation

(L)   admiring

(M)   mournful

(N)   objective

(O)   thrilled optimism

(P)   exaggeration

(Q)   disgusted

(R)   neutral

(S) condescending

(T) indifferent

For a specific question

(U) They were always in danger of being deprived of their power.

(V) Voters were easily misled by mudslinging campaigns.

(W) One-celled organisms could be expected to act in fairly predictable ways.

(X) Only a show of athletic ability can excite an audience.

(Y) Economic events can have political repercussions.

When You've Got It Down to Two

If you've eliminated all but two answers, don't get stuck and waste time. Keep the main idea in the back of your mind and step back.

- Reread the question.

- Look at what makes the two answers different.

- Go back to the passage.

- Which answer is worse? Eliminate it.

When You Are Done
Check your answers in Chapter 20.

REVIEW—THE READING PLAN

The Passages

After I read each paragraph, I _____ it.

After I read an entire passage, I ask myself: _____? and _____?

The Questions

The five main types of general questions, and the questions I can ask myself to answer them, are:

_____   _____

_____   _____

_____   _____

_____   _____

_____   _____

To find the answer to a specific question, I can use three clues.

_____

_____

_____

If the question says "in line 22," where do I begin reading for the answer?

_____

The Answers

On a general question, I eliminate answers that are

_____

_____

_____

_____

_____

On a specific question, I eliminate answers that are

_____

_____

_____

When I've got it down to two possible answers, I should

_____

_____

_____

If you had any trouble with these questions, reread this section of the chapter before going further.

When You Are Done
Check your answers in Chapter 20.

PRACTICE DRILL 20—ALL READING TECHNIQUES— LOWER LEVEL

Line

1 The term "tides" has come to represent the cyclical rising
2 and falling of ocean waters, most notably evident along the
3 shoreline as the border between land and sea moves in and out
4 with the passing of the day. The primary reason for this constant
5 redefinition of the boundaries of the sea is the gravitational
6 force of the moon.
7 This force of lunar gravity is not as strong as Earth's own
8 gravitational pull, which keeps our bodies and our homes from
9 being pulled off the ground, through the sky, and into space
10 toward the moon. It is a strong enough force, however, to exert
11 a certain gravitational pull as the moon passes over Earth's
12 surface. This pull causes the water level to rise (as the water is
13 literally pulled, ever so slightly, toward the moon) in those parts
14 of the ocean that are exposed to the moon and its gravitational
15 forces. When the water level in one part of the ocean rises, it
16 must naturally fall in another, and this is what causes water
17 level to change, dramatically at times, along any given piece of
18 coastline.

1. Which one of the following is the most obvious effect of the tides?

   (A) A part of the beach that was once dry is now under water.
   (B) Floods cause great damage during heavy rainstorms.
   (C) The moon is not visible.
   (D) Water falls.

2. The word "lunar" most nearly means

   (A) weak
   (B) strong
   (C) destructive
   (D) related to the moon

3. It can be inferred from the passage that if one were to travel to the moon

   (A) that water would be found on its surface
   (B) that an object, if dropped, would float away from the surface of the moon
   (C) that tides are more dramatic during the day than during the night
   (D) that an object, if dropped, would fall to the moon's surface

4. The author's primary purpose in writing this passage is to

   (A) prove the existence of water on the moon
   (B) refute claims that tides are caused by the moon
   (C) explain the main cause of the ocean's tides
   (D) argue that humans should not interfere with the processes of nature

When You Are Done
Check your answers in Chapter 20.

PRACTICE DRILL 21—ALL READING TECHNIQUES—LOWER LEVEL

Line

1 　　The Brooklyn Bridge in New York has been featured in
2 movies, photographs, and media for over a hundred years, but
3 the bridge is much more than just a pretty sight. It opened on
4 May 24, 1883, and, at 3,460 feet, it was the longest suspension
5 bridge in the world, measuring 50% longer than any previously
6 built. The Brooklyn Bridge was a symbol of American strength
7 and vitality, but its completion followed years of toil and
8 sacrifice.
9 　　John Augustus Roebling, a German immigrant, envisioned
10 the bridge that would link Manhattan to Brooklyn over the
11 East River. While in preparations for building, however, John
12 Roebling was injured when a ferry pinned his foot to a pylon,
13 and he died weeks later of tetanus. This first setback to the
14 building of the bridge was indicative of the problems that would
15 plague its construction as well as the harrowing tenacity that led
16 to its completion.
17 　　Washington Roebling took over the project upon his father's
18 death. Washington persevered through many hurdles in the
19 building of the bridge including fires, accidents, industrial
20 corruption, and loss of public support. He continued, however,
21 in his push to complete the bridge. In fact, it is said that he
22 worked harder and longer than any worker he employed in
23 even the most dangerous circumstances. While working in
24 the caissons, underwater chambers that supported the bridge,
25 he was stricken by the decompression sickness that led to his
26 paralysis. Nothing could stop him, though, and he continued
27 construction by sending messages to the site through his wife,
28 Emily.
29 　　Fourteen years after construction began, the Brooklyn
30 Bridge celebrated its grand opening. The total cost to build the
31 bridge was fifteen million dollars, and 27 people died in its
32 construction, but it stood as a tribute to American invention and
33 industry.

1. The primary purpose of the passage is to

(A) convince the reader that the Brooklyn Bridge is the longest suspension bridge in the world

(B) describe Washington Roebling's rise to success

(C) show that Americans have an inborn talent for inventiveness

(D) describe how the Brooklyn Bridge was a great success despite the hardships faced in building it

2. It can be inferred from the third paragraph that Washington Roebling

   (A) was injured by a ferry
   (B) was determined to build the bridge despite many setbacks
   (C) suffered from depression after his injury
   (D) had a son who completed the building of the bridge

3. Which one of the following is given as a difficulty faced in building the Brooklyn Bridge?

   (A) An excessive number of pylons in the East River
   (B) An outbreak of tetanus among the workers
   (C) The death of the man who envisioned the bridge
   (D) A lack of funds to keep building

4. Washington Roebling can best be described as

   (A) persistent
   (B) weak
   (C) clumsy
   (D) dangerous

5. Which of the following is NOT stated about the Brooklyn Bridge?

   (A) It was a sign of American power.
   (B) It cost millions of dollars to build.
   (C) It was not worth the money lost in building it.
   (D) It has been seen in the movies.

When You Are Done
Check your answers in Chapter 20.

PRACTICE DRILL 22—ALL READING TECHNIQUES—ALL LEVELS

Line

1   Immediately following the dramatic end of World War II
2   came a realization that the United States now had to turn its
3   attention inward. Years of fighting battles around the globe had
4   drained the country of important resources. Many industries
5   (such as housing) suffered, as both materials and workers
6   were used elsewhere in the war effort. Once the soldiers began
7   returning, it became clear that new jobs and new homes were
8   among their biggest needs. The homes needed to be affordable,
9   since few people had the time or ability to save much during the
10 war.
11   It was in this situation that many house developers saw a
12 business opportunity. Amid such a pressing demand for new
13 homes, developer William Levitt realized the need for a new
14 method of building. He sought a way to build homes cheaper
15 and faster than ever before.
16   He wasn't the only developer to realize this, but he was one
17 of the best in making it happen. He applied the same ideas to
18 homes that Henry Ford had used 50 years earlier in making
19 cars. Levitt did not build a factory with an assembly line of
20 fully formed homes rolling out of some giant machine. Instead,
21 he adapted the assembly line formula into a system in which
22 the workers, rather than the product, moved for a streamlined,
23 efficient building process.
24   Previously, a developer who completed four homes a year
25 had been moving at a good pace. Levitt planned to do that
26 many each week, and succeeded. He created specialized teams
27 that focused on only one job each and moved up and down the
28 streets of new homes. Teams of foundation-builders, carpenters,
29 roofers, and painters worked faster by sticking to just one task
30 as they moved, factory-style, from house to house. The time
31 and money saved allowed Levitt to build cheap homes of good
32 value.
33   With this new approach, Levitt oversaw the building of some
34 of the first towns that would eventually be called suburbs—
35 planned communities outside the city. Some critics blame
36 developers like Levitt for turning farmland into monotonous,
37 characterless towns. However, most agree that his contribution
38 to the country following a bitter war was mostly positive. He
39 did vary the style of home from street to street, and his work
40 on simpler home features was influenced by the work of
41 architecture great Frank Lloyd Wright.
42   In the end, Levitt's success speaks for itself. After his first
43 success—building thousands of homes in Long Island, New
44 York—he went on to found several more "Levittowns" in
45 Pennsylvania, New Jersey, and elsewhere. Levitt gave home

Line

46 buyers what they wanted: nice pieces of land with nice homes
47 on top. In a way, by creating houses that so many families
48 could afford, William Levitt made the American dream a more
49 affordable reality.

1. The primary purpose of the passage is to

   (A) discuss the final days of World War II
   (B) suggest that suburban housing is unaffordable
   (C) describe one person's contribution to an industry
   (D) prove that the economy changed after World War II

2. Which of the following statements about William Levitt is best supported by the passage?

   (A) He invented the word "suburb."
   (B) He was unconcerned with the appearance of the homes he built.
   (C) His homes were built in Ford-style factories.
   (D) His efficient methods helped make homes more affordable.

3. Which of the following best describes Levitt?

   (A) Courageous patriot
   (B) Strict businessman
   (C) Ground-breaking entrepreneur
   (D) Financial mastermind

4. It can be inferred from the passage that

    (A)   Levitt was the only developer working in New York following World War II.

    (B)   Levitt and Henry Ford created homes the same way.

    (C)   Other developers did not know how to use the concept of assembly line construction.

    (D)   Levitt built homes much faster than was customary before World War II.

5. The passage mentions all of the following as reasons for the postwar housing demand EXCEPT the

    (A)   destruction of American homes during the war

    (B)   difficulty of saving money during the war

    (C)   search for new jobs and new homes by returning soldiers

    (D)   use of home-building materials elsewhere during the war

6. The passage suggests that a potential drawback to "assembly-line style" houses is that they can be

    (A)   hard to sell

    (B)   not very sturdy

    (C)   similar-looking

    (D)   horrible for the environment

PRACTICE DRILL 23—ALL READING TECHNIQUES—ALL LEVELS

Line

1   Etymology, the study of words and word roots, may sound
2   like the kind of thing done by boring librarians in small, dusty
3   rooms. Yet etymologists actually have a uniquely interesting
4   job. They are, in many ways, just like archeologists digging up
5   the physical history of people and events. The special aspect
6   of etymology is that it digs up history, so to speak, through the
7   words and phrases that are left behind.
8   The English language, in particular, is a great arena in which
9   to explore history through words. As a language, English has an
10   extraordinary number of words. This is in part due to its ability
11   to adapt foreign words so readily. For example, "English" words
12   such as *kindergarten* (from German), *croissant* (from French),
13   and *cheetah* (from Hindi) have become part of the language
14   with little or no change from their original sounds and spellings.
15   So English language etymologists have a vast world of words
16   to explore.
17   Another enjoyable element of etymology for most word
18   experts is solving word mysteries. No, etymologists do not
19   go around solving murders, cloaked in intrigue like the great
20   fictional detective Sherlock Holmes. What these word experts
21   solve are mysteries surrounding the origin of some of our most
22   common words.
23   One of the biggest questions English language experts have
24   pursued is how English came to have the phrase *OK*. Though it
25   is one of the most commonly used slang expressions, its exact
26   beginning is a puzzle even to this day. Even its spelling is not
27   entirely consistent—unless you spell it *okay*, it's hard even to
28   call it a word.
29   Etymologists have been able to narrow *OK*'s origin down to
30   a likely, although not certain, source. It became widely used
31   around the time of Martin Van Buren's run for president in
32   1840. His nickname was Old Kinderhook. What troubles word
33   experts about this explanation is that the phrase appeared in
34   some newspapers before Van Buren became well known. As a
35   result, it's unlikely that Van Buren could be called its primary
36   source. Like bloodhounds following a faint scent, etymologists
37   will doubtless keep searching for the initial source. However, it
38   is clear that *OK*'s popularity and fame have exceeded those of
39   the American president to whom it has been most clearly linked.

1. It can be inferred from the second paragraph that English vocabulary

   (A) is easy to learn for speakers of other languages
   (B) can claim many sources
   (C) has a longer history than that of many other languages
   (D) affects American politics

2. The author mentions the words "kindergarten," "croissant," and "cheetah" most likely because

   (A) they are words with unknown origins
   (B) etymologists dispute words like these
   (C) they represent words that are similarly spelled and spoken in two languages
   (D) English speakers find them difficult to pronounce

3. According to the passage, etymologists are

   (A) investigators of word history
   (B) lovers of vocabulary words
   (C) scientists of the five senses
   (D) archeologists of extinct languages

4. Which of the following best states the purpose of the fourth and fifth paragraphs?

   (A) to illustrate another non-English word
   (B) to define the phrase "OK"
   (C) to show an interesting aspect of etymology
   (D) to compare American phrases

5. The primary purpose of the passage is to

   (A) provide information about the English language
   (B) discuss enjoyable aspects of the study of words
   (C) show that language plays an important role in politics
   (D) describe the origin of the phrase "OK"

PRACTICE DRILL 24—ALL READING TECHNIQUES—
UPPER LEVEL

Line

1   Bob Dylan was born on May 24, 1941 in Duluth, Minnesota,
2 but his name wasn't Dylan. He was born Robert Allen
3 Zimmerman, one of two sons born to Abraham and Betty
4 Zimmerman. Nineteen years later, he moved to New York
5 City with his new name and a passion to pursue his dream of
6 becoming a music legend.
7   Bob Dylan's career began like those of many musicians.
8 He began to play in New York City at various clubs around
9 Greenwich Village. He began to gain public recognition as a
10 singer/songwriter and was even reviewed by the *New York Times*
11 his first year in New York. He signed his first record deal with
12 Columbia Records a mere ten months after moving to New
13 York. From that point on, his career skyrocketed.
14   What is unique about Bob Dylan, given his huge success, is
15 his vocal quality. Dylan's singing voice was untrained and had
16 an unusual edge to it. Because of this, many of his most famous
17 early songs first reached the public through versions by other
18 performers who were more immediately palatable. Joan Baez
19 was one of these musicians who performed many of Dylan's
20 early songs. She furthered Dylan's already rising performance
21 career by inviting him onstage during her concerts, and many
22 credit her with bringing Dylan to his vast level of national and
23 international prominence.
24   In his career, which spans more than four decades, Dylan
25 has produced 500 songs and more than 40 albums. This king
26 of songs has thirteen songs on *Rolling Stone* magazine's Top
27 500 Songs of All Time, including his most famous song, "Like
28 a Rolling Stone," which tops the list. In 2004, Bob Dylan was
29 ranked second in *Rolling Stone* magazine's 100 Greatest Artists
30 of All Time, surpassed only by the Beatles.
31   In a recent television interview, Bob Dylan was asked why
32 he became a musician. He replied that from a very early age, he
33 knew it was his destiny to become a music legend. Certainly,
34 that destiny has been realized!

1. Which of the following best states the main idea of the passage?

   (A) The beginning of Bob Dylan's music career is similar to the beginnings of the careers of most other musicians.
   (B) It is extremely important to follow your dreams.
   (C) Bob Dylan never really knew what he wanted to be in life.
   (D) Bob Dylan had great success despite his unusual style of singing.

2. The word "prominence" at the end of the third paragraph most nearly means

   (A) perception
   (B) status
   (C) obviousness
   (D) protrusion

3. The passage most strongly supports which of the following statements about Joan Baez?

   (A) She was jealous of Bob Dylan's superior vocal training.
   (B) She grew up in Minnesota.
   (C) She has performed more of Bob Dylan's songs than of her own.
   (D) She helped Bob Dylan to become a music legend.

4. The phrase "king of songs" near the beginning of the fourth paragraph refers to

   (A) Bob Dylan's prolific nature as a singer/songwriter
   (B) Bob Dylan's ownership of *Rolling Stone* magazine
   (C) how most musicians regarded Bob Dylan as a king
   (D) Bob Dylan's perception of himself

When You Are Done

Check your answers in Chapter 20.

5. Which of the following is best supported by the passage?

   (A) Bob Dylan has two brothers.
   (B) Bob Dylan was reviewed by Columbia Records his first year in New York.
   (C) "Like a Rolling Stone" is considered by some to be the best song of all time.
   (D) Without Joan Baez, Bob Dylan would never have succeeded.

PRACTICE DRILL 25—ALL READING TECHNIQUES—MIDDLE AND UPPER LEVEL

Line

1   It is easy to lose patience with science today. The questions
2   are pressing: How dangerous is dioxin? What about low-
3   level radiation? When will that monstrous earthquake strike
4   California? And why can't we predict weather better? But the
5   evidence is often described as "inconclusive," forcing scientists
6   to base their points of view almost as much on intuition as on
7   science.
8   When historians and philosophers of science listen to these
9   questions, some conclude that science may be incapable of
10   solving all these problems any time soon. Many questions seem
11   to defy the scientific method, an approach that works best when
12   it examines straightforward relationships: If something is done
13   to variable A, what happens to variable B? Such procedures
14   can, of course, be very difficult in their own ways, but for
15   experiments, they are effective.
16   With the aid of Newton's laws of gravitational attraction, for
17   instance, ground controllers can predict the path of a planetary
18   probe—or satellite—with incredible accuracy. They do this
19   by calculating the gravitational tugs from each of the passing
20   planets until the probe speeds beyond the edge of the solar
21   system. A much more difficult task is to calculate what happens
22   when two or three such tugs pull on the probe at the same time.
23   The unknowns can grow into riddles that are impossible to
24   solve. Because of the turbulent and changing state of the earth's
25   atmosphere, for instance, scientists have struggled for centuries
26   to predict the weather with precision.
27   This spectrum of questions—from simple problems to those
28   impossibly complex—has resulted in nicknames for various
29   fields of study. "Hard" sciences, such as astronomy and
30   chemistry, are said to yield precise answers, whereas "soft"
31   sciences, such as sociology and economics, admit a great degree
32   of uncertainty.

1. Which of the following best tells what this passage is about?

    (A) How the large variety of factors some scientists deal with makes absolute scientific accuracy impossible

    (B) How Newton solved the problem of accuracy and science

    (C) How "hard" science is more important than "soft" science

    (D) Why science now uses less and less conclusive evidence

2. According to the passage, it can be inferred that the scientific method would work best in which of the following situations?

   (A) Predicting public reactions to a set of policy decisions
   (B) Identifying the factors that will predict a California earthquake
   (C) Predicting the amount of corn that an acre will yield when a particular type of fertilizer is used
   (D) Calculating how much a cubic centimeter of water will weigh when cooled under controlled conditions

3. The author suggests that accurately predicting the path of a planetary probe is **more** difficult than

   (A) forecasting the weather
   (B) determining when an earthquake will occur
   (C) predicting economic behavior
   (D) determining the gravitational influence of one planet

4. According to the passage, "hard" science can be distinguished from "soft" science by which of the following characteristics?

   (A) Finding precise answers to its questions
   (B) Identifying important questions that need answers
   (C) Making significant contributions to human welfare
   (D) Creating debates about unresolved issues

5. The author implies that when confronted with complex questions, scientists base their opinions

   (A) on theoretical foundations
   (B) more on intuition than on science
   (C) on science and intuition, in varying degrees
   (D) on experimental procedures

When You Are Done
Check your answers in Chapter 20.

Chapter 20
Answer Key to
ISEE Drills

ISEE MATH

Practice Drill 1—Lower Level

1. D
2. D
3. B
4. C
5. D
6. B
7. D
8. C
9. B
10. C
11. D
12. A
13. C
14. D
15. C

Practice Drill 2—Middle and Upper Levels

1. A
2. B
3. D
4. B
5. B
6. B
7. D
8. D
9. D
10. A
11. C
12. C
13. A
14. C
15. A

More Practice: Upper Level Only

16. A
17. B
18. C
19. D
20. B
21. D
22. D
23. C
24. D
25. D
26. B
27. D
28. C
29. B

Practice Drill 3—Ratios

1. C
2. C
3. C

Practice Drill 4—Average Pie

1. A
2. B
3. A
4. A

More Practice: Lower Level

1. A
2. B
3. D

Practice Drill 6—Plugging In

1. B
2. D
3. C

More Practice: Middle and Upper Levels

5. C
6. C

Practice Drill 7—Plugging In The Answers

1. C
2. B
3. D

More Practice: Middle and Upper Levels

4. C
5. B

More Practice: Lower Level

1. B
2. B

More Practice: Upper Level

7. B
8. B
9. D
10. D
11. B
12. B
13. C

More Practice: Lower Level

4. D
5. B

Practice Drill 5—Percent Change

1. D
2. C

More Practice: Middle Level

3. C
4. C

More Practice: Middle and Upper Levels

6. D
7. D
8. A
9. C
10. A

Extra Practice—Geometry—Shaded Regions

1. B
2. B

Practice Drill 8—Functions

1. B
2. C
3. D
4. D
5. A

Practice Drill 9—Charts

1. D
2. D
3. D
4. D
5. B
6. D
7. B
8. C

Practice Drill 10—Quantitative Comparison

1. C
2. A
3. B
4. B
5. C
6. D

Practice Drill 11—Quantitative Comparison—Plugging In

1. B
2. C
3. D
4. A
5. D
6. D

Practice Drill 12—Quantitative Comparison

1. C			
2. D	12. D	23. B	34. D
3. D	13. C	24. A	35. C
4. C	14. D	25. C	36. B
5. A	15. A	26. C	37. C
6. A	16. C	27. A	38. C
7. B	17. B	28. C	39. A
8. B	18. C	29. D	40. B
9. A	19. B	30. C	41. C
10. A	20. C	31. C	42. B
11. A	21. B	32. B	43. D
	22. D	33. C	44. A
			45. D

Math Review

1. Yes
2. It is neither positive nor negative.
3. Addition
4. Multiplication
5. The quotient
6. Yes; No
7. Exponents
8. Yes; No
9. No; Yes
10. Zero
11. Two
12. $2 \times 2 \times 2 = 8$
13. Over 100 $\left(\dfrac{x}{100}\right)$
14. Multiplication
15. Total
16. Average Pie
17. Plug in a number
18. Add; all four
19. Multiply; two (or square one, since the sides of a square are the same)
20. 180
21. 3; 180
22. 360
23. 2; equilateral
24. Hypotenuse; right angle
25. Area (of a triangle) = $\dfrac{1}{2}$ base × height

REVIEW—THE VERBAL PLAN

Pacing and Verbal Strategy

I will do the verbal questions in this order.

1. Synonyms with words I know
2. Synonyms with words I sort of know
3. Sentence completions

I should spend less than ten minutes on synonyms.

I will always eliminate wrong (or "worse") answers.

If possible, I will eliminate answer choices before I guess, but *even if I can't eliminate any*, I will still guess productively.

No, I cannot eliminate answer choices that contain words I do not know.

SYNONYMS

Practice Drill 1— Write Your Own Definition

Possible Definitions
1. Weird
2. Introduction
3. Giving
4. Doing the right thing
5. Change
6. Circle around
7. Optimistic
8. Stick around
9. Help
10. Build
11. Bend down
12. Honest
13. Tease
14. Rough
15. Self-centered
16. Calm
17. Use
18. Full of life
19. Stretch out
20. Help

Practice Drill 2—Write Another Definition

Look up these seven words in a dictionary to see how many different meanings they can have.

Practice Drill 3— Easy Synonym Techniques

1.	C	11.	C
2.	A	12.	B
3.	C	13.	D
4.	D	14.	B
5.	D	15.	A
6.	D	16.	C
7.	B	17.	D
8.	C	18.	C
9.	D	19.	B
10.	A	20.	C

Practice Drill 4—Making Your Own Context

Possible Contexts (Answers Will Vary)

1. Common cold; common man
2. Competent to stand trial
3. Abridged dictionary
4. Untimely demise; untimely remark
5. Homogenized milk
6. Juvenile delinquent; delinquent payments
7. Inalienable rights
8. Paltry sum
9. Auspicious beginning; auspicious occasion
10. Prodigal son

Practice Drill 5—Using Your Own Context

1. C
2. D
3. D
4. C
5. A
6. B
7. C
8. A
9. C
10. A

Practice Drill 6—Decide Positive/Negative

1. –
2. –
3. –
4. +
5. +
6. +
7. –
8. +
9. +
10. –

Practice Drill 7—Use Positive/Negative
Answers remaining should be

1. B	6. C D	11. A B	16. A D
2. A B	7. B D	12. A B D	17. A B C
3. A C	8. B D	13. D	18. A B
4. C D	9. B	14. A	19. B
5. A B D	10. A C D	15. A D	20. B C

You should have more answers remaining than are listed above if you encountered words you did not know in the answer choices. Don't eliminate those!

Practice Drill 8—Identifying Parts of Speech

1. Noun or verb
2. Noun
3. Noun or verb
4. Adjective
5. Noun
6. Adjective

Review—The Synonyms Plan

When I know the stem word, I write down my own definition.

If I don't see a definition close to mine, I write another definition.

When I sort of know the stem word, I can use the following techniques:
- Use my own context.
- Use word parts to put together a definition.
- Use "positive/negative."
- Eliminate wrong parts of speech.

If I've never seen the stem word before, I don't spend time on the question, but I guess my letter-of-the-day.

No, I cannot eliminate answer choices that contain words I do not know.

Practice Drill 9—All Synonyms Techniques

1.	B	11.	B	21.	C	31.	B
2.	A	12.	C	22.	B	32.	B
3.	C	13.	D	23.	B	33.	B
4.	A	14.	C	24.	D	34.	D
5.	D	15.	D	25.	D	35.	D
6.	A	16.	B	26.	D	36.	C
7.	D	17.	C	27.	C	37.	C
8.	B	18.	B	28.	C	38.	D
9.	C	19.	D	29.	A	39.	B
10.	B	20.	B	30.	D	40.	D

SENTENCE COMPLETIONS

Practice Drill 10—
Coming Up with Your Own Word

These words are just to give you an idea of what you could use. Any words that accurately fill the blank, based on the clue and the direction word, will do.

1.	good	12.	produce	23.	annoyed
2.	rare	13.	changed	24.	on time
3.	remarkable	14.	strong	25.	skill
4.	awake	15.	not necessary	26.	variety
5.	lucky	16.	repetitive	27.	creative
6.	thoughtful	17.	risky	28.	sharing
7.	alike	18.	outgoing	29.	flexible
8.	waste time	19.	healthy	30.	inborn
9.	frugal	20.	generous	31.	affable; talkative
10.	movement	21.	steadfast		
11.	simple	22.	intimidated; shy	32.	awestruck

Practice Drill 11—Eliminating Answers Based on Your Word

Below are the correct answers to the problems. You should have eliminated the other answer choices.

1.	D	17.	B
2.	B	18.	A
3.	C	19.	C
4.	D	20.	C
5.	A	21.	B
6.	A	22.	D
7.	D	23.	A
8.	C	24.	B
9.	B	25.	A
10.	A	26.	C
11.	D	27.	B
12.	D	28.	B
13.	B	29.	C
14.	C	30.	B
15.	D	31.	A
16.	C	32.	C

Practice Drill 12—Using Positive/Negative

1. +
2. +
3. −
4. +
5. −
6. +
7. −
8. −
9. −
10. +

Practice Drill 13—Eliminating Based on Positive/Negative

1. A
2. C
3. B
4. D
5. C
6. A
7. C
8. D
9. A
10. C

Practice Drill 14—Two-Blank Sentence Completions

1. B
2. C
3. A
4. A
5. D
6. A
7. C
8. C
9. A
10. C

Review—The Sentence Completions Plan

For each and every sentence completion, the first thing I do is cover the answers.

I look for the clue, and I mark it by underlining it.

I look for any direction words, and I circle them.

Then I come up with my own word for the blank. If I have trouble coming up with a word for the blank, I decide if the blank is positive or negative (or neither).

Then I eliminate answer choices, and I guess from the remaining choices.

For each and every sentence completion, the first thing I do is cover the answers.

I look for the clue, and I mark it by underlining it.

I look for any direction words, and I circle them.

If the sentence completion has two blanks, I do them one at a time.

I do the blank that is easier first—the one that has the better clue.

I come up with a word for one of the blanks, and when I uncover the answer choices, I only uncover the words for the blank that I am working on, and I eliminate based on those.

Then, I go back to the sentence and come up with a word for the other blank, uncover the answer choices that are left, and eliminate.

No, I cannot eliminate answer choices that contain words I do not know.

If I can only eliminate one or two answer choices, then I guess from the remaining choices.

If the sentence or vocabulary looks so difficult that I can't come up with a word or decide if the blank is positive or negative, then I fill in my "letter-of-the-day."

I spend my last minute filling in the "letter-of-the-day" for any questions I have not gotten around to answering.

I should never leave a question unanswered because there is no penalty for guessing.

READING COMPREHENSION

Practice Drill 15—All Sentence Completion Techniques

1.	A	11.	D
2.	C	12.	A
3.	B	13.	B
4.	A	14.	C
5.	D	15.	A
6.	B	16.	B
7.	B	17.	C
8.	C	18.	D
9.	C	19.	A
10.	B	20.	D

Practice Drill 16—Getting Through the Passage

You should have brief labels like the following:

1st Label:	Norway → Iceland
2nd Label:	Iceland → Greenland
3rd Label:	Lost
4th Label:	Saw America; landed Greenland
What?	A Viking
So What?	Found America early
Passage type?	History of an event—social studies

Practice Drill 17— Answering a General Question

1. D
2. C
3. D

Practice Drill 18— Answering a Specific Question

1. C
2. A   Lead word: Iceland
3. B
4. D   Lead word: Greenland

Practice Drill 19—Eliminating Answers

For a general question

A   Too big—you can't do that in a few paragraphs
C   Extreme
D   Extreme
E   Extreme
F   Extreme
H   Too small—this is only a detail

For a specific question

U   Extreme
V   Extreme
X   Extreme and against common sense

For a general tone/attitude question

J
K
M
O   Still too extreme, even though it's positive!
P
Q
S
T   Why would anyone write about something she doesn't care about?

Review—The Reading Plan

After I read each paragraph, I label it.

After I read an entire passage, I ask myself: What? and So what?

The five main types of general questions, and the questions I can ask myself to answer them, are:

- Main idea: What was the "What? So what?" for this passage?
- Tone/attitude: How did the author feel about the subject?
- General interpretation: Which answer stays closest to what the author said and how he said it?
- General purpose: Why did the author write this?
- Prediction: How was the passage arranged? What will come next?

To find the answer to a specific question, I can use three clues.

- Paragraph labels
- Line or paragraph reference
- Lead words

If the question says "In line 22," then I begin reading at approximately line 17. On a general question, I eliminate answers that are

- Too small
- Not mentioned in the passage
- In contradiction to the passage
- Too big
- Too extreme
- Against common sense

On a specific question, I eliminate answers that are

- Too extreme
- Contradicting passage details
- Not mentioned in the passage
- Against common sense

When I've got it down to two possible answers, I

- Reread the question
- Look at what makes the two answers different
- Go back to the passage
- Eliminate the answer that is worse

Practice Drill 20—All Reading Techniques—Lower Level

What? Tides

So what? Are caused by the moon

1. A
2. D
3. D
4. C

Practice Drill 21—All Reading Techniques—Lower Level

What? Brooklyn Bridge

So what? There were problems building it.

1. D
2. B
3. C
4. A
5. C

Practice Drill 22—All Reading Techniques—All Levels

What? William Levitt

So what? Built homes efficiently

1. C
2. D
3. C
4. D
5. A
6. C

Practice Drill 24—All Reading Techniques—Upper Level

What? Bob Dylan

So what? Was destined to be a musician

1. D
2. B
3. D
4. A
5. C

Practice Drill 23—All Reading Techniques—All Levels

What? Etymology

So what? Has many words to explore

1. B
2. C
3. A
4. C
5. B

Practice Drill 25—All Reading Techniques—Middle and Upper Level

What? Science

So what? Doesn't have all the answers

1. A
2. D
3. D
4. A
5. C

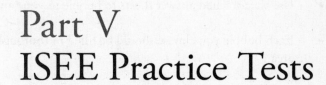

Part V
ISEE Practice Tests

HOW TO TAKE A PRACTICE TEST

Here are some reminders for taking your practice test.

- Find a quiet place to take the test where you won't be interrupted or distracted, and make sure you have enough time to take the entire test.

- Time yourself strictly. Use a timer, watch, or stopwatch that will ring, and do not allow yourself to go over time for any section.

- Take a practice test in one sitting, allowing yourself breaks of no more than two minutes between sections.

- Use the attached answer sheets to bubble in your answer choices.

- Each bubble you choose should be filled in thoroughly, and no other marks should be made in the answer area.

- Make sure to double check that your bubbles are filled in correctly!

Upper Level Practice Test

Be sure each mark *completely* fills the answer space.

SECTION 1

1 Ⓐ Ⓑ Ⓒ Ⓓ	9 Ⓐ Ⓑ Ⓒ Ⓓ	17 Ⓐ Ⓑ Ⓒ Ⓓ	25 Ⓐ Ⓑ Ⓒ Ⓓ	33 Ⓐ Ⓑ Ⓒ Ⓓ
2 Ⓐ Ⓑ Ⓒ Ⓓ	10 Ⓐ Ⓑ Ⓒ Ⓓ	18 Ⓐ Ⓑ Ⓒ Ⓓ	26 Ⓐ Ⓑ Ⓒ Ⓓ	34 Ⓐ Ⓑ Ⓒ Ⓓ
3 Ⓐ Ⓑ Ⓒ Ⓓ	11 Ⓐ Ⓑ Ⓒ Ⓓ	19 Ⓐ Ⓑ Ⓒ Ⓓ	27 Ⓐ Ⓑ Ⓒ Ⓓ	35 Ⓐ Ⓑ Ⓒ Ⓓ
4 Ⓐ Ⓑ Ⓒ Ⓓ	12 Ⓐ Ⓑ Ⓒ Ⓓ	20 Ⓐ Ⓑ Ⓒ Ⓓ	28 Ⓐ Ⓑ Ⓒ Ⓓ	36 Ⓐ Ⓑ Ⓒ Ⓓ
5 Ⓐ Ⓑ Ⓒ Ⓓ	13 Ⓐ Ⓑ Ⓒ Ⓓ	21 Ⓐ Ⓑ Ⓒ Ⓓ	29 Ⓐ Ⓑ Ⓒ Ⓓ	37 Ⓐ Ⓑ Ⓒ Ⓓ
6 Ⓐ Ⓑ Ⓒ Ⓓ	14 Ⓐ Ⓑ Ⓒ Ⓓ	22 Ⓐ Ⓑ Ⓒ Ⓓ	30 Ⓐ Ⓑ Ⓒ Ⓓ	38 Ⓐ Ⓑ Ⓒ Ⓓ
7 Ⓐ Ⓑ Ⓒ Ⓓ	15 Ⓐ Ⓑ Ⓒ Ⓓ	23 Ⓐ Ⓑ Ⓒ Ⓓ	31 Ⓐ Ⓑ Ⓒ Ⓓ	39 Ⓐ Ⓑ Ⓒ Ⓓ
8 Ⓐ Ⓑ Ⓒ Ⓓ	16 Ⓐ Ⓑ Ⓒ Ⓓ	24 Ⓐ Ⓑ Ⓒ Ⓓ	32 Ⓐ Ⓑ Ⓒ Ⓓ	40 Ⓐ Ⓑ Ⓒ Ⓓ

SECTION 2

1 Ⓐ Ⓑ Ⓒ Ⓓ	9 Ⓐ Ⓑ Ⓒ Ⓓ	17 Ⓐ Ⓑ Ⓒ Ⓓ	25 Ⓐ Ⓑ Ⓒ Ⓓ	33 Ⓐ Ⓑ Ⓒ Ⓓ
2 Ⓐ Ⓑ Ⓒ Ⓓ	10 Ⓐ Ⓑ Ⓒ Ⓓ	18 Ⓐ Ⓑ Ⓒ Ⓓ	26 Ⓐ Ⓑ Ⓒ Ⓓ	34 Ⓐ Ⓑ Ⓒ Ⓓ
3 Ⓐ Ⓑ Ⓒ Ⓓ	11 Ⓐ Ⓑ Ⓒ Ⓓ	19 Ⓐ Ⓑ Ⓒ Ⓓ	27 Ⓐ Ⓑ Ⓒ Ⓓ	35 Ⓐ Ⓑ Ⓒ Ⓓ
4 Ⓐ Ⓑ Ⓒ Ⓓ	12 Ⓐ Ⓑ Ⓒ Ⓓ	20 Ⓐ Ⓑ Ⓒ Ⓓ	28 Ⓐ Ⓑ Ⓒ Ⓓ	36 Ⓐ Ⓑ Ⓒ Ⓓ
5 Ⓐ Ⓑ Ⓒ Ⓓ	13 Ⓐ Ⓑ Ⓒ Ⓓ	21 Ⓐ Ⓑ Ⓒ Ⓓ	29 Ⓐ Ⓑ Ⓒ Ⓓ	37 Ⓐ Ⓑ Ⓒ Ⓓ
6 Ⓐ Ⓑ Ⓒ Ⓓ	14 Ⓐ Ⓑ Ⓒ Ⓓ	22 Ⓐ Ⓑ Ⓒ Ⓓ	30 Ⓐ Ⓑ Ⓒ Ⓓ	
7 Ⓐ Ⓑ Ⓒ Ⓓ	15 Ⓐ Ⓑ Ⓒ Ⓓ	23 Ⓐ Ⓑ Ⓒ Ⓓ	31 Ⓐ Ⓑ Ⓒ Ⓓ	
8 Ⓐ Ⓑ Ⓒ Ⓓ	16 Ⓐ Ⓑ Ⓒ Ⓓ	24 Ⓐ Ⓑ Ⓒ Ⓓ	32 Ⓐ Ⓑ Ⓒ Ⓓ	

SECTION 3

1 Ⓐ Ⓑ Ⓒ Ⓓ	9 Ⓐ Ⓑ Ⓒ Ⓓ	17 Ⓐ Ⓑ Ⓒ Ⓓ	25 Ⓐ Ⓑ Ⓒ Ⓓ	33 Ⓐ Ⓑ Ⓒ Ⓓ
2 Ⓐ Ⓑ Ⓒ Ⓓ	10 Ⓐ Ⓑ Ⓒ Ⓓ	18 Ⓐ Ⓑ Ⓒ Ⓓ	26 Ⓐ Ⓑ Ⓒ Ⓓ	34 Ⓐ Ⓑ Ⓒ Ⓓ
3 Ⓐ Ⓑ Ⓒ Ⓓ	11 Ⓐ Ⓑ Ⓒ Ⓓ	19 Ⓐ Ⓑ Ⓒ Ⓓ	27 Ⓐ Ⓑ Ⓒ Ⓓ	35 Ⓐ Ⓑ Ⓒ Ⓓ
4 Ⓐ Ⓑ Ⓒ Ⓓ	12 Ⓐ Ⓑ Ⓒ Ⓓ	20 Ⓐ Ⓑ Ⓒ Ⓓ	28 Ⓐ Ⓑ Ⓒ Ⓓ	36 Ⓐ Ⓑ Ⓒ Ⓓ
5 Ⓐ Ⓑ Ⓒ Ⓓ	13 Ⓐ Ⓑ Ⓒ Ⓓ	21 Ⓐ Ⓑ Ⓒ Ⓓ	29 Ⓐ Ⓑ Ⓒ Ⓓ	
6 Ⓐ Ⓑ Ⓒ Ⓓ	14 Ⓐ Ⓑ Ⓒ Ⓓ	22 Ⓐ Ⓑ Ⓒ Ⓓ	30 Ⓐ Ⓑ Ⓒ Ⓓ	
7 Ⓐ Ⓑ Ⓒ Ⓓ	15 Ⓐ Ⓑ Ⓒ Ⓓ	23 Ⓐ Ⓑ Ⓒ Ⓓ	31 Ⓐ Ⓑ Ⓒ Ⓓ	
8 Ⓐ Ⓑ Ⓒ Ⓓ	16 Ⓐ Ⓑ Ⓒ Ⓓ	24 Ⓐ Ⓑ Ⓒ Ⓓ	32 Ⓐ Ⓑ Ⓒ Ⓓ	

SECTION 4

1 Ⓐ Ⓑ Ⓒ Ⓓ	11 Ⓐ Ⓑ Ⓒ Ⓓ	21 Ⓐ Ⓑ Ⓒ Ⓓ	31 Ⓐ Ⓑ Ⓒ Ⓓ	41 Ⓐ Ⓑ Ⓒ Ⓓ
2 Ⓐ Ⓑ Ⓒ Ⓓ	12 Ⓐ Ⓑ Ⓒ Ⓓ	22 Ⓐ Ⓑ Ⓒ Ⓓ	32 Ⓐ Ⓑ Ⓒ Ⓓ	42 Ⓐ Ⓑ Ⓒ Ⓓ
3 Ⓐ Ⓑ Ⓒ Ⓓ	13 Ⓐ Ⓑ Ⓒ Ⓓ	23 Ⓐ Ⓑ Ⓒ Ⓓ	33 Ⓐ Ⓑ Ⓒ Ⓓ	43 Ⓐ Ⓑ Ⓒ Ⓓ
4 Ⓐ Ⓑ Ⓒ Ⓓ	14 Ⓐ Ⓑ Ⓒ Ⓓ	24 Ⓐ Ⓑ Ⓒ Ⓓ	34 Ⓐ Ⓑ Ⓒ Ⓓ	44 Ⓐ Ⓑ Ⓒ Ⓓ
5 Ⓐ Ⓑ Ⓒ Ⓓ	15 Ⓐ Ⓑ Ⓒ Ⓓ	25 Ⓐ Ⓑ Ⓒ Ⓓ	35 Ⓐ Ⓑ Ⓒ Ⓓ	45 Ⓐ Ⓑ Ⓒ Ⓓ
6 Ⓐ Ⓑ Ⓒ Ⓓ	16 Ⓐ Ⓑ Ⓒ Ⓓ	26 Ⓐ Ⓑ Ⓒ Ⓓ	36 Ⓐ Ⓑ Ⓒ Ⓓ	46 Ⓐ Ⓑ Ⓒ Ⓓ
7 Ⓐ Ⓑ Ⓒ Ⓓ	17 Ⓐ Ⓑ Ⓒ Ⓓ	27 Ⓐ Ⓑ Ⓒ Ⓓ	37 Ⓐ Ⓑ Ⓒ Ⓓ	47 Ⓐ Ⓑ Ⓒ Ⓓ
8 Ⓐ Ⓑ Ⓒ Ⓓ	18 Ⓐ Ⓑ Ⓒ Ⓓ	28 Ⓐ Ⓑ Ⓒ Ⓓ	38 Ⓐ Ⓑ Ⓒ Ⓓ	
9 Ⓐ Ⓑ Ⓒ Ⓓ	19 Ⓐ Ⓑ Ⓒ Ⓓ	29 Ⓐ Ⓑ Ⓒ Ⓓ	39 Ⓐ Ⓑ Ⓒ Ⓓ	
10 Ⓐ Ⓑ Ⓒ Ⓓ	20 Ⓐ Ⓑ Ⓒ Ⓓ	30 Ⓐ Ⓑ Ⓒ Ⓓ	40 Ⓐ Ⓑ Ⓒ Ⓓ	

Middle Level Practice Test

Be sure each mark *completely* fills the answer space.

SECTION 1

1 Ⓐ Ⓑ Ⓒ Ⓓ	9 Ⓐ Ⓑ Ⓒ Ⓓ	17 Ⓐ Ⓑ Ⓒ Ⓓ	25 Ⓐ Ⓑ Ⓒ Ⓓ	33 Ⓐ Ⓑ Ⓒ Ⓓ
2 Ⓐ Ⓑ Ⓒ Ⓓ	10 Ⓐ Ⓑ Ⓒ Ⓓ	18 Ⓐ Ⓑ Ⓒ Ⓓ	26 Ⓐ Ⓑ Ⓒ Ⓓ	34 Ⓐ Ⓑ Ⓒ Ⓓ
3 Ⓐ Ⓑ Ⓒ Ⓓ	11 Ⓐ Ⓑ Ⓒ Ⓓ	19 Ⓐ Ⓑ Ⓒ Ⓓ	27 Ⓐ Ⓑ Ⓒ Ⓓ	35 Ⓐ Ⓑ Ⓒ Ⓓ
4 Ⓐ Ⓑ Ⓒ Ⓓ	12 Ⓐ Ⓑ Ⓒ Ⓓ	20 Ⓐ Ⓑ Ⓒ Ⓓ	28 Ⓐ Ⓑ Ⓒ Ⓓ	36 Ⓐ Ⓑ Ⓒ Ⓓ
5 Ⓐ Ⓑ Ⓒ Ⓓ	13 Ⓐ Ⓑ Ⓒ Ⓓ	21 Ⓐ Ⓑ Ⓒ Ⓓ	29 Ⓐ Ⓑ Ⓒ Ⓓ	37 Ⓐ Ⓑ Ⓒ Ⓓ
6 Ⓐ Ⓑ Ⓒ Ⓓ	14 Ⓐ Ⓑ Ⓒ Ⓓ	22 Ⓐ Ⓑ Ⓒ Ⓓ	30 Ⓐ Ⓑ Ⓒ Ⓓ	38 Ⓐ Ⓑ Ⓒ Ⓓ
7 Ⓐ Ⓑ Ⓒ Ⓓ	15 Ⓐ Ⓑ Ⓒ Ⓓ	23 Ⓐ Ⓑ Ⓒ Ⓓ	31 Ⓐ Ⓑ Ⓒ Ⓓ	39 Ⓐ Ⓑ Ⓒ Ⓓ
8 Ⓐ Ⓑ Ⓒ Ⓓ	16 Ⓐ Ⓑ Ⓒ Ⓓ	24 Ⓐ Ⓑ Ⓒ Ⓓ	32 Ⓐ Ⓑ Ⓒ Ⓓ	40 Ⓐ Ⓑ Ⓒ Ⓓ

SECTION 2

1 Ⓐ Ⓑ Ⓒ Ⓓ	9 Ⓐ Ⓑ Ⓒ Ⓓ	17 Ⓐ Ⓑ Ⓒ Ⓓ	25 Ⓐ Ⓑ Ⓒ Ⓓ	33 Ⓐ Ⓑ Ⓒ Ⓓ
2 Ⓐ Ⓑ Ⓒ Ⓓ	10 Ⓐ Ⓑ Ⓒ Ⓓ	18 Ⓐ Ⓑ Ⓒ Ⓓ	26 Ⓐ Ⓑ Ⓒ Ⓓ	34 Ⓐ Ⓑ Ⓒ Ⓓ
3 Ⓐ Ⓑ Ⓒ Ⓓ	11 Ⓐ Ⓑ Ⓒ Ⓓ	19 Ⓐ Ⓑ Ⓒ Ⓓ	27 Ⓐ Ⓑ Ⓒ Ⓓ	35 Ⓐ Ⓑ Ⓒ Ⓓ
4 Ⓐ Ⓑ Ⓒ Ⓓ	12 Ⓐ Ⓑ Ⓒ Ⓓ	20 Ⓐ Ⓑ Ⓒ Ⓓ	28 Ⓐ Ⓑ Ⓒ Ⓓ	36 Ⓐ Ⓑ Ⓒ Ⓓ
5 Ⓐ Ⓑ Ⓒ Ⓓ	13 Ⓐ Ⓑ Ⓒ Ⓓ	21 Ⓐ Ⓑ Ⓒ Ⓓ	29 Ⓐ Ⓑ Ⓒ Ⓓ	37 Ⓐ Ⓑ Ⓒ Ⓓ
6 Ⓐ Ⓑ Ⓒ Ⓓ	14 Ⓐ Ⓑ Ⓒ Ⓓ	22 Ⓐ Ⓑ Ⓒ Ⓓ	30 Ⓐ Ⓑ Ⓒ Ⓓ	
7 Ⓐ Ⓑ Ⓒ Ⓓ	15 Ⓐ Ⓑ Ⓒ Ⓓ	23 Ⓐ Ⓑ Ⓒ Ⓓ	31 Ⓐ Ⓑ Ⓒ Ⓓ	
8 Ⓐ Ⓑ Ⓒ Ⓓ	16 Ⓐ Ⓑ Ⓒ Ⓓ	24 Ⓐ Ⓑ Ⓒ Ⓓ	32 Ⓐ Ⓑ Ⓒ Ⓓ	

SECTION 3

1 Ⓐ Ⓑ Ⓒ Ⓓ	9 Ⓐ Ⓑ Ⓒ Ⓓ	17 Ⓐ Ⓑ Ⓒ Ⓓ	25 Ⓐ Ⓑ Ⓒ Ⓓ	33 Ⓐ Ⓑ Ⓒ Ⓓ
2 Ⓐ Ⓑ Ⓒ Ⓓ	10 Ⓐ Ⓑ Ⓒ Ⓓ	18 Ⓐ Ⓑ Ⓒ Ⓓ	26 Ⓐ Ⓑ Ⓒ Ⓓ	34 Ⓐ Ⓑ Ⓒ Ⓓ
3 Ⓐ Ⓑ Ⓒ Ⓓ	11 Ⓐ Ⓑ Ⓒ Ⓓ	19 Ⓐ Ⓑ Ⓒ Ⓓ	27 Ⓐ Ⓑ Ⓒ Ⓓ	35 Ⓐ Ⓑ Ⓒ Ⓓ
4 Ⓐ Ⓑ Ⓒ Ⓓ	12 Ⓐ Ⓑ Ⓒ Ⓓ	20 Ⓐ Ⓑ Ⓒ Ⓓ	28 Ⓐ Ⓑ Ⓒ Ⓓ	36 Ⓐ Ⓑ Ⓒ Ⓓ
5 Ⓐ Ⓑ Ⓒ Ⓓ	13 Ⓐ Ⓑ Ⓒ Ⓓ	21 Ⓐ Ⓑ Ⓒ Ⓓ	29 Ⓐ Ⓑ Ⓒ Ⓓ	
6 Ⓐ Ⓑ Ⓒ Ⓓ	14 Ⓐ Ⓑ Ⓒ Ⓓ	22 Ⓐ Ⓑ Ⓒ Ⓓ	30 Ⓐ Ⓑ Ⓒ Ⓓ	
7 Ⓐ Ⓑ Ⓒ Ⓓ	15 Ⓐ Ⓑ Ⓒ Ⓓ	23 Ⓐ Ⓑ Ⓒ Ⓓ	31 Ⓐ Ⓑ Ⓒ Ⓓ	
8 Ⓐ Ⓑ Ⓒ Ⓓ	16 Ⓐ Ⓑ Ⓒ Ⓓ	24 Ⓐ Ⓑ Ⓒ Ⓓ	32 Ⓐ Ⓑ Ⓒ Ⓓ	

SECTION 4

1 Ⓐ Ⓑ Ⓒ Ⓓ	11 Ⓐ Ⓑ Ⓒ Ⓓ	21 Ⓐ Ⓑ Ⓒ Ⓓ	31 Ⓐ Ⓑ Ⓒ Ⓓ	41 Ⓐ Ⓑ Ⓒ Ⓓ
2 Ⓐ Ⓑ Ⓒ Ⓓ	12 Ⓐ Ⓑ Ⓒ Ⓓ	22 Ⓐ Ⓑ Ⓒ Ⓓ	32 Ⓐ Ⓑ Ⓒ Ⓓ	42 Ⓐ Ⓑ Ⓒ Ⓓ
3 Ⓐ Ⓑ Ⓒ Ⓓ	13 Ⓐ Ⓑ Ⓒ Ⓓ	23 Ⓐ Ⓑ Ⓒ Ⓓ	33 Ⓐ Ⓑ Ⓒ Ⓓ	43 Ⓐ Ⓑ Ⓒ Ⓓ
4 Ⓐ Ⓑ Ⓒ Ⓓ	14 Ⓐ Ⓑ Ⓒ Ⓓ	24 Ⓐ Ⓑ Ⓒ Ⓓ	34 Ⓐ Ⓑ Ⓒ Ⓓ	44 Ⓐ Ⓑ Ⓒ Ⓓ
5 Ⓐ Ⓑ Ⓒ Ⓓ	15 Ⓐ Ⓑ Ⓒ Ⓓ	25 Ⓐ Ⓑ Ⓒ Ⓓ	35 Ⓐ Ⓑ Ⓒ Ⓓ	45 Ⓐ Ⓑ Ⓒ Ⓓ
6 Ⓐ Ⓑ Ⓒ Ⓓ	16 Ⓐ Ⓑ Ⓒ Ⓓ	26 Ⓐ Ⓑ Ⓒ Ⓓ	36 Ⓐ Ⓑ Ⓒ Ⓓ	46 Ⓐ Ⓑ Ⓒ Ⓓ
7 Ⓐ Ⓑ Ⓒ Ⓓ	17 Ⓐ Ⓑ Ⓒ Ⓓ	27 Ⓐ Ⓑ Ⓒ Ⓓ	37 Ⓐ Ⓑ Ⓒ Ⓓ	47 Ⓐ Ⓑ Ⓒ Ⓓ
8 Ⓐ Ⓑ Ⓒ Ⓓ	18 Ⓐ Ⓑ Ⓒ Ⓓ	28 Ⓐ Ⓑ Ⓒ Ⓓ	38 Ⓐ Ⓑ Ⓒ Ⓓ	
9 Ⓐ Ⓑ Ⓒ Ⓓ	19 Ⓐ Ⓑ Ⓒ Ⓓ	29 Ⓐ Ⓑ Ⓒ Ⓓ	39 Ⓐ Ⓑ Ⓒ Ⓓ	
10 Ⓐ Ⓑ Ⓒ Ⓓ	20 Ⓐ Ⓑ Ⓒ Ⓓ	30 Ⓐ Ⓑ Ⓒ Ⓓ	40 Ⓐ Ⓑ Ⓒ Ⓓ	

Lower Level Practice Test

Be sure each mark *completely* fills the answer space.

SECTION 1

1 Ⓐ Ⓑ Ⓒ Ⓓ	9 Ⓐ Ⓑ Ⓒ Ⓓ	17 Ⓐ Ⓑ Ⓒ Ⓓ	25 Ⓐ Ⓑ Ⓒ Ⓓ	33 Ⓐ Ⓑ Ⓒ Ⓓ
2 Ⓐ Ⓑ Ⓒ Ⓓ	10 Ⓐ Ⓑ Ⓒ Ⓓ	18 Ⓐ Ⓑ Ⓒ Ⓓ	26 Ⓐ Ⓑ Ⓒ Ⓓ	34 Ⓐ Ⓑ Ⓒ Ⓓ
3 Ⓐ Ⓑ Ⓒ Ⓓ	11 Ⓐ Ⓑ Ⓒ Ⓓ	19 Ⓐ Ⓑ Ⓒ Ⓓ	27 Ⓐ Ⓑ Ⓒ Ⓓ	
4 Ⓐ Ⓑ Ⓒ Ⓓ	12 Ⓐ Ⓑ Ⓒ Ⓓ	20 Ⓐ Ⓑ Ⓒ Ⓓ	28 Ⓐ Ⓑ Ⓒ Ⓓ	
5 Ⓐ Ⓑ Ⓒ Ⓓ	13 Ⓐ Ⓑ Ⓒ Ⓓ	21 Ⓐ Ⓑ Ⓒ Ⓓ	29 Ⓐ Ⓑ Ⓒ Ⓓ	
6 Ⓐ Ⓑ Ⓒ Ⓓ	14 Ⓐ Ⓑ Ⓒ Ⓓ	22 Ⓐ Ⓑ Ⓒ Ⓓ	30 Ⓐ Ⓑ Ⓒ Ⓓ	
7 Ⓐ Ⓑ Ⓒ Ⓓ	15 Ⓐ Ⓑ Ⓒ Ⓓ	23 Ⓐ Ⓑ Ⓒ Ⓓ	31 Ⓐ Ⓑ Ⓒ Ⓓ	
8 Ⓐ Ⓑ Ⓒ Ⓓ	16 Ⓐ Ⓑ Ⓒ Ⓓ	24 Ⓐ Ⓑ Ⓒ Ⓓ	32 Ⓐ Ⓑ Ⓒ Ⓓ	

SECTION 2

1 Ⓐ Ⓑ Ⓒ Ⓓ	9 Ⓐ Ⓑ Ⓒ Ⓓ	17 Ⓐ Ⓑ Ⓒ Ⓓ	25 Ⓐ Ⓑ Ⓒ Ⓓ	33 Ⓐ Ⓑ Ⓒ Ⓓ
2 Ⓐ Ⓑ Ⓒ Ⓓ	10 Ⓐ Ⓑ Ⓒ Ⓓ	18 Ⓐ Ⓑ Ⓒ Ⓓ	26 Ⓐ Ⓑ Ⓒ Ⓓ	34 Ⓐ Ⓑ Ⓒ Ⓓ
3 Ⓐ Ⓑ Ⓒ Ⓓ	11 Ⓐ Ⓑ Ⓒ Ⓓ	19 Ⓐ Ⓑ Ⓒ Ⓓ	27 Ⓐ Ⓑ Ⓒ Ⓓ	35 Ⓐ Ⓑ Ⓒ Ⓓ
4 Ⓐ Ⓑ Ⓒ Ⓓ	12 Ⓐ Ⓑ Ⓒ Ⓓ	20 Ⓐ Ⓑ Ⓒ Ⓓ	28 Ⓐ Ⓑ Ⓒ Ⓓ	36 Ⓐ Ⓑ Ⓒ Ⓓ
5 Ⓐ Ⓑ Ⓒ Ⓓ	13 Ⓐ Ⓑ Ⓒ Ⓓ	21 Ⓐ Ⓑ Ⓒ Ⓓ	29 Ⓐ Ⓑ Ⓒ Ⓓ	37 Ⓐ Ⓑ Ⓒ Ⓓ
6 Ⓐ Ⓑ Ⓒ Ⓓ	14 Ⓐ Ⓑ Ⓒ Ⓓ	22 Ⓐ Ⓑ Ⓒ Ⓓ	30 Ⓐ Ⓑ Ⓒ Ⓓ	38 Ⓐ Ⓑ Ⓒ Ⓓ
7 Ⓐ Ⓑ Ⓒ Ⓓ	15 Ⓐ Ⓑ Ⓒ Ⓓ	23 Ⓐ Ⓑ Ⓒ Ⓓ	31 Ⓐ Ⓑ Ⓒ Ⓓ	
8 Ⓐ Ⓑ Ⓒ Ⓓ	16 Ⓐ Ⓑ Ⓒ Ⓓ	24 Ⓐ Ⓑ Ⓒ Ⓓ	32 Ⓐ Ⓑ Ⓒ Ⓓ	

SECTION 3

1 Ⓐ Ⓑ Ⓒ Ⓓ	9 Ⓐ Ⓑ Ⓒ Ⓓ	17 Ⓐ Ⓑ Ⓒ Ⓓ	25 Ⓐ Ⓑ Ⓒ Ⓓ
2 Ⓐ Ⓑ Ⓒ Ⓓ	10 Ⓐ Ⓑ Ⓒ Ⓓ	18 Ⓐ Ⓑ Ⓒ Ⓓ	
3 Ⓐ Ⓑ Ⓒ Ⓓ	11 Ⓐ Ⓑ Ⓒ Ⓓ	19 Ⓐ Ⓑ Ⓒ Ⓓ	
4 Ⓐ Ⓑ Ⓒ Ⓓ	12 Ⓐ Ⓑ Ⓒ Ⓓ	20 Ⓐ Ⓑ Ⓒ Ⓓ	
5 Ⓐ Ⓑ Ⓒ Ⓓ	13 Ⓐ Ⓑ Ⓒ Ⓓ	21 Ⓐ Ⓑ Ⓒ Ⓓ	
6 Ⓐ Ⓑ Ⓒ Ⓓ	14 Ⓐ Ⓑ Ⓒ Ⓓ	22 Ⓐ Ⓑ Ⓒ Ⓓ	
7 Ⓐ Ⓑ Ⓒ Ⓓ	15 Ⓐ Ⓑ Ⓒ Ⓓ	23 Ⓐ Ⓑ Ⓒ Ⓓ	
8 Ⓐ Ⓑ Ⓒ Ⓓ	16 Ⓐ Ⓑ Ⓒ Ⓓ	24 Ⓐ Ⓑ Ⓒ Ⓓ	

SECTION 4

1 Ⓐ Ⓑ Ⓒ Ⓓ	9 Ⓐ Ⓑ Ⓒ Ⓓ	17 Ⓐ Ⓑ Ⓒ Ⓓ	25 Ⓐ Ⓑ Ⓒ Ⓓ
2 Ⓐ Ⓑ Ⓒ Ⓓ	10 Ⓐ Ⓑ Ⓒ Ⓓ	18 Ⓐ Ⓑ Ⓒ Ⓓ	26 Ⓐ Ⓑ Ⓒ Ⓓ
3 Ⓐ Ⓑ Ⓒ Ⓓ	11 Ⓐ Ⓑ Ⓒ Ⓓ	19 Ⓐ Ⓑ Ⓒ Ⓓ	27 Ⓐ Ⓑ Ⓒ Ⓓ
4 Ⓐ Ⓑ Ⓒ Ⓓ	12 Ⓐ Ⓑ Ⓒ Ⓓ	20 Ⓐ Ⓑ Ⓒ Ⓓ	28 Ⓐ Ⓑ Ⓒ Ⓓ
5 Ⓐ Ⓑ Ⓒ Ⓓ	13 Ⓐ Ⓑ Ⓒ Ⓓ	21 Ⓐ Ⓑ Ⓒ Ⓓ	29 Ⓐ Ⓑ Ⓒ Ⓓ
6 Ⓐ Ⓑ Ⓒ Ⓓ	14 Ⓐ Ⓑ Ⓒ Ⓓ	22 Ⓐ Ⓑ Ⓒ Ⓓ	30 Ⓐ Ⓑ Ⓒ Ⓓ
7 Ⓐ Ⓑ Ⓒ Ⓓ	15 Ⓐ Ⓑ Ⓒ Ⓓ	23 Ⓐ Ⓑ Ⓒ Ⓓ	
8 Ⓐ Ⓑ Ⓒ Ⓓ	16 Ⓐ Ⓑ Ⓒ Ⓓ	24 Ⓐ Ⓑ Ⓒ Ⓓ	

Chapter 21
Upper Level ISEE
Practice Test

SECTION 1

VERBAL REASONING

Time: 20 minutes

40 Questions

This section is divided into two parts that contain different types of questions. As soon as you have completed Part One, answer the questions in Part Two. You may write in your test booklet. For each answer you select, fill in the corresponding circle on your answer document.

Part One

Each question in Part One is made up of a word in capital letters followed by four choices. Choose the one word that is most nearly the same in meaning as the word in capital letters.

SAMPLE QUESTION:

SWIFT: (A) clean (B) fancy
(C) fast (D) quiet

Sample Answer

Ⓐ Ⓑ ● Ⓓ

---

1. GRAVE: (A) deadly (B) final (C) open
    (D) solemn

2. FOMENT: (A) articulate (B) dissemble
    (C) instigate (D) praise

3. INARTICULATE: (A) creative (B) friendly
    (C) overly sensitive (D) tongue-tied

4. AMELIORATE: (A) enjoy (B) hinder
    (C) improve (D) restrain

5. THESIS: (A) belief (B) paper (C) report
    (D) study

6. DEBUNK: (A) build (B) discredit
    (C) impress (D) justify

7. DISDAIN: (A) annoy (B) contempt (C) find
    (D) hope

8. RETICENT: (A) anxious (B) aware
    (C) informed (D) reserved

9. PREVALENT: (A) fascinating (B) minority
    (C) old-fashioned (D) predominant

10. SATIATE: (A) deny (B) fill (C) serve
    (D) starve

11. CANDID: (A) defiant (B) dejected (C) frank
    (D) stingy

12. EMULATE: (A) brush off (B) imitate
    (C) perplex (D) permit

13. TAINT: (A) annoy (B) handle (C) infect
    (D) master

14. ENIGMA: (A) effort (B) mystery
    (C) struggle (D) tantrum

15. DETRIMENTAL: (A) considerate (B) desolate
    (C) emphatic (D) injurious

16. METICULOUS: (A) favorable (B) finicky
    (C) gigantic (D) maddening

17. JUXTAPOSE: (A) keep away
    (B) place side by side (C) put behind
    (D) question

18. CONGENIAL: (A) friendly (B) impressive
    (C) inborn (D) magical

19. MITIGATE: (A) bend (B) ease (C) harden
    (D) untangle

20. ELUSIVE: (A) real (B) slippery
    (C) treacherous (D) unhappy

GO ON TO THE NEXT PAGE.

1 1 1 1 1 1 1 1 1 1

Part Two

Each question below is made up of a sentence with one or two blanks. One blank indicates that one word is missing. Two blanks indicate that two words are missing. Each sentence is followed by four choices. Select the one word or pair of words that will best complete the meaning of the sentence as a whole.

SAMPLE QUESTIONS:

Sample Answer

● Ⓑ Ⓒ Ⓓ Ⓔ

Ann carried the box carefully so that she would not ------- the pretty glasses.

(A) break
(B) fix
(C) open
(D) stop

● Ⓑ Ⓒ Ⓓ Ⓔ

When our boat first crashed into the rocks we were -------, but we soon felt ------- when we realized that nobody was hurt.

(A) afraid .. relieved
(B) happy .. confused
(C) sleepy .. sad
(D) sorry .. angry

21. Jane felt ------- about whether to go to the party or not; on one hand it seemed like fun, but on the other, she was very tired.

(A) ambivalent
(B) apathetic
(C) happy
(D) irritated

22. Like the more famous Susan B. Anthony, M. Carey Thomas ------- feminism and women's rights.

(A) championed
(B) defaced
(C) found
(D) gained

23. Morality is not -------; cultures around the world have different ideas about how people should be treated.

(A) debatable
(B) helpful
(C) realistic
(D) universal

24. Although Ms. Sanchez ------ the student that he needed a good grade on the final exam, he did not study at all.

(A) admonished
(B) congratulated
(C) criticized
(D) ridiculed

GO ON TO THE NEXT PAGE.

25. Thomas Jefferson was a man of ------- talents: he was known for his skills as a writer, a musician, an architect, and an inventor as well as a politician.

    (A) abundant
    (B) frugal
    (C) mundane
    (D) overblown

26. Monica could remain ------- no longer; the injustices she witnessed moved her to speak up.

    (A) active
    (B) furious
    (C) helpful
    (D) reticent

27. Louisa May Alcott's *Little Women* is really quite -------; much of the story is based on her experiences as a young woman growing up in Concord, Massachusetts.

    (A) autobiographical
    (B) fictional
    (C) moving
    (D) visual

28. Though his lectures could be monotonous, Mr. Cutler was actually quite ------- when he spoke to students in small, informal groups.

    (A) amiable
    (B) pious
    (C) prosaic
    (D) vapid

29. Craig had ------- that the day would not go well, and just as he'd thought, he had two pop quizzes.

    (A) an antidote
    (B) an interest
    (C) a premonition
    (D) a report

30. Far from shedding light on the mystery, Jason's ------- reponse left people unsure.

    (A) impartial
    (B) opaque
    (C) risky
    (D) systematic

31. Although Marie was a talented and ------- performer, her gifts were often ------- because she didn't know how to promote herself.

    (A) faithful . . supported
    (B) insulting . . overlooked
    (C) promising . . satisfied
    (D) versatile . . ignored

32. Although she was the daughter of a wealthy slaveholder, Angelina Grimke ------- slavery and ------- her whole life for the cause of abolition.

    (A) desired . . picketed
    (B) detested . . dedicated
    (C) hated . . wasted
    (D) represented . . fought

33. Rhubarb is actually quite ------- requiring a large amount of sugar to make it -------.

    (A) bitter . . palatable
    (B) flavorful . . fattening
    (C) nutritious . . sickening
    (D) unpopular . . sticky

GO ON TO THE NEXT PAGE.

34. Because Martha was naturally -------, she would see the bright side of any situation, but Jack had a ------- personality and always waited for something bad to happen.

    (A) cheerful . . upbeat
    (B) frightened . . mawkish
    (C) optimistic . . dreary
    (D) realistic . . unreasonable

35. Although Edgar was not telling the truth, his ------ succeeded: the crowd was ------- to demand that Edgar's competition be rejected.

    (A) antipathy . . questioned
    (B) condone . . encouraged
    (C) fallacy . . incited
    (D) lie . . permitted

36. Even though the critics praised the author's ------- use of words, they found the text ------- at a mere 100 pages.

    (A) hackneyed . . threadbare
    (B) improper . . laconic
    (C) precise . . short
    (D) sure . . banal

37. Erica's mother could not ------- why Erica would study a subject as ------- as the culture of 13th century French winemakers.

    (A) fathom . . esoteric
    (B) intend . . bizarre
    (C) respond . . gruesome
    (D) understand . . interesting

38. The threat of the storm did not ------- Ernie's excitement for the race; he had no ------- running in even the most unpleasant of weather.

    (A) diminish . . reservations about
    (B) improve . . concerns about
    (C) lessen . . inclination to
    (D) understate . . abilities for

39. Always -------, Mr. Sanford refused to spend any money on anything unnecessary; to him, even a meal at a restaurant was a ------- excess.

    (A) parsimonious . . respectable
    (B) penurious . . useful
    (C) spendthrift . . respectable
    (D) stingy . . selective

40. To her -------, Margie was given the unfair label of -------, even though her love of the arts was far from superficial.

    (A) chagrin . . dilettante
    (B) frustration . . adversary
    (C) irritation . . performer
    (D) surprise . . mentor

STOP

IF YOU FINISH BEFORE TIME IS CALLED,
YOU MAY CHECK YOUR WORK ON THIS SECTION ONLY.
DO NOT TURN TO ANY OTHER SECTION IN THE TEST.

GO ON TO THE NEXT PAGE.

SECTION 2

QUANTITATIVE REASONING

Time: 35 minutes

37 Questions

Directions

Any figures that accompany questions in this section may be assumed to be drawn as accurately as possible EXCEPT when it is stated that a particular figure is not drawn to scale. Letters such as x, y, and n stand for real numbers.

(1) Each question in Part One consists of a word problem followed by four answer choices. You may write in your test booklet; however, you may be able to solve many of these problems in your head. Next, take a look at the four answer choices and select the best one.

Example 1	If $3 + x = 5$, what is the value of x ?	Answer
	(A) 0 (B) 1 (C) 2 (D) 3	Ⓐ Ⓑ ● Ⓓ

(2) All questions in Part Two are quantitative comparisons between the quantities shown in Column A and Column B. Using the information given in each question, compare the quantity in Column A to the quantity in Column B and choose one of these four answer choices:

(A)   The quantity in Column A is greater.
(B)   The quantity in Column B is greater.
(C)   The two quantities are equal.
(D)   The relationship cannot be determined from the information given.

	Column A	Column B	
Example 2	3^2	2^3	Answer ● Ⓑ Ⓒ Ⓓ

The quantity in Column A (9) is greater than the quantity in Column B (8), so space A is marked.

Example 3	The cost of 8 apples at 7 cents apiece	The cost of 7 apples at 8 cents apiece	Answer Ⓐ Ⓑ ● Ⓓ

The quantity in Column A (56 cents) equals the quantity in Column B (56 cents), so space C is marked.

GO ON TO THE NEXT PAGE.

2 2 2 2 2 2 2 2 2 2

1. Which of the following is greatest?

   (A) 0.0100
   (B) 0.0099
   (C) 0.1900
   (D) 0.0199

2. Which of the following is NOT the product of two prime numbers?

   (A) 33
   (B) 35
   (C) 45
   (D) 91

3. If x, y, and z are consecutive even integers, then what is the difference between x and z ?

   (A) 0
   (B) 1
   (C) 2
   (D) 4

Questions 4-5 refer to the following chart.

Clothing Close-out

Dresses	Originally $120	Now $90
Coats	Originally $250	Now $180
Shoes	Originally $60	Now $40
Hats	Originally $40	Now $20

4. Which of the items for sale has the greatest percent discount?

   (A) Dresses
   (B) Coats
   (C) Shoes
   (D) Hats

5. Purchasing which item will save the buyer the most dollars?

   (A) Dresses
   (B) Coats
   (C) Shoes
   (D) Hats

GO ON TO THE NEXT PAGE.

6. Amy is three years older than Beth and five years younger than Jo. If Beth is *b* years old, how old is Jo, in terms of *b* ?

    (A) $2b + 3$
    (B) $2b - 3$
    (C) $b + 4$
    (D) $b + 8$

7. If *x* is divided by 5, the remainder is 4. If *y* is divided by 5, the remainder is 1. What is the remainder when $(x + y)$ is divided by 5 ?

    (A) 0
    (B) 1
    (C) 2
    (D) 3

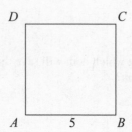

8. What is the perimeter of the square *ABCD* shown above?

    (A)   5
    (B) 15
    (C) 20
    (D) 25

9. At a party, 4 pizzas with 8 slices each were served. If each of the 9 guests had 3 pieces of pizza each, how many slices remained?

    (A) 4
    (B) 5
    (C) 6
    (D) 7

10. Jamie had *x* dollars in the bank. He withdrew $\frac{1}{2}$ to buy a car. He withdrew $\frac{1}{3}$ of what was left to buy a couch. What fraction of the original amount remained in his account?

    (A) $\frac{1}{6}$
    (B) $\frac{1}{5}$
    (C) $\frac{1}{4}$
    (D) $\frac{1}{3}$

11. *J* is a whole number divisible by 4. *J* is also divisible by 3. Which of the following is NOT a possible value for *J* ?

    (A) 12
    (B) 24
    (C) 30
    (D) 36

12. The product of 0.48 and 100 is approximately

    (A)   0.5
    (B)   4.8
    (C)   5
    (D) 50

13. If the length of a rectangle is increased by 20 percent and the width of the rectangle is decreased by 10 percent, what is the percent increase of the area of the rectangle?

    (A)   8%
    (B)   9%
    (C) 10%
    (D) 12%

GO ON TO THE NEXT PAGE.

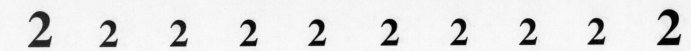

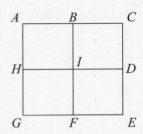

14. Square *ACEG* shown above is composed of 4 squares with sides of 1 meter each. Traveling only on the lines of the squares, how many different routes from *A* to *D* that are exactly 3 meters long are possible?

(A) 2
(B) 3
(C) 4
(D) 5

15. If, in triangle *ABC*, the measure of angle *B* is greater than 90 , and *AB = BC,* what is a possible measure for angle *C* in degrees?

(A) 35
(B) 45
(C) 60
(D) It cannot be determined from the information given.

16. Chumway Motors discounts the cost of a car by 10% and then runs another special one-day deal offering an additional 20% off the discounted price. What discount does this represent from the original price of the car?

(A) 28%
(B) 30%
(C) 40%
(D) 72%

17. David scored 82, 84, and 95 on his first three math tests. What score does he need on his fourth test to bring his average up to a 90?

(A) 90
(B) 92
(C) 96
(D) 99

18. Sam ranks movies on a scale of 1-100. If he adds 2 points to each movie in his collection, and the range of the rankings was 54, what is the range when the 2 points are added?

(A) 50
(B) 52
(C) 54
(D) 56

19. If $p^2 + q^2 = 25$ and $2pq = 10$, what is the value of $(p - q)^2$?

(A) 250
(B) 100
(C) 50
(D) 5

20. The ratio of yellow paint to red paint to white paint needed to make a perfect mixture of orange paint is 3 to 2 to 1. If 36 gallons of orange paint are needed to paint a cottage, how many gallons of red paint will be needed?

(A) 2
(B) 6
(C) 12
(D) 15

GO ON TO THE NEXT PAGE.

Directions: Using the information given in each quesiton, compare the quantity in Column A to the quantity in Column B. All questions in Part Two have these answer choices:

(A) The quantity in Column A is greater.
(B) The quantity in Column B is greater.
(C) The two quantities are equal.
(D) The relationship cannot be determined from the information given.

	Column A	Column B
21.	25% of 50	50% of 25

In a group of 150 books, 60 percent are fiction.

	Column A	Column B
22.	Half the number of fiction books	The difference between the number of fiction books and the number of nonfiction books

Dawn has a drawer filled with socks. The ratio of brown socks to blue socks is 2:3.

	Column A	Column B
23.	$\frac{2}{3}$	The fractional part of the socks in Dawn's drawer that are brown

	Column A	Column B
24.	x^2	x^3

	Column A	Column B
25.	$8 - 20 \ 2 \times 5 + 3$	20

$$(x + 2)(x - 2) = 0$$

	Column A	Column B
26.	x	2

	Column A	Column B
27.	$\sqrt{36} + \sqrt{16}$	$\sqrt{52}$

	Column A	Column B
28.	3^{12}	9^6

The volume of a solid cube is 27.

	Column A	Column B
29.	The height of the cube	3

$$\frac{x + 2}{y + 2} = \frac{x}{y}$$

	Column A	Column B
30.	x	$y + 2$

GO ON TO THE NEXT PAGE.

	Column A	Column B
31.	The sum of the integers from 1 to 100, inclusive	The sum of the even integers from 1 to 200, inclusive

$$\frac{x}{4} = 1.5$$

	Column A	Column B
32.	x	5

	Column A	Column B
33.	$\left(1\frac{1}{5}^{-\frac{1}{2}}\right)$	$\left(1\frac{4}{5}\right)$

A hiker completed a hike, walking at an average rate of 4 miles per hour. Had she averaged 5 miles per hour, the trip would have been completed two hours earlier than it was.

	Column A	Column B
34.	The number of hours in which the hike was completed	10

x is a positive integer.
y is the result of $100x$.

	Column A	Column B
35.	The sum of the digits in x	The sum of the digits in y

36. A box contains 4 cookies, 5 brownies, and 6 doughnuts. Two items are removed from the bag.

	Column A	Column B
	The probability that both items are brownies	The probability that one item is a cookie and the other is a doughnut

37. A triangle has two sides measuring 4 and 6, respectively.

	Column A	Column B
	The greatest possible area of the triangle	12

STOP

IF YOU FINISH BEFORE TIME IS CALLED,
YOU MAY CHECK YOUR WORK ON THIS SECTION ONLY.
DO NOT TURN TO ANY OTHER SECTION IN THE TEST.

SECTION 3

READING COMPREHENSION

Time: 35 minutes

36 Questions

Directions: This section contains six short reading passages. Each passage is followed by six questions based on its content. Answer the questions following a passage on the basis of what is stated or implied in that passage. You may write in your test booklet.

Line   Questions 1-6

1   New Orleans was the site of the last major battle
2   during the War of 1812, a lengthy conflict between
3   British and American troops. The Battle of New
4   Orleans in January 1815 was one of the greatest
5   victories in American military history. However, the
6   great success of this battle did not actually bring
7   about the end of the war. Surprisingly, the Treaty of
8   Ghent, which declared the end of the war, had already
9   been signed by both sides a month earlier.
10   How was that possible? There were two major
11   reasons. The first is that New Orleans was relatively
12   isolated and communication in the growing United
13   States was not as simple as it is today. Thus, it is
14   possible that the British commanders and the American
15   general, Andrew Jackson, did not realize a treaty had
16   been signed before they started their battle. A second
17   reason is that there is a difference between a signed
18   treaty and a ratified treaty. Even if all soldiers fighting
19   in and around New Orleans had known of the treaty,
20   it had not yet been ratified by the U.S. Senate. Thus,
21   though the Treaty of Ghent took place in December
22   prior to the Battle of New Orleans, the war did not
23   officially end until February 1815, when the Senate
24   ratified the treaty.
25   Had the combatants in New Orleans known of
26   the treaty, they might have avoided a tough battle,
27   especially the British. In the battle, a force of about
28   4,000 American troops decisively defeated an enemy
29   of nearly twice its size. At stake for the soldiers was
30   control of the waterways of the Mississippi, and
31   the fighting was fierce. A combination of tactical
32   mistakes and bad weather doomed the British

33   attack, costing them nearly 2,000 soldiers injured or
34   killed. The Americans lost fewer than 200. But was
35   the terrible battle all for nothing? Some historians
36   suggest that victory that day was crucial for the
37   American military in order to enforce and help
38   ratify quickly the peace treaty. Potentially, with an
39   American loss in New Orleans, the British could have
40   found hope to continue the conflict.

1. The primary purpose of the passage is to
    (A) blame the British for fighting an
         unnecessary war
    (B) celebrate the tactical military maneuvers of
         Andrew Jackson
    (C) convince readers that peace treaties are
         often worthless
    (D) provide greater details about the end of a
         historical conflict

2. The passage suggests that all of the following oc-
    curred near the end of the War of 1812 EXCEPT
    (A) Andrew Jackson ignored the orders of
         President Madison
    (B) Communication with the battle line
         commanders was slow
    (C) The Treaty of Ghent was signed
    (D) Weather conditions hurt the efforts of the
         British soldiers

GO ON TO THE NEXT PAGE.

3. Which of the following is implied by the passage?

   (A) Andrew Jackson did not know the difference between a signed treaty and a ratified treaty.
   (B) President Madison did not realize the Battle of New Orleans was possible.
   (C) The British may have had a chance for victory with better conditions and preparation.
   (D) The British troops knew of the treaty but attacked anyway.

4. According to the passage, New Orleans was a strategic battle site because

   (A) it was the only location where American forces were better supplied than the British forces
   (B) the American forces would be trapped in the swamplands if they lost
   (C) the British were attempting to defeat a more numerous force
   (D) the Mississippi River was nearby and control of it was important

5. After which of the following was the War of 1812 officially at an end?

   (A) Both armies signing the Treaty of Ghent.
   (B) British retreat from the Mississippi.
   (C) The Battle of New Orleans.
   (D) The Senate's ratification of the Treaty of Ghent.

6. According to the passage, a treaty

   (A) cannot be signed by the President without the consent of the Senate
   (B) has sometimes been ignored by those in battle
   (C) is always used to end a war
   (D) is not effective until it is ratified by the Senate

GO ON TO THE NEXT PAGE.

Line

Questions 7-12

1   According to game maker Hasbro, approximately
2 750 million people have played the well-known
3 game *Monopoly* since it was invented in the 1930s.
4 Charles Darrow is typically credited as the inventor
5 of the world's most famous board game. However, he
6 likely derived his version of *Monopoly* from one of
7 several other games similarly involving realty buying
8 and selling that were already in existence prior to the
9 1930s when he got his patent for the game.
10   A probable reason that Darrow's *Monopoly* became
11 the hugely successful game that still exists today is
12 that he took a diligent approach to producing it. Other
13 similar games existed, but some of them had no board
14 or regulation pieces. With help from his wife and son
15 who adorned the sets with detail, Darrow personally
16 created the pieces and boards that became the first
17 *Monopoly* game sets. His extra work in creating the
18 entire environment that players needed gave his game
19 something extra that other variations did not have.
20   Darrow had marginal success selling his games in
21 various parts of the country. Several Philadelphia area
22 stores were the first to carry his game and sell it in
23 large quantities. Despite this, Darrow had difficulty
24 selling his game to the major game manufacturer
25 of the time, Parker Brothers. He was told that his
26 game was too complex and had fundamental errors
27 in its design that would limit its appeal. Ultimately,
28 the continued sales he managed on his own forced
29 Parker Brothers to reassess the worth of his game.
30 Eventually, the company agreed to produce the game
31 and shortly thereafter it became the bestselling game
32 in the country.
33   That success turned Charles Darrow into a
34 millionaire, which is the ultimate irony. Darrow
35 initially began work on *Monopoly* to help support
36 himself and his family following the financial
37 troubles tied to the stock market crash of 1929.
38 Thus, Charles Darrow became a millionaire by
39 producing a game that allows "regular" people to feel
40 like they are buying and selling homes and real estate
41 like millionaires.

7. The best title for this passage would be
  (A) "A Comparison of Several Early Real
       Estate Board Games"
  (B) "How Hasbro Introduced Monopoly to the
       World"
  (C) "The Early History of Charles Darrow's
       Game"
  (D) "Two Views of Charles Darrow's Life"

8. It is suggested by the passage that
  (A) Darrow decided to make his game less
       complex after initially meeting with
       Parker Brothers
  (B) Darrow had no other skills to use after the
       stock market crash of 1929
  (C) Parker Brothers probably doubted that a
       complex game could sell well
  (D) Philadelphia was the only major city where
       he could sell his game

9. Based on the passage, "irony" most nearly means
  (A) financial gain
  (B) marketing plan
  (C) satisfying revenge
  (D) unexpected result

GO ON TO THE NEXT PAGE.

10. With which of the following would the author be LEAST likely to agree?

   (A) Charles Darrow chose to continue to sell his game despite criticisms.
   (B) Charles Darrow is not the first person to conceive of a board-based real estate game.
   (C) Charles Darrow preferred to achieve his goals without the help of others.
   (D) Some of the things Darrow chose to do helped make his game sell better than other games.

11. Which of the following was NOT mentioned by the author as contributing to the ultimate success of *Monopoly*?

   (A) Darrow's efforts to initially sell the game on his own.
   (B) The addition of specific pieces and a playing board in each set.
   (C) The adjustments Parker Brothers made to the game.
   (D) The enjoyment people get in pretending to be millionaires.

12. The author suggests in the third paragraph that

   (A) certain errors in *Monopoly* served to limit its appeal
   (B) Charles Darrow sold his game in Philadelphia because he knew it would be popular there
   (C) *Monopoly* was initially too complex to be popular
   (D) some people doubted that *Monopoly* would be popular

GO ON TO THE NEXT PAGE.

Questions 13-18

Line

1 Every year, hundreds of hopeful students arrive
2 in Washington, D.C., in order to compete in the
3 National Spelling Bee. This competition has been
4 held annually since 1925 and is sponsored by E.W.
5 Scripps Company. The sponsors provide both a
6 trophy and a monetary award to the champion speller.
7 In the competition, students under 16 years of age
8 take turns attempting to properly spell words as
9 provided by the moderator. The champion is the sole
10 remaining student who does not make a mistake.
11   Most American students are familiar with the
12 concept of a spelling bee because it is practiced in
13 many schools throughout the country. The National
14 Spelling Bee, however, is a much bigger setting and
15 showcases only the best spellers from all parts of the
16 nation. Students who appear at the National Spelling
17 Bee have already won competitions at local and state
18 levels. Winning the competition nowadays requires
19 the ability to perform under intense pressure against
20 very talented students in front of a large audience. A
21 student who wins the event in the twenty-first century
22 will experience a much different challenge than the
23 first winner, Frank Neuhauser, did in 1925 when he
24 defeated only nine other competitors.
25   Clearly, the 80 years of the National Spelling
26 Bee's existence attests to the importance of spelling
27 in the English language. However, struggles with
28 spelling English words goes back much more than 80
29 years. The captivating thing about spelling correctly
30 in English is that it is in many ways without rules.
31 English language has a powerful capacity to absorb
32 new words from other languages and in doing so
33 make them "English" words. As a result of this
34 ability to borrow from other languages, the sheer
35 number of words in English is much higher than
36 any other language. Thus, spelling in many other
37 languages involves fewer words, fewer rules, and
38 fewer odd exceptions to those rules. It turns out that
39 a spelling bee in most other languages would be a
40 waste of time. Why is that? Well, without the myriad
41 exceptions to common vocabulary, there would be
42 very few words that everyone didn't already know.

13. The author mentions "other languages" in line 39 in order to point out that

(A) English-language spelling bees are unnecessarily complex
(B) one challenge in English-language spelling bees is the number of words that can be tested
(C) spelling bees are at least 80 years old
(D) words are harder to spell in English than in some other languages

14. According to the passage, what is a major difference between the first National Spelling Bee and today's competition?

(A) Spellers in the past did not expect the competition to grow so large.
(B) The competition no longer focuses on only English words.
(C) There are more competitors.
(D) The words used today are significantly harder.

GO ON TO THE NEXT PAGE.

15. In line 40, the word "myriad" most nearly means

   (A) confusing
   (B) dangerous
   (C) linguistic
   (D) numerous

16. Which of the following can be inferred from the passage?

   (A) A competitor at The National Spelling Bee has already won at least one smaller spelling bee.
   (B) E.W. Scripps Company desires to eliminate poor spelling in America.
   (C) Frank Neuhauser would not do well in today's competition.
   (D) The competition has grown too large.

17. The author of the passage intends to

   (A) compare the presentation of the current National Spelling Bee with the structure in the past
   (B) contrast the English language with other languages
   (C) investigate the role that vocabulary plays in our lives
   (D) review the history and current form of the National Spelling Bee

18. The author's attitude toward winners of the National Spelling Bee is

   (A) admiring
   (B) critical
   (C) indifferent
   (D) questioning

GO ON TO THE NEXT PAGE.

Questions 19-24

Line

1   The idea of black holes was developed by Karl
2   Schwarzchild in 1916. Since then, many different
3   scientists have added to the theory of black holes in
4   space. A black hole is usually defined as a very dense
5   celestial body from which nothing, not even light, can
6   escape. But from what do black holes originate?
7   A black hole begins as a star. A star burns
8   hydrogen, and this process, called fusion, releases
9   energy. The energy released outward works against
10 the star's own gravity pulling inward and prevents
11 the star from collapsing. After millions of years of
12 burning hydrogen, the star eventually runs out of fuel.
13 At this point, the star's own gravity and weight cause
14 it to start contracting.
15   If the star is small and not very heavy it will shrink
16 just a little and become a white dwarf when it runs
17 out of fuel. White dwarf stars do not emit much
18 energy, so they are usually not visible without a
19 telescope.
20   If the star is bigger and heavier, it will collapse
21 very quickly in an implosion. If the matter that
22 remains is not much heavier than our sun, it will
23 eventually become a very dense neutron star.
24 However, if the matter that remains is more than 1.7
25 times the mass of our sun, there will not be enough
26 outward pressure to resist the force of gravity, and the
27 collapse will continue. The result is a black hole.
28   The black hole will have a boundary around it
29 called the horizon. Light and matter can pass over
30 this boundary to enter, but they cannot pass back
31 out again—this is why the hole appears black. The
32 gravity and density of the black hole prevent anything
33 from escaping.
34   Scientists are still adding to the black hole theory.
35 They think they may have found black holes in
36 several different galaxies, and as they learn more
37 about them, scientists will be able to understand more
38 about how black holes are formed and what happens
39 as the holes change.

19. The purpose of the question in the first paragraph is to
    (A) illustrate how little we know about black holes
    (B) indicate the source of the facts quoted in the passage
    (C) interest the reader in the topic of the passage
    (D) set a goal for independent research

20. According to the passage, which of the following causes a collapsing star to become a neutron star?
    (A) Mass greater than 1.7 times that of our sun
    (B) Mass less than 1.7 times that of our sun
    (C) Remaining fuel that can be used in fusion
    (D) Slow, brief shrinkage process

21. The passage suggests that if we were to send a satellite to the horizon of a black hole, it would probably
    (A) begin spinning uncontrollably and fly apart
    (B) be immediately repelled from the black hole
    (C) be pulled into the black hole and not come back out
    (D) enter, then immediately exit, the black hole

GO ON TO THE NEXT PAGE.

22. According to the passage, which of the following is an effect of the process of fusion?

    (A) The star does not immediately collapse.
    (B) The star generates hydrogen.
    (C) The star survives millions of years longer than average.
    (D) The white dwarf fails to produce light.

23. Black holes appear black because

    (A) only a little energy escapes them
    (B) only one galaxy contains them
    (C) they are extraordinarily large
    (D) they do not emit light

24. Which of the following best describes the organization of the passage?

    (A) It discusses the biggest, heaviest celestial bodies before moving on to the smaller, lighter ones.
    (B) It introduces the topic and then narrates chronologically the process by which stars become black holes.
    (C) It uses a personal story to introduce the topic, then compares and contrasts black holes.
    (D) It uses the example of one specific black hole in order to generalize.

GO ON TO THE NEXT PAGE.

Line

Questions 25–30

1   Carrie Nation gained notoriety as a hatchet-
2 wielding woman during the early part of the twentieth
3 century. She was married to an alcoholic and spent
4 many years trying to reform him. When that seemed
5 impossible, she left him and married David Nation.
6 Some time after their marriage, Carrie and David
7 Nation moved to Kansas. The sale of alcohol was
8 illegal in Kansas, yet there were many establishments
9 that sold alcoholic drinks. Carrie organized the
10 Women's Christian Temperance Union, which
11 vehemently, and sometimes violently, fought the
12 saloons. She believed that because saloons were
13 illegal, she was within her rights to destroy them,
14 so she wrecked saloons with her hatchet. Carrie
15 was arrested thirty times in many cities around
16 the country. Some say her eccentric behavior was
17 inherited from her mentally ill mother. Whatever the
18 cause, Carrie Nation was a well-known personality in
19 the early 1900s and her efforts most probably helped
20 the cause of temperance, which led to the national
21 prohibition of alcohol in 1920.

25. The main purpose of the passage is to
   (A) examine the reasons that Carrie Nation was
        so eccentric
   (B) explain the causes that led to the national
        prohibition of alcohol in 1920
   (C) present an overview of the life and actions
        of a famous woman
   (D) report on the Women's Christian
        Temperance Union

26. The word "cause" as used in line 18 most closely
    means
   (A) excuse
   (B) goal
   (C) reason
   (D) rebellion

GO ON TO THE NEXT PAGE.

27. Which of the following best expresses the author's attitude toward Carrie Nation?

    (A) Concern
    (B) Disgust
    (C) Neutrality
    (D) Respect

28. According to the author, the most probable legacy of Carrie Nation's actions was

    (A) the destruction of saloons by women around the country
    (B) the inquiry into the genetic link to mental illness
    (C) the legislation prohibiting the destruction of saloons
    (D) the national prohibition of alcohol

29. Which of the following does the passage imply was a reason for Carrie Nation's attitude toward temperance?

    (A) Her first husband's alcoholism
    (B) Her inability to have children
    (C) Her mother's mental illness
    (D) Her move to Kansas

30. The author believes that Carrie Nation's tactics are best described as

    (A) criminal but excusable
    (B) disturbed but entertaining
    (C) justified but ineffective
    (D) peculiar but bold

GO ON TO THE NEXT PAGE.

Questions 31-36

Line

1   He is one of the greatest living scientists of
2 this age. In fact, he is perhaps one of the greatest
3 scientists of any age. Yet he owes much of his success
4 not to mathematics or physics or any other science
5 but to a disease. He is Stephen Hawking.
6   Born in 1942, three hundred years after the death
7 of Galileo, Stephen Hawking had an unimpressive
8 start to his scholarly pursuits. At his revered English
9 primary school, St. Albans, he was considered by
10 his teachers a good, but not exceptional, student. It
11 was not evident at the time that he would become
12 internationally acclaimed as a leader in several
13 scientific fields. He continued this moderately
14 successful academic trend at University College
15 in Oxford. Again, his professors thought him to be
16 intelligent, but not extraordinary in his efforts. Both
17 his cleverness and lack of diligence were noticed by
18 some of his instructors.
19   After graduating from Oxford, he continued
20 to Cambridge, another excellent school. Clearly,
21 Hawking was moving forward into a good
22 science career. However, it was at this time that
23 he encountered a life-changing challenge. He was
24 diagnosed with a disease that affects and damages the
25 nervous system. That meant that he was eventually
26 going to lose control of his muscles and spend his life
27 in a wheelchair. Surprisingly though, Hawking credits
28 this event with making his outlook on life strong
29 again. He claims that until then, he was often bored
30 by life. For a man with such a powerful mind, that
31 makes sense. He was talented, but he saw little use
32 for his talent and felt no pressure to work hard. His
33 diagnosis and impending physical problems forced
34 him to start living life to the fullest.
35   Most of Stephen Hawking's contributions to
36 science have come after learning of his disease.
37 His work in the field of physics has influenced
38 the greatest scientists alive. If the technology ever
39 becomes possible, he plans a trip into space with the
40 help of influential friends. Though he now moves
41 only with a special wheelchair and speaks only with

42 the help of a computerized speech enhancer, he still
43 has the ability to contribute to the world. He credits
44 his disease with forcing him to face the limited time
45 available in one lifetime. Stephen Hawking has made
46 a crippling disease the source of one of the greatest
47 scientific careers the world has known. Through his
48 misfortune, he learned to reach his greatest potential.

31. The best title for this passage might be
    (A) "Great Scientists of the 20th Century"
    (B) "Stephen Hawking's Greatest Influence: His Disease"
    (C) "Stephen Hawking's Scientific Discoveries"
    (D) "The Early Life of Stephen Hawking"

32. The passage suggests which of the following about Stephen Hawking?
    (A) He chose a science career specifically because he knew he would need medical help his whole life.
    (B) He feels that his disease actually forces him to focus his energies and talents in ways that he had not previously.
    (C) He feels that he would achieve even greater success in science without a crippling disease.
    (D) He will continue to pursue a cure for his disease and use his understanding of biology to reach that goal.

GO ON TO THE NEXT PAGE.

33. Which of the following describes Stephen Hawking's attitude toward his disease?

   (A) Actively nonchalant
   (B) Bitterly irate
   (C) Ironically appreciative
   (D) Unreservedly giddy

34. According to the second paragraph, Stephen Hawking was seen by some as

   (A) often disrespectful
   (B) particularly brilliant
   (C) somewhat lazy
   (D) uniquely energetic

35. The passage does all of the following EXCEPT

   (A) demonstrate a connection between Stephen Hawking's disease and his success as a physicist
   (B) describe a goal Hawking hopes to achieve
   (C) note particular theories developed by Hawking
   (D) set forth educational institutions attended by Hawking

36. The passage can best be described as focusing primarily on

   (A) biographical details
   (B) medical diagnoses
   (C) scientific discoveries
   (D) technological advancements

STOP

IF YOU FINISH BEFORE TIME IS CALLED,
YOU MAY CHECK YOUR WORK ON THIS SECTION ONLY.
DO NOT TURN TO ANY OTHER SECTION IN THE TEST.

SECTION 4

MATHEMATICS ACHIEVEMENT

Time: 40 minutes

47 Questions

Each question is followed by four suggested answers. Read each question and then decide which one of the four suggested answers is best.

Find the row of spaces on your answer document that has the same number as the question. In this row, mark the space having the same letter as the answer you have chosen. You may write in your test booklet.

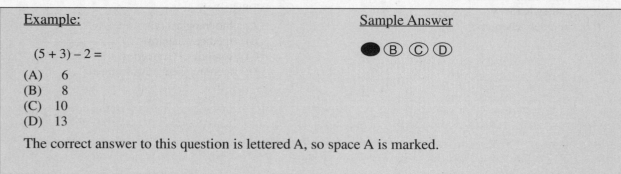

Example:

$(5 + 3) - 2 =$

(A)   6
(B)   8
(C)   10
(D)   13

Sample Answer

● Ⓑ Ⓒ Ⓓ

The correct answer to this question is lettered A, so space A is marked.

1. Which of the following pairs of numbers are the two different prime factors of 36 ?

(A) 2 and 3
(B) 3 and 4
(C) 3 and 12
(D) 4 and 9

2. For what nonzero value of x will the expression

$\dfrac{x - 3}{4x}$ be equal to 0 ?

(A) −3
(B) −2
(C) 1
(D) 3

3. Two positive whole numbers are in a ratio of 3 to 4. If the smaller of the two numbers is 9, what is the average of the two numbers?

(A)   4
(B) 10
(C) 10.5
(D) 12

GO ON TO THE NEXT PAGE.

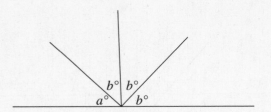

4. The four angles in the figure above share a common vertex on a straight line. What is the value of *b* when *a* equals 42 ?

   (A) 38 degrees
   (B) 40 degrees
   (C) 42 degrees
   (D) 46 degrees

5. What is 85% of 50 ?

   (A) 150.75
   (B) 135
   (C) 42.5
   (D) 39

6. A set of three positive integers has a sum of 11 and a product of 36. If the smallest of the three numbers is 2, what is the largest?

   (A) 2
   (B) 4
   (C) 6
   (D) 9

7. What is two-thirds of one-half?

   (A) $\dfrac{1}{3}$

   (B) $\dfrac{7}{6}$

   (C) $\dfrac{1}{2}$

   (D) $\dfrac{2}{3}$

8. If the distance around an oval-shaped track is 400 meters, how many laps does a runner have to run to cover a distance of 4 kilometers? (1 kilometer = 1,000 meters)

   (A) 4
   (B) 10
   (C) 15
   (D) 1,000

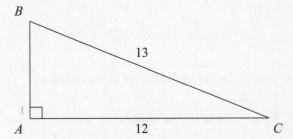

9. In triangle *ABC* shown above, the length of side *AB* is

   (A) 5
   (B) 7
   (C) 11
   (D) 14

10. If $f = 2$, and $f^j = 2f$, what is the value of *j* ?

   (A) 0
   (B) 1
   (C) 2
   (D) 3

11. If $\sqrt{a} + \sqrt{b} + \sqrt{c} = 15$, and $a = 36$ and $b = 25$, what is the value of *c* ?

   (A) 4
   (B) 16
   (C) 49
   (D) 81

GO ON TO THE NEXT PAGE.

12. There are x students is Mrs. Sproul's class, 4 fewer than twice as many as are in Mrs. Puccio's class. If there are y students in Mrs. Puccio's class, then what is the value of y in terms of x ?

(A) $\dfrac{x}{2} + 2$

(B) $2x + 4$

(C) $2x - 4$

(D) $\dfrac{x}{2} - 4$

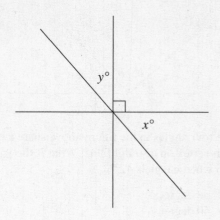

Questions 13-14 refer to the following definition.

For all real numbers x,

$\#x = x^2$ if x is negative;
$\#x = 2x$ if x is positive.

13. $\#(-6) - \#(6) =$

(A) -24
(B) 16
(C) 24
(D) 30

14. What is the value of $\#[\#x - \#y]$ when $x = 3$ and $y = -4$?

(A) -10
(B) 12
(C) 32
(D) 100

15. In the figure above, what is the value of x in terms of y ?

(A) y
(B) $90 - y$
(C) $90 + y$
(D) $180 - y$

16. $\dfrac{4a^4 b^6 c^3}{2a^3 b^5 c^2} =$

(A) $\dfrac{2ac}{b}$

(B) $\dfrac{ac}{b}$

(C) $\dfrac{2b}{c}$

(D) $2abc$

GO ON TO THE NEXT PAGE.

4 4 4 4 4 4 4 4 4

17. In Mr. Johanessen's class, $\frac{1}{4}$ of the students failed the final exam. Of the remaining class, $\frac{1}{3}$ scored an A. What fraction of the whole class passed the test but scored below an A?

(A) $\frac{1}{4}$

(B) $\frac{5}{12}$

(C) $\frac{1}{2}$

(D) $\frac{7}{12}$

18. When buying new clothes for school, Rena spends $20 more than Karen and $50 more than Lynn does. If Rena spends r dollars, then what is the cost of all three of their purchases in terms of r?

(A) $r + 70$

(B) $\frac{r + 70}{3}$

(C) $3r - 70$

(D) $r + 210$

19. In a group of 100 children, there are 34 more girls than there are boys. How many boys are in the group?

(A) 33
(B) 37
(C) 67
(D) 68

20. If $6x - 7 = 17$, then $x + 6 =$

(A) 6
(B) 10
(C) 14
(D) 24

21. At Nicholas's Computer World, computers usually sold for $1,500 are now being sold for $1,200. What fraction of the original price is the new price?

(A) $\frac{1}{10}$

(B) $\frac{1}{5}$

(C) $\frac{3}{4}$

(D) $\frac{4}{5}$

22. If $\frac{3}{x} = \frac{y}{4}$, then

(A) $xy = 12$

(B) $3y = 4x$

(C) $\frac{x}{y} = \frac{4}{3}$

(D) $3x = 4y$

23. The ratio of boys to girls at Delaware Township School is 3 to 2. If there is a total of 600 students at the school, how many are girls?

(A) 120
(B) 240
(C) 360
(D) 400

GO ON TO THE NEXT PAGE.

24. 150% of 40 is

(A) 30
(B) 40
(C) 50
(D) 60

25. Jane studied for her math exam for 4 hours last night. If she studied $\frac{3}{4}$ as long for her English exam, how many hours did she study all together?

(A) 3

(B) $4\frac{3}{4}$

(C) 6

(D) 7

26. $\frac{0.966}{0.42} =$

(A) 0.23
(B) 2.3
(C) 23
(D) 230

27. Nicole was able to type 35 words per minute. If she increased her speed to 42 words per minute, what was the percent increase in her typing speed?

(A) $16\frac{2}{3}\%$

(B) 20 %

(C) 70 %

(D) 71 %

28. The first term in a series of numbers is 50. Each subsequent term is one-half the term before it if the term is even, or one-half rounded up to the next whole number if the term is odd. What is the third term in this sequence?

(A) 13
(B) 24
(C) 30
(D) 40

29. If the average of 7 and x is equal to the average of 5, 9, and x, what is the value of x ?

(A) 2
(B) 5
(C) 7
(D) 9

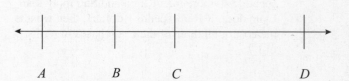

30. On the number line shown above, if segment *BD* has a length of 18, segment *AB* has a length of 5, and segment *CD* has a length of 12, then segment *AC* has a length of

(A) 6
(B) 11
(C) 17
(D) 23

31. The decimal representation of $2 + 40 + \frac{1}{100}$ is

(A) 24.1
(B) 24.01
(C) 42.1
(D) 42.01

GO ON TO THE NEXT PAGE.

32. What is the least possible integer divisible by 2, 3, 4, and 5 ?

    (A) 30
    (B) 40
    (C) 60
    (D) 90

33. If a car travels at x miles per hour, in terms of x and y, how long does it take it to travel y miles?

    (A) $\dfrac{2x}{y}$

    (B) xy

    (C) $\dfrac{y}{x}$

    (D) $\dfrac{x}{y}$

34. Triangles ABC and PQR are similar. The length of $\overline{BC}$ is 4 and the length of $\overline{QR}$ is 12. If the area of ABC is 6, what is the area of PQR?

    (A) 10
    (B) 12
    (C) 18
    (D) 24

35. James buys one halibut steak and two salmon steaks for $30.00. Dave buys two halibut steaks and four salmon steaks for $60.00. If halibut steaks cost x dollars each and salmon steaks cost y dollars each, what is the value of x ?

    (A) $5.00
    (B) $8.00
    (C) $10.00
    (D) It cannot be determined from the information given.

Question 36 refers to the following definition.

For all positive integer values of x,

$$(x) = \frac{1}{2}x \text{ if } x \text{ is even;}$$

$$(x) = 2x \text{ if } x \text{ is odd.}$$

36. $(1 + 5) =$

    (A) 2
    (B) 3
    (C) 4
    (D) 6

37. Which of the following equals $(4z + 1)$?

    (A) $2z + \dfrac{1}{2}$

    (B) $2z + 1$

    (C) $4z + 2$

    (D) $8z + 2$

38. There are eight buildings in Celeste's apartment complex. Each building is directly connected to each of the others with a tunnel. How many tunnels are there?

    (A) 8
    (B) 28
    (C) 36
    (D) 56

39. Zoo A has 3 monkeys. Zoo B has 8 monkeys. Zoo C has 16 monkeys. What is the average number of monkeys at the three zoos?

    (A) 3
    (B) 7
    (C) 9
    (D) 27

GO ON TO THE NEXT PAGE.

40. A steak costs $4 more than a hamburger, and a hamburger costs $4 more than a grilled cheese sandwich. If six grilled cheese sandwiches cost 2x dollars, how much will 4 steaks and 2 hamburgers cost?

    (A) 2x + 40
    (B) 2x + 48
    (C) 6x + 34
    (D) 12x + 40

41. What is the solution set to the inequality $|3-2x|>9$?

    (A) $-3 < x < 6$
    (B) $-6 < x < 3$
    (C) $x < -3$ or $x > 6$
    (D) $x < -6$ or $x > 3$

42. 100xy is what percent of xy ?

    (A)   10
    (B)   100
    (C)   1,000
    (D) 10,000

43. If Matt's home is four miles from school and Laura's home is eight miles from school, then the distance from Matt's home to Laura's home is

    (A) 4 miles
    (B) 8 miles
    (C) 12 miles
    (D) It cannot be determined from the information given.

44. Two partners divide a profit of $2,000 so that the difference between the two amounts is half of their average. What is the ratio of the larger to the smaller amount?

    (A) 6:1
    (B) 5:3
    (C) 4:1
    (D) 2:1

45. What is the total value, in cents, of j coins worth 10 cents each and j + 5 coins worth 25 cents each?

    (A) 35j + 125
    (B) 35j + 5
    (C) 10j + 130
    (D) 2j + 5

46. A box of coins has 6 pennies, 3 nickels, 4 dimes, and 5 quarters. If two coins are selected at random, what is the probability that the first coin is a penny and the second coin is a quarter?

    (A) $\dfrac{11}{18}$

    (B) $\dfrac{17}{18}$

    (C) $\dfrac{6}{18} \times \dfrac{5}{18}$

    (D) $\dfrac{6}{18} \times \dfrac{5}{17}$

47. The formula for the volume of a cone is $\frac{1}{3}\pi r^2 h$, where r is the radius of the circular base and h is the height of the cone. What is the radius of a cone with a volume of 36π and a height of 4?

    (A) 3
    (B) 4
    (C) 8
    (D) 9

STOP

IF YOU FINISH BEFORE TIME IS CALLED,
YOU MAY CHECK YOUR WORK ON THIS SECTION ONLY.
DO NOT TURN TO ANY OTHER SECTION IN THE TEST.

ISEE

UPPER LEVEL

ESSAY TOPIC SHEET

Time - 30 minutes

Directions

You will have 30 minutes to plan and write an essay on the topic printed on the other side of this page. **Do not write on another topic. An essay on another topic is not acceptable.**

The essay is designed to give you an opportunity to show how well you can write. You should try to express your thoughts clearly. How well you write is much more important than how much you write, but you need to say enough for a reader to understand what you mean.

You will probably want to write more than a short paragraph. You should also be aware that a copy of your essay will be sent to each school that will be receiving your test results. You are to write only in the appropriate section of the answer sheet. Please write or print so that your writing may be read by someone who is not familiar with your handwriting.

You may make notes and plan your essay on the reverse side of the page. Allow enough time to copy the final form onto your answer sheet. You <u>must</u> copy the essay topic onto your lined answer sheet in the box provided.

Please remember to write only the final draft of the essay on the lined answer sheet and write it in blue or black pen. Again, you may use cursive writing or you may print.

REMINDER: Please write this essay question on the first few lines of your answer sheet.

Do you think the driving age should be raised to 21? Support your position with specific examples from personal experience, the experience of others, current events, history, or literature.

Notes

STUDENT NAME _____ ID NUMBER _____ GRADE APPLYING FOR _____

Please use a ballpoint pen to write the final draft of your composition on this sheet.

You must write your essay topic in this space.

_____

_____

_____

_____

_____

_____

_____

_____

_____

_____

_____

_____

Chapter 22
Middle Level
ISEE Practice Test

SECTION 1

VERBAL REASONING

Time: 20 minutes
40 Questions

This section is divided into two parts that contain different types of questions. As soon as you have completed Part One, answer the questions in Part Two. You may write in your test booklet. For each answer you select, fill in the corresponding circle on your answer document.

Part One

Each question in Part One is made up of a word in capital letters followed by four choices. Choose the one word that is most nearly the same in meaning as the word in capital letters.

SAMPLE QUESTION:	Sample Answer
SWIFT: (A) clean (B) fancy (C) fast (D) quiet	

1. UNUSUAL: (A) friendly (B) happy (C) new (D) peculiar

2. ASSISTANCE: (A) call (B) disability (C) service (D) teaching

3. REALITY: (A) dream (B) fact (C) rarity (D) security

4. DIMINUTION: (A) assessment (B) leniency (C) reduction (D) restitution

5. CONTENTED: (A) diplomatic (B) disgusted (C) mammoth (D) satisfied

6. BOUND: (A) badgered (B) confused (C) obliged (D) relieved

7. FALTER: A) drop (B) hesitate (C) question (D) replenish

8. CONTAINED: (A) eliminated (B) held (C) raging (D) wooden

9. REVERE: (A) disdain (B) esteem (C) faith (D) reliance

10. DILIGENT: (A) defensive (B) hardworking (C) lazy (D) obsessive

11. DETRIMENTAL: (A) harmful (B) knowledgeable (C) tentative (D) worrisome

12. VOW: (A) argue (B) claim (C) please (D) pledge

13. ASPIRATION: (A) breath (B) hope (C) injury (D) trend

14. BASHFUL: (A) argumentative (B) serious (C) shy (D) tolerant

15. SINISTER: (A) elderly (B) erratic (C) uncomfortable (D) wicked

16. DISCLOSE: (A) hide (B) remove (C) reveal (D) undress

17. CONGEAL: (A) coagulate (B) help (C) recede (D) weaken

18. INUNDATE: (A) enter (B) flood (C) migrate (D) strive

19. STEADFAST: (A) constant (B) optional (C) quick (D) restful

20. RUTHLESS: (A) counterfeit (B) unofficial (C) unsparing (D) victorious

GO ON TO THE NEXT PAGE.

Part Two

Each question below is made up of a sentence with one blank. Each blank indicates that a word is missing. The sentence is followed by four answer choices. Select the one word that will best complete the meaning of the sentence as a whole.

SAMPLE QUESTIONS:

Ann carried the box carefully so that she would not ------- the pretty glasses.

(A) break
(B) fix
(C) open
(D) stop

<u>Sample Answer</u>

---

21. Myron was able to remain completely -------; he never took sides in any of the disagreements around the house.

    (A) biased
    (B) interested
    (C) neutral
    (D) thoughtful

22. Since the great drought left the soil completely useless, the people of that country were forced to ------- food from other countries.

    (A) export
    (B) import
    (C) report on
    (D) sell

23. Because he was annoyed by even the smallest grammatical error, Mr. Jones reviewed all the students' papers ------- before grading them.

    (A) crudely
    (B) helplessly
    (C) inefficiently
    (D) meticulously

24. Eric doesn't merely dislike racism; he ------- it.

    (A) abhors
    (B) moderates
    (C) questions
    (D) studies

GO ON TO THE NEXT PAGE.

25. Sharon's anger was too great: David simply could not ------- her with his charm.

(A) irritate
(B) manipulate
(C) pacify
(D) terrify

26. Even though the accident led to serious damage to our property, our ------- lawyer didn't present a convincing argument and we received no compensation.

(A) discerning
(B) fatalistic
(C) incompetent
(D) professional

27. After months of petty disputes, the two countries finally decided to sit down at a table and have a ------- discussion.

(A) friendly
(B) hostile
(C) lengthy
(D) pressing

28. Although the thief claimed that he accidentally picked up the stolen watch, the jury judged his action -------.

(A) deliberate
(B) frantic
(C) impractical
(D) misguided

29. In order to be a good doctor, you don't need to be ------- yourself, just as a good architect does not have to live in a fancy house.

(A) educated
(B) handsome
(C) healthy
(D) thoughtful

30. Pete ------- his coach when he followed up his winning season with an even better performance this year.

(A) disappointed
(B) gratified
(C) relieved
(D) upset

31. While many species, such as wolves, travel in groups, the cheetah is a ------- animal.

(A) dangerous
(B) pack
(C) solitary
(D) territorial

32. During his years in the Senate, Jones felt ------- about speaking up at all, while most of the other senators were aggressive and argumentative.

(A) blithe
(B) contented
(C) favorable
(D) timid

33. The politician's speech was so ------- that nearly everyone in the room decided not to vote for him.

(A) feeble
(B) monotonous
(C) persuasive
(D) unique

34. The corporation did not have a ------- system for promotions; each department was free to use its own discretion in advancing employees.

(A) dignified
(B) favorable
(C) forgiving
(D) uniform

GO ON TO THE NEXT PAGE.

35. Only from years of training can a gymnast hope to become ------- enough to master Olympic-level techniques.

    (A) agile
    (B) mature
    (C) passive
    (D) strict

36. Though Mr. Fenster was known to be ------- toward his neighbors, he always welcomed their children as trick-or-treaters at Halloween.

    (A) belligerent
    (B) cheerful
    (C) courteous
    (D) direct

37. The ------- young man talked back to his parents and teachers alike.

    (A) dreary
    (B) insolent
    (C) nervous
    (D) respectful

38. While the painting's brushstrokes seem -------, they are actually carefully planned out.

    (A) flagrant
    (B) haphazard
    (C) intricate
    (D) paltry

39. The Declaration of Independence is premised upon ------- principles, such as protecting life, liberty and the pursuit of happiness.

    (A) certain
    (B) lofty
    (C) predictable
    (D) variable

40. Our teacher advised us not to get too caught up in the ------- of the information in the textbook, or we could lose the important "big picture" of its theory by getting bogged down in the details.

    (A) minutiae
    (B) principles
    (C) scope
    (D) thought

STOP

IF YOU FINISH BEFORE TIME IS CALLED, YOU MAY CHECK YOUR WORK ON THIS SECTION ONLY.
DO NOT TURN TO ANY OTHER SECTION IN THE TEST.

GO ON TO THE NEXT PAGE.

SECTION 2

QUANTITATIVE REASONING

Time: 35 minutes

37 Questions

Directions

Any figures that accompany questions in this section may be assumed to be drawn as accurately as possible EXCEPT when it is stated that a particular figure is not drawn to scale. Letters such as x, y, and n stand for real numbers.

(1) Each question in Part One consists of a word problem followed by four answer choices. You may write in your test booklet; however, you may be able to solve many of these problems in your head. Next, take a look at the four answer choices and select the best one.

| Example 1 | If $3 + x = 5$, what is the value of x ? | Answer |
| | (A) 0 (B) 1 (C) 2 (D) 3 | Ⓐ Ⓑ ● Ⓓ |

(2) All questions in Part Two are quantitative comparisons between the quantities shown in Column A and Column B. Using the information given in each question, compare the quantity in Column A to the quantity in Column B and choose one of these four answer choices:

(A) The quantity in Column A is greater.
(B) The quantity in Column B is greater.
(C) The two quantities are equal.
(D) The relationship cannot be determined from the information given.

	Column A	Column B	
Example 2	3^2	2^3	Answer
			● Ⓑ Ⓒ Ⓓ

The quantity in Column A (9) is greater than the quantity in Column B (8), so space A is marked.

Example 3	The cost of 8 apples at 7 cents apiece	The cost of 7 apples at 8 cents apiece	Answer
			Ⓐ Ⓑ ● Ⓓ

The quantity in Column A (56 cents) equals the quantity in Column B (56 cents), so space C is marked.

GO ON TO THE NEXT PAGE.

1. $54 \times 3 =$

   (A) 123
   (B) 150
   (C) 162
   (D) 172

2. What is the area of a square with a side of length 2 ?

   (A) 2
   (B) 4
   (C) 6
   (D) 8

3. $3 \times 2 \times 1 - (4 \times 3 \times 2) =$

   (A) 18
   (B) 6
   (C) −6
   (D) −18

4. Vicky scored 80, 90, and 94 on her three tests. What was her average score?

   (A) 81
   (B) 88
   (C) 90
   (D) 93

Questions 5-6 refer to the following graph.

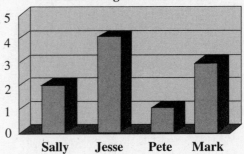

Books Bought at School Fair

5. Who bought the most books at the school fair?

   (A) Sally
   (B) Jesse
   (C) Pete
   (D) Mark

6. Sally and Mark together bought how many more books than Jesse?

   (A) 1
   (B) 2
   (C) 3
   (D) 5

GO ON TO THE NEXT PAGE.

7. $\frac{1}{2} + \frac{3}{4} =$

(A) $\frac{3}{8}$

(B) $\frac{5}{4}$

(C) $\frac{3}{2}$

(D) $\frac{5}{2}$

8. What is the value of the digit 7 in the number 4,678.02 ?

(A) 7
(B) 70
(C) 700
(D) 7,000

9. Jason has several books in his room, 20% of which are fiction. The other books are non-fiction. If he has 5 fiction books, how many non-fiction books does he have?

(A) 5
(B) 10
(C) 20
(D) 25

10. $\frac{7}{0.35} =$

(A) 0.2
(B) 2
(C) 20
(D) 200

11. Which of the following is closest in value to 5 ?

(A) 4.5
(B) 5.009
(C) 5.01
(D) 5.101

12. Janice went to the butcher and bought six pounds of hamburger. If the bill was $18.50, which of the following is closest to the cost per pound of the hamburger?

(A) $2.00
(B) $3.00
(C) $5.00
(D) $6.00

13. Which of the following numbers is closest to the square root of 175?

(A) 9
(B) 13
(C) 22
(D) 30

14. Laurie was reading a book that had an illustration on every odd-numbered page. If there are 32 numbered pages in the book, how many illustrations are there?

(A) 15
(B) 16
(C) 17
(D) 31

15. If $6y + 8 = 20$, what is the value of $3y + 4$?

(A) 2
(B) 8
(C) 10
(D) 12

16. A lecture hall's maximum capacity of 56 has increased by 75%. What is the new seating capacity after the increase?

(A) 42
(B) 70
(C) 98
(D) 112

GO ON TO THE NEXT PAGE.

17. When a number is divided by 8, the quotient is 11 and the remainder is 2. What is the number?

(A) 11
(B) 22
(C) 72
(D) 90

The following graph shows the amount of rainfall in Miller County for the years 1942-1946.

Average Inches of Rainfall in Miller County, 1942-1946

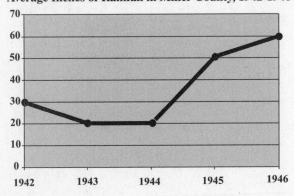

18. When did the greatest increase in rainfall occur in Miller County?

(A) Between 1942 and 1943
(B) Between 1943 and 1944
(C) Between 1944 and 1945
(D) Between 1945 and 1946

19. The temperature at 6 A.M. was 32 degrees. If the temperature increased at a constant rate of 3 degrees per hour all day, what was the temperature at 1 P.M.?

(A) 35 degrees
(B) 43 degrees
(C) 47 degrees
(D) 53 degrees

20. What is the volume of a box with length 4 cm, width 3 cm, and height 2 cm?

(A) 6 cubic centimeters
(B) 9 cubic centimeters
(C) 12 cubic centimeters
(D) 24 cubic centimeters

GO ON TO THE NEXT PAGE.

Directions: Using the informaiton given in each question, compare the quantity in Column A to the quantity in Column B. All questions in Part Two have these answer choices:

(A) The quantity in Column A is greater.
(B) The quantity in Column B is greater.
(C) The two quantities are equal.
(D) The relationship cannot be determined from the information given.

Column A	Column B

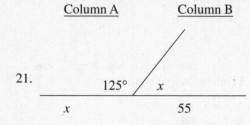

21.
x	55

A rectangle with sides x and y has an area of 12.

22. The length of x | The length of y

---

23. $\sqrt{9} + \sqrt{25}$ | $\sqrt{9 + 25}$

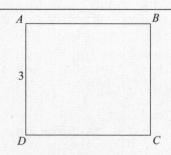

The quadrilateral $ABCD$ has an area of 12

The quadrilateral $ABCD$ has an area of 12.

24. The perimeter of $ABCD$ | 15

Column A	Column B

25. Martha had $20. She gave half of her money to her sister, Linda. Linda now has $30.

The amount of money Martha now has	The amount of money Linda had originally

---

26.
$$4x + 7 = 63$$
$$\frac{y}{3} + 6 = 15$$

x	y

---

27. | The area of a rectangle with length 3 and width 4 | The area of a square with a side of 3 |

---

28. **Number of Cookies Eaten Each Day**

Wednesday	3
Thursday	2
Friday	1
Saturday	3

The average number of cookies eaten each day	The number of cookies eaten on Thursday

GO ON TO THE NEXT PAGE.

	Column A	Column B
29.	$\sqrt{0.64}$	$\sqrt{6.4}$

Amy bought 5 oranges and 6 peaches. The total price of the fruit was $1.10.

	Column A	Column B
30.	The cost of one orange	The cost of one peach

	Column A	Column B
31.	-5^6	$(-5)^6$

a represents an odd integer greater than 9 and less than 15.

b represents an even integer greater than 9 and less than 15.

	Column A	Column B
32.	$a \times 3$	$b \times 4$

A 12-sided die with faces numbered 1 through 12 is rolled.

	Column A	Column B
33.	The probability that the result is even	The probability that the result is prime

Column A   Column B

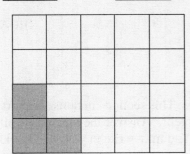

	Column A	Column B
34.	The fractional part of the figure that is shaded	$\dfrac{3}{20}$

Melvin brought home a large pizza with 12 slices.

	Column A	Column B
35.	The number of slices left if Melvin eats 50% of the pizza	The number of slices left if Melvin eats one-third of the pizza

The original price of a shirt now on sale was $50.

	Column A	Column B
36.	The price of the shirt after two 20% discounts	The price of the shirt after a single 40% discount

	Column A	Column B
37.	The slope of the line with points (3, 8) and (5, 2)	The slope of the line $6x - 2y = -8$

STOP

IF YOU FINISH BEFORE TIME IS CALLED, YOU MAY CHECK YOUR WORK ON THIS SECTION ONLY.
DO NOT TURN TO ANY OTHER SECTION IN THE TEST.

SECTION 3

READING COMPREHENSION

Time: 40 minutes

36 Questions

Directions: This section contains six short reading passages. Each passage is followed by six questions based on its content. Answer the questions following a passage on the basis of what is stated or implied in that passage. You may write in your test booklet.

Questions 1-6

Line
1   When most people think of the history of
2   transportation, they think of the invention of the
3   wheel as the starting point. The wheel was invented
4   around 3500 B.C., more than 5,000 years ago.
5   Before then, transportation was a difficult process,
6   especially for those who had anything to carry.
7   During prehistoric times, the only way to get around
8   was to walk. Children and possessions were strapped
9   to someone's back if they needed to be carried. If
10 the load was too heavy for one person, it could be
11 strapped to a pole and carried by two. The sledge was
12 developed as a way to drag a heavy load. Sledges
13 were originally just logs or pieces of animal skin
14 upon which a load was strapped and dragged. In
15 time, runners were put on the sledge, and it evolved
16 to what is now called a sled. Around 5000 B.C., the
17 first animals were domesticated, or tamed. Then,
18 donkeys and oxen were used to carry heavy loads
19 and pull sledges. It wasn't until almost 1,500 years
20 later that wheeled vehicles appeared. It is believed
21 that the wheel was invented in Mesopotamia, in the
22 Middle East. About 300 years later, the Egyptians
23 invented the sailboat. These two inventions changed
24 transportation forever.

1. The primary purpose of the passage is to

    (A) describe some of the things people used for
         transportation long ago
    (B) describe the reasons that led to
         transportation discoveries
    (C) explain the evolution of the sled
    (D) give a detailed history of transportation

2. The passage suggests that prehistoric man used
    all of the following for carrying things EXCEPT

    (A) animals
    (B) children
    (C) poles
    (D) primitive sleds

3. The passage implies that early man

    (A) was incapable of inventing the wheel any
         earlier than 3500 B.C.
    (B) was interested in farming
    (C) was interested in finding ways to help carry
         things
    (D) was outgoing and friendly

4. It can be inferred from the passage that the rea-
    son animals were domesticated was

    (A) to help carry large loads
    (B) to move people and possessions around
         quickly
    (C) to provide family pets
    (D) to ward off danger

5. Which of the following describes the author's
    attitude toward the invention of the wheel?

    (A) Admiration
    (B) Disdain
    (C) Indifference
    (D) Regret

6. The passage suggests that the sledge was

    (A) a precursor to the sled
    (B) invented in conjunction with the wheel
    (C) made exclusively of animal skin
    (D) the only tool used for transportation at the
         time

GO ON TO THE NEXT PAGE.

Line

Questions 7-12

1   Bison and buffalo are not the same animal. For
2 years, American bison were mistakenly referred to
3 as buffalo. Due to this confusion there are many
4 references to buffalo in the United States. There is the
5 City of Buffalo in northwestern New York state. In
6 addition, the buffalo appeared on the U.S. nickel for
7 many years at the beginning of the twentieth century.
8 This is often referred to as the "Buffalo Nickel" to
9 distinguish it from the current nickel with Thomas
10 Jefferson on the front. Buffalo are actually found in
11 Asia, Africa, and South America. Bison roamed the
12 North American western plains by the millions just
13 a couple of centuries ago. Because the bison were so
14 widely hunted, however, their numbers fell greatly. In
15 fact, as of a century ago, there were only about 500
16 left. They were deemed near extinction, but due to
17 conservation efforts, their numbers have increased.
18 There are approximately 50,000 bison living today
19 in protected parks. Though they may never be as
20 abundant as they once were, they are not in danger of
21 extinction as long as they remain protected.

7. The primary purpose of the passage is to

    (A) applaud conservation efforts
    (B) explain the genetic difference between the
           bison and the buffalo
    (C) explain why people confuse the buffalo and
           the bison
    (D) give some background on the American
           bison

8. The passage implies that the primary difference
between the buffalo and the bison is

    (A) their geographic location
    (B) their number
    (C) their size
    (D) when they existed

9. As used in line 16, the word "deemed" most
closely means

    (A) found
    (B) hunted
    (C) ruled
    (D) eaten

10. According to the passage, what can be hoped for
as long as the American bison is protected?

    (A) They will be as plentiful as they once were.
    (B) They will disturb the delicate ecological
           balance in the plains.
    (C) They will face even greater dangers.
    (D) They will probably not die out.

11. According to the passage, the primary reason
that the American bison is no longer near extinction is

    (A) conservation efforts
    (B) lack of interest in hunting them
    (C) loss of value of their fur
    (D) the migration of the animals

12. In line 5, the author mentions the City of Buffalo
in order to

    (A) criticize a hunting practice
    (B) establish the reason for a particular
           currency
    (C) illustrate a common misunderstanding
    (D) pinpoint the first sighting of buffalo in
           New York

GO ON TO THE NEXT PAGE.

Line

Questions 13-18

1   The Greek philosopher Aristotle had many
2 students, but perhaps none so famous as Alexander
3 the Great. As a child, Alexander was known for his
4 intelligence and bravery. The lessons he learned from
5 Aristotle left him with a lifelong love of books and
6 learning. But it was not his love of books that made
7 him famous. Alexander, in 336 B.C., became the king
8 of a small Greek kingdom called Macedonia. He
9 was only twenty at the time. He went on to invade
10 country after country: Persia (now known as Iran),
11 Egypt, and all the way to parts of India and Pakistan.
12 Alexander conquered most of what was then the
13 "civilized world." He brought with him the Greek
14 way of thinking and doing things. He is considered
15 one of the great generals and kings of history
16 and is responsible for the spread of Greek culture
17 throughout much of the world.

13. Which of the following would be the best title
for the passage?

    (A)   "Alexander the Great: King and
           Conqueror"
    (B)   "Aristotle: Teacher of the Kings"
    (C)   "Greek Culture"
    (D)   "The History of Macedonia"

14. As used in line 13, the word "civilized" most
closely means

    (A)   barbaric
    (B)   educated
    (C)   friendly
    (D)   well-mannered

15. The tone of the passage is most like that found in

    (A)   a diary entry from an historian
    (B   a letter from an archeologist
    (C)   a philosophy journal
    (D)   a reference book

16. According to the passage, one of the things that
was so impressive about Alexander was

    (A)   his ability to teach
    (B)   his great integrity
    (C)   his handsome features
    (D)   his intelligence and culture

17. The passage suggests that Aristotle

    (A)   encouraged Alexander to spread culture
    (B)   helped foster Alexander's love of books
    (C)   supported Alexander's military career
    (D)   taught Alexander military strategy

18. According to the passage, when Alexander invaded a country, he

    (A)   enslaved citizens
    (B)   freed oppressed people
    (C)   spread Greek ideas
    (D)   toppled monuments

GO ON TO THE NEXT PAGE.

Questions 19-24

Line

1   Everyone has had attacks of the hiccups, or
2 hiccoughs, at one point in his or her life. Few people,
3 however, think about what is happening to them and
4 how hiccups begin and end.
5   The diaphragm is a large muscle, shaped like a
6 dome, that sits at the base of the chest cavity. As one
7 breathes, the diaphragm gently contracts and relaxes
8 to help the process. Occasionally, an irritation near
9 the diaphragm or a disease may cause the muscle to
10 spasm, or contract suddenly. The spasm will suck
11 air into the lungs past the vocal cords. A small flap
12 called the epiglottis tops the vocal cords so that food
13 will not accidentally enter into the windpipe. The
14 sudden spasm of the diaphragm causes the epiglottis
15 to close quickly. Imagine the pull of air into the vocal
16 cords from the spastic diaphragm hitting the closed
17 epiglottis. This moves the vocal cords, causing the
18 "hic" sound of the hiccup. Although most people
19 don't really worry about the hiccups, attacks may
20 last for days. The exhaustion of hiccuping for days
21 on end has been fatal in certain rare cases. Home
22 remedies abound—from breathing into paper bags to
23 squeezing on pressure points that supposedly relax
24 the diaphragm.

19. The primary purpose of the passage is to

(A) describe a common occurrence
(B) prescribe a treatment
(C) settle a dispute
(D) warn about a danger

20. According to the passage, one possible cause of hiccups is

(A) a sudden rush of air
(B) an irritant near the diaphragm
(C) breathing in and out of a paper bag
(D) the closing of the epiglottis

21. As used in line 19, "attacks" most closely means

(A) advances
(B) assaults
(C) bouts
(D) threats

22. The passage suggests that which of the following makes the "hic" sound of the hiccup?

(A) The diaphragm
(B) The lungs
(C) The stomach
(D) The vocal cords

23. According to the passage, the hiccups can be fatal due to

(A) fatigue from days of hiccuping
(B) home remedies that are toxic
(C) the humiliation of hiccuping for days on end
(D) the irritant to the diaphragm

24. The author mentions "hiccoughs" in line 2 in order to

(A) correct an improper usage
(B) define a technical term
(C) indicate an alternate spelling
(D) weaken a misguided argument

GO ON TO THE NEXT PAGE.

Line

Questions 25-30

1   During the winter months in many regions, food
2 can be extremely scarce. For the wildlife of these
3 areas, this can be a great problem unless animals have
4 some mechanism that allows them to adapt. Some
5 animals migrate to warmer climates. Others hibernate
6 to conserve energy and decrease the need for food.
7 Prior to hibernation, an animal will generally eat a
8 lot to build up a store of fat. The animal's system
9 will "feed" off the fat stores throughout the long
10 cold winter months. When the animal hibernates, its
11 body temperature decreases and its body functions
12 slow down considerably. The dormouse's heartbeat,
13 for example, slows down to just a beat every few
14 minutes. Its breathing also becomes slow and its
15 body temperature drops to just a few degrees above
16 the temperature of the ground around it. All these
17 changes decrease the need for fuel and allow the
18 animal to survive long periods without any food. It is
19 a mistake to think that all hibernating animals sleep
20 for the whole winter. In fact, many animals hibernate
21 for short spurts during the winter. They may wake
22 for an interval of mild weather. Scientists have now
23 discovered the chemical that triggers hibernation. If
24 this chemical is injected in an animal in the summer
25 months, it can cause the animal to go into summer
26 hibernation.

25. The primary purpose of the passage is to

(A) compare the hibernating dormouse to other hibernating animals
(B) debunk some common myths about hibernation
(C) discuss the discovery of the chemical that causes hibernation
(D) explore some basic information about hibernation

26. As used in line 6, the word "conserve" most closely means

(A) expend
(B) help
(C) reserve
(D) waste

27. According to the author, each of the following happens to a hibernating animal EXCEPT

(A) it goes into a dream state
(B) its body temperature drops
(C) its breathing becomes slow
(D) its heartbeat slows

28. Which of the following can be inferred as a reason a hibernating animal may interrupt its hibernation?

(A) A day or two of stormy weather
(B) An overabundance of food
(C) A week in which there was no snow
(D) A week in which the temperature was well above freezing

29. According to the author, if the chemical that triggers hibernation is injected into an animal when it would not normally hibernate, the chemical may

(A) allow the animal to shed extra fat stores
(B) cause an out-of-season hibernation
(C) cause body functions to slow to a halt
(D) decrease an animal's need for food

30. The tone of the passage is best described as

(A) amazed
(B) concerned
(C) indifferent
(D) informative

GO ON TO THE NEXT PAGE.

Questions 31-36

1   The theater is one of the richest art forms. The
2 excitement of opening night can be felt by the
3 people waiting to watch a performance and by the
4 performers and workers backstage waiting for the
5 curtain to go up. Live theater is thrilling because
6 no one really knows how well the play will go until
7 it is performed. Many people collaborate to bring
8 a play to life. There are playwrights, directors, set
9 designers, costumers, lighting technicians, and,
10 of course, actors. If the performance is a musical,
11 the skills of a songwriter, a choreographer (the
12 person who composes the dances), and musicians
13 are also required. The word *theater* comes from the
14 Greek *theatron*, which means "a place for seeing."
15 One concept from Greek theater that is still seen
16 in some plays today is the "Greek Chorus." This
17 consists of several actors/characters watching the
18 action of the play (almost like the audience) and
19 then commenting on what they just saw with either
20 reactions or dialogue. Although most people think
21 of the theater in terms of a play performed on the
22 stage, theater has taken on a much broader meaning
23 in the modern world. You may find yourself walking
24 into the theater, and there are no seats in the rows.
25 Instead, you are seated among the set pieces, which
26 makes you part of the setting. Sometimes theater may
27 come to life on a street corner, or in a classroom. The
28 excitement of theater is in its very nature—it is an
29 art form that changes as it is interpreted in different
30 ways by different people. That is probably why the
31 works of the greatest playwright of all time, William
32 Shakespeare, are still performed and enjoyed today,
33 both in classic and new interpretations.

31. The best title for the passage might be

(A) "A Brief History of Theatrical Productions"
(B) "Modern Theater: Adventures in Acting"
(C) "Shakespeare: Our Greatest Playwright"
(D) "The Excitement of Theater"

32. According to the passage, the primary reason
that theater is so exciting is that

(A) it derives from a Greek custom
(B) it is performed live
(C) plays are often well written
(D) there are so many people working on it

33. The passage suggests which of the following
about modern theater?

(A) It always draws great attention from the
audience.
(B) It has been interpreted in a more varied
fashion.
(C) It is less exciting than classic theater.
(D) There are mostly Shakespearean plays
performed.

34. The author's attitude toward theater can best be
described as

(A) admiring
(B) ambivalent
(C) apathetic
(D) neutral

35. In line 1, the word "richest" is best understood to
mean most

(A) diverse
(B) entertaining
(C) terrifying
(D) wealthy

36. The passage suggests that the plays of
Shakespeare

(A) are more often given new interpretations
today than at any other time
(B) are more popular today than during
Shakespeare's time
(C) have been performed in a variety of ways
(D) will always be considered the world's
greatest

STOP

IF YOU FINISH BEFORE TIME IS CALLED, YOU MAY CHECK YOUR WORK ON THIS SECTION ONLY.
DO NOT TURN TO ANY OTHER SECTION IN THE TEST.

SECTION 4

MATHEMATICS ACHIEVEMENT

Time: 40 minutes
47 Questions

Each question is followed by four suggested answers. Read each question and then decide which one of the four suggested answers is best.

Find the row of spaces on your answer document that has the same number as the question. In this row, mark the space having the same letter as the answer you have chosen. You may write in your test booklet.

Example: Sample Answer

$(5 + 3) - 2 =$ ● Ⓑ Ⓒ Ⓓ

(A)   6
(B)   8
(C)   10
(D)   13

The correct answer to this question is lettered A, so space A is marked.

---

1. In the decimal 0.0987, the digit 9 is equivalent to which of the following?

    (A) $\dfrac{9}{10}$

    (B) $\dfrac{9}{100}$

    (C) $\dfrac{9}{1,000}$

    (D) $\dfrac{9}{10,000}$

2. What is the least common multiple of 6, 9, and 12?

    (A)   3
    (B)   36
    (C)   72
    (D)   324

3. Which of the following equals 5?

    (A) $30 - 12 \div 2 \times (3 + 7)$
    (B) $30 - 12 \div (2 \times 3 + 7)$
    (C) $(30 - 12) \div 2 \times 3 + 7$
    (D) $30 - 12 \div 2 \times 3 + 7$

4. $\dfrac{5}{7} + \dfrac{2}{11} =$

    (A) $\dfrac{10}{17}$

    (B) $\dfrac{10}{77}$

    (C) $\dfrac{7}{18}$

    (D) $\dfrac{69}{77}$

GO ON TO THE NEXT PAGE.

5. $7\frac{1}{2}$ hours is how many minutes more than $6\frac{1}{4}$ hours?

(A) 45
(B) 60
(C) 75
(D) 90

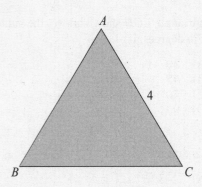

6. What is the perimeter of equilateral triangle *ABC* shown above?

(A) 12
(B) 15
(C) 18
(D) It cannot be determined from the information given.

7. Which of the following is 20% of 200 ?

(A) 20
(B) 30
(C) 40
(D) 100

Questions 8-10 refer to the following chart.

Day	Temperature (in degrees Celsius)	Snowfall (in centimeters)
Monday	2	3
Tuesday	6	3
Wednesday	3	4
Thursday	13	1

8. What was the total amount of snowfall for the four-day period shown?

(A) 44 cm
(B) 40 cm
(C) 11 cm
(D) 10 cm

9. On which day was the snowfall the greatest?

(A) Thursday
(B) Wednesday
(C) Tuesday
(D) Monday

10. What was the average temperature for each day in the four-day period?

(A) 24 degrees
(B) 20 degrees
(C) 11 degrees
(D) 6 degrees

GO ON TO THE NEXT PAGE.

11. $\dfrac{100}{0.25} =$

(A)   4
(B)   40
(C)   400
(D)   4000

12. $5 \times 31 = 100 +$ ____

(A) 55
(B) 51
(C) 50
(D) 36

13. Gwen planted six tomato plants. Half of them died. She then planted one more. How many tomato plants does Gwen have now?

(A) 3
(B) 4
(C) 5
(D) 6

14. The public library charges one dollar to rent a video overnight, with a fifty-cent charge for each day the video is late. If Tracey returns a video three days late, how much does she owe all together?

(A) $1.50
(B) $2.00
(C) $2.50
(D) $3.50

15. $0.45 \times 100 =$

(A) 4,500
(B)   450
(C)   45
(D)   4.5

16. In triangle *FGH* shown above, the value of angle *x*, in degrees, is

(A) 30
(B) 45
(C) 50
(D) 90

17. If a dozen eggs cost $1.20, then 3 eggs cost

(A)   30¢
(B)   36¢
(C)   48¢
(D) $3.60

18. Boris and his friend Bruce collect baseball cards. If Bruce has 12 baseball cards and Boris has three times as many baseball cards as Bruce, what is the average number of cards in the boys' collections?

(A) 7.5
(B) 18
(C) 24
(D) 48

19. What is the perimeter of a rectangle with length 3 and width 2 ?

(A)   6
(B)   8
(C) 10
(D) 12

GO ON TO THE NEXT PAGE.

20. $\dfrac{3}{5} \times \dfrac{2}{7} =$

   (A) $\dfrac{3}{8}$

   (B) $\dfrac{6}{35}$

   (C) $\dfrac{31}{35}$

   (D) $\dfrac{21}{35}$

21. If Kenny can run three miles in 45 minutes, how long will it take him to run five miles?

   (A) 1 hour
   (B) 1 hour 15 minutes
   (C) 1 hour 30 minutes
   (D) 2 hours

22. Which fraction is greater than $\dfrac{5}{11}$?

   (A) $\dfrac{3}{8}$

   (B) $\dfrac{2}{7}$

   (C) $\dfrac{4}{9}$

   (D) $\dfrac{4}{7}$

23. If the perimeter of a square is 36, what is its area?

   (A) 16
   (B) 36
   (C) 64
   (D) 81

24. Maureen studied for two hours before school. After school she studied for twice as long as she had before school. What was the total number of hours she studied in the day?

   (A) 4
   (B) 6
   (C) 8
   (D) 12

25. $\dfrac{40(37 + 63)}{8} =$

   (A) 450
   (B) 500
   (C) 1,250
   (D) 4,000

26. $0.347 =$

   (A) $\dfrac{7}{10} + \dfrac{4}{100} + \dfrac{3}{1,000}$

   (B) $\dfrac{3}{100} + \dfrac{4}{10} + \dfrac{7}{100}$

   (C) $\dfrac{4}{100} + \dfrac{3}{10} + \dfrac{7}{1,000}$

   (D) $\dfrac{3}{10} + \dfrac{4}{1,000} + \dfrac{7}{100}$

27. Which is the prime factorization of 36 ?

   (A) $3 \times 3 \times 3 \times 2$
   (B) $3 \times 3 \times 2 \times 2$
   (C) $3 \times 2 \times 2 \times 2$
   (D) $6 \times 3 \times 2$

GO ON TO THE NEXT PAGE.

Questions 28-30 refer to the following chart.

Train Fares from Monroeville to Perkins' Corner

Fares	Weekday Peak	Weekday Off-Peak	Weekend & Holiday
One Way	$6.00	$5.00	$4.50
Round-Trip	$12.00	$10.00	$9.00
10-Trip Ticket	$54.00	$45.00	$40.00
Children Under 11	$1.00	$0.50	Free with Paying Adult

28. How much would it cost two adults and one child under the age of 11 to travel one way from Monroeville to Perkins' Corner on a weekend?

(A) $25.00
(B) $20.50
(C) $18.00
(D) $9.00

29. The price of a weekday peak fare ten-trip ticket is what percent less than the cost of purchasing ten one-way weekday peak fare tickets?

(A) 10%
(B) 20%
(C) 50%
(D) 100%

30. How much more does it cost for one adult to travel one way during the weekday peak fare period than for one adult to make the trip on the weekend?

(A) $0.50
(B) $0.75
(C) $1.00
(D) $1.50

31. Mr. Schroder swims laps at the community pool. It takes him 5 minutes to swim one lap. If he swims for 60 minutes without stopping, how many laps will he swim?

(A) 8
(B) 10
(C) 12
(D) 14

32. $10^3 =$

(A) 10×3

(B) $10 + 10 + 10$

(C) $10 \times 10 \times 10$

(D) $\dfrac{10}{3}$

33. A DVD player initially cost $100. During a sale, the store reduced the price by 10%. Two days later, the store reduced the new price by 20%. What was the final price?

(A) 68
(B) 70
(C) 72
(D) 80

GO ON TO THE NEXT PAGE.

34. Mr. Hoffman has a rectangular box that is 10 centimeters wide, 30 centimeters long, and 4 centimeters high. What is the volume of the box?

    (A)   44 cm³
    (B)   120 cm³
    (C)   300 cm³
    (D) 1,200 cm³

35. Dr. Heldman sees an average of nine patients an hour for eight hours on Monday and for six hours on Tuesday. What is the average number of patients she sees on each day?

    (A)   54
    (B)   63
    (C)   72
    (D) 126

36. If $q + 9 = 7 - p$, what is the value of $q + p$?

    (A) −16
    (B)   −2
    (C)   2
    (D)   16

37. Which of the following is the product of two consecutive even integers?

    (A)   0
    (B) 15
    (C) 22
    (D) 30

38. Two triangles, *ABC* and *XYZ* are similar. Triangle *ABC* has lengths of 3, 4, and 5. Which of the following could be the corresponding lengths of triangle *XYZ*?

    (A) 3, 3, and 3
    (B) 4, 5, and 6
    (C) 6, 8, and 10
    (D) 13, 14, and 15

39. The perimeter of a square whose area is 169 centimeters is

    (A) 52
    (B) 48
    (C) 44
    (D) 42

40. If three-fourths of the 240 employees at Tigger's Toys are at a party, how many of the employees are NOT at the party?

    (A)   60
    (B)   80
    (C) 120
    (D) 180

GO ON TO THE NEXT PAGE.

41. Jose and Greg are going on a 20-mile walk for charity. If they walk $\frac{1}{4}$ of the distance in the first two hours, and $\frac{1}{5}$ of the entire distance in the next hour and a half, how many miles do they have left to walk?

    (A)   9
    (B)   10
    (C)   11
    (D)   12

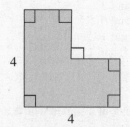

42. What is the perimeter of the shaded area in the figure above?

    (A)   15
    (B)   16
    (C)   24
    (D)   It cannot be determined from the information given.

43. A field hockey player scored an average of 3 goals per game for 12 games. How many points did she score in all 12 games?

    (A)   4
    (B)   20
    (C)   24
    (D)   36

44. What is the volume of a box with length 8, width 4, and height $\frac{1}{4}$?

    (A)   8
    (B) $12\frac{1}{4}$
    (C)   32
    (D)   128

45. The price of a $30 hat is decreased by 20%. What is the new price of the hat?

    (A) $10.00
    (B) $12.00
    (C) $20.00
    (D) $24.00

46. There are 5 oatmeal cookies, 6 brownies, and 8 granola bars in a jar. If an item is selected at random, what is the probability of selecting a brownie?

    (A) $\frac{1}{6}$
    (B) $\frac{6}{19}$
    (C) $\frac{8}{19}$
    (D) $\frac{6}{13}$

47. Which of the following is equivalent to $\frac{2}{3}x = 6 - y$?

    (A) $2x = 6 - 3y$
    (B) $3y - x = 6$
    (C) $2x + 3y = 18$
    (D) $2(x + 3y) = 18$

STOP

IF YOU FINISH BEFORE TIME IS CALLED, YOU MAY CHECK YOUR WORK ON THIS SECTION ONLY.
DO NOT TURN TO ANY OTHER SECTION IN THE TEST.

NO TEST MATERIAL ON THIS PAGE.

ISEE

MIDDLE LEVEL

ESSAY TOPIC SHEET

Time - 30 minutes

Directions

You will have 30 minutes to plan and write an essay on the topic printed on the other side of this page. **Do not write on another topic. An essay on another topic is not acceptable.**

The essay is designed to give you an opportunity to show how well you can write. You should try to express your thoughts clearly. How well you write is much more important than how much you write, but you need to say enough for a reader to understand what you mean.

You will probably want to write more than a short paragraph. You should also be aware that a copy of your essay will be sent to each school that will be receiving your test results. You are to write only in the appropriate section of the answer sheet. Please write or print so that your writing may be read by someone who is not familiar with your handwriting.

You may make notes and plan your essay on the reverse side of the page. Allow enough time to copy the final form onto your answer sheet. You <u>must</u> copy the essay topic onto your lined answer sheet in the box provided.

Please remember to write only the final draft of the essay on the lined answer sheet and write it in blue or black pen. Again, you may use cursive writing or you may print.

REMINDER: Please write this essay question on the first few lines of your answer sheet.

> **If you could change one thing about your school, what would you change and why?**

Notes

STUDENT NAME _____ ID NUMBER _____ GRADE APPLYING FOR _____

Please use a ballpoint pen to write the final draft of your composition on this sheet.

You must write your essay topic in this space.

_____

_____

_____

_____

_____

_____

_____

_____

_____

_____

_____

_____

Chapter 23
Lower Level
ISEE Practice Test

SECTION 1

VERBAL REASONING

Time: 20 minutes

34 Questions

This section is divided into two parts that contain different types of questions. As soon as you have completed Part One, answer the questions in Part Two. You may write in your test booklet. For each answer you select, fill in the corresponding circle on your answer document.

Part One

Each question in Part One is made up of a word in capital letters followed by four choices. Choose the one word that is most nearly the same in meaning as the word in capital letters.

SAMPLE QUESTION: <u>Sample Answer</u>

SWIFT: (A) clean (B) fancy   (A) (B) ● (D)
(C) fast (D) quiet

---

1. BASIN: (A) desk (B) frame (C) mound
(D) sink

2. DRENCH: (A) clean (B) rain (C) soak
(D) twist

3. HASTILY: (A) happily (B) passively
(C) quickly (D) quietly

4. HEAP: (A) grain (B) imprint (C) pile
(D) volume

5. ADORN: (A) average (B) decorate (C) sew
(D) visit

6. UNFURL: (A) close (B) flap (C) gather up
(D) spread out

7. NOVICE: (A) beginner (B) player (C) sickness
(D) story

8. COMPREHEND: (A) compare (B) speak
(C) understand (D) wonder

9. MALICE: (A) fear (B) hatred (C) joy
(D) opinion

10. UNKEMPT: (A) free (B) frequent (C) messy
(D) obvious

11. RUSE: (A) laugh (B) partner (C) sale
(D) trick

12. OBSOLETE: (A) historical (B) old-fashioned
(C) popular (D) uncommon

13. WILY: (A) careful (B) crafty (C) loud
(D) thin

14. BRITTLE: (A) breakable (B) lumpy (C) sharp
(D) small

15. ORATOR: (A) curator (B) listener
(C) orchestra (D) speaker

16. POLL: (A) argument (B) discussion
(C) election (D) survey

17. PLEA: (A) appeal (B) explanation (C) remark
(D) response

GO ON TO THE NEXT PAGE.

1 1 1 1 1 1 1 1 1 1

Part Two

Each question below is made up of a sentence with one blank. The blank indicates that a word is missing. Each sentence is followed by four choices. Select the one word or pair of words that will best complete the meaning of the sentence as a whole.

SAMPLE QUESTIONS:

Ann carried the box carefully so that she would not ------- the pretty glasses.

(A) break
(B) fix
(C) open
(D) stop

<u>Sample Answer</u>

---

18. Sasha's friends think she is outgoing and talkative, but when she meets people for the first time she is often -------.

    (A) friendly
    (B) privileged
    (C) shy
    (D) sociable

19. Ms. Lin reviewed all the essays so that she could ------- each student's writing.

    (A) deny
    (B) emphasize
    (C) evaluate
    (D) ignore

20. A snapping turtle's neck can ------- to catch fish far away from its body.

    (A) blend
    (B) extend
    (C) retract
    (D) wander

21. The young man dressed carefully for his job interview because he wanted to ------- the interviewer.

    (A) annoy
    (B) discourage
    (C) employ
    (D) impress

GO ON TO THE NEXT PAGE.

22. Scientists spend a lot of time studying ants, bees, and other ------- insects that live and work together in large groups.

    (A) aquatic
    (B) social
    (C) uninteresting
    (D) wingless

23. Because the domestic cat cleans its fur thoroughly with its rough tongue, it rarely becomes -------.

    (A) distracted
    (B) soiled
    (C) tidy
    (D) washed

24. Everyone said Jaquinta was an ------- person because she always asked a lot of questions.

    (A) inquisitive
    (B) intense
    (C) organized
    (D) unpredictable

25. Although Wanda has taken violin lessons for three years, her ------- is actually to play sports.

    (A) possibility
    (B) preference
    (C) question
    (D) routine

26. People who obey the law and try not to hurt anyone are not likely to become -------.

    (A) happy
    (B) infamous
    (C) quiet
    (D) serene

27. At one time, Western movies were released -------, but now they are hardly ever made.

    (A) frequently
    (B) informally
    (C) quickly
    (D) seldom

28. Mr. Thomas placed celery in colored water in order to ------- the way plants can absorb liquids.

    (A) compress
    (B) cover
    (C) demonstrate
    (D) ignore

29. Most goods were produced in people's homes before industrialization, but as the factory system became common, ------- production of goods decreased.

    (A) domestic
    (B) energetic
    (C) foreign
    (D) high-speed

GO ON TO THE NEXT PAGE.

30. Frederick Church built a large Moorish home that was ------- as a visitor came up the long driveway, but came into view suddenly at the end.

    (A) beautiful
    (B) concealed
    (C) uninteresting
    (D) visible

31. When Cassidy's baby sister sneezed as loud as Cassidy's father sneezes, -------.
    (A) Cassidy hoped she would develop allergies
    (B) everyone in the family laughed
    (C) Cassidy's father promised to stop sneezing
    (D) Cassidy helped to change the baby's diaper

32. Even though most of the students looked confused, the teacher -------.
    (A) wondered what she would have for lunch
    (B) explained the solution to the problem a second time
    (C) sent a student to the principal's office for misbehaving
    (D) moved on to a new topic without asking whether anyone had questions

33. Although the weather forecast predicted freezing temperatures and wet snow, Jason -------.
    (A) decided to learn how to ski
    (B) did not wear a coat when he went outside
    (C) worked twice as hard as he usually does
    (D) put on his favorite wool sweater

34. Because Ronnie was terrified of the ocean and never learned to swim, -------.
    (A) she did not accept an invitation to her friend's beach house
    (B) her parents never took her on their vacations to Kansas
    (C) she became an A student and was the president of two clubs
    (D) her brother decided to try out for the Olympic swimming team

STOP

IF YOU FINISH BEFORE TIME IS CALLED, YOU MAY CHECK YOUR WORK ON THIS SECTION ONLY.
DO NOT TURN TO ANY OTHER SECTION IN THE TEST.

SECTION 2

QUANTITATIVE REASONING

Time: 35 minutes

38 Questions

<u>Directions</u>

Any figures that accompany questions in this section may be assumed to be drawn as accurately as possible EXCEPT when it is stated that a particular figure is not drawn to scale. Letters such as x, y, and n stand for real numbers. Each question consists of a word problem followed by four answer choices. You may write in your text booklet; however, you may be able to solve many of these problems in your head. Next, look at the four answer choices given and select the best answer on the answer sheet.

<u>Example</u>	If $3 + x = 5$, what is the value of x? (A) 0 (B) 1 (C) 2 (D) 3	Answer
		Ⓐ Ⓑ ● Ⓓ

1. Which is seven hundred ninety thousand twelve?

   (A)   7,912
   (B)   79,012
   (C) 709,012
   (D) 790,012

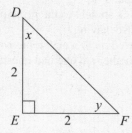

2. Which of the following must be true of triangle *DEF* above, which is drawn to scale?

   (A) $x = 45$

   (B) $\overline{DF} = 2$

   (C) $\overline{DF} = 4$

   (D) $x + y > 90$

GO ON TO THE NEXT PAGE.

3. Which number shows 9 in the thousands place?

   (A) 1,039
   (B) 7,920
   (C) 9,437
   (D) 94,016

4. Which of the following is the product of two distinct prime numbers?

   (A) 1
   (B) 4
   (C) 8
   (D) 14

5. Which is the smallest fraction?

   (A) $\dfrac{2}{5}$

   (B) $\dfrac{3}{8}$

   (C) $\dfrac{3}{4}$

   (D) $\dfrac{4}{9}$

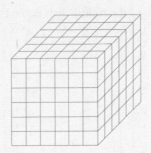

6. The number of smaller cubes that make up the solid object above is

   (A) 36
   (B) 108
   (C) 216
   (D) 46,656

7. It takes Ms. Weiss ten minutes to drive 4 miles. If she continues to drive at the same speed for 25 more minutes, how many more miles will she have driven?

   (A) 4
   (B) 10
   (C) 14
   (D) 25

8. A painter uses 3 gallons of paint to cover 2 square yards on the inside of a house. How many gallons will it take for him to cover a wall that is 12 feet tall and 60 feet long? <u>Note</u>: 3 feet = 1 yard.

   (A) 40
   (B) 120
   (C) 180
   (D) 240

GO ON TO THE NEXT PAGE.

9. Which of the following is equal to $\frac{1}{6}$?

    (A) $\frac{3}{6}$

    (B) $\frac{3}{9}$

    (C) $\frac{3}{18}$

    (D) $\frac{3}{24}$

10. When a number is divided by 8, the remainder is 3. Which could be the number?

    (A) 11
    (B) 14
    (C) 17
    (D) 21

11. Which of the following equals 90 ?

    (A) 5×18
    (B) 5×16
    (C) 4×15
    (D) 9^{10}

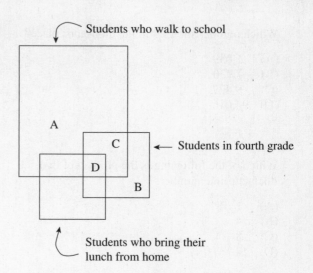

Students who walk to school

Students in fourth grade

Students who bring their lunch from home

12. In which region of the figure above would you find Stephanie, a fourth-grade student who walks to school and buys her lunch in the cafeteria?

    (A) A
    (B) B
    (C) C
    (D) D

GO ON TO THE NEXT PAGE.

13. Which of the following shows a line of symmetry?

(A)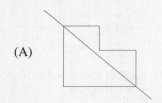

(B)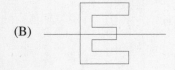

(C)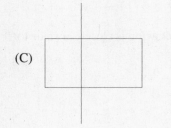

(D)

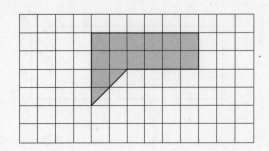

14. What is the area of the shaded region in the figure above?

(A) 12
(B) 13
(C) 14
(D) 24

$$16$$
$$\times M$$
$$\overline{A0}$$

15. In the multiplication problem shown above, if A and M represent distinct positive integers, which of the following is the value of A ?

(A) 0
(B) 4
(C) 8
(D) 9

GO ON TO THE NEXT PAGE.

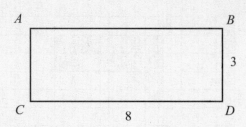

16. What is the perimeter of rectangle *ABCD* above?

    (A) 5
    (B) 11
    (C) 22
    (D) 24

17. Which shows 7 in the hundreds and thousandths places?

    (A) 2,793.4701
    (B) 5,704.2371
    (C) 7,421.9783
    (D) 8,072.7634

18. Which is seventy two thousand fourteen?

    (A) 7,214
    (B) 72,014
    (C) 72,140
    (D) 720,014

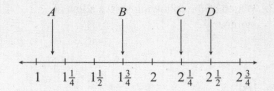

19. Which point on the number line above indicates the correct placement of $\frac{10}{4}$?

    (A) *A*
    (B) *B*
    (C) *C*
    (D) *D*

20. Which of the following is closest in value to 7?

    (A) 6.8
    (B) 7.009
    (C) 7.01
    (D) 7.1

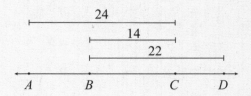

21. The length of *AD* in the figure shown above is

    (A) 30
    (B) 32
    (C) 38
    (D) 46

GO ON TO THE NEXT PAGE.

22. Which of the following shows three-fourths?

(A)

(B)

(C)

(D)

23. Which of the following is NOT equal to 16 ?

(A) $2^2 \times 4$
(B) 2^3
(C) 2^4
(D) 4^2

24. Which is the largest fraction?

(A) $\dfrac{3}{5}$
(B) $\dfrac{2}{3}$
(C) $\dfrac{1}{6}$
(D) $\dfrac{1}{2}$

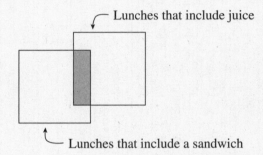

Lunches that include juice

Lunches that include a sandwich

25. Which lunch menu can be found in the shaded part of the figure above?

(A) yogurt and soda
(B) ham sandwich and apple juice
(C) pizza and milk
(D) cheese sandwich and water

GO ON TO THE NEXT PAGE.

26. Which of the following shows a reflection?

(A)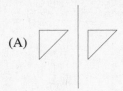

(B)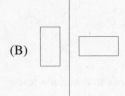

(C)

(D)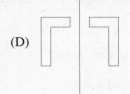

27. Which of the following produces a remainder of 3 ?

(A) $72 \div 9$
(B) $57 \div 6$
(C) $49 \div 9$
(D) $39 \div 7$

28. Sam's Pizza uses 24 slices of pepperoni on 8 pieces of pizza. How many slices of pepperoni would be used on 6 pieces of pizza?

(A) 3
(B) 12
(C) 18
(D) 48

29. Evan is making a quilt out of 6-inch squares of material. How many squares will he need to make a quilt that is 6 feet long and 5 feet wide? Note: 1 foot = 12 inches.

(A) 15
(B) 30
(C) 60
(D) 120

GO ON TO THE NEXT PAGE.

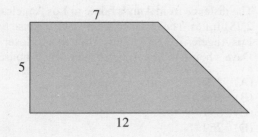

30. What is the area of the figure shown above?
    (A) 24
    (B) 35
    (C) 47.5
    (D) 60

31. Which of the following shows 48 as a product of primes?
    (A) 3×8
    (B) $2^4 \times 3$
    (C) $2^3 \times 6$
    (D) 2×3

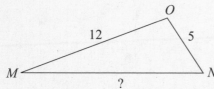

Note: Figure not drawn to scale.

32. Which of the following CANNOT be the length of side MN in triangle MNO, shown above?

    (A) 8
    (B) 11
    (C) 16
    (D) 19

33. When a number is divided by 8, the remainder is 2. What is the number?

    (A) 11
    (B) 22
    (C) 72
    (D) 90

34. What is the perimeter of a square with a side of length 2 ?

    (A) 8
    (B) 6
    (C) 4
    (D) 2

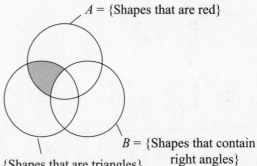

35. Which of these shapes would fall into the shaded region of the figure shown above?

    (A) a red right triangle
    (B) a red equilateral triangle
    (C) a green rectangle
    (D) a blue circle

GO ON TO THE NEXT PAGE.

36. Melissa had 20 words on her spelling test. If she spelled $\frac{1}{4}$ of the words incorrectly, how many words did she spell correctly?

    (A) 4
    (B) 5
    (C) 15
    (D) 16

37. $\frac{2}{3} \times \frac{1}{8} =$

    (A) $\frac{1}{12}$

    (B) $\frac{1}{24}$

    (C) $\frac{19}{24}$

    (D) $\frac{1}{4}$

38. The distance from Amy's home to Los Angeles is 2,281 miles. The distance from Dave's house to Los Angeles is 1,912 miles. How much closer is Dave's house to Los Angeles than Amy's house?

    (A) 379
    (B) 369
    (C) 359
    (D) 269

STOP

IF YOU FINISH BEFORE TIME IS CALLED, YOU MAY CHECK YOUR WORK ON THIS SECTION ONLY.
DO NOT TURN TO ANY OTHER SECTION IN THE TEST.

2 2 2 2 2 2 2 2 2 2

NO TEST MATERIAL ON THIS PAGE.

SECTION 3

READING COMPREHENSION

Time: 25 minutes

25 Questions

<u>Directions</u>: This section contains five short reading passages. Each passage is followed by five questions based on its content. Answer the questions following each passage on the basis of what is <u>stated</u> or <u>implied</u> in that passage. You may write in the test booklet.

<u>Questions 1-5</u>

Line

1   "What's that noise?" my brother asked.
2   I listened carefully. Just when I thought I heard a
3   small noise, the thunder crashed again. The rain was
4   hitting the roof hard, too, making it difficult to hear
5   anything. "I don't hear it," I said.
6   "What do you mean you don't hear it? It's so
7   loud!" my brother whispered. Then I heard it. It was
8   a *click-click-click*, and it sounded like it was coming
9   from the bathroom.
10   "Maybe it's a monster. We should go get Mom,"
11   my brother said. I didn't want to be a scaredy-cat, and
12   I knew Mom was probably asleep. Besides, I'd have
13   to walk past the bathroom to get to her.
14   *Click-click-click*. I told my brother to go to sleep,
15   but he said, "I can't. We have to see what it is."
16   "Okay," I said. I pretended I was very brave, and
17   got up and marched to the bathroom. When I saw
18   what was making the noise, I laughed out loud. My
19   brother came running down the hall, asking, "What
20   is it?"
21   Then, he poked his head in the door and looked
22   in the bathtub. There was our dog, Mack. He was
23   so scared of the thunder that he was hiding in the
24   tub! He sat there with his head down, shivering. His
25   toenails went *click-click-click* against the ceramic tub
26   as he turned to look at us.
27   "Poor Mack! He's more scared than we were," I
28   said. We brought Mack into our bedroom and petted
29   him until he stopped shaking. Then, we all went to
30   sleep.

1.   At the beginning of the story, the narrator's brother thinks the noise is made by

   (A)   a monster
   (B)   his mother
   (C)   the dog
   (D)   the narrator

2.   When the narrator says, "Besides, I'd have to walk past the bathroom," (lines 12-13), you know that he

   (A)   is afraid of getting in trouble
   (B)   is not familiar with the house
   (C)   is scared to go near the noise
   (D)   would rather go to the kitchen

3.   In line 17, "marched" most nearly means

   (A)   hopped loudly
   (B)   ran sneakily
   (C)   sang a military song
   (D)   walked with a purpose

GO ON TO THE NEXT PAGE.

4. Why does the narrator "laugh out loud" (line 18) when he gets to the bathroom?

    (A) He is amused because he sees that it is just the dog making a noise.
    (B) He is happy that there is nothing making a noise in the bathroom.
    (C) He is nervous about opening the door.
    (D) His brother has just told him a good joke.

5. According to the passage, the dog was in the bathtub because

    (A) he needed a bath
    (B) he was hungry
    (C) he was trying to hide from the brothers
    (D) he was trying to hide from the thunder

GO ON TO THE NEXT PAGE.

Questions 6-10

This story is adapted from an African folktale that explains why the sun and moon are in the sky.

Line
1   Long ago, the sun and the moon and the water all
2   lived on Earth. The sun and moon were married and
3   they were friends with the water. The sun and moon
4   often went to visit the water where he lived, but the
5   water never returned their visits.
6   One day, the moon said to the water, "Why do you
7   never come to visit us?"
8   The water replied, "My people and I take up a lot
9   of room. I do not think you have enough room in your
10 house for all my people and me. I would like to visit
11 you, but I do not want to crowd your home."
12   The moon said, "Well, then we shall build a bigger
13 house so that you can visit."
14   "I would like that," said the water, "but it must be a
15 very big place."
16   So the moon and the sun built a huge palace. It
17 took many months, but finally it was finished. They
18 sent word to the water to come and visit.
19   The next day, the water came. It stayed outside the
20 gates and called inside. "I have arrived, my friends.
21 Shall I come in?"
22   The sun and moon said together, "Yes, of course.
23 Come in." So the water came through the gates.
24 So, too, came the fishes and the crabs and the other
25 water-dwelling creatures.
26   The water filled the palace so much that the sun
27 and moon were forced to move up to the top floor.
28 "Are you sure you want me to continue?" the water
29 asked.
30   "Of course, come in," said the sun and moon. So
31 the water continued.
32   Soon the water had filled the house completely, and
33 the sun and moon were perched on the roof. "Are you
34 sure?" asked the water.
35   "Yes, yes. You are welcome here," said the moon
36 and sun. And so the water flowed more, until the
37 moon and sun had to jump into the sky. They have
38 stayed there ever since.

6. The primary purpose of this passage is to

    (A) describe how to build a large and expensive palace
    (B) describe how water flows in a flood
    (C) explain how the sun and moon got into the sky
    (D) provide information about sea creatures

7. The sun and moon can best be described as

    (A) assertive
    (B) friendly
    (C) grumpy
    (D) selfish

8. In the beginning of the story, why does the water never come to visit the sun and moon?

    (A) The sun and moon have never invited the water to their home.
    (B) The water does not really like the sun and moon.
    (C) The water lives too far away from the sun and moon to make the trip.
    (D) The water thinks there is not enough space where the sun and moon live.

9. When the water says "my people" in line 8, he is referring to

    (A) the creatures that live in the trees
    (B) the creatures that live in the water
    (C) the sun and the moon
    (D) the workers who build the palace

10. In line 33, "perched" most nearly means

    (A) got very thirsty
    (B) laughed heartily
    (C) looked like a fish
    (D) sat on the edge

GO ON TO THE NEXT PAGE.

Line

Questions 11-15

1   Not all bees live in colonies. Some bees live all
2   alone in a nest built for one. Most of us, however,
3   when we think of bees and wasps, think of huge
4   groups of insects, working together in a cohesive
5   social unit. The hive is, in many ways, a perfect
6   example of a social system. Inside the hive, bees raise
7   their young and store honey. The queen honeybee,
8   for example, may lay up to 1,500 eggs a day in the
9   summer. The drone bees mate with the queen and die.
10 The worker bees gather food, care for the hive and
11 the young, and protect the hive. The stored pollen
12 and honey will feed the colony throughout the cold
13 winter months. Inside a hive there is one queen, a few
14 hundred drones, and as many as 40,000 workers. The
15 expression "busy as a bee" is certainly appropriate
16 when you consider the work that bees perform.

11. According to the passage, the purpose of the drones
    is to

    (A)   care for the hive
    (B)   gather food
    (C)   mate with the queen
    (D)   supervise the workers

12. According to the passage, the purpose of the honey
    and pollen is to

    (A)   attract a queen to the hive
    (B)   fertilize flowers
    (C)   provide a place for the queen to lay her
          eggs
    (D)   provide food for the hive

13. According to the passage, the hive is an example
    of a social system because

    (A)   different members of the hive perform
          different jobs, yet they work together
    (B)   the queen rules over all the bees
    (C)   there are workers to do all the work
    (D)   there is no conflict in the hive

14. The word "cohesive" in line 4 most nearly means

    (A)   connected
    (B)   hardworking
    (C)   sacred
    (D)   sticky

15. The tone of the passage is most like that found
    in a

    (A)   diary entry of a modern naturalist
    (B)   general science textbook
    (C)   laboratory report
    (D)   letter to a friend

GO ON TO THE NEXT PAGE.

Questions 16-20

Line
1 A wealthy contributor to the arts, Isabella Stewart
2 Gardner was born in New York in 1840. She married
3 John Lowell Gardner, a wealthy heir, and settled in
4 Boston, Massachusetts. When her only son died as a
5 young child, she devoted her life to the arts. Assisted
6 by Bernard Berenson, a young art critic, she began
7 collecting important works of art. After her husband
8 died in 1898, she purchased land for the construction
9 of a museum and worked for years overseeing its
10 creation. She actually lived in the museum until her
11 death in 1924. Her museum became a gathering
12 place for artists, writers, and celebrities. She was
13 considered quite eccentric, often shunning Boston
14 "society" in favor of more colorful characters. She
15 gave her wonderful museum to the city of Boston, to
16 be preserved as a public museum. Today, if you visit
17 Boston, you can admire the work of Isabella Stewart
18 Gardner.

16. Which title would be most appropriate for the passage?

(A) "An Eccentric Woman"
(B) "Isabella Stewart Gardner—A Life"
(C) "The Beginnings of a Museum"
(D) "Two Deaths in a Family"

17. In line 14, the word "colorful" most nearly means

(A) beautiful
(B) brilliant
(C) unusual
(D) vivid

18. The passage suggests that Isabella Stewart Gardner began collecting art

(A) after the death of her husband
(B) after the death of her son
(C) to impress art critics
(D) to spend her husband's money

19. According to the passage, the museum built by Isabella Stewart Gardner was used for all of the following EXCEPT

(A) a place for artists to congregate
(B) a place for art to be viewed
(C) a school for aspiring artists
(D) her home

20. The author's attitude toward Isabella Stewart Gardner can best be described as

(A) admiring
(B) critical
(C) jealous
(D) skeptical

GO ON TO THE NEXT PAGE.

Line

Questions 21-25

1   Charlotte Perkins Gilman lived from 1860 to
2 1935. She lived during a time when most women
3 in America and Europe had few educational
4 opportunities. For most of Gilman's life, women
5 could not even vote. Gilman had many ideas for how
6 to improve women's lives.
7   Because she grew up in a family that was not
8 wealthy, Gilman read a lot in order to educate herself.
9 When she was eighteen, however, she attended the
10 Rhode Island School of Design. She worked her way
11 through school by tutoring and teaching.
12   Gilman eventually began publishing books,
13 articles, poems, and even a monthly magazine of her
14 own. She also lectured to large groups. Much of her
15 writing and speaking focused on allowing women to
16 use their natural talents and intelligence by giving
17 them access to education and jobs that paid well. By
18 offering lots of different ideas and ways to change
19 society, Gilman helped women gain the right to live
20 full, productive lives.

21. The primary purpose of the passage is to
    (A) convince the reader that women are able to work and study outside the home
    (B) describe how one woman focused on helping to improve others' lives
    (C) prove that people who are not wealthy can still gain access to education
    (D) show that everyone needs to find a way to help others

22. According to the passage, during Gilman's life women did not have
    (A) any ideas about how to change things
    (B) any way to publish their writing
    (C) a way to travel between America and Europe
    (D) many options for school and work

23. It can be inferred from lines 7-8 that Gilman
    (A) did not like to read by herself
    (B) planned to become a writer and speaker when she was young
    (C) preferred to spend time alone
    (D) was not able to attend school very often as a child

24. The main point of the third paragraph (lines 12-20) is that
    (A) Gilman enjoyed writing and speaking to large groups
    (B) Gilman worked to spread ideas about how women could live fuller lives
    (C) it was very easy to publish your own magazine at the turn of the century
    (D) most women did not have access to education and well-paying jobs

25. Based on the information in the passage, you could most likely expect one of Gilman's books to be titled
    (A) *Europe: A History*
    (B) *Growing Up Rich*
    (C) *Why Women Don't Need to Vote*
    (D) *Women and Economics*

STOP

IF YOU FINISH BEFORE TIME IS CALLED, YOU MAY CHECK YOUR WORK ON THIS SECTION ONLY.
DO NOT TURN TO ANY OTHER SECTION IN THE TEST.

SECTION 4
MATHEMATICS ACHIEVEMENT
Time: 30 minutes

30 Questions

Each question is followed by four suggested answers. Read each question and then decide which one of the four suggested answers is best.

Find the row of spaces on your answer document that has the same number as the question. In this row, mark the space having the same letter as the answer you have chosen.

Example:

$(5 + 3) - 2 =$

(A)   6
(B)   8
(C)   10
(D)   13

Sample Answer

● Ⓑ Ⓒ Ⓓ

The correct answer to this question is lettered A, so space A is marked.

---

1. $6\frac{1}{2}$ hours is how many minutes more than 5 hours?

(A) $1\frac{1}{2}$

(B)   30

(C)   60

(D)   90

2. Which numeral represents twenty-four thousand, six hundred and three?

(A)   2,463
(B)   20,463
(C)   24,603
(D)   24,630

3. $\frac{2}{3} + \frac{8}{9} =$

(A) $\frac{14}{9}$

(B) $\frac{28}{27}$

(C) $\frac{10}{9}$

(D) $\frac{9}{14}$

GO ON TO THE NEXT PAGE.

Questions 4-6 refer to the pictograph shown below.

Letters Delivered on Mrs. Adler's Mail Route

Monday	🗳🗳🗳🗳🗳
Tuesday	🗳🗳🗳
Wednesday	🗳🗳🗳🗳

Note: Each 🗳 represents 2 letters.

4. How many letters did Mrs. Adler deliver on Tuesday?

   (A) None
   (B) 2
   (C) 3
   (D) 6

5. How many more letters did Mrs. Adler deliver on Monday than on Wednesday?

   (A) 1
   (B) 2
   (C) 3
   (D) 4

6. How many letters did Mrs. Adler deliver on Monday and Tuesday?

   (A) 24
   (B) 18
   (C) 16
   (D) 8

7. In the decimal 0.42537, the digit 2 is equivalent to which of the following?

   (A) $\dfrac{2}{10}$

   (B) $\dfrac{2}{100}$

   (C) $\dfrac{2}{1,000}$

   (D) $\dfrac{2}{10,000}$

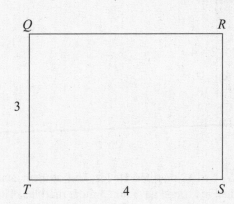

8. What is the perimeter of rectangle *QRST* shown above?

   (A) 7
   (B) 10
   (C) 12
   (D) 14

GO ON TO THE NEXT PAGE.

9. $\dfrac{1,000}{25} =$

   (A) 400

   (B) 40

   (C) 4

   (D) $\dfrac{1}{4}$

10. $3 \times 64 =$

   (A) 128
   (B) 182
   (C) 192
   (D) 256

11. $3 \times 2 + 4 =$

   (A) 7
   (B) 10
   (C) 14
   (D) 16

12. Wu had 18 marbles. He lost half of them, and then his friend gave him 3 more marbles. How many marbles does Wu have now?

   (A) 6
   (B) 9
   (C) 12
   (D) 21

School Supplies	
Pad of Paper	$1.25
Notebook	$1.50
Box of Pencils	$2.00
Pens	$1.00

13. Ian visits the store and buys 2 pads of paper, 1 notebook, and 3 boxes of pencils. How much money does he spend?

   (A) $10.00
   (B) $8.00
   (C) $5.75
   (D) $4.75

14. $\dfrac{1}{5} \times 400 =$

   (A) 20
   (B) 40
   (C) 80
   (D) 120

15. Evan has 26 comic books. Mark has twice as many comic books as Evan has. How many comic books does Mark have?

   (A) 13
   (B) 26
   (C) 42
   (D) 52

GO ON TO THE NEXT PAGE.

16. If 12 eggs cost $1.80, then how much will 36 eggs cost?

    (A) $0.60
    (B) $1.80
    (C) $3.60
    (D) $5.40

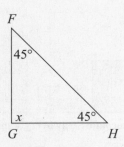

17. In triangle *FGH* shown above, the value of angle *x* in degrees is

    (A) 30
    (B) 45
    (C) 90
    (D) 180

Questions 18-19 refer to the following graph.

Amount of Time Alicia Spent Doing Homework

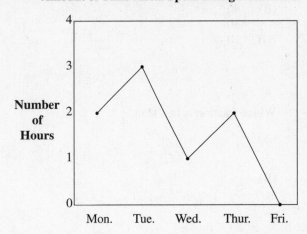

18. On which day did Alicia spend the same amount of time doing homework as she spent on Monday?

    (A) Tuesday
    (B) Wednesday
    (C) Thursday
    (D) Friday

19. How many more hours did Alicia spend doing her homework on Tuesday than on Wednesday?

    (A) 1
    (B) 2
    (C) 3
    (D) 4

GO ON TO THE NEXT PAGE.

20. $6 \times 20 = 150 -$ ___

(A) 130
(B) 90
(C) 30
(D) 10

21. Which fraction is less than $\dfrac{3}{4}$?

(A) $\dfrac{2}{3}$

(B) $\dfrac{5}{6}$

(C) $\dfrac{7}{8}$

(D) $\dfrac{9}{10}$

22. All of the following are multiples of 3 EXCEPT

(A) 120
(B) 210
(C) 462
(D) 512

Questions 23-24 refer to the graph shown below.

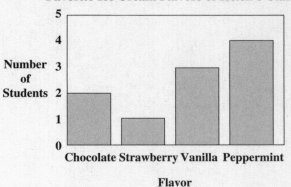

Favorite Ice Cream Flavors of Helen's Class

23. How many students chose vanilla ice cream as their favorite?

(A) 1
(B) 2
(C) 3
(D) 4

24. Which flavor was the favorite of the greatest number of students?

(A) Peppermint
(B) Vanilla
(C) Chocolate
(D) Strawberry

25. If the perimeter of a square is 36, what is the length of one side?

(A) 6
(B) 8
(C) 9
(D) 18

GO ON TO THE NEXT PAGE.

26. If 1 pound = 16 ounces, which of the following is equivalent to 2.5 pounds?

    (A) 18 ounces
    (B) 24 ounces
    (C) 32 ounces
    (D) 40 ounces

27. Jessica worked $5\frac{1}{2}$ hours on Tuesday and $3\frac{3}{4}$ hours on Wednesday. How many hours did she work on Tuesday and Wednesday?

    (A) $1\frac{3}{4}$

    (B) $2\frac{1}{2}$

    (C) $8\frac{1}{4}$

    (D) $9\frac{1}{4}$

Questions 28-30 refer to the price list shown below.

Fast Ferry Price List

	ADULTS	CHILDREN
Weekday Mornings	$15.00	$9.00
Weekday Afternoons	$12.00	$6.00
Weekends	$10.00	FREE

28. How much will it cost for 2 adults and 1 child to ride the Fast Ferry on a weekday afternoon?

    (A) $30.00
    (B) $27.00
    (C) $24.00
    (D) $18.00

29. How much less will it cost 1 adult and 2 children to ride the Fast Ferry on a weekday afternoon than it would cost them to ride on a weekday morning?

    (A) $6.00
    (B) $8.00
    (C) $9.00
    (D) $18.00

30. The price for 2 adults and 1 child to ride the Fast Ferry on a weekend is what fractional part of the price for 2 adults and 1 child to ride the Fast Ferry on a weekday afternoon?

    (A) $\frac{1}{2}$

    (B) $\frac{1}{3}$

    (C) $\frac{2}{3}$

    (D) $\frac{3}{4}$

STOP

**IF YOU FINISH BEFORE TIME IS CALLED, YOU MAY CHECK YOUR WORK ON THIS SECTION ONLY.
DO NOT TURN TO ANY OTHER SECTION IN THE TEST.**

ISEE

LOWER LEVEL

ESSAY TOPIC SHEET

Time - 30 minutes

Directions

You will have 30 minutes to plan and write an essay on the topic printed on the other side of this page. **Do not write on another topic. An essay on another topic is not acceptable.**

The essay is designed to give you an opportunity to show how well you can write. You should try to express your thoughts clearly. How well you write is much more important than how much you write, but you need to say enough for a reader to understand what you mean.

You will probably want to write more than a short paragraph. You should also be aware that a copy of your essay will be sent to each school that will be receiving your test results. You are to write only in the appropriate section of the answer sheet. Please write or print so that your writing may be read by someone who is not familiar with your handwriting.

You may make notes and plan your essay on the reverse side of the page. Allow enough time to copy the final form onto your answer sheet. You <u>must</u> copy the essay topic onto your lined answer sheet in the box provided.

Please remember to write only the final draft of the essay on the lined answer sheet and write it in blue or black pen. Again, you may use cursive writing or you may print.

REMINDER: Please write this essay question on the first few lines of your answer sheet.

If you could plan your perfect vacation, what would you do?

Notes

STUDENT NAME ———————————— ID NUMBER ———————— GRADE APPLYING FOR———

Please use a ballpoint pen to write the final draft of your composition on this sheet.

You must write your essay topic in this space.

Chapter 24
Answer Key to
ISEE Practice Tests

ISEE UL VERBAL 1

1. D	5. A	9. D	13. C	17. B	21. A	25. A	29. C	33. A	37. A
2. C	6. B	10. A	14. B	18. A	22. A	26. D	30. B	34. C	38. A
3. D	7. B	11. C	15. D	19. B	23. D	27. A	31. D	35. C	39. A
4. C	8. D	12. B	16. B	20. B	24. A	28. A	32. B	36. C	40. A

ISEE UL QUANTITATIVE 2

1. C	5. B	9. B	13. A	17. D	21. C	25. B	29. C	33. B	37. C
2. C	6. D	10. D	14. B	18. C	22. A	26. D	30. B	34. C	
3. D	7. A	11. C	15. A	19. B	23. A	27. A	31. B	35. C	
4. D	8. C	12. D	16. A	20. C	24. D	28. C	32. A	36. B	

ISEE UL READING 3

1. D	5. D	9. D	13. B	17. D	21. C	25. C	29. A	33. C
2. A	6. D	10. C	14. C	18. A	22. A	26. C	30. D	34. C
3. C	7. C	11. C	15. D	19. C	23. D	27. C	31. B	35. C
4. D	8. C	12. D	16. A	20. B	24. B	28. D	32. B	36. A

ISEE UL MATH 4

1. A	6. C	11. B	16. D	21. D	26. B	31. D	36. B	41. C	46. D
2. D	7. A	12. A	17. D	22. A	27. B	32. C	37. D	42. D	47. A
3. C	8. B	13. C	18. C	23. B	28. A	33. C	38. B	43. D	
4. D	9. A	14. D	19. A	24. D	29. C	34. C	39. C	44. B	
5. C	10. C	15. B	20. B	25. D	30. B	35. D	40. A	45. A	

ISEE ML VERBAL 1

1. D	5. D	9. B	13. B	17. A	21. C	25. C	29. C	33. A	37. B
2. C	6. C	10. B	14. C	18. B	22. B	26. C	30. B	34. D	38. B
3. B	7. B	11. A	15. D	19. A	23. D	27. A	31. C	35. A	39. B
4. C	8. B	12. D	16. C	20. C	24. A	28. A	32. D	36. A	40. A

ISEE ML QUANTITATIVE 2

1. C	5. B	9. C	13. B	17. D	21. C	25. B	29. B	33. A	37. B
2. B	6. A	10. C	14. B	18. C	22. D	26. B	30. D	34. C	
3. D	7. B	11. B	15. C	19. D	23. A	27. A	31. B	35. B	
4. B	8. B	12. B	16. C	20. D	24. B	28. A	32. B	36. A	

ISEE ML READING 3

1. A	5. A	9. C	13. A	17. B	21. C	25. D	29. B	33. B
2. B	6. A	10. D	14. B	18. C	22. D	26. C	30. D	34. A
3. C	7. D	11. A	15. D	19. A	23. A	27. A	31. D	35. B
4. A	8. A	12. C	16. D	20. B	24. C	28. D	32. B	36. C

ISEE ML MATH 4

1. B	6. A	11. C	16. D	21. B	26. C	31. C	36. B	41. C	46. B
2. B	7. C	12. A	17. A	22. D	27. B	32. C	37. A	42. B	47. C
3. D	8. C	13. B	18. C	23. D	28. D	33. C	38. C	43. D	44. A
4. D	9. B	14. C	19. C	24. B	29. A	34. D	39. A	44. A	
5. C	10. D	15. C	20. B	25. B	30. D	35. B	40. A	45. D	

ISEE LL VERBAL 1

1. D	5. B	9. B	13. B	17. A	21. D	25. B	29. A	33. B
2. C	6. D	10. C	14. A	18. C	22. B	26. B	30. B	34. A
3. C	7. A	11. D	15. D	19. C	23. B	27. A	31. D	
4. C	8. C	12. B	16. D	20. B	24. A	28. C	32. B	

ISEE LL QUANTITATIVE 2

1. D	5. B	9. C	13. B	17. B	21. B	25. B	29. D	33. D	37. A
2. A	6. C	10. A	14. C	18. B	22. A	26. D	30. C	34. A	38. B
3. C	7. B	11. A	15. C	19. D	23. B	27. B	31. B	35. B	
4. D	8. B	12. C	16. C	20. B	24. B	28. C	32. D	36. C	

ISEE LL READING 3

1. A	5. D	9. B	13. A	17. C	21. B	25. D
2. C	6. C	10. D	14. A	18. B	22. D	
3. D	7. B	11. C	15. B	19. C	23. D	
4. A	8. D	12. D	16. C	20. A	24. B	

ISEE LL MATH 4

1. D	5. B	9. B	13. A	17. C	21. A	25. C	29. C
2. C	6. C	10. C	14. C	18. C	22. D	26. D	30. C
3. A	7. B	11. B	15. D	19. B	23. C	27. D	
4. D	8. D	12. C	16. D	20. C	24. A	28. A	

Chapter 25
Scoring Your
Practice ISEE

CHECK YOUR ANSWERS

Use the Answer Key to determine how many questions you answered correctly and how many you answered incorrectly. You should not have left any answer blank, even if you didn't get to work through the problem!

COUNT THE NUMBER OF QUESTIONS YOU ANSWERED CORRECTLY

There are no deductions for incorrect answers, so simply count up the number of questions you got right. Write those totals here.

Verbal _____ (total for both sections)

Quantitative _____ (total for both sections)

Reading _____

Mathematics _____

These are your raw scores.

WHAT ABOUT SCALED SCORES AND PERCENTILES?

In addition to raw scores, you will receive two other types of scores for each section of the ISEE. First, your raw scores will be converted to scaled scores, which range from the upper 700s to the lower 900s, differing by test level and section. Then, your scaled scores will be compared with the scores of the students in your grade level who took the ISEE to determine a percentile. This percentile, which will range from 1 to 99, gives you the percentage of test takers whose score was *below* yours in each area. A percentile of 80, for instance, means that you did better than 80 percent of the students in your grade level who took the test (during the naming period of test development).

Unfortunately, we cannot provide the other types of scores you will find on an ISEE score report for your practice test. Each version of the ISEE uses a different conversion table to translate raw scores into scaled scores, and percentile scores can only be determined by comparing your performance with that of all the other students who took the ISEE. We encourage you to contact ERB for more information about their scoring procedures and to request any practice or scoring materials they can make available. ERB's publication, *What to Expect on the ISEE,* provides some general guidelines to allow you to determine a range of possible scaled scores and percentiles that you might expect to receive, based on your raw score.

Find Your Raw Score on the Conversion Chart

On the following pages, you will find conversions charts for all three test levels. For each subject (Verbal, Quantitative, Reading, and Math), the chart shows the range of scaled scores that are associated with each raw score. These scales are subject to change.

Please note that for each subject in each chart, the top raw score does not equal the total number of questions in that section. This is because some of the questions in each section are experimental and do not count towards your raw score. *For this reason, you will need to approximate a raw score.* The most cautious approach would be to reduce your raw score by the number of experimental questions. For example, because there are 36 questions in Upper Level Reading Comprehension but a maximum raw score of 30 appears in the chart, you would reduce your raw score by 6 points.

Upper Level ISEE Score Ranges

Verbal Reasoning		Quantitative Reasoning		Reading Comprehension		Mathematics Achievement	
Raw	Scaled Range	Raw	Scaled Range	Raw	Scaled Range	Raw	Scaled Range
35	905–935	32	918–940	30	923–940	42	920–940
34	902–932	31	915–940	29	920–940	41	917–940
33	899–929	30	911–940	28	917–940	40	914–940
32	896–926	29	908–938	27	913–940	39	912–940
31	892–922	28	905–935	26	910–940	38	909–939
30	889–919	27	902–932	25	907–937	37	906–936
29	886–916	26	899–929	24	904–934	36	903–933
28	883–913	25	895–925	23	900–930	35	901–931
27	880–910	24	892–922	22	897–927	34	898–928
26	877–907	23	889–919	21	894–924	33	895–925
25	874–904	22	886–916	20	890–920	32	893–923
24	871–901	21	882–912	19	887–917	31	890–920
23	868–898	20	879–900	18	884–914	30	887–917
22	865–895	19	876–906	17	881–911	29	885–915
21	862–892	18	873–903	16	877–897	28	882–912
20	859–889	17	869–899	15	874–904	27	879–900
19	855–885	16	866–896	14	871–901	26	876–906
18	852–882	15	863–893	13	868–898	25	874–904
17	849–879	14	860–890	12	864–894	24	871–901
16	846–876	13	857–887	11	861–891	23	868–898
15	843–873	12	853–883	10	858–888	22	866–896
14	840–870	11	850–880	9	855–885	21	863–893
13	837–867	10	847–877	8	851–881	20	860–890
12	834–864	9	844–874	7	848–878	19	858–888
11	831–861	8	840–870	6	845–875	18	855–885
10	828–858	7	837–867	5	842–872	17	852–882
9	825–855	6	834–864	4	838–868	16	849–879
8	822–852	5	831–861	3	835–865	15	847–877
7	818–848	4	827–857	2	832–862	14	844–874
6	815–845	3	824–854	1	829–859	13	841–871
5	812–842	2	821–821	0	825–855	12	839–869
4	809–839	1	818–848			11	836–866
3	806–836	0	815–845			10	833–863
2	803–833					9	830–860
1	800–830					8	828–858
0	797–827					7	825–855
						6	822–852
						5	820–850
						4	817–847
						3	814–844
						2	812–842
						1	809–839
						0	806–836

Middle Level ISEE Score Ranges

Verbal Reasoning		Quantitative Reasoning		Reading Comprehension		Mathematics Achievement	
Raw	Scaled Range	Raw	Scaled Range	Raw	Scaled Range	Raw	Scaled Range
35	896–926	32	897–927	30	914–940	42	877–907
34	892–922	31	894–924	29	910–940	41	874–904
33	889–919	30	891–921	28	907–937	40	872–902
32	886–916	29	887–917	27	903–933	39	870–900
31	883–913	28	884–914	26	899–925	38	867–897
30	879–909	27	881–911	25	895–925	37	865–895
29	876–906	26	877–907	24	891–921	36	862–892
28	873–903	25	874–904	23	887–917	35	860–890
27	870–900	24	871–901	22	884–914	34	857–887
26	866–896	23	867–897	21	880–910	33	855–885
25	863–893	22	864–894	20	876–896	32	852–882
24	860–890	21	861–891	19	872–902	31	850–880
23	856–886	20	857–887	18	868–898	30	847–877
22	853–883	19	854–884	17	864–894	29	845–875
21	850–880	18	851–881	16	861–891	28	843–873
20	847–877	17	847–877	15	857–887	27	840–870
19	843–873	16	844–874	14	853–883	26	838–868
18	840–870	15	841–871	13	849–879	25	835–865
17	837–867	14	837–867	12	845–875	24	833–863
16	834–864	13	834–864	11	841–871	23	830–860
15	830–860	12	831–861	10	837–867	22	828–858
14	827–857	11	828–858	9	834–864	21	825–855
13	824–854	10	824–854	8	830–860	20	823–853
12	821–851	9	821–821	7	826–856	19	821–851
11	817–847	8	818–848	6	822–852	18	818–848
10	814–844	7	814–844	5	818–848	17	816–846
9	811–841	6	811–841	4	814–844	16	813–843
8	808–838	5	804–834	3	811–841	15	811–841
7	804–834	4	801–831	2	807–837	14	808–838
6	801–831	3	808–838	1	803–833	13	806–836
5	798–828	2	798–828	0	799–829	12	803–833
4	795–825	1	794–824			11	801–831
3	791–821	0	791–821			10	798–828
2	788–818					9	796–826
1	785–815					8	794–824
0	782–812					7	791–821
						6	789–819
						5	786–816
						4	784–814
						3	781–811
						2	779–809
						1	776–806
						0	774–804

Lower Level ISEE Score Ranges

Verbal Reasoning		Quantitative Reasoning		Reading Comprehension		Mathematics Achievement	
Raw	Scaled Range	Raw	Scaled Range	Raw	Scaled Range	Raw	Scaled Range
30	873–903	35	881–911	20	883–913	25	869–899
29	869–899	34	878–908	19	877–897	24	865–895
28	865–895	33	875–905	18	871–901	23	861–891
27	861–891	32	871–901	17	865–895	22	857–887
26	857–887	31	868–898	16	859–889	21	853–883
25	853–883	30	865–895	15	853–883	20	849–879
24	849–879	29	862–892	14	848–878	19	845–875
23	846–876	28	858–888	13	842–872	18	841–871
22	842–872	27	855–885	12	836–866	17	837–867
21	838–868	26	852–882	11	830–860	16	833–863
20	834–864	25	848–878	10	824–854	15	829–859
19	830–860	24	845–875	9	818–848	14	825–855
18	826–856	23	842–872	8	812–842	13	821–851
17	822–852	22	838–868	7	806–836	12	817–847
16	818–848	21	835–865	6	800–830	11	813–843
15	814–844	20	832–862	5	794–824	10	809–839
14	811–841	19	829–859	4	788–818	9	805–835
13	807–837	18	825–855	3	782–812	8	801–831
12	803–833	17	822–822	2	776–806	7	797–827
11	799–829	16	819–849	1	770–800	6	793–823
10	795–825	15	815–845	0	764–794	5	789–819
9	791–821	14	812–842			4	785–815
8	787–817	13	809–839			3	781–811
7	783–813	12	805–835			2	777–807
6	779–809	11	802–832			1	773–803
5	776–806	10	799–829			0	769–799
4	772–802	9	796–826				
3	768–798	8	792–822				
2	764–794	7	789–819				
1	760–790	6	786–816				
0	760–786	5	782–812				
		4	779–809				
		3	776–806				
		2	772–802				
		1	769–799				
		0	766–796				

ABOUT THE AUTHORS

Elizabeth Silas is the former Director of Research and Development for The Princeton Review. She developed and edited books for kindergarten through high school students.

Reed Talada has worked in various capacities with The Princeton Review for more than a decade in New Jersey, Boston, and New York City. He is the former head of Educational Content Development for the K–12 Services division of the The Princeton Review. A graduate of Drew University, he lives in New Jersey with a brilliant cat named Tigger.

ISEE NOTES

ISEE NOTES

ISEE NOTES

ISEE NOTES

ISEE NOTES

ISEE NOTES

ISEE NOTES

ISEE NOTES

ISEE NOTES

ISEE NOTES